GREAT CAMPAIGNS

The Battle of Britain

The Battle of Britain
And the American Factor

July–October 1940

David Alan Johnson

COMBINED PUBLISHING
Pennsylvania

PUBLISHER'S NOTE

The headquarters of Combined Publishing are located midway between Valley Forge and the Germantown battlefield, on the outskirts of Philadelphia. From its beginnings, our company has been steeped in the oldest traditions of American military history and publishing. Our historic surroundings help maintain our focus on military history and our books strive to uphold the standards of style, quality and durability first established by the earliest bookmakers of Germantown and Philadelphia so many years ago. Our famous monk-and-console logo reflects our commitment to the modern and yet historic enterprise of publishing.

We call ourselves Combined Publishing because we have always felt that our goals could only be achieved through a "combined" effort by authors, publishers and readers. We have always tried to maintain maximum communication between these three key players in the reading experience.

We are always interested in hearing from prospective authors about new books in our field. We also like to hear from our readers and invite you to contact us at our offices in Pennsylvania with any questions, comments or suggestions, or if you have difficulty finding our books at a local bookseller.

For information, address:
Combined Publishing
P.O. Box 307
Conshohocken, PA 19428

Library of Congress Cataloging-in-Publication Data
Johnson, David, 1950-
     The Battle of Britain / David A. Johnson.
         p. cm.
     Includes bibliographical references and index.
ISBN 0-938289-88-8
1. Britain, Battle of, 1940. I. Title.
D756.5.B7J625   1998
940.54'211—dc21   97-46496

Printed in the United States of America.
Maps by Paul Dangel.

Contents

Maps

To Laura—

Thanks for staying out of the way

The Most Important Factor

"...he mobilized the English language and sent it into battle."
President John F. Kennedy, proclaiming Winston Churchill an honorary citizen
of the United States. 9 April, 1963.

Mention the Battle of Britain to most Americans, and likely response will be something like: "Oh, I know. Winston Churchill. "Their Finest Hour." Spitfires and Messerschmitts. The Luftwaffe against the Royal Air Force." If anyone mentioned the fact that the Battle is as much a part of American history as it is Britain's "Finest Hour," our average American would probably be very surprised. But in fact, the battle, its outcome, the way in which it was fought, and especially the way in which it was reported to Americans, had as much of an effect upon America's future as it had upon Britain's.

The Battle of Britain pushed Americans out of their isolationist cocoon, kicking and screaming, into what has become known as "the international arena." Before the battle, America had been stridently neutral; by the time it ended, the U.S. had been led into participation in the war, and had begun its role as a world power.

In July 1940, when the battle was just starting, the United States was still bound by two of the three Neutrality Acts that had passed through Congress in the 1930s. These acts had been designed to keep the country from involvement in any "entangling alliances," to use Thomas Jefferson's phrase, and were quite effective. (The last of the three acts would not be repealed until November 1941, just a few weeks before Pearl Harbor.)

The vast majority of Americans enthusiastically backed the Neutrality Acts and what they represented—an almost violent determination to stay out of European affairs. Charles Lindbergh, the flying hero from the 1920s who had become a well-publicized supporter of American isolationism, spoke for the majority of his fellow countrymen when he said that "the security of our country lies in the strength and character of our own people, and not in fighting foreign wars."

But Britain needed America as an ally—specifically, she needed American money and materiel. Prime Minister Winston Churchill was determined to persuade the maddeningly noncommital Yanks that Britain's war was America's war as well, and set about to use all his powers of persuasion—which were considerable—to turn American public opinion to Britain's side.

Churchill had a lot of help—from his own Ministry of Information and from American reporters and broadcasters. Reporters such as Edward R. Murrow, Quentin Reynolds, and Raymond Daniell of *The New York Times* sent reports from Britain that told about the war from a decidedly pro-British point of view. None of these men made any bones about their pro-British prejudice; Quentin Reynolds wrote stories that were so biased that they even succeeded in embarrassing some British officials.

The Ministry of Information gave these reporters a good deal of latitude in filing their stories—with the censor always hovering nearby—and made certain that they were given access to information that would place Britain in a favorable light. (Such as fighter pilots' inflated claims on the number of enemy aircraft shot down.)

Churchill had entertained hopes that his propaganda campaign might persuade the United States to become a combatant in the war against Germany, and possibly even to declare war on Germany. It never did that, but it did heavily influence American opinion—it made Americans see the war from Britain's side. By the end of the 114-day battle, the majority of Americans were *on* Britain's side. In an opinion poll conducted in the autumn of 1940, most said that they favored sending arms and assistance to Britain, and were committed—cynics would say "re-signed"—to an Anglo-American alliance.

The Battle of Britain was responsible for bringing the United States into war. If the battle had not taken place—for instance, if Hitler had used a U-boat blockade to starve the British into submission instead of trying to knock out the RAF as a prelude to invading England—no one can say when the United States would have entered the war in Europe. (The Japanese bombing of Pearl Harbor had no connection at all with Hitler and the war against Germany.)

News stories of heroic RAF pilots defending their country against Nazi air fleets caught the public's imagination. Americans were becoming pro-British in spite of themselves and 160 years of historical prejudice.

And when the Luftwaffe began bombing London in September, Americans became even more sympathetic. Reports were broadcast to the U.S. during actual bombing attacks—with the full permission and cooperation of the Ministry of Information. The London "Blitz," as it came to be known, and the reporting of it by Edward R. Murrow and his fellow American journalists, was instrumental in turning American opinion against Nazi Germany.

Germany had a propaganda campaign of its own aimed at the United States, a campaign to keep America neutral. Its main thrust was to convince Americans that the Nazis were not such a bad lot of fellows after all, and that they meant no harm to the U.S. In July, Reichsmarschall Hermann Göring made a point of telling an audience of reporters that Germany had no plans to invade the United States. "The German Air Force has no planes of sufficient range for trans-Atlantic operations," he said. "Even if you don't like us, give us some credit for common sense and reason."

Hitler's govement also spent a lot of money on the U.S. presidential campaign of 1940, specifically to keep President Franklin D. Roosevelt from being re-elected. Hitler did not have much regard for Roosevelt (and the feeling was mutual). To Hitler's way of thinking, Roosevelt was too unreasonable—meaning not pro-German enough. An attache in the German embassy in Washington placed pro-isolationist advertisements in *The New York Times*, and contributed to other "non-interventionist" causes. It did no good, though—a few days after the Battle officially ended on 31 October, Roosevelt was re-elected for a third term.

By this time, American public opinion had reversed itself—more than 50 per cent then favored all possible aid to Britain "even at the risk of getting into war ourselves." This shift did not represent just a moral victory for Britain—it meant financial backing and a steady supply of war materiel, as well. It also meant a major propaganda victory. Such a turnaround did not just happen all by itself; it came as the result of months of work by Churchill and his government.

Two examples of the success of this campaign: In September 1940, 50 World War I vintage destroyers were transferred from retirement in American navy yards to the British fleet. Shortly after the Battle of Britain ended officially, the Lend-Lease bill was introduced in Congress. Under Lend-Lease (known as Lease-Lend in Britain), the United States would be able to "lend" the British tanks, warplanes, and other urgently needed war goods. Churchill can properly take credit for having persuaded President Franklin D. Roosevelt into "lending" Britain the destroyers, as well as into introducing Lend-Lease.

As the battle went on, Hitler came to realize that the United States was not going to remain neutral; by the time it ended, he could see that the country was already an enemy. Even before the destroyer deal and Lend-Lease, Americans had not been very friendly toward Nazi Germany. The Americans who joined Britain's Royal Air Force also angered Hitler—even though they had joined without either the knowledge or permission of the U.S. government. (These volunteers had violated the Neutrality Acts, and had lost their U.S. citizenship by joining the armed forces of a "belligerent" nation.)

Documents discovered after the war disclosed that Hitler blamed the United States for being "a forceful factor in this war" throughout 1940 and 1941 and an active ally of Britain—which is why he declared war on America three days after Pearl Harbor, on 11 December 1941. If he ever wondered why the U.S. had been such a "forceful factor" during this time, when by all rights she should have remained neutral, Hitler might have consulted a quote by Otto von Bismarck. Bismarck remarked that the most important factor of the 19th century was that Americans spoke English—a factor that obviously continued into the mid-20th century.

So the United States was not blasted into the Second World War at Pearl Harbor, as many Americans seem to think. The country was talked into the war during the summer of 1940—talked by some extremely forceful British persuasion. It can safely be said that the United States was persuaded into the war.

With a battle being fought over southern England every day, Americans realized that they would have to take sides in the fight, sooner or later. After hearing stories about the Luftwaffe's attacks on Britain, they knew that they could never choose Nazi Germany. And after listening to warnings that they would be next on Hitler's list if Britain surrendered, they knew that they could not choose neutrality either.

The Battle of Britain may not have been America's finest hour, as it was Britain's. But it did mark the beginning of American maturity—which may not have been as heroic as Britain's defense in the battle or her endurance in the Blitz, but it produced results that were just as far reaching.

Beginning with the summer of 1940, Americans began thinking about the part they occupied in world affairs, and not just about their own problems at home. And their part—the role of Great Arsenal of Democracy and ultimately Britain's great wartime ally—was given to them in a script written by Winston Churchill and his Ministry of Information.

Churchill knew that he had to convince the United States that Britain was able to win the war, and that the British were worthy of American backing and support—a formidable task after the fiasco in France in May of 1940 and the evacuation of the British army at Dunkirk. Without the backing of the U.S., he knew that Britain's chances against the German war machine were virtually nil. In short, as British writer Len Deighton said in his study of the battle, "winning the Battle was only marginally more important than convincing the USA that they were winning."

Churchill went about his task of persuasion with his usual energy and enthusiasm. When it became clear that the Germans would not invade England and that Britain had indeed won the Battle of Britain (at least for 1940), Churchill was determined to persuade Americans that a German victory over Britain would mean disaster for the United States—if Hitler beat the British, the next target would be the U.S.A.

In other words, Churchill worked hard to persuade Americans that their own best interest rested in a "grand alliance," to use his own words, with Great Britain against Adolf Hitler and Nazi Germany.

He was so successful that he not only convinced Americans, but also managed to convince Adolf Hitler as well. Four days after Pearl Harbor had been bombed, Hitler declared war on the United States—solving Churchill's problem of American neutrality once and for all, and forging the "Grand Alliance" against Nazi Germany.

The Royal Air Force won the battle in the air over southern England, but the propaganda battle for American opinion ultimately won the war.

This campaign of persuasion was every bit as important as the day-to-day air fighting over southern England. Its results would be felt throughout the war and—for better or worse—for many years afterward.

Chapter I

"A Landing Operation Against England..."

In the early 1990s, two gray-haired war veterans got together to talk about old times, as they had done on several previous occasions. Both men were fit and prosperous. Ted Shipman was well-known for his work with the Red Cross. Hans Kettling had a successful business in Düsseldorf.

During their reunion, there was much talk and many reminiscences—about the war, and about what they had said and done when they were both still fairly young and foolish. Their meeting was probably not very different from any one of a thousand other such reunions, except for one detail—at their first encounter, Ted Shipman had tried to kill Hans Kettling, and had very nearly succeeded.

The first time they met was 15,000 feet over Yorkshire, in the summer of 1940. At the time, Ted Shipman was Pilot Officer Edward Shipman, Royal Air Force, of 41 Squadron; he was at the controls of a Supermarine Spitfire Mark I. Hans Kettling was an Oberleutnant in the German Luftwaffe, piloting a Messerschmitt Bf 110.

Oberleutnant Kettling's unit, The Richthofen Geschwader, had taken off from Stavanger, Norway, as an escort to Heinkel 111 bombers that were to attack air bases in the Englsih Midlands. Before they reached the coast of England, however, Pilot

Officer Shipman and the rest of 41 Squadron were up to intercept. P/O Shipman attacked two Bf 110s without any results before getting behind Oberleutnant Kettling.

Shipman fired "a long burst" at the Bf 110, saw the starboard engine begin to smoke heavily, and watched Kettling's fighter make an "erratic" turn to port, "apparently out of control." Kettling dove for the clouds, but was attacked by more Spitfires before he could make good his escape.

When his second engine was hit and his rear gunner shot, Kettling made a crash-landing in a field. He and his gunner, Obergefreiter Fritz Volk, were taken prisoner by "cut-throats with sticks, stones, and hayforks." The cut-throats quickly surrendered their prisoners to the police, much to the relief of the two Germans.

In the police cells, Volk's wounds were treated; both he and Kettling were given "an excellent dinner." They spent the next few months in England. Kettling was eventually sent to Canada, where he spent the rest of the war.

Many years after the war had ended, Shipman and Kettling were re-united by a British aviation enthusiast. In their old age, the two former adversaries became good friends. But in 1940, they were deadly enemies—two young fliers at each other's throats. "I would have shot Ted Shipman without a thought," Kettling said. Shipman probably felt the same way about Kettling.

Britain and Nazi Germany were also at each other's throats in the summer of 1940, as they faced each other across the narrow English Channel—or, as the Germans called it, "der Kanal." The war had been a one-sided affair up to that point, all in favor of Germany. In six weeks, the Wehrmacht had overrun Belgium and the Netherlands; had overwhelmed France, and forced the once-magnificent French army to surrender; and had trapped the British army against the Channel on the beaches of Dunkirk. Only good luck, and bad judgment on the part of the Germans, allowed most of the British forces to escape—plucked off the French beaches and evacuated back to England by a makeshift navy of small boats and pleasure craft, in the "Miracle of Dunkirk."

Britain now faced the enemy alone. Soon after France surrendered in June, German forces moved into position just across the Channel from southern England and waited for the order to attack. Adolf Hitler hoped that no such attack would be necessary. He thought that Britain's position was hopeless, and was convinced that the government in London would ask for an armistice, just as the French had done. The German Chief of Staff, Alfred Jodl, predicted: "The final victory over England is now only a question of time."

But Hitler and his General Staff had misjudged the opposition. The British made it very clear that they had no intention of surrendering. Winston Churchill, who had warned of the consequences of German re-armament during the 1930s, had become Prime Minister on 10 May—the same day that the "Phoney War" came to an abrupt end when German forces invaded the Low Countries. In a speech before the House of Commons, Churchill eloquently summarized the British position:

> What General Weygand has called "The Battle of France" is over. The Battle of Britain is about to begin. The whole fury and might of the enemy must very soon be turned on us. Hitler knows that he will have to break us in this island or lose the war. If we can stand up to him, all Europe may be free, and the life of the world may move forward into broad, sunlit uplands. But if we fail, the whole world, including the United States, including all that we have known and cared for, will sink into the abyss of a new Dark Age, made more sinister and perhaps more protracted by the lights of a perverted science. Let us therefore brace ourselves to our duties, and so bear ourselves that if the British Empire and its Commonwealth last for a thousand years, men will still say, "This was their finest hour."

Britain may not have thought of the time as their finest hour, but now they knew what their position was—there had been talk of an armistice in London as well. They also knew that there were some very rough times in store for them.

Hitler and his General Staff now knew the British position, as well, and they were incredulous. They knew—better than the British public—how desperate Britain's position was; German intelligence kept them well informed. Although the British army had been rescued from captivity at Dunkirk, the High Command knew that all of their equipment had been left behind in France. Some soldiers did not even have rifles; many who took their rifles back to England had no ammunition for them.

On 19 July, Adolf Hitler made his famous "peace offer" to Britain in a speech in Berlin's Reichstag, an "appeal to reason and common sense" which was meant to persuade the British to end the war. The British response was quick and emphatic—in the words of William L. Shirer, "a great big No." No specific terms were mentioned by Hitler, but Britain made it quite clear that they wanted no part of Hitler or his guarantees of peace.

Hitler realized that he would now have to prepare for war with Britain, which would mean an invasion of England. He did not want this war; he feared that it might prove long and costly, and might cost more than he could afford. But now he had no choice.

At that point in time, no invasion plans existed—which was one of the main reasons Hitler wanted to avoid war with Britain. His generals were masters of land warfare—as they had just proved in France—but had no idea of the sea or of amphibious operations. The Wehrmacht could have crushed the British army, if they had the chance to fight. But separating the German armies from their enemy—and from domination of Europe—was the English Channel. Hitler's armies would have to cross the Channel if they intended to win the war.

The invasion of England was not something that Hitler looked forward to; he knew enough about history to realize that no one had succeeded in a cross-Channel invasion in nearly 900 years. But he had great faith in his military forces, which had perfected the *blitzkrieg*, "lightning war," which combined the forces of infantry, armor, and air power to crush and overwhelm the enemy. In just six weeks, the German army and Luftwaffe had done something that the Kaiser's armies had not been able to accomplish in more than four years during the First World War—force France to surrender.

Hitler would have preferred an armistice. But if the British wanted war, he would see to it that his Luftwaffe would give them all the war they wanted. On 16 July, the Führer's Headquarters issued "Directive No. 16 on the Preparation of a Landing Operation against England":

> Since England, despite her militarily hopeless situation, still shows no sign of willingness to come to terms, I have decided to prepare a landing operation against England, and if necessary to carry it out.
>
> The aim of this operation is to eliminate the English homeland as a base for the carrying on of the war against Germany and, if it should become necessary, to occupy it completely.

Britain was now Nazi Germany's only active enemy. The United States and the Soviet Union were not yet involved. The Russians were Germany's implicit ally—they would continue to sell oil to Germany, oil which would fuel the bombers that would attack London. The United States would remain stubbornly neutral—a growing cause of resentment among the British.

Germany and her war machine had just crushed France and the Low Countries. Now, German forces were beginning preparations for "Operation Sea Lion," the invasion of England. During the month of July, Luftwaffe bomber and fighter units began moving to bases in northern France, a few minutes" flying time from southern England.

For Germany, the coming battle would decide the outcome of the war. Britain, however, had two battles. The first was for survival against the Luftwaffe. The second, equally desperate, was to win allies in their war against Germany.

The fight for a strong, dependable ally, especially an American ally, would become as important as the battle against Germany and the Luftwaffe. As much time and effort would be spent on the propaganda war, time and effort to convince Americans that Britain could win the battle, as was spent on the battle itself.

Even in the history of warfare, where the unusual tends to be commonplace, the Battle of Britain is unique. In previous wars, campaigns lasted for a matter of days or weeks, but the Battle of Britain went on for 114 days—the official dates are from 10 July to 31 October 1940. It was also history's first great air battle. Its outcome was decided entirely by aircraft, and the daily fighting was carried out by a comparative handful of pilots and aircrew on either side.

Historians have divided the battle into phases, but do not always agree on how many phases, or when they began or ended—Some insist upon four phases; others say five phases. Some German historians consider the first phase of the battle, *der Kanalkampf*, to be a separate battle, since the Luftwaffe considered it an attack on shipping in the Channel instead of an air battle.

In addition to being a source of controversy, the battle has also become the greatest source of romantic myth and legend since the fall of Troy. All sorts of words, true and otherwise, have been expended on the subject. One American writer thought the British people had found "a fearful elation" in the knowledge that "they would soon be fighting for their very survival," and that the country exhibited "a mood of Shakespearean poetry-drama."

An actual participant in the battle was no less rhapsodic. "They were wonderful, weird, exciting days," said one squadron leader. "High summer, 1940—that is a time to look back upon with wonder," wrote Hugh Dundas, a Spitfire pilot with 616 Squadron. And British writer Richard Collier could not restrain himself from going on about the "chivalrous jousting of the skies."

Reality was a good deal less romantic, however. Britain was unprepared for Operation Sea Lion. Winston Churchill knew it; so did his war cabinet and all senior military commanders, although they tried to convince America otherwise.

The fact was that only one fully-equipped division could be activated against a German landing. The Admiralty admitted that the navy would not have the strength or the numbers to

Troops of the British Expeditionary Force waiting at Dunkirk for evacuation. Over 300,000 British and French troops were rescued. Although photos like these were meant to raise morale, and show the British public that "The Miracle of Dunkirk" had been a triumph over Germany, they had the opposite effect in the United States. Pictures of Dunkirk served to convince Americans that Germany was on the verge of overwhelming Britain as easily as it had France and Poland, and gave isolationists more ammunition for staying out of the "British war."

prevent the crossing of a German invasion fleet. And RAF Fighter Command had lost nearly half its strength in the French campaign—one hundred aircraft had been shot down at Dunkirk alone.

German commanders realized that the Luftwaffe would have to win control of the air over the Channel if an invasion were to succeed. Otheriwise, the army and naval landing units would be mauled by the RAF before they could get anywhere near the English landing beaches.

German army High Command (OKH—Oberkommando des Heeres) originally planned to land 40 divisions on the south coast, between Ramsgate, Kent, and Lyme Bay, and advance north to Maldon, Essex. This would isolate London, which could then be taken at leisure. This plan was scaled down to a landing of nine divisions between Folkstone and Brighton, a much narrower front, which would be supported by two parachute divisions—a total of 200,000 men.

Senior naval staff officers drafted a reply to the army's plan, suggesting a small landing force and stressing the problems that the navy would face during a large amphibious landing. Although the army and the navy did not see eye to eye, both sides agreed on one item: air supremacy would be vital to the success of any invasion.

Luftwaffe units, of both Bomber and Fighter Command, were already moving into position. On 26 July, Jagdgeschwader 26 was ordered from its bases near the Rhine to the Channel coast. (*Jagdgeschwader* is normally translated as "Fighter Wing.") The Geschwader's three *gruppen* (squadrons) occupied three airfields near Calais: Audembert; Marquises Ost; and Caffiers. Both Caffiers and Marquises had been used by the Royal Flying Corps—the predecessor of the Royal Air Force—in 1914-18. Major Adolf Galland, soon to become almost legendary for his abilities in flying and shooting, would command III Gruppe (about 30 Messerschmitt Bf 109s).

Reichsmarschall Hermann Göring, the Luftwaffe's flamboyant (and drug-addicted) commander-in-chief, was confident that his air force would have absolutely no trouble in subduing the RAF. Overconfident, in fact. He predicted that the RAF wouldn't last a month—one of several remarks that would come back to haunt him.

But Göring could be excused for having too much faith. Morale among pilots and aircrew was high—they had just destroyed France's *Armee de l'Air* in just over a month, and believed that they would do the same to the RAF. The Luftwaffe's Chief of Staff, Generaloberst Hans Jeschonnek, reflected the German air force's optimism when he predicted, "The Luftwaffe [alone] will conquer England in a matter of weeks."

In Britain, the mood could not have been more different. The Luftwaffe had come away from the Battle of France in triumph;

the RAF escaped in tatters. At the beginning of June, in the wake of their losses in France, Fighter Command had only 413 serviceable aircraft: 79 Blenheims (used primarily as night fighters); 9 Defiants (obsolete 2-man fighters); 162 Spitfires; and 163 Hurricanes.

Air Chief Marshal Sir Hugh Dowding, Commander-in-Chief of Fighter Command, said that he would not be able to guarantee air superiority for more than 48 hours if the Luftwaffe "developed a heavy air attack on this country at this moment."

The optimistic attitude of the Luftwaffe in the spring of 1940 is evident in Oberleutnant Hans Ulrich Kettling, who joined the air force in the late 1930s. He decided to join Fighter Command, and was assigned to the Richthofen Geschwader, which flew the brand-new Messerschmitt Bf 109.

Originally, young Hans had intended to join the merchant navy, but vacancies were scarce—it was the middle of the Depression, and more young men than usual were anxious to get away from an economically devastated Germany. In 1936, his school's headmaster addressed the top class; the message was that the new Luftwaffe was looking for recruits. The Luftwaffe offered another way to get out of the Depression.

Hans listened to his headmaster's talk, and became "desperately interested." He had read about the pilots of the First World War, especially Manfred von Richthofen, and considered himself a "patriotic German." He also belonged to the Nazi Youth movement, although he says that he was not an "ardent Nazi."

After he completed his training, Kettling was assigned to the Richthofen Geschwader. "Can you imagine that for a young man's pride?" he asked—joining a unit that was named after one of Germany's leading heroes, and one of his own personal idols.

But Kettling and his fellow pilots were not being trained to bolster their pride. By 1937, Germany was already preparing for war on a number of fronts—against Austria; against "Red" Spain; against Czechoslovakia; against France—and had drafted two *Kriegsfalle* (literally "war plans") for war on two fronts. In

1938, with the Munich crisis, Germany nearly precipitated war when its forces occupied Sudeten Czechoslovakia.

Like most Germans, Kettling believed the official word from Berlin concerning these events. "We were told that we were going into other countries to protect our borders from foreign intrigue by Russia and France," Kettling recalled. "Perhaps we wanted to believe. Perhaps we were young."

And perhaps he really didn't care. Adolf Hitler had transformed Germany from a weak and anxious little country into a strong and aggressive power. The means by which he had accomplished this did not concern Kettling; it also did not matter very much to millions of other Germans. It was this mentality that allowed Hitler to become absolute dictator, and to start a war that would devastate half the world.

War finally came when German troops invaded Poland on 1 September 1939; two days later, Britain declared war on Germany. But war seemed a happy adventure to a young and inexperienced Luftwaffe officer; Kettling didn't worry. His unit was equipped with the Bf 109; pilots who had flown them in the Spanish Civil War, as part of the Fascist "Condor Legion," said that the 109 was the best fighter in the world. Kettling had flown a few combat sorties in Czechoslovakia, where his unit met "a bit of resistance" from a few obsolete bi-planes. Most of the Czech fighters had been destroyed on the ground. "War, it seemed, was very easy," he recalled.

Before war was declared, Kettling's *Staffel* was transferred. His unit would now fly the twin-engined Messerschmitt Bf 110 *Zerstörer* (destroyer). Kettling was impressed with the new aircraft. "Not a fighter. A destroyer. Heavy armour. Two engines. Longer range .... in front, we had two cannon and four guns, all controlled by a switch on the stick. Lovely! You could break up a bomber with one squirt, clear a road, scatter a regiment."

During the Polish campaign in the autumn of 1939, the Luftwaffe fought against obsolete airplanes, mostly bi-planes with fixed landing wheels. Kettling speaks of the campaign in Poland as "lovely days" of excitement, and of "free hunting" against targets of opportunity.

Kettling also fought in the Norwegian campaign of early 1940. His *Staffel* had been ordered to an airfield that was thought to have been captured by German paratroops. But when Kettling and his unit arrived, they discovered that the field was still in British hands. Their Bf 110s were attacked by obsolete Gloster Gladiator bi-planes, which shot down one of the Messerschmitts.

The airplanes were low on fuel, so they had no choice but to land. On the ground, Kettling and his radioman/gunner carried the rear machine gun out of the plane, "and started fighting like infantry." A short while later, a couple of Junkers troop carriers also landed; the troops they carried rescued the two fliers from the British army. This operation earned Kettling the Iron Cross.

But in spite of these encounters—or maybe because of them—war was still an adventure for Kettling. The Luftwaffe had not yet come up against a modern air force—airplanes that could compete with Messerschmitt fighters, flown by determined pilots. In the coming months, Kettling's opinion that war was "very easy," as well as the Luftwaffe's aircraft, pilots, and methods, would face its first real test.

If Hans Kettling thought war was an easy adventure, Ted Shipman hadn't thought about war at all. "We spent most of our time in tents, playing cards. Talking. There was no real emotion or apprehension for most of us. A war was on, so what? That's what we had trained for. What's to worry about. It showed how little we know."

Shipman had been in the Royal Air Force for ten years by the time the Battle of Britain was approaching. He joined in 1930 because he was "tired of hoeing turnips" on his father's small farm. But memories of the First World War also influenced his decision to join. He remembered FE-2 bi-planes landing at a nearby aerodrome between 1914 and 1918, and had heard stories of two older cousins in the Royal Flyng Corps.

Civilian instructors, not the RAF, taught him to fly. A fellow aircraftsman went to get a free test flight at a flying school; Shipman went along for company. When the instructor asked,

"How about you, too, son?" Shipman said yes. Six months later, he was awarded his "A" license.

Shipman did a bit of flying as part of his duties; he was personal fitter to an air commodore, and sometimes "took the stick" of the commodore's personal bi-plane. But he was not taken on as a pilot until 1935, when world events began to look ominous. Benito Mussolini, dictator of Fascist Italy, had invaded Ethiopia in 1935, and Adolf Hitler was making belligerent noises in Germany. The British Air Ministry were becoming increasingly concerned (unlike their American counterparts).

"I don't think anyone believed there was going to be another big war," Shipman said. "But there was enough going on in Europe for someone to think we ought to have a few more pilots." Shipman trained as a fighter pilot in obsolete bi-planes, like the Gloster Gladiator, and received instruction in obsolete tactics—flyng in tight "V" formation. The V, or "vic," formation may have looked very impressive at an air show, but would prove lethal to British pilots in combat—emphasis was placed upon keeping tight formation and watching the flight leader, instead of looking out for the enemy.

In June 1939, however, conditions took a definite turn for the better—41 Squadron was equipped with the Supermarine Spitfire Mark I. These early Spitfires had their limitations, Shipman remembers. They only had "a single wooden propeller, and you had to pump up the wheels by hand. But it was marvelous. It gave you everything you loved about flying—and ten times more. As a fighting machine? No, no, no ... we still didn't think we'd be using it for that. It was just a superb aeroplane to fly."

Although the situation over on the Continent was going from bad to worse, with Hitler making threats to invade both Poland and Czechoslovakia, the pilots of 41 Squadron carried on with their training, and tried not to think about what might happen. When Germany invaded Poland on 1 September, and Britain and France declared war two days later, nothing much changed. For the first few weeks, war was "a seamless continuation of the previous not-very real training." In October, however, reality revealed its unwanted presence in the form of a German patrol craft on the prowl.

Pilot Officer Shipman's flight scrambled to intercept the intruder over the North Sea, and was vectored to the area by the ground controller; "Suddenly, at 10 o'clock, this distant plane." Nobody had seen a German machine up to that time. Shipman led his section down to have a good look—"I was anxious about ID," and did not want to shoot down a British plane by mistake.

Changing from a peacetime mentality to a war mentality was not an easy transition, even for a fighter pilot. Firing eight Browning .303 caliber machine guns at a tow target was one thing; shooting at a real airplane, with real men inside of it, was something else again. P/O Shipman wanted to make very sure of his quarry before be pressed the firing button.

> And, oh God, it was! One of them! The last thing I wanted to see was there—black and white crosses. Nothing else for it; I had to go to war.
>
> I dropped behind him and gave him a real pasting. He started to go down in a long spin. The others then had a bash. We watched him go into the sea, saw several figures get into a dinghy, and radioed the position to base.

Shipman does not identify the type of aircraft that he and his flight shot down. He only added that he asked permission to visit the three surviving German crewmen in the hospital (and was refused permission). He didn't want to talk much about 41 Squadron's—and his own—first kill. "It was a big shock." he says.

Following this somewhat violent start, P/O Shipman and 41 Squadron had a quiet winter. Over Dunkirk, they also had a rather quiet time—Shipman flew seven sorties over the beaches, thinks that he saw one German plane, and never fired a shot. After Dunkirk, 41 Squadron were transferred to Catterick, in North Yorkshire. From Catterick, they flew patrols against intruding enemy bombers, and waited to be called down to the battle over southern England.

Shipman and his fellow pilots had confidence in themselves and in their Spitfires. But they were not overly eager to go down and join the battle—they had heard all about the losses. Shipman realized that he would have to go if called. "But jumping up and down for the chance? No."

Shipman was right about the losses suffered by Fighter Command—in July and August, the number of pilots who were killed and wounded was staggering. The RAF were pressing every pilot they could get into service to fill the vacancies. The Royal Navy transferred 75 pilots to Fighter Command. A few Army pilots, trained to fly unarmed reconnaissance aircraft, were also transferred to RAF fighter squadrons following an "accelerated"—meaning rushed—training course.

Fighter Command did manage to acquire some combat-seasoned pilots from countries that had been occupied by the Germans: Belgians, French, Czechs, and Poles. The problem was that there were so few of them—only 12 French pilots managed to escape to England, and only 29 Belgians got away.

But these pilots also had their drawbacks. Many were not accustomed to advanced fighters like the Spitfire and the Hurricane. Most had flown planes without retractable landing wheels—out-of-date bi-planes, which was one reason why the Luftwaffe enjoyed such great success. After giving an expert display of rolls, loops, and dives, these foreign pilots would sometimes wreck their planes when they forgot to put their wheels down before landing.

The language problem was another drawback. The Poles, for instance, were among the best, and most determined, pilots in Fighter Command. The only trouble was that they didn't speak any English; they didn't understand ground controllers, and could not be vectored to intercept an incoming flight of enemy aircraft. Before they could be classified as operational, the Poles would at least have to learn the basic rudiments of English. They would also have to learn flight jargon, such as "angels," "vector," "bogey," and "bandit." Without the ability to communicate with ground control, the Poles would be as good as useless, for all their experience and determination.

Because of the desperate shortage of pilots, Fighter Command also decided to accept American volunteers. The Yanks might

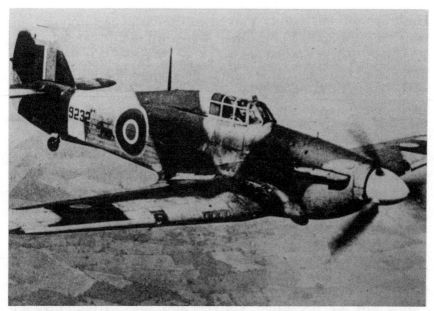

A Hawker Hurricane Mark II. Although not as advanced or sophisticated as the Spitfire, the Hurricane marked a radical departure from bi-planes like the Gloster Gladiator—it was a monoplane, with no struts or supporting cables, and featured an enclosed cockpit. The Hurricane was more rugged than the Spitfire, was a steadier gun platform, was much more stable in landings and take-offs, and was present in greater numbers than its more glamorous contemporary during the battle.

not have the combat experience of the Poles or the Czechs, but at least they spoke a language that was roughly similar to English. They could be vectored toward an incoming enemy bomber formation by ground control, and could sometimes even be understood when they spoke. (They might also prove useful as a propaganda device, to sway the opinion of neutral America.) The official records of the Royal Air Force list only seven Americans as having served with RAF Fighter command during the summer of 1940.[1]

Flight Lieutenant James Davies was one American who is not included in the RAF's official records. Jimmy Davies was born in Bernardsville, New Jersey, in 1913, and attended Morristown

High School. His family moved to Connecticut before he finished high school; Jimmy then went to the Gilbert School in Winstead. When he was about 18 or 19 years old, he and his parents moved again, this time to Bridgend in South Wales. He couldn't quite decide what he wanted to do with himself—he studied radio at Cardiff College for a while, and "did this and that for a year or two." In 1936, he decided to join the Royal Air Force. He took a short service commission, and was posted to a fighter squadron. Davies flew bi-planes until just before the war broke out. In 1939, his squadron, 79 Squadron, was re-equipped with Hawker Hurricanes. By this time, Davies had been promoted twice, to the rank of Flight Lieutenant. (The U.S. Army Air Force equivalent is Captain.)

At the time, F/Lt. Davies and the rest of 79 Squadron were stationed at Biggin Hill aerodrome in Kent. In the coming Battle of Britain, Biggin Hill would acquire the dubious distinction of being one of the most active—and most frequently attacked—RAF stations. But at the beginning of the war, it was just another fighter base; its pilots and ground crews spent most of their time waiting for something to happen. Things first began to happen for 79 Squadron on 21 November. F/Lt. Davies was leading a section of four Hurricanes near Dover on that particular day, when a Dornier Do 17 "flying pencil" bomber was spotted at 12,000 feet, about 2,000 feet below the Hurricanes. No one had seen a German airpane up to that time, so "we went down carefully to make sure."

British fighters had already shot down other RAF aircraft on at least one occasion—on 6 September, a group of Spitfires

---

1   The seven "official" Americans in Fighter Command during the summer of 1940 are:
   Pilot Officer Arthur Donahue: 64 Squadron;
   Pilot Officer J.K. Haviland: 151 Squadron;
   Pilot Officer W.M.L. Fiske: 601 Squadron;
   Pilot Officer Vernon Keough: 609 Squadron;
   Pilot Officer Phil Leckrone: 616 Squadron
   Pilot Officer Andrew Mamedoff: 609 Squadron;
   Pilot Officer Eugene Tobin: 609 Squadron

destroyed two Hurricanes, thinking them Messerschmitts; and anti-aircraft gunners shot down a twin-engine RAF Blenheim. Nobody wanted to be responsible for another fiasco like that one.

It didn't take very long to recognize the intruding aircraft as a Dornier; its thin pencil of a fuselage was unmistakable. Davies went after him, got close behind him "and gave him three sharp bursts of fire." Another member of his section, a Sergeant Pilot Brown, also got in several good shots. The Dornier turned over on its back, began an inverted dive toward the Channel, and crashed into the water with a huge splash.

When Davies returned to Biggin Hill, he was handed a package—a bottle of champagne, compliments of the station commander. It had been 79 Squadron's first fight with a German aircraft, and they had won. The Dornier had also been the first enemy airplane destroyed over British home waters of the Second World War, and had been Biggin Hill's first German aircraft. "In those days, one German aircraft was something to celebrate," Davies said. During the coming months, Biggin Hill and its pilots would see hundreds of German aircraft; at the end of August 1940, the station itself would be attacked almost on a daily basis.

After spending a quiet winter, Davies was sent to France when German forces invaded the Low Countries in May 1940. His second victory came on 14 May, when he shot down a Messerschmitt Bf 110. His squadron was in France only for eleven days; they were withdrawn to England after covering the evacuation of British and French forces at Dunkirk. By the end of June, Davies had been credited with six enemy aircraft destroyed, and had been awarded the Distinguished Flying Cross. On the day that he was to have been presented with the DFC by George VI, 25 June 1940, Davies was himself shot down and killed.

Following the presentation ceremony at Biggin Hill that day, the King asked about the remaining DFC on the table. He was told about the expatriate American. A squadron mate of Davies thought that the King was "quite moved."

No. 65 Squadron Spitfires in 1939. The Supermarine Spitfire owed its famous graceful lines—and its speed—to its early ancestors. It evolved from a series of successful racing seaplanes that were designed in the 1920s and 1930s by Reginald J. Mitchell, racers that won the Schneider Trophy in 1929 and again in 1931 and set a world speed record of 407.5 miles per hour.

Davies' six enemy aircraft destroyed by the end of June 1940 would make him the first American ace of the war. American record books do not recognize him, however; his achievement, being the first American to destroy five or more enemy planes, seems to have been overlooked rather than snubbed. Which seems incredible, in light of Britain's attempts to convince the United States that the war was America's fight. Jimmy Davies was born in America, spent most of his life there, became the first American to win the Distinguished Flying Cross—and almost no mention was given either to him or his accomplishments. But there would be other opportunties, and other Americans, that would present themselves in the coming weeks; this time, the Ministry of Information would use their publicity value to the fullest advantage. (A great deal of time, energy, and effort—and money—has been expended over the question: Who was the first American killed in the Battle of Britain? F/Lt Davies was killed two weeks before the battle officially began, on 10 July 1940, yet very little mention is made of him.)

On 2 July 1940 OKW (Oberkommando der Wehrmacht, which is usually translated as High Command of the Armed Forces) issued this directive:

The Führer and Supreme commander has decided: That a landing in England is possible, providing that air superiority can be attained and certain other necessary conditions fulfilled. The date of commencement is still undecided. All preparations to begin immediately.

"... provided that air superiority can be attained ..."The beginning of history's first great air battle was just a week away. Its outcome would be decided by factors unheard of and undreamed of by leaders of previous wars.

THE SUPERMARINE SPITFIRE AND THE HAWKER HURRICANE

Britain's defence against the coming battle with the Luftwaffe depended largely upon two single-seat fighters: the Hawker Hurricane and the Supermarine Spitfire. The fact that the RAF had these two fighters at all in the summer of 1940 was because of the efforts of three men: Hugh Dowding; Reginald J. Mitchell, of the firm Vickers-Supermarine; and Sidney Camm, of Hawker Aircraft Ltd.

R. J. Mitchell's design for the Spitfire evolved from a series of highly successful racing seaplanes. In fact, the name "Supermarine" was chosen because it means "above water"—the opposite of "submarine." Mitchell's racers were among the fastest in the world. In 1927, his S.4 racer won the Schneider Trophy with a speed of 281.6 miles per hour. Four years later, his elegant S.6 captured the Schneider Trophy outright for Britain with a world speed record of 406.99 mph.

During this time, the Air Ministry began looking for a replacement for the RAF's bi-plane fighters, the Bristol Bulldog and the Gloster Gladiator. Mitchell decided to make a bid for the Air Ministry's contract to build this fighter. The Supermarine firm had been taken over by the industrial giant Vickers by this time; the new corporation was known as Vickers-Supermarine.

The first prototype of the aircraft that would become known as the Spitfire was an odd-looking ma-chine called the F.7/30, a gull-winged monoplane with an open cockpit and "spatted" undercarriage. But the F.7/30 was not a success; it was too slow, too heavy, and did not climb quickly enough. So Mitchell began to experiment. He added a larger engine, enclosed the cockpit, gave his new fighter smaller, thinner wings, and retractable undercarriage. These thin, eliptically-shaped wings would become the fighter's most prominent feature.

Mitchell continued to modify his design throughout 1933 and 1934. The larger engine he had in mind was supplied by Rolls Royce—a new, twelve-cylinder, liquid-cooled powerplant called simply PV-12. Rolls Royce would rename this engine the Merlin.

This new fighter, now called F.10/35, developed into a low-winged interceptor with retractable undercariage, flaps, enclosed cockpit, and oxygen for the pilot. For armament, Mitchel gave his fighter four wing-mounted machine guns.

It is at this point that Air Vice Marshal Hugh Dowding enters the story. Dowding had been in charge of the RAF's technical development since 1930, and held the title Air Member for Supply and Research.

Dowding was favourably impressed by Mitchell's F.10/35 except for one item: he wanted eight machine guns. During the 1930s, Squadron Leader Ralph Sorley, a highly-qualified armament officer, carried out a number of tests involving aerial gunnery. These tests showed that no fewer than 256 hits from calibre .303 ammunition would be needed to inflict "lethal damage" to an all-metal bomber. Tests also showed that a fighter attacking a bomber flying at 180 miles per hour would probably not be able to bring guns to bear on the target for more than two seconds. As such, eight machine guns—each firing 1,000 rounds per minute—would be needed to shoot down an enemy bomber.

Dowding had the future in mind. He knew that the new Luftwaffe was expanding, and that Adolf Hitler's ambition for his New Order would probably lead to an armed conflict between Britain and Germany. His far-sightedness would pay off eight years later, when he would be chief of RAF Fighter Command.

Because of his aircraft's elliptical wings, R. J. Mitchell was able to fit four Browning .303 machine guns into each wing without increasing drag or radically altering design. With this armament, and with the Rolls Royce Merlin engine, Mitchell knew that his fighter would be a match for any airplane that the German Luftwaffe might produce. Now, all he had to do was to convince the Air Ministry.

Mitchell's fighter first took to the air on 5 March 1936. By this time, it had been given a name—Spitfire. (Mitchell himself didn't like the name very much; he called it "a bloody silly name.") This Spitfire prototype, K5054, flown by Vickers test pilot Joseph "Mutt" Summers

from Eastleigh in Hampshire, was unarmed and fitted with a fixed-pitch airscrew. After landing, Summers told his ground crew, "I don't want anything touched"—although alterations were made in the airplane, he realized from just one flight that the Spitfire was an outstanding fighter.

Two days after Mutt Summers' test flight, 35,000 German troops reoccupied the "demilitarised" Rhineland. This was in direct violation of the Versailles Treaty, and was also Adolf Hitler's first act of military aggression—his first step on the road to war.

The Air Ministry in London eventually agreed with Mutt Summers' evaluation of the Spitfire, after listening to some persuasive argument from Air Vice Marshal Dowding. On 3 June 1936, a contract was placed with Vickers-Supermarine for three hundred Spitfires. In 1937, six hundred more were ordered. By the time Britain went to war with Germany on 3 September 1939, the war that Dowding had forseen, a total of 2,160 Spitfires were on order for the RAF.

But Reginald J. Mitchell never lived to see the success of his creation. In 1937, at the age of 42, Mitchell died of cancer of the colon.

The Spitfire was the product of one man's imagination. The Hawker Hurricane was the result of evolution that began with fabric-covered bi-planes of the First World War.

The Hurricane was revolutionary for its time—it was the RAF's first monoplane fighter, and the first RAF fighter to exceed 300 miles per hour. Its basic construction was conventional, however—a wire-supported framework of metal tubing, which wsa held together by elliptical wooden formers and stringers, the same as the bi-planes in service during the 1930s. One writer referred to the Hurricane as "a halfway house between the old bi-planes and the new Spitfires."

The leading force behind the Hurricane's development was Sidney Camm, Hawker Aircraft's chief designer. In the early 1930s, when the Air Ministry began to look to replace bi-planes with more modern fighters, Camm already had a design for what he called his "Fury monoplane"—a modification of the graceful and highly manoeuverable Fury bi-plane. The Fury was the direct descendent of the Sopwith Camel and Sopwith Tri-plane of the First World War— Hawker Aircraft Ltd. had begun its life as Sopwith Ltd.

Apart from the fact that the Hurricane was a monoplane, its major differences from the Fury were power plant and armament. The Fury was powered by the Rolls Royce Kestrel, which gave it a maximum speed of 184 miles per hour. But the Kestrel was much too small for the Hurricane. When Sidney Camm heard about Rolls Royce's PV-12 engine, he modified his new monoplane to accomodate it. The PV-12 was re-named the Merlin.

Original armament of the Hawker monoplane fighter ocnsisted of two Vickers Mark V machine guns mounted in the fuselage, and two Browning machine guns

mounted in the wings. But when Hugh Dowding concluded that eight guns would be needed to destroy an enemy bomber, a conclusion based upon Squadron Leader Sorley's tests, Camm changed his design.

Just as Reginald Mitchell had done with his Spitfire, Camm incorporated eight Browning .303 machine guns in his new fighter, four in each wing. But while Mitchell spaced the Spitfire's guns across the wing's leading edge, Camm grouped four guns together on each wing. Many pilots claimed that this made for an accurate, and more destructive, concentration of fire.

When the new Hawker fighter made its first test flight on 6 November 1935—four months before Mutt Summers took the Spitfire up for the first time—it was still without a name. The Air Ministry did not approve "Hurricane" until June 1940. The maiden flight impressed the Air Ministry, but there were still some who had their doubts about such an "unconventional" airplane—one that had such unusual features as eight machine guns, an enclosed cockpit, and retractable undercarriage. The first order of six hundred Hurricanes was not placed until seven months after the initial test flight.

It may seem strange, even bizarre, to think that both the Spitfire and Hurricane met with a good deal of opposition by members for the Air Ministry because they were thought to be too unorthodox. High-ranking officers who had been pilots during the First World War were

34

used to open cockpits, fixed undercarriages, and struts and supporting cables and two sets of wings. Wood-and-fabric bi-planes were familiar; monicoque monoplanes with enclosed cockpits and retractable undercarriages were new and strange. These "old school" types had a good deal of influence in the pre-1939 Royal Air Force.

Some First World War pilots even insisted that the monoplane would always be outclassed by the bi-plane, simply because a bi-plane could always out-manoeuvre any monoplane. If these officers had their way, RAF Fighter Command would have faced the Luftwaffe's Messerschmitt Bf 109s with outdated Bristol Bulldogs and Gloster Gladiators in the spring and summer of 1940.It was this line of thinking that made Dowding's job of upgrading and modernizing the RAF more difficult than it should have been. The bi-plane lobby did not take kindly to the changes in aircraft design made by the likes of Sidney Camm and R. J. Mitchell. They also did not like Dowding very much; what annoyed them even more was the fact that Dowding really didn't give a damn what anyone thought of him.

Hugh Dowding could be charming and gracious to friends, but was distant and domineering with opponents. Author Len Deighton said that Dowding was "totally devoid of charm and made no attempt to be diplomatic to men who questioned his judgment." And the "chairborne types" at the Air Ministry frequently questioned both Dowding and his judgment.

Dowding's insistence that RAF Fighter Command be equipped with the "unconventional" Spitfire and Hurricane would pay huge dividends in the summer of 1940. But his manner and personality in dealing with superiors at the Air Ministry made him lasting and bitter enemies.

The first RAF squadron to be equipped with the Hawker Hurricane was Number 111 Squadron, which received its new fighters late in 1937. The first Spitfire was delivered to Number 19 Squadron on 4 August 1938; the unit would not be completely converted to Spitfires until 19 December. By the time was war declared, 16 squadrons had been converted to the Hawker Hurricane, and nine squadrons were equipped with the Spitfire.

R. J. Mitchell, Sidney Camm, and Hugh Dowding had done their job. The outcome of the forthcoming Battle of Britain would now have to be decided by pilots of RAF Fighter Command.

TACTICS: "VIC" VS. "FINGER FOUR"

Flight tactics used by RAF Fighter Command proved themselves hopelessly inadequate; many a pilot paid for these shortcomings with his life. Senior RAF officers insisted upon obsolete movements and formations, including the standard pe-war "vic" formation. These may have been impressive during a peacetime air display but were not practical for combat. Luftwaffe pilots used a more mobile and flexible grouping, called the *Schwarm*.

Compared with the Schwarm, the tight "vic'" or "vee" formation—consisting of three fighters flying in close formation—had several serious shortcomings. One of the most glaring disadvantages of this tight grouping was loss of manoeuverability.

In a turn, for instance, the two inside aircraft had to reduce speed, while the outside aircraft was forced to accelerate. If this throttling back and forth was not done properly, the tight formation would break. Which meant that a formation turn had to be done slowly and gently—not the best policy during an air battle over the Channel! Also, a sudden move might leave one (or more) pilots alone in a hostile sky—the most dangerous possible situation for a fighter pilot.

Squadron formations consisted of four "vics" of three fighters each. To maintain this strict formation, pilots had to concentrate on watching each other instead of lookng out for enemy fighters. Someitmes, an "ass-end Charlie" was stationed behind the rest of the squadron; his job was to weave back and forth and keep watch for approaching enemy fighters. But his position—alone and behind everybody else in the formation—was so vulnerable that he often did not live long enough to do his job. (As Red Tobin of 609 Squadron nearly found out.) As time went on and lessons were learned, "ass-end Charlie" was discontinued.

Luftwaffe pilots used tactics better suited to air fighting, tactics that had been developed during the Spanish Civil War. The basic German formation was the *Rotte*, a two-fighter unit made up of a leader and his wingman. Two *Rotten* made up a *Schwarm*. The four fighters of the *Schwarm* flew a loose formation, and kept at different altitudes. This allowed each pilot to keep an eye out for the enemy, and allowed increased manoevrability without reducing speed.

RAF Fighter Command eventually adopted the Luftwaffe Schwarm, after individual squadrons had been using it unofficially—that is, without permission—throughout the Battle of Britain. The RAF called it "finger four" formation. (The U.S. Army Air Force also flew the "finger four" formation in its campaign against Germany.)

This new method of formation flying was considerably more successful than the old "vics." The change in tactics greatly improved the effectiveness of RAF fighter units and, in spite of initial opposition by senior RAF commanders, undoubtedly spared the lives of many fighter pilots.

Chapter II

DER KANALKAMPF
The Battle of Attrition
10 July - 11 August

The first "official" day of one of history's most celebrated battles, a battle that would be compared with Marathon, Waterloo, and Gettysburg, was very nearly called off because of bad weather.

The sky over southern England on the morning of Wednesday 10 July 1940 was gloomy and despondent—cloudy, windy, rainy, and nasty. Pilots took one look out the window from their bases in southern England, and decided to go back to sleep—it did not look as though there would be any flying that morning.

During the past few days, the pilots of Fighter Command had quite a lot of activity. The Luftwaffe had made its presence known over the Channel on the 8th and 9th; fighter pilots put in a good many "office hours" on both of these days. On Monday 8 July, for instance, Fighter Command flew more than 300 sorties to protect coastal convoys—about the same number they flew each day during Dunkirk—and had lost 12 pilots and 15 aircraft since 20 June. But on the 10th, it looked as though Fighter Command would have the day off.

But Dover Chain Home RDF[2] station picked up a German reconnaissance flight while the aircraft was still over France; other CH (Chain Home) stations detected more enemy aircraft. The Luftwaffe were sending flights to check the weather and give reports on targets of opportunity in the Channel and off the coast of Norfolk and Suffolk.

Fighter Command's Spitfires and Hurricanes were scrambled to intercept. A Dornier Do 17 was shot down over the sea near Great Yarmouth by Spitfires of 66 Squadron. Spitfires from 74 Squadron, based at Manston, damaged another Do 17; this Dornier made it back across the Channel, where it crash-landed near Boulogne. Before it had been shot up by the Spits from Manston, the Dornier's crew sent word of a large British convoy heading for the Straits of Dover. This news sent the Luftwaffe into action, and set the stage for the real fighting of 10 July.

Reports of the convoy, given the code-name "Bread," reached Luftwaffe intelligence at about 10 am. About 25 minutes later, a Staffel (about 12 aircraft) of Bf 109s were sent across the Channel on a *frei jagd*, literally "free hunt" or "free chase." The Messerschmitts were supposed to entice RAF fighters to come up and fight, so that they would be out of fuel and ammunition when the real attack took place later on. They were only partly successful. Nine Spitfires from Biggin Hill intercepted the 109s and lost one aircraft, flown by Squadron Leader Andrew Smith; the German fighters suffered no casualties.

At about 1:30 pm, the Luftwaffe's main attack began. The weather had improved radically by this time; rain had given way to scattered cloud and large stretches of blue sky. Chain Home radar stations on the south coast detected a large gathering of enemy aircraft south of Calais—about 70 planes, made up

---

2   RDF, Radio Direction Finding. It was known as DeTe by the Germans, for Decimeter Telegraphy. In 1943, the name was changed officially to radar, for Radio Direction and Ranging; this was to adopt the American name for the device.

of about 20 Do 17s and an escort of several Staffeln of Bf 109s and Bf 110s.

Six Spitfires from 32 Squadron were already on station over convoy Bread; four fighter squadrons were scrambled to reinforce—56 Squadron (Hurricanes) from Manston; 111 Squadron (Hurricanes) from Croydon; 64 Squadron (Spitfires) from Kenley; and 74 Squadron (Spitfires) from Hornchurch. Thirty-two RAF fighters and 70 Luftwaffe fighters and bombers headed toward each other on an interception course.

The two sides caught sight of each other at just about the same time. A naval pilot, assigned to the RAF by the Fleet Air Arm, observed "Waves of enemy bombers coming from direction of France in waves of six." The Luftwaffe had the advantage in numbers, but the RAF had the vital edge of altitude—they flew at heights several thousand feet above the Germans.

Number 32 Squadron's pilots had trouble finding the enemy—the Dorniers kept flying in and out of drifting clouds. But the Spitfire pilots of 74 Squadron found the enemy straight away, and attacked—one Dornier was shot down, and an escorting Bf 109 was damaged. Dover's anti-aircraft barrage also joined the fight, which was now increasing in tempo. The Hurricanes of 111 Squadron flew right through the flak in-line abreast, and charged head-on at a formation of Dorniers of Kampfgeschwader 2.

The Dornier pilots were shaken by the sight of 12 Hurricanes charging right at them—the combined closing speed was about 600 miles per hour—and scattered as the fighters tore through their formation. The Hurricanes, led by Squadron Leader John Thompson, turned round and began chasing the frightened German bombers. They caught up with one, and shot it down with a series of deflection attacks. Anti-aircraft batteries at Dungeness also claimed to have hit the Dornier. It crashed into the Channel; one NCO crewman was saved.

Over Dungeness, Flying Officer Tom Higgs collided with a Dornier, unit markings U5+FL of KG 2, and chopped off one of the bomber's wings. It crashed near Dungeness buoy at about 2 pm.; two of the four crew members survived, and were taken prisoner. F/O Higgs' Hurricane also lost a wing in the collision, and crashed not far from the Dornier. Although Higgs managed to bale out, he did not survive; his body washed up on the Dutch coast at Noordwijk over a month later, on 15 August.

The fight went on above convoy Bread, well within sight of the Kentish shore. And, for those who were not frightened into shelters, there was a great deal to see—huge splashes of exploding bombs that missed the convoy; fighters chasing their quarry at low-level; sometimes, an airplane trailing a long streamer of smoke before splashing into the Channel.

When 56 Squadron's Blue Section attacked a formation of Bf 110s, the three pilots were surprised to see the big twin engine fighter form a defensive circle—flying in a ring, so that the guns of each machine covered the tail of the fighter in front. This tactic didn't do them much good; their circle was soon broken up by the Hurricanes. Three of the *Zerstörers* were shot down; two others returned to base with .303 bullet holes in their wings and fuselage. Reichsmarschall Göring's vaunted Destroyer, in which he had placed so much hope, was clearly overmatched by the Hurricane, as well as by the Spitfires.

The Luftwaffe had more success in the west of the British Isles. A force of 63 Junkers Ju 88s attacked Falmouth, in Cornwall, and Swansea, Wales. In the attacks, thirty people were killed, a 6,000 ton vessel was sunk at Falmouth, and dock facilities were damaged. Although Spitfires of 92 Squadron were scrambled to intercept, they arrived too late. All of the Ju 88s returned safely to France.

Convoy Bread—which was in ballast and was not carrying cargo—lost one ship in the action off Dover. The Luftwaffe had 13 of its aircraft destroyed, and several others that made it back to base with damage caused by fighters and anit-aircraft fire. The RAF lost six airplanes and one pilot (P/O Higgs of 111 Squadron).

On this Wednesday, the air war over southern England and the Channel had taken a turn. The attacks by the Luftwaffe, and the RAF response, were not the small-scale activities of earlier in the month. The German air fleets had come in force, and had

A low-level attack on a coastal convoy, as seen from a Heinkel He 111. By early August, the Channel and Straits of Dover belonged to the Luftwaffe. Convoys, and their escorting destroyers, were being decimated by German bombers. Despite heavy losses in shipping—and RAF losses in both aircraft and pilots—the navy refused to abandon the convoy system. Their cargoes could very easily have been carried by rail, but the Admiralty insisted in continuing the coastal convoys for reasons of national prestige.

attacked in numbers previously unknown; RAF Fighter Command answered with 609 sorties.

"This afternoon, one of the greatest air battles of the war has been going on," Sir Edward Grigg, Parliamentary Secretary at the Ministry of Information, told the House of Commons. At the time, it certainly seemed like a great air battle—609 sorties by Fighter Command and 13 German aircraft destroyed seemed fairly overwhelming. In the weeks to come, however, these numbers would come to seem very small and insignificant.

On 30 June, Reichsmarschall Hermann Göring had ordered increased attacks against supply convoys in the Channel, as well as against English port towns. The ultimate goal of this campaign was, in Winston Churchill's estimation, that "our Air Force should be tested, drawn into battle, and depleted," and also that "damage should be done to those seaside towns marked as objectives for the forthcoming invasion"—especially between Dover and Plymouth. This phase of the battle would be called *der Kanalkampf*—the Battle of the Channel. It would be a battle of attrition against the RAF, an attempt to wear it down in both strength and numbers. Both sides would lose hundreds of aircraft, as well as many experienced pilots and aircrew.

11 July, Thursday

The Luftwaffe's activities against both the RAF and the Channel convoys continued on 11 July, in spite of cloud and overcast. At about 7:30 am., CH stations on the south coast plotted two enemy formations heading toward a convoy in Lyme Bay. Six Spitfires of 609 (West Riding) Squadron, based at Warmwell, and six Hurricanes of 501 Squadron, based at Middle Wallop, were vectored to intercept.

The Hurricanes arrived on the scene just before 8 am., and found about 10 Ju 87 Stukas moving into postion to attack the convoy. At about the same time, about 10 Bf 109s found the Hurricanes. In their attack, one Hurricane was shot down by Oberleutnant Franziket of JG 27; the pilot of the Hurricane, Sgt. Fred J.P. Dixon, baled out but drowned in the Channel.

A few minutes afterward, the six Spitfires of 609 Squadron met the Stukas just as the bombers were preparing to push over into their dives. Three Spits flew protective cover; the other three made ready to attack the Stukas. But once again, the Bf 109 escort struck first. The Messerschmitts of JG 27 flew right through the protective screen, and shot down two of the three attacking Spitfires. The pilots of both Spitfires were killed.

Losses of the RAF were three aircraft and three pilots; the Luftwaffe suffered no casualties. But the convoy lost no ships; the attacks of the RAF fighters were successful in distracting the Stukas.

Throughout the day on 11 July, single German aircraft made their annoying presence known to RAF Fighter Command; author Len Deighton called the day "an endless stream of German bombers." One of the earliest actions, and one of the best known, came at about 6:15 am. It was between a Dornier Do

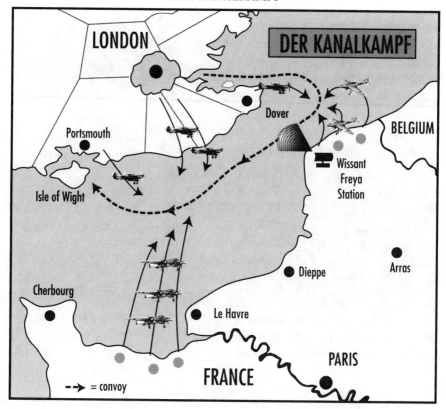

LONDON

DER KANALKAMPF

Dover

BELGIUM

Portsmouth

Wissant
Freya
Station

Isle of Wight

Dieppe

Arras

Cherbourg

Le Havre

PARIS

- ▸ = convoy

FRANCE

17 of KG 2 and Squadron Leader Peter Townsend of 85 Squadron, at the controls of a Hawker Hurricane.

One fighter was scrambled from Martlesham Heath, near Suffolk's North Sea coast, when the lone German aircraft was plotted. S/L Townsend took the call, and was vectored toward the enemy airplane. Near Lowestoft, he spotted the Dornier, but it was flying in the opposite direction. Townsend turned his Hurricane around, and began his attack.

The Dornier's gunner began shooting first, but from too far away. When Townsend was satisfied that he was close enough, he "pressed the tit and things warmed up inside the Dornier." Two of the crew were hit; fragments of metal were blown about the inside of the bomber. But the gunner was not among those injured, and kept shooting at Townsend.

Rare shot of a Spitfire maneuvering to attack a Dornier Do 17. This technique for approaching an aircraft with a rear firing gunner dated from the First World War.

Townsend was still behind the Dornier when "suddenly there was a large orange explosion in the cockpit in front of me"—his engine had been hit by the Dornier's machine gunner, and began to seize up. He began trailing black smoke, and dove away from the German bomber.

"Am hit and bailing out at sea," Townsend reported to ground control. Underneath his right wing, he caught sight of a ship; it looked so small that it reminded him of a toy boat. After grabbing hold of his parachute's ripcord ring, Townsend jumped from his crippled fighter. During the minutes while he drifted down toward the cold North Sea, he watched his Hurricane, squadron markings VY-K, crash vertically into the frigid blue-grey water.

The crew of the small boat was watching, as well. They saw a pilot come down in the sea, less than a mile away, and sent a small boat to pick him up. The verbal exchange betwen Townsend and the boat's crew may not rank with Stanley's first meeting with Livingstone, but it deserves an honorable mention.

Four sailors rowed the small boat; a fifth rode in the stern, holding a boathook. Sailors are notorious at aircraft identification, and apparently even worse at identifying pilots by nationality. "Blimey, if he aint a fucking Hun," the fifth man shouted in a broad North Country accent.

"I'm not," Townsend replied. "I'm a fucking Englishman." His eloquence was rewarded by being hauled aboard the boat and rowed to the trawler *Cap Finisterre*, where he was given several generous tots of rum.

The trawler's crew took Townsend back to England; he was back on patrol in a new Hurricane later that day. He was told that *Cap Finisterre* had been well off-course and in the middle of a minefield when he had been picked up—his rescue had been the purest kind of luck. Many other pilots would not be nearly so fortunate in the weeks to come.

Townsend's Dornier, or rather the Dornier that shot Townsend down, made it back to France in spite of being severely damaged. Its wiring circuitry had been shot away; its undercarriage would not come down; and it still had bombs on board. But it took its wounded crew back to St. Leger, where the pilot made a wheels-up landing. The gunner that shot S/L Townsend's engine to pieces wrote that the brave Do 17 "got us home despite 220 hits in the engines, fuel tanks, and other vital parts."

If Townsend's Hurricane had been equipped with 20 mm cannon instead of .303 caliber machine guns, he probably would have destroyed the Dornier. The RAF actually did experiment with 20 mm cannon in 1940, but gave them up as too unreliable—frequent jamming was the major complaint.

Pilots favored the DeWilde incendiary shells over the standard .303 ball ammunition; the DeWilde shell did a lot more damage to enemy aircraft than solid shot. They also exploded with a bright flash on impact which, in the words of the New Zealand ace Alan Deere, allowed pilots "to confirm their aim," which is to say that they let the pilot know where his shots were hitting. If Townsend's armorers had loaded his guns with DeWilde ammunition, along with solid shot, he also would have stood a very good chance of destroying the Dornier—those hits in the fuel tanks mentioned by the bomber's gunner would have set the airplane on fire.

But S/L Townsend had no complaint about his fight over the North Sea—he was lucky to be alive. At this stage of the Battle, British air-sea rescue was virtually non-existent. A British pilot who baled out over the Channel or the North Sea "had to rely on luck, the Navy, the coast guards, or a passing convoy."

The Luftwaffe had a well-organized rescue operation, which included about thirty Heinkel He 59 seaplanes to save pilots from the sea. While waiting to be picked-up by a He 59, the pilot was equipped with inflatable rubber dinghies and other items that saved many a German pilot from death either by drowning or exposure. But the RAF had no such system, which cost many pilots and aircrew that might have been saved.

Britain was enjoying a lot more success against the Luftwaffe than in her battle to convince the United States to join her as an ally. Prime Minister Winston Churchill realized that Britain needed American help—there was nowhere else to turn. But he was having a difficult time convincing the Americans that Britain was worth the effort. The United States made it clear that it did not want to involve itself in a war with Germany. But the country also seemed convinced that Britain was losing the war, and that any help given the British would be a waste of time and materiel.

In the summer of 1940, the United States was solidly isolationist. In May of that year, a Gallup poll indicated that 64% of Americans favored staying out of the war instead of helping Britain. Americans made it very clear that they wanted no part of the British or their war with Germany. Charles Lindbergh, the American aviation hero of the 1920s and now an outspoken isolationist, spoke bluntly for the majority of his countrymen. "We must not be misguided that our frontiers are in Europe," he insisted. "What more could we ask for than the Atlantic Ocean on the East, and the Pacific on the West?"

Britain was insulted. "The United States administration is pursuing an almost entirely American policy, rather than one of all possible aid to Britain," Foreign Secretary Anthony Eden complained to Winston Churchill.

The American ambassador to Great Britain, Joseph P. Kennedy (father of future U.S. President John F. Kennedy), added to the insult and resentment. Kennedy told anyone who would listen, including American journalists, that Britain was not only losing the war but had no chance of winning it. Britain's only chance, he told a group of American officers, was for the U.S. to "pull them out."

When Ambassador Kennedy returned to the United States, he was quoted in the *Boston Globe* as predicting that "Democracy is finshed in England" and "if we get into the war, it will be in this country, too." (Kennedy protested that he had been misquoted, and that his interview had been off the record.)

Although Kennedy's sentiments made him something less than popular in Britain, he was actually reflecting the thoughts of many of his fellow Americans. Throughout the United States, men and women of all backgrounds and occupations believed that Britain was losing the war. When a member of President Roosevelt's cabinet called Britain a good risk, Missouri Senator Bennett C. Clark expressed his astonishment at this point of view.

There were those who opposed helping "the damn Redcoats" because Britain had been America's traditional enemy for generations, or because they resented the British trying to drag Americans into their war. But the most popular sentiment was pure isolationism, deeply ingrained in the American character—"whatever the British do, 3,500 miles away, is none of our concern."

President Roosevelt favored aid to Britain. He saw that the ambitions of Adolf Hitler would one day bring Germany into conflict with the United States, and that if Britain surrendered, Americans would face Germany alone. But Roosevelt had to be very careful. He had decided to run for an unprecedented third

Winston Churchill's statue in Parliament Square. Because he refused to compromise with Hitler after France had surrendered, Churchill is remembered mainly for his resolution in war, and for his role as a wartime leader. But he should also be remembered as a master of propaganda.

term as President; he did not want to ruin his chances of being re-elected by being labelled a war monger by the Republicans.

It is difficult to grasp how isolationist, and isolated, the U.S. had become. "People who spoke out against Hitler... or joined anti-Nazi organizations were seen vaguely as too far left, too liberal," wrote an American social historian. An anti-Nazi Hollywood screenwriter, who had gone on record as being against Hitler, was rejected when he tried to join the U.S. Army—he was labelled a "premature anti-fascist."

So Winston Churchill already had a two-front war in the summer of 1940. The first was against Adolf Hitler and his war machine, particularly his Luftwaffe. The second front was against an America that was determined to remain neutral and detached no matter what: against a defeatist Ambassador Kennedy; against an antagonistic Charles Lindbergh; and against a politically pragmatic Franklin Roosevelt.

At first, Churchill tried to frighten Roosevelt with the prospect of an early German victory, and what that would mean to America. But he soon gave up that idea—if Americans thought that the Germans were sure to win, they would be even less inclined to back Britain's war effort.

And so, Churchill and Britain's Ministry of Information used the opposite approach. The myth of "Their Finest Hour" was created—the gallant young pilots of the RAF fighting the ruthless Hun over southern England, and shooting them down in record numbers.

The Ministry of Information gave U.S. reporters and correspondents all the help they needed—and made certain that British censors gave stories a pro-British slant. And the American fliers who crossed the Atlantic to join the Royal Air Force, the Yanks in the RAF, were also put to good use by Britain's propaganda machine—persuading the stubborn Americans that some of their fellow countrymen were already fighting Hitler.

If reason did not persuade the Americans to join the fight, there were other, more subltle ways. A British writer said that the Prime Minister was "obsessed with getting America into the war." Churchill may or may not have been obsessed, but he certainly was determined that the defiantly neutral—and sometimes blatantly anti-British—Americans would have their views turned around.

* * *

Both the Luftwaffe and the RAF spent the month of July getting the measure of each other—each other's aircraft, each other's tactics, each other's strengths and weaknesses. During the first two weeks of the battle, the Luftwaffe's main plan seemed to be working, at least up to a point. RAF Fighter Command was rising to the bait—coming up to protect the coastal convoys that traveled from the Thames Estuary through the Straits of Dover.

But the results were not always what the Luftwaffe's senior officers had anticipated. Fighter Command's strength was being worn down, as had been planned, but the Luftwaffe was also suffering its share of losses. Between 10 July and 23 July, the RAF lost 45 aircraft (mostly fighters), while the Luftwaffe lost 82 aircraft (of all types).

Possibly because of exaggerated claims, Luftwaffe High Command seemed to believe that the RAF had the higher loss ratio. "In these encounters," a Luftwaffe historian wrote about the Channel battle, "the RAF definitely came out second-best." This sort of wishful thinking would continue, not only throughout the battle but all during the war. It would often cause German commanders to underestimate their opponents, usually with disastrous results.

Which is not to imply that the RAF was winning the battle. For although the Luftwaffe were losing more aircraft, these included bombers, fighters, and even HE 59 seaplanes; the RAF's losses were mainly fighters. Writer Len Deighton points out that the RAF fighter losses were increasing at such a rate that Fighter Command "would cease to exist within six weeks" (of 19 July).

Between 12 July and 23 July, losses by RAF Fighter Comand resulting from combat are given below. Luftwaffe fighter losses are also given:

DATE	RAF FIGHTER LOSSES	LUFTWAFFE FIGHTER LOSSES
12 July, Friday	5	0
13 July, Saturday	3	2 (1 Bf109, 1 Bf 110)
14 July, Sunday	1	2 (both Bf 109s)
15 July, Monday	2	0
16 July, Tuesday	0	0
17 July, Wednesday	1	0
18 July, Thursday	3	1 (Bf 109)
19 July, Friday	10 (including 6 Blenheims of 141 Sq.)	3 (Bf 109s)
20 July, Saturday	8	5 (Bf 109s)
21 July, Sunday	0	2 (1 Bf 109, 1 Bf 110)
22 July, Monday	0	0
23 July, Tuesday	0	0
Total for 12 days	33	15

One of the reasons behind the RAF's high loss rate in fighters was their outdated air fighting tactics. "Area Attacks" were employed as the basic combat tactic—these were basically parade-ground formations, which looked impressive but did not allow pilots room to maneuver. Typical of these formations was the "V," or "Vic," where pilots were too busy watching their neighbor's wingtip to watch out for the enemy. (The in-line abreast formation was another Area Attack, used with such success by 111 Squadron because it was done as a head-on charge.)

German fighter pilots relied upon the four-fighter *Schwarm*, later known as "finger four formation" by British and American pilots. It involved two pairs of aircraft, each pair consisting of a leader and his wingman. This formation was loose and maneuverable, with each pilot guarding the vulnerable tail of another in the formation.

The *Schwarm*, as well as the leader-and-wingman system called the *Rotte*, were devised by Werner Mölders during the Spanish Civil War. By the summer of 1940, Luftwaffe pilots were experienced in flying this formation, and used it to its maximum advantage against the RAF and their outdated Area Attacks. Although Fighter Command would adopt the finger four, it would require some time before its pilots were able to learn it.

24 July, Wednesday

The Luftwaffe's attacks against Channel shipping continued, in spite of frequent showers, rain, haze, and cloud. On 24 July, JG 26—Adolf Galland's *Geschwader*—and JG 52 each lost three Bf 109s; 54 Squadron and 610 (County of Chester) Squadron lost three Spitfires between them. All this happened even though the day was rainy and cloudy.

25 July, Thursday

On the following day, the skies cleared; the weather looked to be fine for the first time in a couple of weeks. In the south of

England, it was a good day for sunbathing. It was also a good day for flying. And for fighting.

Shortly after noon, about 60 Stukas of StG 65 and a cover of Bf 109s from JG 26 and JG 52, attacked convoy C.W. 8, code named "Peewit," in the Straits of Dover. Peewit consisted of 21 colliers and other small coastal vessels, escorted by the destroyers *Boreas* and *Brilliant*.

The Messerschmitts arrived on the scene first. They approached the convoy at sea level. They hoped to bring the inevitable RAF fighters down low, so that the vulnerable Stukas would be left alone.

The Spitfires of 65 Squadron, operating from Hornchurch, Essex, were scrambled and intercepted the enemy fighters. The resulting free-for-all was carried out at such low level that a Bf 109 of JG 52 flew straight into the Channel during a fight with a Spitfire, killing the pilot instantly.

Hurricanes from 32 Squadron, based at Biggin Hill, as well as of 65 Squadron from Kenley, were vectored to join the fight. While they were occupied with Messerschmitts at low altitude, the Stukas arrived. With no fighters to interfere with them the Stuka attacks were slow, deliberate, and accurate. In just a few minutes, the dive bombers demonstrated why they had been the terror of Poland and France.

The collier *Tamworth* was bracketed by near misses; columns of white water rose to six or seven times the height of her masts. One of the bombs exploded beneath the ship, literally blowing it out of the water and stopping its engines. The ship just astern, *Leo*, took a direct hit and capsized. A Dutch coaster up ahead also suffered a direct hit and sank. Almost as soon as this group of Stukas pulled out of their dives, a second wave began its attack. The cement carrier *Summity* was hit and had to be beached to prevent her from sinking. The collier *Henry Moon* was also bombed; she capsized and sank.

By the time the third formation of Stukas arrived, the convoy was no longer holding any sort of formation. More bombs fell from the undersides of the swooping dive bombers, and more ships were hit. Near misses drenched officers on the bridge of the destroyer *Boreas*.

The commander of der Kanalkampf [3] watched the attack from his mobile headquarters at Cap Blanc Nez. It was quite a spectacle, and for Oberst Fink a highly satisfying one—his Stukas peeling off into almost impossibly steep dives; the tall geysers from exploding bombs; the debris from the coastal vessels as they rolled over and sank. At the height of the action, destroyers Boreas and Brilliant broke away from the convoy and headed across the Channel for Oberst Fink's headquarters, which was visible from the two ships. Both destroyers fired at Fink's command post; no damage was reported, except to Oberst Fink's composure. But before the destroyers could get away, they were also attacked by Stukas—an officer on the bridge thought he counted twenty-four of them. After a lot of near misses, one of which put Boreas' steering gear out of action for a few minutes, the destroyer's luck ran out.

Two bombs hit *Boreas*' bridge. Neither exploded on contact; both penetrated to the lower decks and exploded in the galley, killing 50 sailors. *Boreas* had to be towed back to Dover by *Brilliant*.

More fighter support was called for. Nine Spitfires from 54 Squadron were sent from Rochford, and met a swarm of Bf 109s—including 36 from III/JG 26,[4] led by Major Adolf Galland. While 54 Squadron's pilots were preparing to attack the Stukas, the Spitfires were "bounced" by Galland's Messerschmitts.

Galland later wrote that "in this conflict we had clear superiority, the English aircraft fighting almost without exception singly"—the *Schwarm* once again gave German pilots a vital

---

3   Oberst Johannes Fink. Oberst Fink's official designation was *Kanalkampfführer*, Channel Battle Leader. He was also known as Chief Sewage Worker, *kanal* translating as "sewer." Fink accepted this as the joke it was meant to be.

4   This indicates the third *Gruppe* of *Jagdgeschwader* (fighter or literally "hunter" *Geschwader*) 26. A *Geschwader* was roughly the equivalent of an RAF Wing or a USAAF Group all of which consisted of about 36 aircrafts.

edge over RAF pilots. Two of the Spitfires were shot down. One crash-landed near Dover; the other, piloted by F/Lt B.H. "Wonky" Way, crash-landed into the Channel. The pilot did not survive. None of the Messerschmitts were lost.

The day's fighting was not over yet. At about 2.30, roughly 30 Junkers Ju 88s approached what was left of the badly mauled convoy. The RAF Senior Controller sent 8 Spitfires of 64 Squadron to intercept; the Spits attacked, but were jumped by the Bf 109 escort. No losses were reported on either side, but the Ju 88s continued their course toward the convoy.

The remaining three Spitfires of 64 Squadron were also sent for, as well as the Hurricanes of 111 Squadron from Croydon. When 111 Squadron arrived over the Channel, the squadron leader formed his pilots into the unit's favorite tactic—a line abreast head-on attack right through the German formation.

This was a nerve-jangling experience for both sides—closing with each other at a combined speed of about 600 miles hour. This time, as usual, it was the bomber pilots who flinched. The Ju 88s broke formation and headed back toward France. Their Bf 109 escort went with them.

But the afternoon was still not over. As Peewit passed Folkstone, it came under attack by yet another group of Stukas; at least one more ship was sunk. When the Stukas had finished, a force of German motor torpedo boats, or E-boats, came out from the vicinity of Calais and went after the convoy. No hits were reported, but the attack did nothing to improve either the nerves or the disposition of anyone in the convoy.

By the time the sun set on Thursday, 25 July, five ships out of the 21 of convoy Peewit were on the bottom of the Straits of Dover. Another six were dead in the water. Both escorting destroyers were damaged; one of them would not be back in service for quite some time. During the night, E-boats came out and sank three more of the surviving ships.

In the confusing air melee above the convoy, the Luftwaffe lost 18 aircraft; the RAF lost seven. Of the eighteen German aircraft, 7 were Messerschmitt Bf 109s. Surprisingly, only 3 were

Stukas. One of the Stukas was shot down by Pilot Officer Geoffrey Page of 56 Squadron.

Pilot Officer Page, along with Barry Sutton and F/Lt "Jumbo" Gracie, did not see the dive bombers at first. The first thing that caught their attention was the flashes of anti-aircraft fire from the guns of *Boreas* and *Brilliant*; then, they saw the German planes "swarming above the ships," formed in two layers. The three of them dived on the lower level, which consisted of Stukas that had already made their attacks and were on their way back to base in France.

Page's Stuka was putting up a fight. The pilot zig-zagged left and right, trying to spoil Page's aim while giving his rear gunner a better shot at the attacking Hurricane. But Sutton had an easy target. His Stuka executed a climbing turn to starboard, right across Sutton's sights. "The worst shot in the world couldn't have missed," he said.

Sutton pressed the firing button on the Hurricane's control column; bullets from his eight Browning maching guns tore pieces from the Stuka. He watched as the stricken bomber plunged into the Channel. Sutton was surprised that it did not make a bigger splash when it hit.

P/O Page was not having such an easy time of it as Sutton. The Stuka's rear gunner kept shooting at Page, but the battle was entirely one-sided. A burst from his eight .303 machine guns set the enemy bomber on fire. Page watched it glide down; he thought it took a very long time before it crashed into the water, and imagined that the crew had already been killed by his guns. After the Stuka finally hit, all that remained on the surface was one tire and some burning oil.

It was Page's first kill, his first air victory. He should have been elated—and was, up to a point. But he was also repelled. He wrote to an old friend from his days at the RAF Cadet College, Cranwell, "I enjoy killing. It fascinated me beyond belief to see my bullets striking home and then to see the Hun blow up before me. It also makes me feel sick."

But Page did not have the luxury of being sick of fighting. The Channel battle showed no signs of ending. The Luftwaffe were gathering strength in northern France, and were about to intensify their attacks.

26 July, Friday

On 26 and 27 July, cloud and rain curtailed operations. But the Luftwaffe attacks continued, in spite of the poor visibility.

Fighter Command logged 581 sorties on 26 July, but only 4 RAF aircraft were lost, as well as 2 German. On that same day, the War Cabinet reported that "many fresh German troops" were arriving in Belgium and Holland, "of which a high proportion belong to the Air Force."

27 July, Saturday

On the 27th, two convoys were attacked in the morning, and the destroyer *Wren* was sunk. The port of Dover also came under attack—a destroyer in the harbor was hit, and docking facilities, as well s the barracks, suffered bomb damage. Four German aircraft were lost, against one for the RAF.

Dover had been given the nickname "Hell Fire Corner" by the press, and lately had been living up to it. On 28 July, the Admiralty decided not to use Dover as a forward base for its anti-invasion destroyers—too many were being sunk or damaged. The destroyers were withdrawn to Portsmouth. Also, fighter cover for Dover was increased to 28 operational squadrons. If the Luftwaffe had not yet cleared the RAF from southern England, it had already begun to force the Royal Navy to withdraw from the Straits of Dover.

28 July, Sunday

The Luftwaffe's main attack did not begin until afternoon. One fighter unit that would take part in the day's activities was *Jagdgeschwader* 51, under the command of Major Werner Mölders. This would be Mölders' first trip across the Channel, even though he already had 25 enemy aircraft to his credit—including 14 that he had shot down as a member of the Condor Legion in Spain. It was also his first day as *Kommodore* of JG 51.

Major Werner Mölders, who became Kommodore of Jagdgeschwader 51 in July, learned the tricks of the fighter pilot's trade during the Spanish Civil War. In 1938, Mölders became a member of the Legion Kondor (along with his colleague and rival Adolf Galland of JG 26). In Spain, he developed the four-man schwarm, or "finger four formation," which was eventually adopted by the RAF.

Altogether, it would turn out to be a very memorable day for him.

Werner Mölders was acknowledged the Luftwaffe's leading fighter pilot, its top ace. His leading rival, Adolf Galland—who would end the war with 104 enemy aircraft destroyed—admitted that it was Mölders who "taught me how to shoot and bring down aircraft." Mölders was known as "Vati" (Daddy) because of his serious demeanor, and had earned a great deal of respect—on both sides—for his shooting ability. He became the first fighter pilot to be awarded the Knight's Cross of the Iron Cross, and would become General of Fighters (*General der Jagdflieger*) before reaching the age of 29.

It is surprising that Mölders became a fighter pilot at all, let alone that he rose to such a high rank. He suffered from air sickness to such a degree that it nearly prevented him from flying. But he was so determined to become a pilot that he suffered through the pain and discomfort. He was also a devout Roman Catholic, and was completely unsympathetic toward the Nazi regime—two items that probably would have ended the career of a pilot with lesser abilities. But the Luftwaffe needed fighter pilots, especially outstanding pilots, and chose to overlook Mölders' differences.

Spitfires attacked the Bf 109s of Mölders' JG 51. A Messerschmitt from Mölders' formation was shot down "in flames." At that point, he found himself "in the middle of a clump of Englishmen, and they were all very angry with me." They all rushed at him, and were in such a hurry to score a kill that they got in each other's way.

One of the Spitfire pilots got clear of the pack and got behind Mölders. The editors of *The Battle of Britain Then and Now* claim that the pilot was F/Lt Webster of 41 Squadron. Len Deighton thought that it was none other than A.G. "Sailor" Malan, the legendary South African fighter ace. Whoever it was, they held Mölders in their gunsight long enough to put a long burst into his Messerschmitt. Mölders was lucky to be able to fly across the Channel and belly-land on the French coast—Len Deighton said that he never would have made it if Spitfires had been armed with 20 mm cannon.

Mölders was taken to a hospital in France with leg wounds, and was not able to fly again for a month. His Messerschmitt Bf 109E-3 was a loss.

He had been shot down once before, during the Battle of France. Mölders had been able to crash-land that time, as well, but he came down behind French lines and was taken prisoner. When France surrendered in June, he was returned to the Luftwaffe and, in Winston Churchill's words, had to be shot down "a second time."

Werner Mölders would be involved in one more air crash; his third which would also be his last. In November 1941, Generaloberst Ernst Udet, Germany's Director of Air Armament, committed suicide after a bitter dispute with Reichsmarschall

Hermann Göring. Because of Udet's rank in the Luftwaffe and his record as a fighter pilot in the First World War—62 enemy aircraft shot down—he was given a state funeral. Mölders was ordered to attend the funeral, along with other prominent Luftwaffe officers. The Heinkel He 111 in which Mölders was traveling to the funeral stalled and crashed; he was killed instantly.

Fighting on 28 July cost the Luftwaffe 18 aircraft; RAF losses came to five. Attacks on shipping were completely frustrated by Fighter Command; no bombs were dropped.

29 July, Monday

Another convoy was attacked off Dover on 29 July. About 50 Ju 87 Stukas, with a cover of about 80 Bf 109s, approached the coastal convoy at about 8am. This force was intercepted by Spitfires and Hurricanes, which shot down 4 Stukas and damaged another for the loss of one Spitfire. Later in the day, Junkers Ju 88s made another attack near Worthing; one bomber was destroyed.

Also on the 29th, RAF pilots were given official permission to shoot down Heinkel He 59 seaplanes of German air-sea rescue. Although these seaplanes were painted white and marked conspicuously with red crosses, they were frequently spotted near coastal convoys and were suspected of reporting their position. In other words, the He 59s were performing reconnaissance patrols under the protection of the red cross.

Three He 59s had been destroyed on 28 July—Dr. Josef Goebbels, the German progaganda minister, called the pilots murderers. Now, the Air Ministry officially sanctioned attacking the seaplanes.

30 July, Tuesday

Weather once again curtailed operations on 30 July, but the Luftwaffe were up and looking for a fight. The drizzle worked against the German bombers; in their attacks, they failed to score any hits. The RAF did not seem to have any trouble finding the bombers, however. They shot down five bombers, without any losses to themselves.

31 July, Wednesday

Fighting began at about 11am. over the Dover coast. Luftwaffe attacks on shipping were carried out in full view of news correspondents, the majority of whom appear to have been American.

Dover had become "lodestone for the news media"—the diving Stukas, the bursting anti-aircraft shells, and the white contrails of the twisting and turning fighters against the blue sky were all clearly visible. "You could lie on your back with glasses," said American reporter Drew Middleton, "and look up, and there was the whole goddamn air battle."

Then Dover itself came under attack by about 80 bombers; the exploding bombs made the ships in the harbor bob about "like corks," according to one eyewitness.

During early afternoon, isolated raids around Harwich on the North Sea Coast harrassed the east coast defenses. And later on, Dover came under attack again when about 18 Bf 109s went after the harbor's balloon barrage—the balloons were a hindrance to the bombers because they kept attackers at a respectful height.

By the end of the day, the Luftwaffe had lost five machines. The RAF lost three.

* * *

At about the same time that Dover harbor was being bombed, Adolf Hitler went into a meeting at his Berghof, his "Eagle's Nest" in Bavaria. Also present were Feldmarschall Wilhelm Keitel and General Alfred Jodl, General Franz Halder and Feldmarschall Walther von Brauchitsch, and Grossadmiral Erich Raeder. The topic under discussion was to be the invasion of England, Operation Sea Lion. Reichsmarschall Hermann Göring, the head of the Luftwaffe and the man from whom so much would be needed, was not present—Hitler apparently did not think it important for him to attend.

Hitler asked Grossadmiral Raeder how far the German navy, the *Kriegsmarine*, had come in its preparations for the invasion. Raeder was his usual windy self that particular Wednesday, and gave his answer in several thousand well-chosen words.

Preparations were proceeding on schedule, Raeder said, and the navy was doing its best. But he would need calm weather for an invasion; if the Channel turned stormy, landing barges would sink and supply ships would not be able to unload. He did not want to be held responsible for the weather. Also, he strongly recommended a shortened landing front—he did not want to be responsible for the army if it found itself stranded on the damn English beaches. He finished by telling Hitler and the senior army chiefs that, all things considered, "the best time for this operation would be May 1941."

Hitler was used to the Grossadmiral, as well as his gassing and his gloominess, and was not dissuaded from his invasion plans. He did not want to wait until the spring of 1941, which would give the British time to build up their defenses. Also, he had his eyes on the vast plains of Russia—"When we speak of new territory in Europe today," he wrote in *Mein Kampf*, "we must think principally of Russia and her border vassal states." Britain was only a temporary stumbling block, and would be dealt with in the same manner as the Belgians, the Dutch, the Poles, and the French. The sooner Britain was eliminated, the sooner he would be able to turn his full attention to Russia.

And so, Hitler decided, the invasion had to be prepared by 15 September 1940. This was the date given by Raeder as the earliest possible time for completion of preparations. The Luftwaffe would begin an intensified campaign against targets in southern England as a preliminary to invasion. After two weeks of concentrated attacks against the Royal Air Force, naval bases, and ports, Hitler himself would decide whether or not the invasion would be carried out in 1940. Otherwise, it would be postponed until 1941.

In other words, Hitler had taken the main burden away from the Kriegsmarine and placed it on the Luftwaffe. And Herman

Göring, the Luftwaffe Commander in Chief, was not even at the meeting.

On the following day, 1 August, Führer Directive No. 17 was issued. In it, Hitler made clear his intent "to intensify air and sea warfare against the English homeland." Specifically, he ordered:

1. The Luftwaffe is to overpower the Royal Air Force...
2. After achieving temporary, or local, air superiority, the air war is to be carried out aginst harbours...

After these two items had been accomplished, "The Luftwaffe is to stand by in force for Operation Sea Lion."

Grossadmiral Raeder was not happy about the Führer's decision regarding Operation Sea Lion—he still thought that his navy would be overtaxed by such an operation. But Hermann Göring was delighted. He called a meeting of senior Luftwaffe officers at the Hague to discuss the imminent battle against the RAF. For the occasion, the always-flamboyant Göring—his detractors said that he was vulgar—wore a brand-new white uniform, complete with all of his medals and decorations.

"The Führer has ordered me to crush Britain with my Luftwaffe," he told the gathering. "By delivering a series of very heavy blows, I plan to have the enemy, whose morale is already at its lowest, down on its knees in the nearest future so that our troops can land on the island without any risk."

Hermann Göring had a tendency to believe his own propaganda. For instance, he believed that the Americans would be unable to produce a fighter that could compete with the Messerschmitt Bf 109 because Americans were only good at producing consumer products. They were very good at refrigerators, children's toys, and sewing machines, but had no flair for fighter planes. When the Luftwaffe first encountered the Republic P-47 Thunderbolt, and the North American P-51 Mustang the year following, Göring was astonished to discover that the toy-makers could have made two such outstanding airplanes.

In the summer of 1940, Göring convinced himself that the British suffered from a terminal case of low morale, and also that

RAF pilots lacked the courage to confront the Luftwaffe—in spite of the fact that Fighter Command had been giving a very good account of itself for the past several weeks.

Göring's inability, or unwillingness, to deal with facts was one of his glaring weaknesses. It would end up costing the Luftwaffe, and himself, everything they had.

One of the Luftwaffe commanders at the Hague meeting, Theo Osterkamp of JG 51, argued that the RAF were not cowards, that their fighters were damn formidable, and that they had been giving the Luftwaffe one hell of a row over the Channel. Göring brushed Osterkamp aside, saying that the RAF were too cowardly to engage German fighters.

The plan to destroy the RAF was to be called Eagle Attack, *Adlerangriff*, which would take about two weeks. The start of the big offensive, on *Adlertag*—Eagle Day, which would be the first day of the attack—would be determined as soon as preparations were complete and the reports promised fair weather.

* * *

Nobody really knows how many "secret Americans" served in the Royal Air Force during the summer of 1940, or how many Canadians who joined the RAF were actually Americans who kept their nationality a secret. The editors of *The Battle of Britain Then and Now* give the number of U.S. citizens who took part in the battle as 11 (the official number is 7), but the real figure is probably many times higher. The only traces of their true nationality are nicknames, buried in squadron rosters—"Tex," or "America," or "Uncle Sam."

Three Americans who went to England by way of Canada—and managed to conceal their identities from prying FBI agents at the Canadian border—were Andrew Mamedoff, Eugene Q. "Red" Tobin, and Vernon C. "Shorty" Keough. The three managed to outsmart U.S. authorities on both sides of the Atlantic, and wound up in 609 (West Riding) Squadron in time to take part in the height of the battle.

Red Tobin and Andy Mamedoff had originally signed up as pilots for Finland's air force. Russian troops had invaded

Finland in November 1939, and the Finns were in desperate need of pilots. Neither had any experience with fighter planes or military flying, but the pay of $100 per month and the excitement of foreign service sounded intriguing. That was all the incentive they needed to leave sunny California.

But Finland gave up the fight in the winter of 1940, before Tobin and Mamedoff had the chance to leave California. They still wanted to be fighter pilots, though, and found out that the French *Armee de l'Air* was looking for men. The French air force looked as good to them as the Finnish air force, so they signed up with *l'Armee* and set off for France.

Before crossing the border into Canada, Tobin and Mamedoff met Vernon Keough, a 4-foot-10-inch former parachute jumper with the appropriate nickname "Shorty." During his career, Shorty managed to survive 486 jumps at air shows and county fairs. If anyone asked why he was so short (which did happen occasionally), he would reply that he used to be of normal height until he became a jumper—the impact of all the landings had pushed his legs right up inside his body. You ask a stupid question, you get a stupid answer.

The three arrived in France a very short time before the French army surrendered. They never got to fly with *l'Armee;* they had a hard enough time keeping away from the advancing Wehrmacht, sleeping in haystacks and living like refugees. On 22 June, the day that France formally asked for an armistice, Keough, Tobin, and Mamedoff reached the French port of St. Jean de Luz and boarded the steamer *Baron Nairn*—the last ship to leave occupied France. Two days later, they disembarked at Plymouth. Having missed joining the Finnish air force and *l'Armee*, they decided that they might as well try the RAF. "If you go looking for a fight," Red Tobin said, "you can always find one."

Although the three had managed to evade the Wehrmacht and were now safely in England, their troubles were far from over. They went to the U.S. Embassy in London for assistance, and were very nearly deported for their efforts when they announced their intention to join the Royal Air Force. Ambassador

Joseph P. Kennedy was not overjoyed to hear that three U.S. citizens were trying to join the armed services of a foreign country,[5] and tried to have them sent back to the United States. By joining the Royal Air Force, Red Tobin, Shorty Keough, and Andy Mamedoff would be violating the U.S. Neutrality Acts that had been passed by the Congress of the United States in the 1930s.[6]

American authorities were quite serious about preventing U.S. nationals from joining the Royal Air Force. Six potential volunteers from California found out about the Neutrality Act, and the enforcement of it, the hard way. They had decided to join the RAF and, in late 1940, headed for Canada to sign up.

When their train made its first stop inside Canada, the six young fellows were met by agents of the Federal Bureau of Investigation. The FBI men gave them a choice—either go back home, or go to prison. It wasn't a hard decision—the six went back to California. But they did try again. On the second try, they made it past the border guards and, finally, over to England.[7]

But Tobin, Keough, and Mamedoff managed to get around Ambassador Kennedy with the help of a friendly Member of Parliament. The MP got them into the RAF—at which point, the

---

5   Adolf Hitler referred to American isolationists as "American radical
     nationalists." In Kennedy's case, it was more a matter of being anti-British than
     radically pro-American.
6   Actually, three Neutrality Acts passed through Congress between 1935 and 1937.
     The Acts that prohibited the sale of US arms and munitions to a "belligerent
     nation," as well as the use of American ships to carry any such weapons, were
     repealed in 1939. But it was still against the law to join the armed forces of a
     "belligerent nation;" Americans who did so had their US citizenship revoked. It
     is interesting to note, however, that American pilots who flew with the the
     American Volunteer Group in China, the famous Flying Tigers, had no
     restrictions, and these were military pilots, trained by U.S. taxpayers' money.
     Which gives an indication of the American attitude toward Britain in 1940.
7   One of the six was Chesley Peterson, a Mormon from Utah. Peterson became a
     member of the first Eagle Squadron, and rose to the rank of Major General in
     the U.S. Air Force.

Three Yanks in the RAF. Left to right: Eugene "Red" Tobin; Vernon "Shorty" Keough, and Andrew "Andy" Mamedoff, all members of 609 (West Riding) Squadron. Here, they are displaying the brand-new "Eagle Squadron" patch—Tobin, Keough, and Mamedoff were the first members of the all-American 71 (Eagle) Squadron, which was formed at the end of September 1940. All three were killed on active service with the RAF in 1941.

three Yanks lost their citizenship and technically became fugitives from justice.

The Air Ministry sent them off to No. 7 Operational Training Unit at Hawarden, in Cheshire. In a four week course at Hawarden, they learned to fly Spitfires and, from OTU, all three of them were sent as replacements ot 609 (West Riding) Squadron, based at Warmwell aerodrome in Dorset.

The three brand-new pilot officers fit in very well with their new squadron, and seemed to have been well-liked. Nobody had ever seen a real live Yank before—they had seen them in films, of course, but that did not really count—and now there were three of them, right in the officers' mess.

Everybody in the squadron seemed to have been amused by their trans-Atlantic squadron mates. Lanky Red Tobin, with his wisecracks and easy-going manner, was thought to be typically American. Since he was from California, which every Briton knew was somewhere out in the Wild West, Red was compared with a film cowboy—"he might have stepped straight out of a Western," Peter Townsend commented.

Andy Mamedoff, stocky and mustached, was known for his over-fondness of gambling—he would make a bet with anybody on just about anything. And Shorty Keough, at 4' 10", was known for being short.

A squadron mate said that Shorty was "the smallest man I ever saw, barring circus freaks." Keough needed two cushions in order to fly a Spitfire. He sat on one, so that he could see over the top of the plane's instrument panel. The second went in the small of his back, which pushed him forward in the seat and allowed his legs to reach the rudder bar. But even with the pillows, "all you could see of him was the top of his head and a couple of eyes peering over the edge of the cockpit."

Shortly after the three Americans joined 609 Squadron, Warmwell was visited by Air Commodore the Duke of Kent. The Yanks had only just arrived in the country, and had never met a duke before. "Say," Shorty wanted to know, "What do we call this guy—Dook?" He was told that "Sir" would do very nicely, which must have put his mind at ease since Shorty and the Dook indulged in a long bi-lingual—English and Brooklynese—conversation.

The squadron seemed to accept the three Yank replacements without any sign of condescension. Which was surprising, considering that 609 Squadron was Auxiliary. Auxiliary units were made up mainly of wealthy young men of social standing, and have been referred to as "reservoirs of snobbery and class prejudice." In pre-war days, pilots were selected for Auxiliary squadrons because of their school, their club, and their social connections rather than their talent for flying.

Auxiliary pilots usually treated members of the Volunteer Reserve—and all three Americans were with the Volunteer Reserve—as being of inferior rank, if not absolutely sub-human. The standard auxiliary joke about VR pilots was: "A regular

RAF officer was an officer trying to be a gentleman; an Auxiliary was a gentleman trying to be an officer; and a Volunteer Reservist was neither, trying to be both." There were no jokes about American VRs. Or, at least, none were ever repeated ouside the officers' mess.

But there was no snobbishness shown toward the three Yanks. "They were typical Americans," said one of their fellow squadron member, "amusing, democratic, always ready with some devastating wisecrack (frequently at the expense of authority), and altogether excellent company. Our three Yanks became quite an outstanding feature of the squadron."

According to the findings of a British opinion poll, the British tend to look upon the average American with a "slightly distant familiarity" which is tempered by "a recognition of certain defects of character"—most of which have their origins in the Declaration of Independence in 1776. The men of 609 Squadron even seemed willing to overlook this last flaw.

Great things were expected from the three Yanks in the field of gunnery. From the Hollywood cowboy and gangster films, everybody knew that Americans were "good with guns," and each Spitfire had eight .303 Browning machine guns. The squadron's commander did not share in this enthusiasm, however. Squadron Leader Horace "George" Darley was not about to let the three "new boys" go up against the Luftwaffe until they could look after themselves. The Yanks may have been keen, courageous, and all that, but that was no substitute for solid training. And four weeks at OTU was not Darley's idea of training pilots for combat.

And so S/L Darley assigned the Americans to non-combat duties. Mostly, they did ferrying chores—delivering a Sptifire to another base, and being flown back to Warmwell in a twin-seat Miles Magister trainer. In between, they flew Spitfires until they got to know the airplane intimately—its strengths and its weaknesses. Tobin, Keough, and Mamedoff were not happy with this arrangement. Nearly every day, they would hear other pilots talking about their encounters with the enemy, while all they were allowed to do was run errands. But they knew their turn was coming. With each passing day, the Luftwaffe seemed to be getting stronger.

While waiting for *Adlertag*, the Luftwaffe continued to go after shipping in the Channel.

1 August, Thursday

Thursday 1 August, the day that Hitler issued Directive No. 17, was a clear day. By early afternoon, any lingering haze had been burnt off by the sun. Two German raiders, a Junkers Ju 88 and a Dornier Do 17, were plotted by radar as they approached convoys "Agent" and "Arena" off the North Sea coast. The raiders were intercepted by 607 Squadron (Hurricanes) and 616 Squadron (Spitfires), but turned away before either side could begin an attack. Another raid attacked the city of Norwich. A timber mill was burned, a factory was damaged, and other scattered bomb damage was done.

Two enemy raids were intercepted over the Channel at about 3 pm. Hurricanes from 145 Squadron were scrambled to intercept—two of the raiders were shot down; a Hurricane was shot down by return fire from one of the German bombers.

Five German aircraft were shot down, for a loss of the Hurricane of 145 Squadron and its pilot. Also, an RAF Battle was destroyed by British fighters because of mistaken identity.

2 August, Friday

Four enemy aircraft failed to return from operations on this Friday. Targets were, once again, shipping in the Channel and the North Sea. The RAF lost no aircraft.

During the next five days, a partial lull settled over the air battle. This was partly because of weather, partly because of the Luftwaffe's build-up for *Adlertag*, and partly because of lack of British shipping.

3 August, Saturday

Five small raids wre intercepted over the Channel. The Luftwaffe lost four aircraft; the RAF lost none.

4 August, Sunday

Only reconnaissance sorties were flown by the Luftwaffe, in spite of fair weather. Neither side lost any aircraft from enemy action.

5 August, Monday (Bank Holiday)

Spitfires of 65 Squadron destroyed a Bf 109 over the Straits of Dover at about 8 am. The Messerschmitt went into the Channel off Calais with a huge splash. Two other Bf 109s were damaged during this early attack, but managed to get back to their base in France.

In the afternoon, Spitfires of 41 Squadron and Hurricanes of 151 Squadron intercepted a German raid of about 40 aircraft. One Bf 109 was destroyed, bringing the total of German aircraft brought down this Monday to six. One RAF aircraft, a Spitfire from 64 Squadron, was lost.

6 August, Tuesday

Cloud and strong wind curtailed activities. Seven German aircraft attacked the coast; one was shot down. One RAF fighter was reported destroyed, and a Spitfire from 616 Squadron was damaged by return fire from a Junkers JU 88 over Flamborough Head, Yorkshire.

Hermann Göring had originally ordered *Adlertag* for 10 August, "provided weather is favourable," on this Tuesday. But bad weather would force a postponement of Göring's plan.

7 August, Wednesday

This Wednesday was another day of convoy reconnaissance and limited air activity. Two German aircraft were reported lost during operations off the east coast of England, and a convoy off Cromer, on the northeast coast of Norfolk, was attacked. The RAF lost no aircraft.

Red Tobin, one of 609 Squadron's three Yanks, said that the recent lull was because Göring was resting the Luftwaffe for their next attack—Göring knew that Red and his pals Shorty

Keough and Andy Mamedoff had arrived. Tobin was partially correct, at that—Göring was saving his strength for *Adlertag*. But he was also waiting for a target in the Channel that was worthy of the Luftwaffe's full attention.

8 August, Thursday

A worthy target presented itself on the night of 7-8 August—25 merchant ships and colliers (or 20, depending upon which source is used) of convoy C.W. 9, code-named "Peewit", sailed from the Thames Estuary under cover of darkness. A German mobile radar station on the cliffs on Cap Blanc Nez, opposite Dover, discovered the convoy as it entered the Straits of Dover. (This mobile radar, called *Freya*, was stationed for the sole purpose of locating coastal convoys.) French-based E-boats attacked the convoy, sinking 3 ships, damaging 2 more, and causing a collision that resulted in another sinking.

By dawn on Thursday, the ships were scattered all over the Channel—there was no more convoy. Stukas of General Wolfram von Richtofen's *Fliegerkorps VIII* arrived to attack the straggling ships. But low cloud cover—the overcast was at about 2,000 feet—the cables of the ships' barrage balloons, and interference from no fewer than six RAF fighter squadrons prevented the Stuka pilots from making any successful attacks.

The Stukas came again in the afternoon—57 of them, escorted by Bf 109s and Bf 110s, at about 12:45. Spitfires and Hurricanes were there to meet them, but this time the Messerschmitts were more effective. In the fighting, airplanes of all types were shot into the Channel—Spitfires, Hurricanes, Messerschmitts, Stukas—but the dive bombers were able to carry out their attacks; they sank four more of the ships, and damaged several others.

At about 5 pm., a third attack was carried out; the pilots of the Stukas were ordered to sink every ship that remained of "Peewit". Eighty-two of the dive bombers, escorted by Bf 109s and Bf 110s, once again were confronted by squadrons of Spitfires and Hurricanes.

Peter Townsend reported that the three Hurricane squadrons of the Tangmere sector—Numbers 43, 145, and 601—had a field day. Pilot Officer J.L. Crisp noted in his report: "Met large quantities of assorted Hun aircraft over convoys off I. of Wight, fired at some, no certs, (Very scared)." But the Stukas were able to bomb again. They hit six rescue ships which had come out to assist the crippled convoy, and stopped them dead in the water.

Only four ships from Peewit reached their destination of Swanage, Dorset. The rest were either disabled somewhere between the Isle of Wight and the Straits of Dover, or else were at the bottom of the Channel.

In Berlin, Greater German Radio announced that 8 August had been a great day for the Luftwaffe, and claimed that the Stukas, in another demonstration of their pinpoint accuracy, had virtually wiped out another British coastal convoy, which was true. But the broadcast went on to report that 49 RAF fighters had been shot down, which was not true. The actual number was 19 RAF fighters destroyed.

Inflated reports such as this were responsible for Luftwaffe High Command's underestimating the strength of their enemy. Also responsible was the fact that Air Chief Marshal Dowding was holding back much of his fighter force; he had no intention of wasting his Spitfires and Hurricanes over the Channel, when he knew that the Battle of Britain was only beginning. These two factors made the Luftwaffe believe that RAF Fighter Command was lacking in pilots and aircraft.

The RAF did their fair share of inflating combat reports, as well. Fighter Command announced that their pilots had shot down 60 German aircraft on 8 August; they had, in fact, destroyed 31, half the official number. But how much of this sort of overstatement was believed? It is difficult to say. Senior RAF officers realized that the numbers were optimistic, to put it mildly. American reporters took it for granted that the figures were exaggerated—much to the annoyance of both the RAF and the Ministry of Information. Air Chief Marshal Dowding certainly did not use them as a basis for any decision-making. He realized that the Luftwaffe was far from being on the verge of destruction, and that the brunt of the battle still lay ahead.

In spite of the disaster of convoy Peewit, however, Fighter Command did get some good news out of it. The best news was that the Hawker Hurricane was more than able to hold its own against the Bf 109—if any further proof was needed. Ten Bf 109s were destroyed on 8 August; 9 of them had been shot down by Hurricanes.

9 August, Friday

Coming after the fighting in and over the Channel the previous day, 9 August was relatively quiet. Convoys in the North Sea came under attack. Two bombers, a Ju 88 and a Heinkel He 111, were shot down over Plymouth. A total of five German aircraft were shot down; the RAF lost three more fighters.

Also on this Friday, Reichsmarschall Göring announced *Adlertag* for 13 August. It had been planned for the 10th, but reports of bad weather caused Göring to delay.

10 August, Saturday

Bad weather once again interferred with operations; strong, gusty winds and thunderstorms kept most of the Luftwaffe's air fleets on the ground. Norwich was attacked; so was the aerodrome at West Malling, when a Dornier Do 17 dropped 11 small high explosive bombs at 7:30 am. But no interceptions were made by the RAF, and neither side suffered any losses.

11 August, Sunday

Even though the weather had cleared by Sunday morning, no convoys ventured into the Channel—following the catastrophe of three days before, merchant ships were kept away from the Straits of Dover and the Luftwaffe, which meant that one step toward making Operation Sea Lion a reality had been accomplished—the Channel had been closed to British shipping. This provided a great source of amusement for the Germans—the English were no longer able to sail in the English Channel.

But other shipping targets still presented themselves. Convoys traveled southward along the North Sea coast and into the Thames Estuary, bringing their cargo to the Port of London. At about 1 pm., a convoy in the North Sea was attacked by the fighter-bomber Bf 110s of *Erprobungsgruppe* 210 (usually translated as "Experimental Group"). The twin-engined Messerschitts bombed accurately, crippling two ships, and got away; escorting Bf 109s held off an attack by the Spitfires of 74 Squadron. But 74 Squadron would have a day to remember, in spite of this early setback.

The main attacks of the day came at Dover, in the early morning, and later at Portland naval base. The attacks on Dover were meant to draw fighters away from the Portland area, which was actually the primary target. Radar had warned of the approaching raid on Dover; 74 Squadron, commanded by "Sailor" Malan, were over the harbor at 8 am. Malan led a charge out of the sun and surprised eight Bf 109s that were on course for Dover; they struck and disappeared before any other German fighters could intervene. The Spitfire pilots claimed all eight Messerschmitts as destroyed. Malan himself accounted for one of them.

Adolph " Sailor" Malan was born in Wellington, South Africa. He had been in the merchant navy before joining the RAF in 1935. By the summer of 1940, Malan was all of 30 years old, an old man by Fighter Command standards. But in spite of his age, or maybe because of it, Malan was determined to become an outstanding pilot. He also became an excellent shot—he was an ace with the Distinguished Flyng Cross by the end of July.

About an hour after 74 Squadron surprised the eight Bf 109s, Malan had another brush with Messerschmitts above Dover. His radio had been damaged by a bullet, which prevented the rest of his squadron from hearing his order to attack. So Malan attacked by himself.

"I attacked two Me 109s at 25,000," Malan reported, "delivered two two-second bursts with deflection at the rearmost one and saw my bullets entering the fuselage"—his DeWilde shells were leaving their mark. He caught sight of eight other Bf 109s diving at him, and executed a climbing right-hand turn to bring his guns to bear. The enemy fighters overtook him and dove right past him without firing a shot. Malan was a good pilot and an excellent shot and, perhaps even more important, he was lucky.

During the afternoon, 74 Squadron had two more fights. The first was a "hell of a dog-fight" against Bf 110s off the coast of Suffolk—the Spitfire pilots claimed ten destroyed. Two Spitfires were shot down into the sea off Harwich; both pilots, P/O Cobden and P/O Smith, were killed. About four hours later, Malan took eight Spitfires up to meet another attack on the coast of Kent near Folkstone. Malan claimed another German aircraft destroyed. This action ended the squadron's frantic day.

An attack on Portland began to take shape during the late morning, about 10:30. Some 150 German airplanes, bombers flying with a fighter escort, approached from the southeast. Fighters from surrounding aerodromes intercepted including Number 609, based at Middle Wallop. Squadron Leader Darley still would not allow his three highly-publicized Yanks, Red Tobin, Andy Mamedoff, and Shorty Keough, to fly combat operations. The rest of the pilots were in the air, throttles forward and climbing for altitude.

When they spotted a formation of Bf 110s, the Spitfires had the advantage of height—they dived on the twin-engined Messerschmitts, and claimed five shot down. None of 609 Squadron's Spitfires were lost. S/L David Crook was satisfied with the results of the attack—they all did what they were supposed to do, came right down on the enemy fighters, fired at close range, and got away.

The only problem was that they failed to stop the bombers. The Luftwaffe's attack broke through the fighter interception, and did no small amount of damage to Portland's docks, gas works, and port facilities.

It had been a confused day of scattered fighting; the air battlefield stretched from Norfolk to the Isle of Wight. RAF Fighter Command claimed 60 German aircraft destroyed, against 20 Hurricanes and 5 Spitfires lost in combat. Berlin

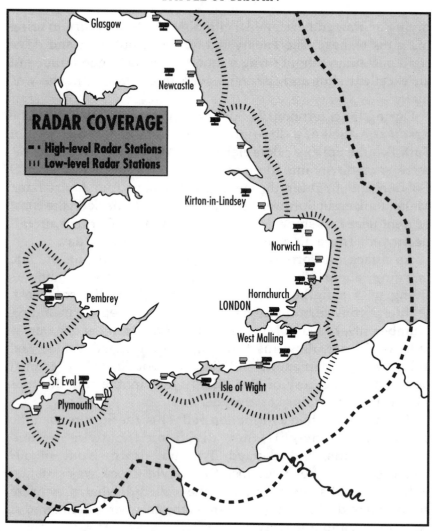

claimed that the Luftwaffe shot down 93 British airplanes. The actual numbers turned out to be 32 RAF aircraft shot down, and 38 Luftwaffe machines destroyed.

The importance of Britain's early warning system was becoming evident to the Luftwaffe high command. The RDF chain gave RAF Fighter Command advance warning of every attack—whenever German aircraft approached the coast of Britain, regardless of the height or the direction fo the attack, or the number of aircraft involved, RAF fighters were always there to intercept. It was now apparent to Göring and his commanders that these warning stations would have to be destroyed before RAF Fighter Command could be eliminated.

Nobody in the Luftwaffe, including Generalmajor Wolfgang Martini, the head of Luftwaffe Signals Service, knew exactly how RDF worked. Martini thought it had something to do with radio waves on the 12-meter band, but could not say precisely what. But although Luftwaffe High Command had no idea what the RDF stations were, just about everybody knew where they were located. The 350-foot tall aerials were visible to anybody with a pair of binoculars. Martini insisted that the RDF stations should be attacked. Reichsmarschall Göring agreed, and decided to switch targets. Since the mysterious aerials were so important to the RAF, they would have the distinction of being put at the top of the Luftwaffe's target priorities.

The knock-out blow to RAF Fighter Command, *Adlertag*, was ordered for 13 August. But Göring decided that the attack against the giant aerials, as well as against fighter airfields near the coast, would begin on the day before *Adlertag*. With the early warning stations knocked out, and the forward bases bombed, the main attack on *Adlertag* should face a lot less opposition.

The Battle of the Channel, *der Kanalkampf*, had not been a clear-cut and decisive victory for the Luftwaffe, but it had given the German air force a decided edge. RAF Fighter Command were certainly being winnowed down. During the month of July, Fighter Command had lost 148 aircraft, along with a good many senior pilots whose absence would be sorely felt in coming months. The aircraft could be replaced—Lord Beaverbrook, the Minister of Aircraft Production, was working minor miracles in supplying the depleted fighter squadrons with replacement aircraft. But there was no replacing the pilots. The new pilot officers from training units may have been keen, but they were also inexperienced.

The other battle, the effort to sway the American public to the British side, was also not going as well as Prime Minister Churchill would have liked. The American news media continued to tell about the air war over the Channel and southern England, and most Americans were interested in hearing about the new kind of warfare. But the opinion of the U.S. had not changed during July. The country preferred to stay neutral.

For both the Luftwaffe and the RAF, 12 August would begin a new phase of the Battle of Britain. No longer would the battle be one of attrition against Fighter Command. From the 12th, the air squadrons and their RDF warning systems would come under direct attack. Generalobrst Hans Jeschonnek, Göring's Chief of Staff, issued the order: "British DeTe stations are to be attacked in force, and put out of action in the first wave."

RDF—BRITAIN'S VITAL EDGE

If the Battle of Waterloo was won on the playing fields of Eton, then the Battle of Britain was surely decided on the dismal gravel beaches of Orfordness, Suffolk.

Orfordness was the site of the first RDF (radar) installation in the British Isles, and was also the original center for its research and development. RDF—for "Radio Direction Finding"—had been given a practical demonstration on 26 February 1935, and found to be feasible as an early detection apparatus—a primitive transmitter tracked an RAF bomber for about eight miles, to the excitement of the observers. But although the device had great potential, it was still only an elaborate novelty, and had a long way to go before it could be used as a practical instrument for detecting aircraft. The place where all the necessary testing and evaluating would be carried out, it had been decided, was grim, forbidding Orfordness.

Orfordness was chosen as the research site precisely because it was so bleak and uninviting—its wind and tides would discourage the curious from getting too nosy. It was picked by Robert Watson Watt, the self-styled "father of radar" who had become one of Britain's leading radio research experts.

Robert Watson Watt's expertise in the technical aspects of radio was more than compensated for by his almost total lack of tack and diplomacy. He was a sarcastic, opinionated, egotistical Scot who seemed to go out of his way to be insulting

and make enemies. But he also believed implicitly in the future of his project. He encouraged his six-man research team at Orfordness to give their best and then some, impressing upon them that they were in a race against time—he predicted that there would be war with Germany in 1938.

His research team took Watson Watt's urgings to heart. They "lived and breathed their enterprise," and made astonishing progress in developing it. Watson Watt himself was usually only present during weekends, however; life at Orfordness was too harsh and spartan for his taste. He preferred luxury, and left the hard living, and the hard work, to his underlings.

And they certainly did work hard. By the end of 1935, Watson Watt's research unit was tracking aircraft at ever-increasing distances—40 miles, 50 miles, finally 80 miles off the coast. Both the RAF and Whitehall were impressed. The government approved £1,000,000 to build five RDF stations along the coast—a measure backed by Hugh Dowding—and alotted a further £24,000 for a new, more luxurious, test site.

The new test site was established at Bawdsey Manor, one of England's Stately Homes, not far from Orfordness. It had all the amenities that Orfordness had conspicuously lacked: stables; gardens; a fish pond; and great, panelled rooms filled with elegant furnishings. This was more to Watson Watt's liking; he decided to move in with his growing number of bright young scientists.

From their new quarters, the research crew went ahead with their work, always experimenting with ways to improve their new weapon. Watson Watt realized that they did not have the time to "perfect" RDF before the war he had predicted would begin. He coined the phrase "Second Best Tomorrow" as Bawdsey's motto—develop the best system possible as quickly as possible, because they would not have the years they would need to create the sophisticated system they would have liked.

Which is exactly what happened. The Chain Home system in existence at the outset of the war certainly had its share of flaws—operators could not tell whether an approaching airplane was in front of them or behind them, for exam-

ple. But it worked; they system gave warning of approaching enemy aircraft, even if the warning was a bit primitive.

Work continued on the CH network during the "Phoney War" period and throughout the disastrous campaign in France. During this time, RDF became more advanced and dependable. By July 1940, the Chain Home network gave RAF Fighter Command a vital edge over the German Luftwaffe—by giving RAF pilots the height, range, and course of an incoming raid, as well as a course for intercepting enemy aircraft. RDF eliminated the need for stressful standing patrols.

RDF had come a long and vital way since its first primitive days at Orfordness. Without it, the outcome of the Battle of Britain would almost certainly have been quite different.

THE CHAIN HOME SYSTEM

Germany had its own verson of RDF before the war began, as good as Britain's if not better. By 1939, they had the *Freya* early warning system, as well as the excellent *Würzberg* anti-aircraft device.

But these mainly operated as individual units; the various sets of each type of radar were not coordinated within an overall defence network. This is where Britain's CH system had an advantage over the German radar. Britain's widely separated RDF units, spread out all along the

coastline, were plugged into a sophisticated communications network which gave senior RAF commanders access to the information being gathered at each of these units.

Twenty nine Chain Home stations stretched from the east coast of Scotland to the west coast of Wales. Each of these stations, which had a receiving aerial about 300 feet tall, could detect an airplane at a range of about 120 miles. Chain Home Low stations, which used a shorter wavelength than the CH stations, were able to plot a low-flying plane about 50 miles off the coast.

But it is what happened to these radio contacts after they were received—how each one was passed along to Fighter Command Headquarters, where it would be examined and sent along to fighter stations near the Channel coast—that made RDF effective as an early warning screen. Operating individually, these stations would never have been able to consolidate Fighter Command's defense against the Luftwaffe during the summer of 1940. Singly, each individual station was severely limited; linked together by an advanced communications system, the CH network became a formidable weapon.

The detection of an incoming flight of enemy aircraft at a Chain Home station triggered a series of events that followed a set pattern.

First contact with an incoming enemy raid was made by operators at work only a short distance from the station's tall masts. Technicians inside the station's receiver huts saw a "blip" appear on cathode ray tubes—a radio pulse had bounced off one or more aircraft. This contact was then telephoned to the Filter Room at Fighter Command Headquarters, Bentley Priory—estimates of height, bearing, and number of aircraft.

"Hello, Stanmore," the operator would report, "I have a plot of twenty-plus hostiles at 100 miles. Height fifteen thousand. Let me give you a bearing on that..."

At Stanmore, this plot was checked against reports from other CH stations. Each one was placed on a huge table map in the Filter Room. Here, every aircraftt or formation was identified as "friendly," "hostile," "doubtful," or "unknown." Updated information on an incoming raid was received constantly. The position of each raid was moved across the face of the table map by a team of WAAFs using long, magnet-tipped plotting rods.

This "filtered" data—with all misinformation hopefully removed—was then passed along to the Operations Room, just next door to the Filter Room at Bentley Priory. The Operations Room had a table map identical to the map in the Filter Room, and was also updated by a team of WAAFs.

While the WAAFs were kept busy updating plots, the Operations Duty Controller relayed the updated information to Group Operations. Each Group had its own headquarters; 11 Group Headquarters was at Uxbridge, Middlesex. The Group Controller then alerted its sector airfields—such as Biggin Hill and Tangmere—of the approaching enemy aircraft.

The Sector Controller ordered the fighter squadrons under his command to states of readiness. When the enemy raid had committed itself to a definite course, squadrons were then ordered to scramble, to intercept the raiders.

When the enemy flight crossed the coast, the RDF stations could no longer maintain contact—the CH network faced only one direction, out to sea. Now, the Observer Corps took over, tracking the airplanes visually. On cloudy days, they judged the height and course by the sound of the airplanes' engines.

This system sounds slow and inefficient by latter day standards. Average elapsed time between first contact and the ringing of the telephone in Biggin Hill's operations room spanned only about six minutes. But it was efficient enough to frustrate the pilots of all three German fleets. Anytime they approached the coast of Britain, with rare exceptions, the RAF fighters were always there to meet them.

Chapter III

"Very Soon, The Big Lick"
12 August - 23 August

*R*eichsmarschall Hermann Göring had great hopes for this next phase of the battle against Fighter Command. Across the Channel, everyone in southern England waited to see what would happen next. And on the other side of the Atlantic, President Franklin D. Roosevelt also watched and waited, along with the rest of America.

12 August, Monday

"We had just settled down to the inevitable game of cards in our dispersal hut at Manston," Flying Officer Alan Deere of 54 Squadron wrote, "when the telephone shrilled." Everyone in the hut immediately stopped whatever they were doing.

The orderly picked up the receiver, listened intently for a few seconds, and shouted, "Hornet Squadron scramble!" The almost eerie silence instantly changed to bedlam, as "table, cards, and money shot into the air as first one and then all the pilots dived headlong for the door."

Within a couple of minutes—literally—the squadron's Spitfires would be in the air and headed for Dover.

By the time 54 Squadron arrived in the vicinity of Dover, the day's fighting had been going on for several hours. It had begun at about 7:30 am., when the Luftwaffe sent several decoy flights over the Channel. But the real attack began about an hour later, when the fighter-bombers of *Erprobungsgruppe* 210, commanded by Swiss-born Hauptmann Walter Rubensdörffer, attacked four CH stations on the south coast—Dunkirk, Dover, Rye, and Pevensey.

Erprobungsgruppe 210 had been formed for the purpose of evaluating both the Bf 109 and Bf 110 as light bombers. The idea was for these fighters to carry out low-level precision attacks on specific targets and, after dropping their bombs, take on the role of their own fighter escort.

The tall south coast CH towers were tailor-made for Rubensdörffer's *Erpro* 210. His Bf 110s and Bf 109s could approach their targets without being spotted, make their bombing runs, and be on their way home before the RAF fighters could get after them. And when *Adlertag* began on the following day, four of the enemy's early detection stations would already be out of action.

Hauptmann Rubensdörffer led his sixteen specially-equipped aircraft on a westerly course down-Channel at 18,000 feet—it had taken longer than usual to reach that height because of their bombs. They continued due west for as long as possible, to make the job of the CH operators more difficult—no one would be able to guess at the target until the planes actually turned north to attack.

Just before 9 am., *Erpro* 210 broke into four groups and banked toward the coast; each group of four aircraft went after a different target. Rubensdörffer headed for Dunkirk; Hauptmann Martin Lutz aimed for the towers at Pevensey; Oberleutnant Wilhelm-Richard Rössinger's target was the CH station at Rye; Oberleutnant Hintze turned his four Bf 109s sharply northwest, toward Dover. The Bf 110s each carried two 500 kg (1,100 lb) bombs; the Bf 109s each had a single 250 kg (550 lb) bomb.

The first CH station to pick up the incoming raid was Rye; Oberleutnant Rössinger's Bf 110s were heading right at them. Eighteen-year-old WAAF Corporal Daphne Griffiths reported the plotting to the Filter Room at Fighter Command Headquarters, Stanmore, Middlesex: "Hostile four at 25 miles. Height twenty thousand." Stanmore told her to mark the incoming aircraft with an "X," meaning "unknown aircraft." Daphne Griffiths seemed annoyed at Stanmore's instruction—she could tell from the way they were acting that the four incoming planes were not "unknown!"

Oberleutnant Rössinger and the other Zerstörers bored in toward the masts at Rye. The towers could hardly be overlooked: 350-foot tall, lattice-work aerials looming over a scattering of huts and buildings. When they had their target in sight, the four pilots pushed over into their dive. There was no opposition: no anti-aircraft and no fighters. The greatest threat came from the towers themselves—it would not be difficult to dive too low and crash into one of them.

In the operations hut, Daphne Griffiths heard the station adjutant suggest to the NCO in charge, "I think it would be a good idea if we had our tin hats." A moment later, the hut was overwhelemed by the noise of Rössinger's attacking Bf 110s.

Rössinger's section dropped their 500 kg bombs and pulled out of their dive. The operations hut shook; Daphne Griffiths' screen went dark. Explosions of earth shot 400 feet in the air, splattering the steel towers and covering the concrete bases with dirt and debris. The cook house was blasted into splinters and a clutter of kitchen utensils. Every building except one, the transmitting and receiving block, was damaged.

Stanmore wanted to know what all the noise was about. "Your 'X' raid is bombing us," Corporal Griffiths told them, with some reproach in her voice.

At Pevensey, Dover, and Dunkirk, the same situation prevailed. Telephone lines were severed; power connections were knocked out; buildings and huts were blown up; airmen and WAAF were killed and injured. At Dunkirk, the blast from a 500 kg bomb moved the concrete transmitter block two to three inches.

Erpro 210 had certainly lived up to its reputation. The sixteen aircraft had come in fast, dropped their bombs with almost frightening accuracy, and had disappeared before the RAF had time to recover.

None of the RDF masts had been destroyed, which came as a disappointment to Generalmajor Martini and some other senior Luftwaffe officers. In fact, the towers would prove to be immune to anything except a direct hit—blast waves passed right through the lattice-work without causing damage. But all of the stations, except for Dunkirk, had been put out of action temporarily. It would only be for a couple of hours, but meanwhile there was a 100-mile gap in Britain's Chain Home network.

While technicians hurried to repair the damage caused by *Erpro* 210, another attack was already on the way. About 15 Junkers Ju 88s were approaching the coast of Kent, on their way to bomb the fighter bases at Lympne and Hawkinge. The damage done to the CH network would help them to make their approach undetected.

Both Hawkinge and Lympne suffered serious damage. At Hawkinge, two hangars were hit by bombs; the fighters inside them were destroyed. Repair shops were blown up, the telephone system was pulverized, and there were bomb craters everywhere. And the raiders had not been detected until they were almost on top of their target, when it was much too late to do anything about it.

Two convoys, code-named "Agent" and "Arena," also came under attack during the RDF blackout. The twelve attacking Stukas were actually detected by Foreness CHL (Chain Home Low, for plotting low-level attacks), which had not been attacked that morning. But the Stukas were able to dive-bomb the convoy before the Hurricanes of 111 Squadron and the Spitfires of 174 Squadron had time to intercept.

Just before noon, Poling CH station—which also had not been bombed that morning—picked up a very large formation heading for the south coast. While it was sitll over the Channel, the formation—consisting of about seventy-five Ju 88s of KG 51; one hundred twenty Bf 110s of ZG 2 and ZG 76; and fighter cover provided by twenty-five Bf 109s of JG 53—made a turn toward Portsmouth and the Isle of Wight.

Barrage balloons were one way of keeping enemy raiders from attacking at low altitude. If an airplane struck a balloon cable, it would lose enough air speed to make it crash; sometimes, a cable could take a plane's wing right off. Balloons were especially effective at night, when they were not as easily seen; a number of night raiders came to grief when wandering into the balloon barrage.

The formation approached Portsmouth, turned through a gap in the barrage balloons, and burst into the harbor. Although it seemed as though every gun for miles around was shooting at them, from 4.5 inch anti-aircraft batteries on shore to 20 mm cannon and machine guns aboard ships at anchor, the Ju 88s made an excellent approach. And they did a thorough job of demolishing Portsmouth.

Dock installations suffered heavy bomb damage. The city of Portsmouth was also bombed, and had several outbreaks of fire. In the harbor, the battleship *Queen Elizabeth* was attacked, but was not hit. Anti-aircraft fire may not have been very accurate, but there was enough of it to make up for the lack of accuracy. Two of the German bombers were hit, and crashed into the sea.

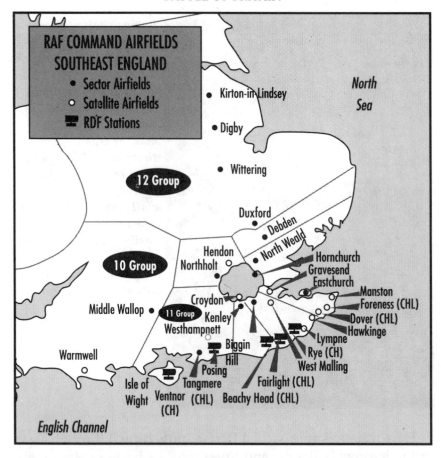

RAF COMMAND AIRFIELDS
SOUTHEAST ENGLAND
• Sector Airfields
○ Satellite Airfields
▆ RDF Stations

North
Sea

Kirton-in-Lindsey

Digby

Wittering

12 Group

Duxford

Debden

North Weald

Hendon

10 Group   Northholt

Hornchurch
Gravesend
Eastchurch
Manston
Foreness (CHL)
Dover (CHL)
Hawkinge

Middle Wallop •

Croydon

11 Group   Kenley

Westhampnett

Biggin

Lympne

Warmwell

Hill

Rye (CH)

Posing

West Malling

Isle of   Tangmere   Fairlight (CHL)

Wight   Ventnor (CHL)   Beachy Head (CHL)

(CH)

English Channel

But fifteen of the Ju 88s did not follow the main formation into Portsmouth. This detachment, led by the *Geschwader Kommodore*, Oberst Fisser, broke away and turned south, flew across the Isle of Wight, and attacked Ventnor CH station from the landward side. Ventnor's masts, over 300 feet tall and situated on hills would have been difficult to miss. And Oberst Fisser's Junkers did not miss—fifteen 500 kg bombs landed right on target, demolishing or damaging every building on the station. Even the steel latticework of the towers themselves had been damaged. The plotters'screens went dark, and stayed that way for three days. Another link in the CH chain had been knocked out.

But the fighting had not been entirely one-sided. Spitfires of 152 and 609 Squadrons had been scrambled, and arrived over Portsmouth and the Isle of Wight after the attack had started. "I was staggered by the number of Huns in the sky," wrote David Crook of 609 Squadron. Crook and his section dove on a circle of Bf 110s. He "blazed madly away" at one of them, nearly had a collision with another, and watched as a third Bf 110 "enveloped in a sheet of flame, fell past within 200 yards of me."

Hurricanes of 213 Squadron had also joined in the fight. Squadron Leader Hector McGregor managed to get behind a Bf 110 in spite of the rear gunner's machine gun fire—among many Zerstörer crews, this rear machine gun was known as a "marmalade thrower'—and shot it down.

Two more Hurricanes of 213 Squadron, joined by two Spitfires of 152 Squadron, latched on to the Ju 88 of Oberst Fisser, KG 52's *Kommodore*. Fisser was killed by the murderous .303-caliber gunfire. Another crew member apparently took over as pilot, and succeeded in making a semi-controlled crash-landing at Godshill Park on the Isle of Wight. The bomber broke in half when it hit the ground. The three crewmen miraculously survived, and were taken prisoner.

The attack had been short and violent. Ventnor had been left in ruins, and Portsmouth was a shambles. Ten of the Ju 88s were shot down by fighters and anit-aircraft fire. By 12:40, all of the German aircraft that would ever return were on their way back to base.

The four RDF stations that had been bombed that morning were now operating at partial capacity—Dunkirk had not been knocked out; Pevensey, Rye, and Dover had been restored with emergency equipment. But the latter three were not operating at full power and efficiency. Because of this, an attack against RAF fighter bases at Lympne, Hawkinge, and Manston arrived over the Kentish coast with little advance warning.

Manston, a forward station right on the coast, came under attack at about 1:30. The Luftwaffe had sent fifteen Bf 110s of *Erprobungsgruppe* 210, on their second cross-Channel trip of the day. Some of the pilots from 65 Squadron managed to get their

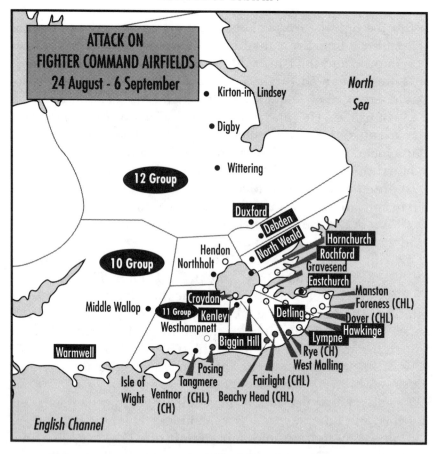

ATTACK ON
FIGHTER COMMAND AIRFIELDS
24 August - 6 September

Kirton-in Lindsey

North
Sea

Digby

Wittering

12 Group

Duxford

Debden

North Weald

Hornchurch
Rochford
Gravesend
Eastchurch

10 Group

Hendon
Northholt

Manston
Foreness (CHL)

Croydon

Middle Wallop

11 Group
Kenley
Westhampnett

Detling

Dover (CHL)
Hawkinge

Biggin Hill

Lympne

Warmwell

Rye (CH)
West Malling

Pasing

Isle of
Wight

Tangmere
Ventnor
(CH)

Fairlight (CHL)

(CHL) Beachy Head (CHL)

English Channel

Spitfires off the ground in spite of the attack. One of the Spits had its engine stopped by a bomb blast just prior to take-off; the airplane was not damaged, however, and the pilot was unhurt.

As soon as *Erpro* 210 dropped their bombs and departed for France, the airfield was given a thorough going-over by eighteen Dornier Do 17s of KG 2. Bombs hit hangars and workshops, and blew craters in the runways. When Alan Deere landed with the rest of 54 Squadron later in the afternoon, he discovered that Manston "was a shambles of gutted hangars and smoldering dispersal buildings, all of which were immersed in a thin film of white chalk dust that drifted across the airfield."

Hawkinge and Lympne were next. Both were attacked for the second time. Lympne was bombed while an RAF Inspector-General was on the station; the Ju 88s prevented him from making his tour, which probably marks the first time that an enemy air attack ever came as a godsend to a Station Commander. Hawkinge was also given another demolishing by Ju 88s. More hangars and other buildings were destroyed, the runway was cratered again—someone counted 28 of them—and craters that had been filled in following the morning raid were re-opened.

After dropping their bombs on Manston, the Do 17s of KG 2 were jumped by Hurricanes of 56 Squadron. Flight Lieutenant "Jumbo" Gracie led the attack. One of his pilots was Pilot Officer Geoffrey Page.

Page closed to within 50 yards of the leading Dornier—probably the *Kommodore's* plane—and pressed the firing button. He could see his bullets hitting the port engine. Then his Hurricane was hit—the fuel tank, just behind the fighter's instrument panel, blew up. Instantly, the cockpit became a raging furnace; Page's hands and face were severely burned.

"I took a hit," Page recalled many years later, "and my plane burst into flames. I bailed out over the Channel, but my hands were badly burned, and I wondered if I could even pull the ripcord on my parachute."

He did manage to pull the ripcord, in spite of his burns, and was picked up in the Channel by a motor launch—as in the case of Peter Townsend's rescue, the launch's crew would not believe that Page was RAF until he cursed them up and down. But unlike Townsend, Geoffrey Page had been critically injured. After months in the hospital, and following several skin-grafting operations, he returned to flying operations. Page is officially credited with having destroyed 17 enemy aircraft.

At about the same time that Geoffrey Page was bailing out of his burning Hurricane, the Spitfire pilots of 64 Squadron were intercepting the Ju 88s that had just laid waste to Hawkinge. One of the pilots was P/O Arthur Donahue, the squadron's resident Yank from St. Charles, Minnesota.

Donahue had originally applied for a commission in the U.S. Army Air Corps. But he was very young and extremely impatient, and became disgusted by all of the Army's delay and red-tape—he wanted to fly, not fill out paperwork and forms. So he went to Canada and, in spite of the Neutrality Act and the border patrols, joined the RAF. He arrived in England on 4 August, "a foggy Sunday morning," and was assigned to 64 Squadron at Kenley.

Although the three Yanks of 609 Squadron, Red Tobin, Shorty Keough, and Andy Mamedoff, had been put on probation until they could fend for themselves in combat, the squadron leader of 64 Squadron apparently had no such scruples. P/O Donahue fired his first shots in anger on 5 August—the day after he landed in England, and following only three weeks training in Canada.

On his first operational sortie, Donahue shot at a Bf 109—after making absolutely certain that it really was a Messerschmitt—and claimed it as "damaged." He also had his own Spitfire damaged by a German cannon shell. The 20 mm shell severed several control cables, and blew out the battery connection that operated his gunsight. When he brought his Spitfire back to Kenley, it needed a new fuselage.

He scored a "probable" on 8 August. Donahue's flight was on patrol over the Channel when the six Spitfires were jumped by a "gruppe" of about 27 Messerschmitt 109s. Donahue tried to lock onto the tail of an enemy fighter, and did get off a few shots at several Bf 109s, "just firing whenever I saw something with a black cross in front of me." His maneuverings brought him right behind one German fighter; he fired a good burst into it, and claimed it as "probably destroyed."

Four days later, a German fighter got behind P/O Donahue and shot him down. The details of this action, however, are thoroughly confusing. Some sources say that he was hit by the rear gunner of a Ju 88 that he was pursuing; others insist that he was brought down by a Bf 109. Donahue is not much help in the matter himself; he insists that his nemesis was flying a Heinkel

He 113. There is no record of any He 113s being anywhere near the vicinity.

Once again, German cannon shells proved his undoing. (Which rules out the rear gunner of a Ju 88.) Donahue heard an alarming "Powp! Powp!"—20 mm shells exploding against the metal skin of his Spitfire. He noticed at once that his control cables were gone. He could not turn the plane, and his control column "just flopped limply all the way forward" when he tried to dive.

Donahue now presented an easy target. Because the Spit's control cables had been shot away, he could only fly straight and level—a maneuver not recommended for pilots who wished to enjoy a long and healthy life. A second attack from behind shattered his instrument panel and set his fuel tank on fire. Donahue could see "a little hot bonfire in one corner of the cockpit."

As Donahue was preparing to bail out, the "bonfire" blew up; he was badly burned by the explosion. He did manage to get out of his Spitfire, and parachute into an oat field. A detachment of soldiers happened to be nearby; they obligingly called for an ambulance. Donahue spent the next seven weeks in the hospital.

For his nine days' service as a fighter pilot during the Battle of Britain, P/O Donahue's record was not a bad one. (It was probably remarkable, in view of the amount of training he had received.) He had been credited with one "damaged" and one "probable." Unfortunately, he also had one Spitfire damaged, and another shot out from under him. (A good many participants in the battle blazed away at any number of targets, and never hit a thing—or, at least, were never credited with hitting a thing.)

But Donahue's most valuable contribution began after he was released from the hospital. He went back to the United States on leave, where he described his experiences with Number 64 Squadron RAF to a variety of audiences. In addition, Donahue wrote an article for the *Saturday Evening Post* as well as a book, *Tallyho: Yankee In A Spitfire*.

He did not make himself seem very heroic in any of these accounts. If anything, he plays down his own part in the battle, making himself seem a well-meaning amateur in the ranks of dedicated professional fighter pilots. But Donahue contributed a great deal to the mystique of the heroic few defending their island nation against a ruthless enemy. In one part of the *Saturday Evening Post* article, he talks about his squadron being outnumbered by odds of 5 to 1—30 Germans against 6 Spitfires—but overcoming these odds by skill and determination.

During this time back in the United States, Donahue provided the real worth of the Yanks in the RAF. The Americans were needed as pilots—there was still a critical shortage—but were even more useful to the British war effort as ministers of propaganda in their native country. Arthur Donahue accomplished more for Britain by speaking and writing about what he had seen and done in the battle, than if he had shot down an entire *Geschwader* of Messerschmitts single-handedly.

Donahue's account of 12 August begins with the Air Ministry's official summary of the day's activities: "In these operations, thirteen of our aircraft were lost and twelve pilots." He added, "I am that thirteenth pilot."

Dramatic, but not quite accurate. Although RAF Fighter Command did lose thirteen fighters, only eight pilots were numbered as killed or missing.[8] Luftwaffe losses totaled 45 aircraft. On the face of it, the RAF got the better of the fighting.

But the Luftwaffe had accomplished most of its aims. Five coastal RDF stations had been damaged; Ventnor had been put out of action for several days. (Either ten or eleven days, depending upon which source is believed, although signals sent from another transmitter fooled the Germans into believing that Ventnor was back in service on the following day.)

The fighter bases at Lympne, Hawkinge, and Manston had also received major bomb damage—at Manston, some aircrafts-

---

8   Two Handley-Page Hampden bombers (out of 10) were lost that night in an RAF attack on the Dortmund-Ems canal near Münster.

men went down into the station's bomb shelters and refused to come out for several days. These bases were put back into operating condition as quickly as possible, with power and telephone restored and runway craters filled in. But they obviously could not operate at peak efficiency.

For the Luftwaffe, the day had been both rewarding and disappointing. The resilience of the RDF stations had come as a shock—those damn 350-foot towers simply refused to fall down! But they realized that they had blown a gap in the early-warning chain, and were convinced that they would do better next time. They also knew that they had hit the RAF's fighter bases, and had hit them hard; the feeling was that if these attacks continued, RAF Fighter Command would not be able to hold out for very long.

Air Chief Marshal Dowding and Air Vice Marshal Keith Park, the commander of 11 Group, were both inclined to agree with the Luftwaffe's assessment. The quickness of the repairs to both RDF stations and fighter stations was encouraging. So was the reception given to the German raiders, and the losses suffered by them. But if the enemy continued to attack in such force, both men recognized that RAF Fighter Command would be in serious trouble.

In other words, the damage done to RAF Fighter Command had not been fatal, but the Luftwaffe's strategy seemed to be working.

13 August, Tuesday (*Adlertag*)

Enlisted men in every army tend to be cynical and sarcastic about generals and their far-reaching plans. The soldiers and airmen are prone to regard most general officers as conceited, pompous, self-congratulating asses, and frequently laugh at all the grand strategies as inept and unworkable, at best.

This point of view was certainly justified regarding the planning and execution of *Adlertag*, and gave everyone in the enlisted men's mess a good, dirty laugh for several weeks. The grand strategy for the day, given the far-fetched name *Eagle Day* (couldn't they have come up with a better name?) opened with a typical announcement from none other than *der Dicke* (Fatso) himself, Reichsmarschall Hermann Göring:

FROM REICHSMARSCHALL GÖRING TO ALL UNITS OF AIR FLEETS TWO, THREE, AND FIVE. OPERATION EAGLE. WITHIN A SHORT TIME YOU WILL WIPE THE BRITISH AIR FORCE FROM THE SKY. HEIL HITLER.

Riggers and fitters at Luftwaffe fields across France and the Low Countries made their preparations for Eagle Day, and wondered silently what was going to go wrong and spoil *der Dicke's* plans.

The men did not have long to wait. For although Luftwaffe High Command had planned well in advance for Operation Eagle, there was always something that could go wrong in such a large operation. And all of Göring's planners and commanders forgot one thing—they neglected to consult with Mother Nature on her plans for the day.

Early morning weather for 13 August was supposed to have been clear and bright. It turned out to be nothing of the sort. When pilots woke up on the morning of the *Adlertag*, they looked out of their windows and saw solid overcast mixed with drizzle. It was certain that there would be not operational flying through that, Reichsmarschall Göring notwithstanding.

The Reichsmarschall agreed, and personally delayed the beginning of the offensive. His Chief of Staff, *Generaloberst* Hans Jeschonnek, advised him that the weather would be much improved by afternoon; Göring postponed the attack until 2 pm. Immediately, the word went out—*Adlertag* had been postponed. But enlisted men have another proverb: "There is always some damn fool that never gets the word." *Oberst* Johannes Fink of KG 2, who had nearly been shot down over Manston the day before, was leading his 74 Dornier Do 17s toward the English coast at about 5 am. But Fink's Dorniers had not been fitted with the proper crystals for their radio sets, and missed the recall signal; the crew were unable to receive on the pre-arranged wavelength.

When the Dorniers arrived over St. Omer, *Oberst* Fink was glad to see his fighter escort—Bf 110s of ZG 26, commanded by the one-legged *Oberstleutnant* Joachim-Friedrich Huth. But Fink was less than pleased when one of the big, twin-engined fighters began climbing and diving in front of his Dornier's nose, and then turned to make a head-on pass at the bomber. He did not appreciate the playful aerobatics, and planned to lodge a formal complaint when he returned to base at Arras.

But *Oberstleutnant* Huth had not been indulging in fun and games at Fink's expense. He had merely been trying to get Fink's attention. Huth had only just heard the recall order himself, and was doing his best to relay the message to the Dornier formation. But he had no luck—Fink had no idea what Huth was up to, and continued on toward his target.

His target was the airfield at Eastchurch, on the Isle of Sheppy off the north coast of Kent. Fink dived on the base just after 7 am.; the Dorniers released their bombs from 1,500 feet. The bombing was accurate, and Eastchurch was hit hard—a hangar was badly damaged, several aircraft were destroyed on the ground, the base's ammunition supply blew up in a colossal explosion, and a number of airmen were killed. After they had dropped their bombs, the suddenly lighter Dorniers pulled up and headed for the clouds.

Before they were able to reach cloud cover, however, Fink's Dorniers were overtaken by the Hurricanes of 111 Squadron. Pilots of "treble-one" shot down four of the Dorniers; the rest escaped to the safety of the clouds. A fifth Dornier was destroyed by a Hurricane flown by Flight Lieutenant Roddick Lee Smith of 151 Squadron. F/Lt. Smith's Hurricane was one of the few to be equipped with 20 mm cannon instead of .303 Brownings; his cannon shells set fire to the bomber's fuel tanks at a range of about 300 yards.

Although 20 mm cannon had a greater range than the .303 machine gun, as well as much greater destructive power, not many RAF pilots were very enthusiastic about it. For one thing, the cannon was extremely prone to jamming. Also, the big guns made the already too-slow Hurricane even slower and less

Do 17s at low altitude, half hidden by their camouflage markings. The specialty of Dornier crews was the low-level attack—especially an attack from a shallow dive. In spite of their limited bomb loads, Dorniers did considerable damage to 11 Group's airfields in late August and early September.

maneuverable; each cannon was mounted beneath the wing in a pod, which was the size of a small bath tub, and which added weight and decreased air speed. F/Lt. Smith was one of the few pilots who actually preferred the cannon-equipped Hurricane. His squadron had two of them—one with two cannon, the other with four cannon—and they were flown almost exclusively by Smith, since nobody else wanted any part of them.

Oberst Fink arrived back at Arras literally in a screaming rage. He made straight for a telephone, and got in touch with *Feldmarschall* Albert Kesselring, commander of *Luftflotte 2*, at his underground headquarters at the Pas de Calais.

Fink shouted his morning's experiences at the chastened Kesselring—five of his Dorniers shot down, five more returning to base badly shot up (Sailor Malan's 74 Squadron had joined the fray and added their share of the damage), and his damn fool fighter escort had turned for home before his bombers reached the English coast.

Fink would have been even more upset had he known that Eastchurch was not even a Fighter Command airfield; it had been assigned to Coastal Command. On 13 August, Spitfires of 266 Squadron happened to have been based there temporarily. Fink's Dorniers only destroyed one of them, not the ten he claimed.

Kesselring decided to make a personal visit to Arras, to try and smooth things over by explaining what had happened. It did not help much; KG 2 was still minus ten aircraft—five destroyed and five badly damaged. But at least it gave Fink an idea of why everything had gone wrong that morning.

Events did not improve very much for the Luftwaffe as the day went on. The next phase of *Adlertag* was to have been an attack on the RAF facilities at Odiham and Farnborough in Hampshire—neither of which had any connection with Fighter Command. The raiders, Ju 88s escorted by Bf 110s and Bf 109s, were intercepted by Hurricanes of 43 Squadron and 601 Squadron from Tangmere. Low cloud, and the unwelcome attentions of the Hurricanes, prevented the bomb aimers from hitting either target.

When these Junkers turned for home, another pack of them arrived—according to 601 Squadron's Operations Record Book, there were about 24 Ju 88s with a fighter escort. One of the bombers was shot down by Pilot Officer Billy Fiske, a wealthy American from Chicago, Illinois. His squadron mates, along with the pilots from 43 Squadron, prevented the rest of the Ju 88s from reaching their objective.

Just before noon, 23 Bf 110s of ZG 2 appeared on RDF screens as they headed for Portland. They were supposed to be escorting a bomber strike, but their escort stood them up. (Actually, the attack had been called off, but ZG 2 never heard the recall.) Instead, Spitfires from 609 Squadron made the rendezvous. The pilots shot down five of the twin-engined Zerstörers, and damaged five others; 609 lost no Spitfires.

Members of 601 (County of London) Squadron sprint toward their Hurricanes after receiving the "Scramble." The letters "UF," 601 Squadron's identification letters, are plainly visible on the fusilages.

By 3:30, another raid was on its way. This one was aimed at the docks at Southampton and at the nearby fighter airfields at Warmwell and Middle Wallop. Warmwell was the home of 609 (West Riding) Squadron as well as 152 Squadron, while close by Southampton were the well-known Spitfire works at Woolston.

But this attack did not fare any better than the Luftwaffe's earlier efforts. Although Southampton was heavily bombed, and its docks, where luxury liners berthed in peacetime, suffered damage and heavy loss of life, the Spitfire works were not touched. They were probably not even marked as a target. And the attacks on Middle Wallop and Warmwell were, in the words of General Wolfram von Richtofen of *Fliegerkorps VIII,* "a flop... our own formations returned without releasing their bombs."

The air strikes of *Adlertag* had been either ineffective or totally meaningless. The early evening attack on Detling airfield, near Maidstone, Kent, might be cited as an example. Eighty-seven

Stukas dive-bombed the base, while Bf 109s of Adolf Galland's JG 26 took on the Spitfires of 65 Squadron. The Ju 87 Stukas demolished buildings, cratered the runways, destroyed 22 aircraft, killed 67 people, and got away without a loss.

Once again, however, the Luftwaffe had targeted a non-Fighter Command airfield. So although the air raid had been well-planned and was carried out with thoroughness, and the target had been badly damaged, the operation would not have any real effect on the battle or its outcome.

What was probably the last action of the day involved Ju 87s of StG 2. Spitfires of 609 Squadron caught the Stukas without any fighter escort off the Dorset coast near Lyme Regis. It had been a busy day for 609 Squadron, and it would end on an encouraging note—the Spitfire pilots shot down six of the nine Stukas, and damaged another.

The only unhappy members of 609 Squadron were its three Yanks: Pilot Officers Tobin, Keough, and Mamedoff. Squadron Leader Darley was still not completely satisfied that the three Americans were ready to go up against the Luftwaffe, and kept them confined to ferrying jobs and other errands. When they heard the other pilots talking about their adventures that day—at least Tobin, Keough, and Mamedoff thought of the combats as "adventures"—the three nearly went purple in the face with envy.

On the day, the Luftwaffe lost 45 aircraft, while the RAF lost 13 fighters. (Fourteen, counting the fighter destroyed on the ground at Eastchurch.) Nothing seemed to have gone right for the Luftwaffe; the Day of the Eagle turned out to be the day of the flounder.

Although senior Luftwaffe officers argued that operations on 13 August had worn down RAF Fighter Command by virtue of the fact that so many attacks had been made over such a scattered area—which was true, up to a point—it was a hollow argument. It was as though a heavyweight boxer claimed to have damaged his opponent's fist by bashing his nose into it. All arguments and excuses aside, the day had not been a good one for the Luftwaffe.

14 August, Wednesday

Following the previous day's frenzy, both sides braced themselves for another frantic day. But clouds kept the Luftwaffe grounded until nearly noon.

Before the fighting began on this Wednesday, Adolf Hitler had a meeting with Göring and Admiral Raeder at Göring's estate, Karinhall, about 40 miles northeast of Berlin. Hitler first presented eight new field marshals with their batons, and then went on to say a few words about Operation Sea Lion.

Hitler told his audience that he had no intention of carrying out any sort of operation that would pose too much of a risk—"Britain's defeat does not depend upon invasion alone." But he also emphasized that he wanted to go ahead with invasion preparations, and that all preparations should be completed by 15 September.

As far as particulars were concerned, Hitler said that the invasion would be confined to Brighton area and would not, as had been previously planned, spread over a wide area. This was a concession to Admiral Raeder, who still groused about the Navy's part in the operation. Raeder still did not favor the prospect of a landing of any size. But he was convinced that Hitler meant to go through with Sea Lion in spite of any protests.

As a prelude to invasion, a sort of opening round, a Luftwaffe memorandum suggested a "ruthless air attack" on London. This air raid should, if possible, be launched on the day prior to the landings; it would cause mass panic and a frenzy of Londoners leaving the city, which would block roads for miles. Hitler read the memo, but did not comment.

Just before noon, Air Vice-Marshal Park, the commander of 11 Group, received some unwelcome news from his CH stations on the south coast: a large enemy force was forming over the Pas de Calais. As soon as the formation gathered strength, it turned north and, once again, headed for Manston and Lympne.

The "large formation" was, in fact, Walter Rubensdörffer's *Erprobungsgruppe* 210. Unescorted by fighters, the Bf 110s came in low and blasted their targets with their usual thoroughness. Manston's anti-aircraft gunners returned the compliment. A 40 mm shell literally blew the tail off Unteroffizier Hans Steding's Bf 110. The plane crashed, but the rear gunner, Gefreiter Ewald Schank, baled out at the height of 500 feet and survived.

When Schank was taken to shelter, completely dazed and with an apparent head injury, he kept muttering in broken English: "The big lick. Very soon, the big lick."

The message was not lost on Schank's captors. They were bracing themselves for the "big lick," but no one had any idea when it would be coming.

About a half hour later, at least one hundred Messerschmitt Bf 109s made their presence known over Dover. They shot down seven barrage balloons before they were intercepted by a mixed force of Spitfires and Hurricanes. The result was what an American observer called "one hell of a goddamn brawl." JG 26 and JG 52 each lost a Bg 109; 615 Squadron lost two Hurricanes, as well as their pilots. The Varne lightship had also been sunk.

The brawl carried over into the afternoon, as "scattered raids" of two or three bombers swooped in on airfields and other targets throughout southern and southwest England. One of these raids found Middle Wallop airfield, apparently by accident. Red Tobin was walking to Hangar No. 5, where he was to ferry a Spitfire to the Hamble repair facility, when he heard an airplane approaching at very low level.

Tobin looked up and saw a Ju 88 a few hundred feet above; its two Jumo engines looked enormous. It released four 500 kg bombs. At least one of them hit Hangar Number 5.

"I hit mother earth and stayed there," Red later recounted. When he got up, his head was ringing from the bomb's concussion, and he was covered by chalky white soil. But he was a lot better off than some others who were in the vicinity of the hangar. Three airmen were crushed to death when a gigantic steel door, blasted by the explosion, fell on top of them. "One man's foot was blown off," Red recalled, "another one's arm up to the shoulder blades."

Pilots of 609 Squandron were already taking off to intercept. But the pilot of an already-airborne Spitfire caught the bomber first, and sent it crashing in flames five miles away from the field. The attack had cost 609 several Spitfires destroyed. In addition, 3 Bristol Blenheims had been destroyed. As far as casualties were concerned, three men had been injured, and three had been crushed by the falling door. All of this cost one Junkers Ju 88 as well as the lives of its pilot and crew. Reichsmarschall Göring would have thought it a fair exchange.

Red Tobin co-wrote a series of articles for *Liberty* magazine about this experience, as well as about his pals Andy Mamedoff and Shorty Keough and their experiences with 609 Squadron. Although the articles were not published until several months after the battle had ended—they appeared in the United States in March and April 1941—they helped persuade Americans that Britain was steadfast and reliable, and was likely to hold its own against Nazi Germany and its Luftwaffe. The *Liberty* pieces were part of Britain's fairly relentless and very thorough propaganda campaign in America.

On 14 August, the Luftwaffe lost 19 aircraft, while the RAF suffered 8 aircraft destroyed—all fighters. It had not been a decisive day for either side—although the Luftwaffe lost more aircraft, they also damaged several RAF airfields and had been able to get through to their targets in spite of enemy fighter opposition.

But Dowding had an idea that the Germans might have something more forceful and threatening in their immediate plans. The forecast for the next day called for fair weather. Since the enemy's activities of the day just past had been relatively light, Dowding had a presentiment that the Luftwaffe's efforts would be heavy and intense come morning.

15 August, Thursday

Actually, the weather turned out to be something less than dazzling after all—the morning began as cloudy and overcast. But the clouds had all but disappeared by mid-morning, and meteorologists' reports predicted fine weather for the rest of the day.

The Chief of Staff of *Fliegerkorps II*, *Oberst* Paul Deichmann, saw that the weather was clearing, and decided to give the order that would launch the day's offensive. The order went out on teletype machines to Heinkel He 111 units, to Junkers Ju 88 *Geschwader*, and to Stuka *Staffeln* throughout northern France—*Grosseinsatz*. (The U.S. Army Air Force equivalent would be a "maximum effort.") After the bombers had taken off from their bases and began to form up, their fighter escort took off to join them. All of these forces had been set in motion without any official sanction at all—Deichmann had no authority to give such an order.

Deichmann drove to Kesselring's underground headquarters at Cap Blanc Nez, known sarcastically as *Heiliger Berg* (Holy Mountain), to report his actions. Kesselring himself was away at a meeting with Göring at Karinhall, so Deichmann spoke to the operations officer, Major Hans-Jürgen Rickhoff. Rickhoff had just received a directive from Berlin: the day's operations were to be cancelled because of the weather. Deichmann was not fazed in the slightest by this bit of information. "Too late," he said, "They've already gone!"

This off-hand decision to launch the attack began a chain of events that, in the words of a German writer, "was destined to spark off one of the most bitter combat days of the whole Battle of Britain." Units from Norway and Denmark, from Normandy and Brittany, and from all points in between, began preparations for a major assault on RAF airfields in southern England.

Chain Home RDF stations on the northeast coast picked up a plot, estimated at 30 aircraft, at about 12:15. The pilots of 72 Squadron were scrambled, and intercepted the German formation over the North Sea. Only there were not 30 aircraft—the Spitfire pilots saw about 65 He 111s of KG 26, the *Löwengeschwader* based at Stavanger, Norway, as well as about 25 Bf 110s of ZG 76, also from Stavanger.

Actually, 72 Squadron's Spitfires were supposed to have been drawn away from the attacking force by 17 decoy seaplanes; the

A Heinkel He 111 on its way to England during the Battle, with wheels still down. Although the Heinkel was well-liked by the men who flew it, the bomber was already nearly obsolete when the Battle began.

seaplanes approached the Scottish coast and turned back to base, just as they had been told to do. But the Heinkels made an error in navigation, and flew almost parallel with the seaplanes. As a result, an RDF plotted the decoys and the bombers as one force, and the Spitfires came up to get them.[9]

The Spitfires divided: half went after the Bf 110s; the rest attacked the bombers. One of the first planes to go down was the leading Zerstörer, flown by *Hauptmann* Werner Restemeyer. Restemeyer's Bf 110 carried a long-range drop tank—and no rear gunner, to save weight. The tank would not jettison properly when the pilot released it, and a bullet from an attacking

---

9   Acting Squadron Leader Ted Graham was asked by the ground controller, "Have you seen them?" Graham's reply has become almost mandatory in any book about the Battle of Britain. "Of course I've seen the b-b-b-bastards," he stuttered. "I'm trying to w-w-w-work out what to do."

Spitfire set it off. The twin-engined aircraft disintegrated in a flash.

Other RAF squadrons also joined in the interception: 41, 79, and 605 Squadrons. Fifteen German aircraft were destroyed—12 He 111s and 3 Bf 110s—and one RAF fighter was shot down.

A second North Sea coast attack was made by Ju 88s of KG 30, the *Adler Geschwader*, stationed at Aalborg, Denmark. These Junkers did not have any fighter escort at all—Bf 109s did not have the fuel capacity to reach the English coast, let alone make the round-trip from Denmark.

The pilots of 616 Squadron at Leconfield, just north of Hull, were having lunch when the tinney loudspeaker barked, "Six-one-six Squadron scramble! Six-one-six squadron scramble all aircraft!" As soon as the initial shock wore off, the pilots ran to their Spitfires, climbed into the cockpits, and were strapped in. Hugh Dundas recalled that he rammed the throttle "through the gate," for maximum power on take-off, and headed for the coast without stopping to join up into flights.

About fifteen miles from the coast, Dundas caught sight of "the thin, pencil shapes of twin-engined German bombers, flying in a loose, straggling, scattered formation toward the coast." He switched on his gunsight, set the range to 250 yards, turned the gun safety to "fire," and executed a diving turn toward the nearest Junkers. When he was in position astern of the bomber, Dundas could see a small, winking light—the rear gunner was shooting at him.

Dundas lined up the bomber in his gunsight and pressed the firing button on the Spitfire's control column; the return fire abruptly stopped. Immediately afterward, the Junkers began losing height as "a steady stream poured back from its engine cowlings." It continued to drop toward the North Sea.

Through the Spitfire's plexiglass, Dudas could see fighters shooting at bombers on all sides—six Hurricanes of 73 Squadron were also on the scene—and also caught sight of a Junkers that already had been damaged. He charged after the bomber, caught up with it, and made certain that it would never return to Denmark.

By this time, he was just about out of ammunition. "Hot and elated," Dundas set course back to Leconfield. When he arrived, the rest of the squadron were also "straggling in" by ones and twos. It had been only 25 minutes since he had taken off.

The pilots of KG 30 did manage to reach their target, the RAF base at Driffield, Yorkshire, and destroyed 10 Whitley bombers on the ground. But they paid the price: seven of the Ju 88s were shot down, and three others crash-landed on the Continent. (To give some idea of how wishful thinking inflates a fighter pilot's outlook: Hugh Dundas' 616 Squadron claimed 8 Junkers destroyed, as well as 4 probables and 2 damaged.) RAF Fighter Command admitted no losses.

The Luftwaffe lost about 20% of its attacking force in this foray—a major shock, since fighter opposition along the northeast coast was thought to be minimal. This outing proved beyond all doubt—if any further proof was needed—that a Messerschmitt Bf 109 escort was essential to the survival of bomber formations.

Because of the Bf 109's severely limited range, an escort across the North Sea from either Norway or Denmark would be impossible. Which meant that *Luftflotte* 5, formed after the Scandinavian countries were overrun earlier in 1940, was now effectively out of the battle.

To the south, however, the day's activities were only just beginning. The sky was clearing to a fine blue and the temperature was rising; the machines of *Luftflotten* 2 and 3 began to stir. Bombers of all varieties—Ju 88s, He 111s, Do 17s, Stukas—and their escorts were soon airborne and on their way to targets in southern England.

First on the Luftwaffe's list were the RAF bases at Hawkinge, Lympne, and Manston—again. Channel coast RDF stations plotted the large enemy formations while they were still over the Continent—60-plus over Ostend; 120-plus near Calais. Three squadrons had been scrambled, and ten others were at immediate readiness.

First contact was made when 40 Stukas of *Lehrgeschwader* 1 ran into Spitfires of 54 Squadron and Hurricanes of 501 Squad-

The airfield at Manston came under attack six times in mid-August—it was an easy target for the Luftwaffe's bombers and fighter-bombers, because it was situated right on the coast of Kent. The station's seventh attack came on 24 August; this time, it was put out of action.

ron. Two of the dive bombers were shot down before they could push over to bomb their targets. But the Messerschmitt escort intervened and shot down four fighters. (All four pilots safely bailed out.) The target had been Hawkinge; one hangar had been damaged by the Stukas, along with a housing block.

Damage to Lympne was much more severe. The Stukas blew up the hospital, hit several other buildings, knocked out all power and water, and cratered the runway again. As an active fighter station, Lympne would be non-operational for two days. Just by chance, the same Inspector General who had visited the base when it had been bombed two days before decided to turn up again—probably feeling like a latter-day Typhoid Mary.

The Spitfire pilots did their best to stop the bombing, or at least waylay the attackers, but were badly outnumbered. They admired the precision of the Stukas as they "swept towards the airfield and peeled off to attack," but could do little to stop them because of the diving Messerschmitts. After exhausting their ammunition, with little to show for it, they returned to base at Manston to re-arm and re-fuel.

No sooner did 54 Squadron reach Manston than the field came under attack by Bf 110s. The Spitfires immediately got out of the way of the incoming attack—and out of the range of "friendly" anti-aircraft gunners. About 10 minutes after the raid ended, the pilots landed and inspected the damage. Two Spitfires had been destroyed on the ground; 16 airmen had been killed and wounded by machine gun and cannon fire.

The Zerstörers of Walter Rubensdörffer's *Erprobungsgruppe* 210 were also in action again. Their target was the fighter base at Martlesham Heath in Suffolk, about seven miles from Ipswich. Sixteen of Rubensdörffer's Bf 110s, and nine Bf 109s, executed another of their perfected hit-and-run raids. They swept in so suddenly that the air raid warning did not sound until after the attack had actually begun.

Four and a half minutes later, when *Erpro* 210 departed, Martlesham Heath was a thorough wreck—two hangars were in ruins, the runway was badly cratered, and the officers' mess had been badly damaged. The climax of the raid came when a visiting Fairey Battle blew up; it had been carrying 1,000 lb bombs for the German invasion barges across the Channel. Rubensdörffer and the other 24 fighter-bombers got away before the RAF had the chance to intercept.

The attacks seemed to go on without end. About 90 Dornier Do 17s of KG 3, escorted by nearly 200 Messerschmitt 109s (including 60 from Adolf Galland's JG 26), pushed their way toward Kent. The formation split into three groups to bomb Eastchurch, Hawkinge (for the second time that day), and Rochester. Three RAF squadrons—Numbers 64, 111, and 151—managed to break through the fighter screen. Between them, they shot down two Do 17s and damaged several others, while losing nine of their own aircraft.

Three squadrons were not about to stop this onslaught. All three targets were hit. Rochester suffered the heaviest damage. The airfield was cratered, and the Short Brothers and Pobjoys Aircraft Works nearby had repeated hits. Production of Short's four-engine Stirling bomber was set back for weeks; nearly 200 finished bombers had been destroyed by 18 Do 17s. All in all, it had been a highly satisfying afternoon's work for the Dornier crews.

The Luftwaffe's plan of overwhelming the defenses, and for causing widespread confusion and destruction by overwhelming widely scattered targets, seemed to be having success. The strategy certainly caused its share of confusion among fighter squadrons. Peter Townsend led 85 Squadron toward the enemy formation "at full bore," but could not find it. The ground controller was not much help; he "seemed to have lost the thread of the battle," according to Townsend.

Other squadrons did not fare any better. Number 17 Squadron was vectored "here and there over the North Sea," before being ordered to land at Martlesham Heath. When the pilots landed their Hurricanes, they found Martlesham "a heap of smoking rubble"—courtesy of Hauptmann Rubensdörffer and *Erpro* 210.

So far, the air offensive had been carried out by Kesselring's *Luftflotte* 2, which was based in eastern France, Belgium, and the Low Countries. But the rest of the day would belong to Feldmarschall Hugo Sperrle's *Luftflotte* 3, based in western France. *Luftflotte* 3's targets would be far to the west of *Luftflotte* 2's objectives—Portland, and the fighter bases of 10 Group.

Had Sperrle's *Luftflotte* 3 carried out their attacks in cooperation with *Luftflotte* 2 and begun their operations immediately after Kesselring's units had landed, the RAF would have had its hands more than full. But cooperation between the two *Luftflotten* left a lot to be desired—for nearly two hours, no German aircraft crossed the Channel. This lull allowed Fighter Command time to re-arm and re-fuel its Spitfires and Hurricanes, and also gave the harried pilots a chance to catch their breath.

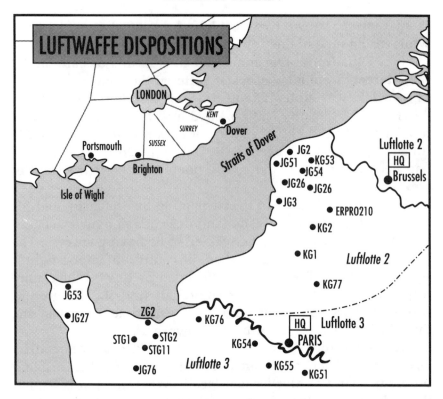

The lull ended at about 5:30 pm., when RDF stations on the south coast began to pick up large enemy formations over Normandy. These plots were larger than any that had been seen previously by RAF operators—an unnerving experience! Before long, the plots formed up and began moving northward, across the Channel.

At bases throughout southern England, pilots sat near their planes in the warm afternoon sun, and waited. They did not have very long to wait.

Fourteen squadrons from 10 Group and 11 Group were scrambled—a total of about 160 Spitfires and Hurricanes—to intercept the raiders. As the pilots climbed toward the Channel coast, they could see a group of specks ahead. The specks soon sprouted wings and became Ju 88s and Stukas, heading toward Portland and other targets in the area.

Hauptmann Joachim Helbig of LG 1 saw the English Channel at about the same time that the Spitfires spotted him. His Ju 88 and 15 others were on their way to bomb the naval air station at Worthy Down, a few miles away from Southampton. The charging Spitfires made them break formation and scatter.

Helbig and his rear gunner, *Oberfeldwebel* Franz Schlund, managed to save their Ju 88 and themselves from destruction by quick maneuvering and good shooting. When Helbig turned sharply to port, Schlund opened fire on an attacking Spitfire with his single .30 caliber machine gun. The fighter shot past, trailing smoke. But there were too many enemy fighters for Helbig to out-maneuver all of them—when he brought the bomber back to Orleans, it had 130 bullet holes in it.

But Helbig and Schlund were a lot luckier than most in their unit—13 of the 15 Junkers in their gruppe had been shot down. Most of the other German bombers in this particular raid met with heavy fighter opposition, as well. A few bombed Portland, their assigned target; the rest jettisoned their bombs in the Channel. About 12 Ju 88s eluded the fighters and dived on Middle Wallop airfield.

According to David Crook, a Spitfire pilot with 609 Squadron, the Junkers "dived out of the sun, dropped thier bombs, and then streamed back toward the coast as hard as they could go." Two hangars were hit, and six aircraft destroyed. The Spitfire pilots went up after the Junkers and, according to Crook, "shot down at least five." It had been Middle Wallop's fourth attack in three days.

While 609 Squadron's pilots were hastening the departure of LG 1, RDF stations at Dover and Rye picked up another 100 plus incoming aircraft—headed for Biggin Hill and Kenley airfields. But it would be poor navigating that would prove to be the undoing of these two raids, not RAF Fighter Command.

By mistake, the Dorniers assigned Biggin Hill found West Malling, which was incomplete. They did inflict considerable damage to some new wooden huts in their attack, and killed two RAF airmen. Biggin Hill, several miles to the northwest, was not even sighted, let alone bombed.

Hauptmann Rubensdörffer's *Erpro* 210 accounted for some of the aircraft plotted by Dover and Rye. His 15 Bf 110s and 8 Bf 109s had already been up today; Martlesham Heath was a fine shambles as the result of their low-level raid. Now, with the sun low on the horizon, they would try to do the same thing to Kenley.

Rubensdörffer had missed his fighter escort, and was now having a hard time finding his target because of the ground haze. But in spite of these setbacks, he decided to press on with his attack. The 23 aircraft bolted across Kent at low level, frightening pedestrians and sheep with their noise, and swung round to the northwest to attack Kenley from the north.

His plan was to make a fast due-south strafing and bombing run, and then to head straight for the Channel with wide-open throttles. If all went well, *Erpro* 210 would be halfway to the coast before the defenses could figure out what was happening.

At about 7 pm., Rubensdörffer saw an airfield—red brick administration buildings, hangars, and four runways—and led *Erpro* 210 in a diving attack. But after he had pushed over into his 45-degree dive, he caught sight of several green-and-brown camouflaged airplanes flying alongside. They were not his fighter escort, but nine Hurricanes of 111 Squadron.

The Hurricanes had been circling the airfield for half an hour, ever since being scrambled from Croydon. When Rubensdörffer's fighter-bombers made their appearance, S/L John "Tommy" Thompson led a diving attack on them and began shooting, trying to spoil *Erpro* 210's diving attack. They certainly succeeded. Although three hangars, the control tower, and the armory all were hit, many bombs went wide of their marks and hit buildings outside the airfield's boundaries. Both the N.S.F. engineering works and the Bourjois scent factory were damaged in the attack—nearby residents could smell Evening in Paris cologne through their open windows. Several civilian houses also were bombed in error; 62 people were killed.

Erpro 210's efforts had all been for nothing. Rubensdörffer had not even bombed his objective—he had missed Kenley by several miles and attacked Croydon. Croydon airport had been

London's air link with the Continent before the war. It had also been put on Adolf Hitler's list of prohibited targets, since Croydon was a suburb of London.

After dropping their bombs, *Erpro's* Bf 110s went into their usual defensive circle; the Bf 109s turned to confront the Hurricanes. But 9 more Hurricanes from 32 Squadron arrived, and the situation immediately became more uncomfortable. The German aircraft were running low on fuel. Whenever they could, the Messerschmitts broke away and fled for the Channel.

What followed is usually referred to as a running fight—the Hurricane pilots snapped at their quarry all the way to the coast. S/L Thompson went after a Bf 110 that was in an almost vertical climb; when he opened fire, he saw pieces of wing blow off. The German pilot managed to make a wheels-up landing in a field; both pilot and rear gunner were captured.

Sometimes, the fight was taken down to rooftop level. Thompson saw another Bf 110 scuttling southward at very low level. He began chasing it, pressing the Hurricane's firing button whenever the enemy crossed into his line of sight. At one point, he saw his bullets blow the roofing tiles off a house. Thompson immediately broke off his attack—he was afraid that he might kill some civilians.

Hauptmann Rubensdörffer was also hedgehopping toward the Channel coast at full throttle. A Hurricane was right behind him, shooting at the big Messerschmitt with his eight Brownings; Rubensdörffer tried desperately to shake off the enemy fighter—sometimes twisting and turning, sometimes flying a matter of a few feet off the ground. But the Hurricane stayed right behind him, firing every time his guns came to bear, rattling the rooftops and pavements below with spent .303 cartridge cases.

The Hurricane pilot's persistence began to have its effect. A burst of machine gun fire hit one of Rubensdörffer's engines. The Bf 110 slowed as the engine caught fire and stopped. Rubensdörffer did his best to keep the plane in the air, but the burning Zerstörer lost height, smashed into the ground at about 350 miles per hour, and blew up with a huge fireball.

Erprobungsgruppe 210 had flown the Luftwaffe's last sortie of the day. Of the 23 aircraft that had taken off from Calais-Marck, 7 had been shot down—6 Bf 110s and 1 Bf 109. The loss of Hauptmann Rubensdörffer would be sorely felt by *Erpro* 210; Rubensdörffer had led the way in fighter-bomber tactics, and was an energetic leader and a positive influence.

When Adolf Hitler was informed about the raid on Croydon, he launched himself into a monumental temper tantrum—Hitler still hoped for a negotiated peace with Britain, and had forbidden any attacks on London. Croydon was considered to be part of London; *Erpro* 210's loop to the north had set off air raid sirens in south London for the first time. Göring demanded a court martial for the officer responsible. But all that was left of Hauptmann Rubensdörffer was a burnt corpse in a mangled airplane.

Losses for the day were grossly exaggerated by both sides—as usual. The Luftwaffe claimed over 100 RAF fighters destroyed—either 101 or 111 depending upon which source is believed.[10] Official RAF figures put the figure at 34.

RAF claims were just as optimistic—182 German aircraft brought down. This was later modified to 75 aircraft. German sources insist that the true number is more like 55, mostly bombers and Bf 110s. Whatever the true losses were, to the Luftwaffe this day, 15 August, would henceforth be known as *der schwarze Donnerstag*—black Thursday. Prime Minister Churchill called it "one of the greatest days in history."

It was certainly one of the most active days. *Luftflotten* 2,3, and 5 had flown 1,786 sorties[11]—a colossal effort. And the damage done to RAF airfields would be felt for some time to come. Although the bomb craters were quickly filled in at Hawkinge, Lympne, Manston, and the other stations, gutted hangars, repair shops, administration offices, and other buildings could not be put right so quickly or easily. As a result of

---

10   German Fighter Pilots' Association or Bekker's *Luftwaffe War Diaries*.
11   Some German sources put the number at 2,000-plus sorties.

today's raids, the efficiency of each bombed airfield deteriorated, and would continue to decline with each raid. Efficiency of fighter pilots also began to wane. This day's air battle had lasted nine hours, and had been scattered over hundreds of miles—six major attacks, along with a number of minor ones. The pilots of Fighter Command made repeated flights against the Luftwaffe—intercepting and attacking an enemy raid, landing for re-fueling and re-arming, and being scrambled again. Alan Deere of 54 Squadron made 6 sorties during these nine hours, the average sortie lasting forty minutes. This should give some idea of the strain under which the pilots were operating, strain that led to exhaustion.

Pilots could not go on like this—flying repeated combat sorties day after day. The campaign to cripple RAF airfields was only three days old, and fighter pilots were already beginning to lose some of their concentration and alertness. This loss would affect the pilots' performance in combat, and would cause the fiery death of some of them.

The American press and news media published all of the exaggerated figures that were given to them by the British Ministry of Information—although they did not necessarily believe them. All of the American newspapers and magazines, including *The New York Times* and *Life* magazine, printed the figure of 182 German aircraft destroyed on 15 August, and went on about how the gallant young men of the RAF bravely fought the Luftwaffe's air fleets.

But although the American press was sympathetic toward Britain, their stories were not always very encouraging. The underlying feeling in most news aritcles dated 15 August was of overwhelming German strength—the Luftwaffe might not be invincible, but it was going to take a hell of a lot to beat them.

Reporters filed stories about the destruction of "182 Nazi raiders," but also told about the fact that over 1,000 German planes had been in the air. The RAF pilots—including the American volunteers—might be gallant, brave, and all that, but it looked to the American press that it was going to take a lot more than pluck and nerve to stop the Germans and their air force.

16 August, Friday

The weather was clear once again on Friday the 16th, which allowed the Luftwaffe to continue its onslaught against the RAF's forward fighter bases.

West Malling was first. At about 11:00 am., 18 Dorniers of KG 76 dropped their loads of high explosives on the airfield, devastating the fighter station. The previous day's bomb damage had not yet been repaired. Runways were re-cratered, and new bomb damage brought all operations to a dead stop. West Malling would remain inactive for another four days because of this attack.

But the Germans did not get away unmolested. Hurricanes of 111 Squadron had been scrambled to intercept; S/L Tommy Thompson led his pilots in the squadron's patented head-on attack. But closing at a combined speed approaching 600 miles per hour did not give very much time to react. Flight Lieutenant Ferriss misjudged his attack and crashed head-on with one of the Dorniers. "There was a tremendous explosion." reported Thompson, "and very little left except a few pieces floating down."

The head-on charge accomplished its aim—it broke up the bomber formation and allowed the Hurricane pilots to take on the bombers one at a time. "Treble One" Squadron claimed four Dorniers destroyed.

Just after noon, another large enemy force was picked up by CH stations. These were actually three separate raids, about 350 aircraft each, on their way to scattered targets along the south coast. Ventnor CH station, on the Isle of Wight, was bombed again by five Stukas. As a result, it would be non-operational until 23 August.

The RAF fighter station at Tangmere was also attacked. Stukas of StG 2, and Ju 88s of KG 51, approached from the south and dive-bombed the station in several waves. An RAF aircraftsman had to admit that the bombing was magnificent—"They got all the hangars, all the buildings round the square...." They also got the workshops, stores, sick quarters, pumping station, and fourteen aircraft—including seven Hurricanes.

The hangar belonging to 43 Squadron, which had been built by German prisoners during the First World War, was a ruin. But the squadron's Hurricanes, along with the Hurricanes of 601 (County of London) Squadron, were in the air and after the German bombers. They got to the Stukas; four were shot down, and several others returned to base with .303 caliber bullets in them. Anti-aircraft fire accounted for a fifth Stuka.

Both 43 Squadron and 601 Squadron lost a Hurricane during this interception. Only one pilot was killed—Pilot Officer Billy Fiske, 601's American member.

Chicago-born William Meade Lindsley Fiske III was one American who made no secret of his U.S. citizenship—he had enough money and social connections to ignore both the Neutrality Act and its consequences.

Billy Fiske was the son of an international banker, and had attended Cambridge University. After leaving Cambridge, he lived a life of wealth and leisure, became a champion bobsledder, and entered society when he married the former wife of the Earl of Warwick. Fiske settled in England, where he did weekend flying during the 1930s. Because of his influential friends and family connections, he had no trouble at all in joining the RAF Auxiliary in 1940.

Number 601 Squadron was probably even more class-and-money snobbish than most auxiliary units; it was nicknamed "the Millionaire's Squadron." "They wore red linings in their tunics, and mink linings in their overcoats," according to Mr. Fiske. "They were arrogant and looked terrific, and probably the other squadrons hated their guts." A researcher who investigated Fiske's life history commented that "it wasn't by chance that Billy was posted to No. 601 with all his pals."

He was highly thought of by his squadron mates. His commander, Flight Lieutenant Archibald Hope, called Fiske "the best pilot I've ever known... natural as a fighter pilot. He was

William Meade Lindsley Fiske III came from a wealthy New York banking family. With his political and social connections, as well as his money, Fiske had no trouble at all getting into the Royal Air Force, in spite of the objections of US Ambassador Joseph P. Kennedy. Fiske's death in combat was used for all of its propaganda value—another attempt to change the opinion of the maddeningly neutral Americans. His funeral was given full press coverage.

also terribly nice, and extraordinarily modest. He fitted into this squadron very well."

On 16 August, Fiske's Hurricane was hit by enemy fire and began to burn. There are several versions of what happened. One is that he was jumped by Messerschmitt 109s; another story has it that the damage was done by return fire from a Stuka. Whatever happened, Fiske was able to crash-land his shot-up fighter on Tangmere's grass landing field.

An ambulance crew lifted Fiske out of the Hurricane's cockpit. F/Lt. Hope saw him lying on the grass next to the fighter; Fiske was burned on the face and hands, but did not seem to be seriously injured. Hope told Fiske that he would be alright, since he was only suffering from a few minor burns.

When the squadron's adjutant visited Fiske in the hospital that night, what he saw seemed to confirm Hope's optimism. "Billy was sitting up in bed, perky as hell." But, Hope recalls,

Commemorative plaque for Billy Fiske at St. Paul's Cathedral.

PILOT OFFICER
WILLIAM MEADE LINDSLEY
FISKE III
ROYAL AIR FORCE

AN AMERICAN CITIZEN
WHO DIED
THAT ENGLAND MIGHT LIVE

AUGUST 18ᵀᴴ 1940

"The next thing we heard, he was dead. Died of shock." He died on 17 August, the day after he had been shot down.

Pilot Officer Fiske's obituary in *The Times* of 19 August ran for 39 lines—highly unusual for such a junior officer. The standard obituary for officers ran 7 or 8 lines. Senior officers sometimes received 15 or 20 lines. The reason Fiske was given so much space was partly because he was married to the former Countess of Warwick, and partly because he was American. Fiske's death as a result of combat with the Germans presented Britain with a golden opportunity—now that a well-known American citizen had been killed in the battle, it could be said to Americans that their fellow countrymen were already involved in the war.

The Times obituary was a small part of this publicity campaign. Throughout the United States, newspapers and magazines carried stories about Billy Fiske's funeral—including a full-page photo spread in *Life* magazine. Fiske's death was made into a centerpiece of the program to arouse American sympathy, as well as to enlist American support for Britain.

Billy Fiske was buried in the churchyard of Boxgrove Parish Church in West Sussex, not far from Tangmere. He is also commemorated by a memorial plaque in the crypt of St. Paul's Cathedral in London—which cynics insisted was just another propaganda attempt to sway neutral America to Britain's side. The plaque is dedicated to W.M.L. Fiske; "An American Citizen Who Died That England Might Live."

A great deal has been made over whether or not Billy Fiske was the first American to lose his life in the Second World War. He was certainly the first "official" American to be killed. Flight Lieutenant Jimmy Davies of Bernardsville, New Jersey, died on 25 June, many weeks before Billy Fiske, which has been overlooked. (He was killed before the Battle of Britain officially began on 10 July, which may have something to do with it.) Some U.S. citizens who volunteered for the RAF as Canadians may have lost their lives even earlier—because they kept their nationality a secret, no one will ever know for certain.

At the same time that Tangmere was being worked over, the naval air station at Lee-on-Solent and the Coastal Command field at Gosport, both to the west of Portsmouth, also were bombed. At Lee-on-Solent, two hangars and the aircraft inside them were destroyed—mostly Albacores and Skuas, which were blasted into wreckage. Damage at Gosport was not nearly as severe, although more than one hangar was hit by bombs.

Flight Lieutenant James Nicolson and two other Hurricane pilots of 249 Squadron were flying at about 15,000 feet in the vicinity of Gosport. In his report, Nicolson reported seeing "3 E/A [enemy aircraft] some distance to the left;" he was ordered to investigate by his squadron commander. Before he could get anywhere near the enemy formation, 12 Spitfires showed up and started shooting at the enemy planes. Nicolson turned to re-join the rest of his squadron.

He started climbing to 17,000 feet when he heard "Tally-ho" from another pilot. Immediately, his Hurricane was hit by four cannon shells, "damaging hood, firing reserve tank, and damaging leg and thigh." The other two Hurricanes in his section were also attacked and damaged.

Nicolson decided to bail out of the burning fighter. He had climbed up on the pilot's seat, in preparation for jumping, when he was overtaken by a Bf 110—which may or may not have been his attacker. By this time, the cockpit must have resembled the interior of a furnace; the fire from the fuel tank had badly burned his face and hands. In spite of the fact that his Hurricane was on fire, and disregarding his own pain, Nicolson went after the enemy fighter.

Nicolson closed on the Bf 110, "opened fire at approx. 200 yds., and fired until I could bear heat no more." After a very short time, probably only a few seconds, he lost sight of the Messerschmitt. There was nothing for him to do now but bail out. He was wounded, and had his own Hurricane shot out from under him, but Nicolson had the satisfaction of putting a good burst of .303 machine gun fire into the enemy before he had to jump.

It seemed to him that the Messerschmitt 110 crashed into the Channel off Southampton. Eyewitnesses on the ground claimed that it zig-zagged and dived after Nicolson's attack, but no one actually saw it crash.

Nicolson's parachute opened and, for an anxious couple of minutes, he descended upon the Southampton suburb of Mill-brook. Before he hit the ground, a Home Guard spotted Nicolson and, deciding it wisest to shoot first and ask questions later, fired his shotgun at the parachute. Nicolson was hit on the right side, "in the buttocks," according to his report.

What followed could have been a scene from a slapstick comedy. A butcher's delivery boy came to Nicolson's rescue. When he saw the RAF officer lying on the ground with buckshot wounds, the boy began punching the Home Guardsman. Next, it was the Home Guardsman's turn to be rescued; a policeman came along and pulled the boy off. An ambulance had been called for Nicolson, but the Guardsman had been so badly beaten that he was put into it and taken to the hospital instead. Eventually, Nicolson was taken to Royal Southampton Hospital—in an old van. He remained hospitalized until mid-November, which gives some idea of the extent of his wounds. On 24 November, Nicolson was awarded the Victoria Cross by George VI at Buckingham Palace—the only fighter pilot to receive Britain's highest decoration during the Second World War.

A good many myths and half-truths have become associated with this well-known incident. Various sources have claimed that Nicolson was attacking a formation of Ju 88s when his Hurricane was hit by cannon fire (it was not); that his attacker was a Bf 109 (it probably was not); that the plane shot down by Nicolson had been the fighter that set his Hurricane on fire (it may have been, but not necessarily); and that the wreckage of the Bf 110 has been found and positively identified (it has not).

Not very far from where F/Lt. Nicolson won his Victoria Cross, 609 Squadron's three Yanks were preparing for their first operational sortie. Squadron Leader Darley finally decided that Pilot Officers Mamedoff, Keough, and Tobin were ready for combat.

When the scramble came, the three ran for their Spitfires along with the other pilots. Red Tobin shouted "Saddle her up! I'm ridin'!" to his gound crew, much to everyone's amusement—one thing about these Yanks, they had a style all their own.

As junior men in the squadron, the Americans would be "Ass-End Charlie" in their three-man formation—weaving and turning to protect the tail of the section leader and his wingman. The only trouble was that there was nobody to warn if enemy fighters were attacking *his* tail. Which is why Ass-end Charlie did not enjoy a very long life expectancy. (And which is why this three-man formation was abandoned in favor of the much more practical "finger four" formation.)

At 18,000 feet, Red got the word—"OK, Charlie. Weave." He began flying a weaving-snaking path behind the other two Spitfires, who kept flying straight and level. Over his headset, he heard someone call: "Many, many bandits, three o'clock." He looked off to his left and could see them, more than 50 of them. Another call said that there were still more bandits, at 12 o'clock, straight overhead. But Red could not find these, which put him into a panic—the veterans said that it was always the ones you couldn't see that got you.

Tobin's leader went into a sharp dive, followed by his wingman. Tobin followed them but could not see if they were going after a formation of enemy bombers or trying to evade enemy fighters. After they pushed over, he lost sight of them. The only other plane in sight was a Bf 110, which had seen Tobin and was turning to evade him.

He pushed his throttle forward and closed to within firing distance of the twin-engined Zerstörer, and pressed the firing button. From his stream of tracer, he could see that his shots were going wide—over anxious, he thought. He pulled back on the Spitfire's stick to correct his aim.

But he pulled much too hard, and the Spitfire almost performed a loop. The violence of this maneuver pulled all the blood from his brain, causing him to black out momentarily. When he recovered, the Messerschmitt was gone and he was all alone in the sky—not another plane to be seen, where there had been dozens only a few moments before.

With his flight leader nowhere in sight and his ammunition supply nearly exhausted, Tobin decided that he had better head back to Warmwell.

When he landed, Tobin discovered that all of 609's time and effort had been a complete and total waste. The Luftwaffe had got through, and Middle Wallop had been bombed for the second time that month. The station was still open, but just barely—the runway was cratered by bomb blasts; hangars and workshops had either been blown up or badly damaged, and the aerodrome was dotted by unexploded bombs, which might go off at any moment.

The nearby satellite station at Warmwell, one of Middle Wallop's auxiliary fields, had not been bombed. But this was not because of 609 Squadron's efforts—the Luftwaffe had not tried to bomb it, probably because they did not know it was there.

But they had tried, and had mainly succeeded, in their attacks against RAF stations all along the south coast—Ventnor, on the Isle of Wight; Tangmere had suffered fourteen planes destroyed on the ground; and other airfields and vital communications centers had suffered a similar fate.

So far, the day had been a highly frustrating one, both for Red Tobin and RAF Fighter Command. In his first operational flight, Tobin had burned 80 gallons of gasoline, fired 2,000 rounds of .303 caliber ammunition, and had not one damn thing to show for it. He had not come all the way from sunny California for this.

The frustration was not over yet. In the early evening hours, two Ju 88s attacked the training airfield at Brize Norton, Oxfordshire. The pilots lowered their undercarriage—pretending to make a landing approach, so that they might be mistaken for Bristol Blenheims.

It was a ruse right out of a Hollywood war film, but it worked. The two Junkers dropped 16 bombs each, and were out of sight before anyone on the ground realized what had happened. They blew up several hangars and the airplanes inside them—46 Airspeed Oxford trainers, as well as 11 Hurricanes. Several other buildings also suffered considerable damage. But in spite of all the damage, only 10 people were injured.

But the Luftwaffe had also suffered its share of disappointments. As devastating as their raids had been, the German commanders had expected to accomplish even more—Debden, Duxford, Hornchurch, and North Weald airfields had also been marked as targets, but the bomber crews could not find them through the clouds. These stations were well to the north of the battle area, and as such were not as important to the Luftwaffe's immediate interests as the south coast airfields. But it would have been nice to have given them a good pasting, just to show the RAF what the Luftwaffe could *really* do. A German writer complained that "the weather was in league with the British."

That day, Luftwaffe losses came to 45 aircraft; the RAF lost 21. But Fighter Command was not impressed by these figures. "In spite of heavy losses," RAF Intelligence warned, "large scale attacks by GAF [German Air Force] on airfields and industry are likely to continue."

The intelligence report went on to predict that the Luftwaffe "probably overestimates considerably our own losses," and further forecast that the "GAF is prepared to suffer heavily in the attempt to obtain air superiority."

Peter Townsend of 85 Squadron put it a different way: "...the Luftwaffe was closing in, and we braced ourselves to meet the assault."

17 August, Saturday

Saturday turned out to be a fine, clear day. Everyone in southern England—including American reporters and broadcasters—expected another day of heavy fighting, another maximum effort. But the Luftwaffe's air fleets stayed on the ground.

German reconnaissance units made their usual camera outings over southern England, photographing damage done the previous day, but no massive raids were launched. The Luftwaffe lost 3 aircraft on this Saturday—one of which was shot down by German anti-aircraft fire when it strayed over a flak belt. The RAF lost no airplanes.

Both sides made good use of their day off—the strain of the past couple of days, physical and emotional, had taken its toll. Some pilots went off on leave, and tried to forget the battle for a while. Others remained on station and caught up on their sleep, which was another means of escape.

But the commanders did not rest. Dowding managed to convince the Air Minstry to take pilots away from other duties. Five Fairey Battle pilots were transferred to Fighter Command; Dowding hoped that the transition from light bombers to fighters would not prove too difficult a process. He could only get five pilots, though; Bomber Command did not want to weaken its units any further, especially with the German invasion threatening.

Squadron leaders of Spitfire and Hurricane squadrons were not so sure that these pilots would be such an asset, after all. Flying a light bomber was a far cry from flying a high-performance interceptor. Even an experienced Fairey Battle pilot would not have any idea of deflection shooting or the finer points of making a head-on attack. But, in accordance with Dowding's demand, the five pilots were sent to an Operational Training Unit (OTU) for a cram course on fighters. (Three Army pilots were sent to the same OTU.)

Fighter Command's shortage of pilots was reaching the crisis stage. Squadron leaders desperately missed the pilots they had lost in July's Channel battle. It was especially galling to think that many might have been saved from drowning had Air Sea Rescue been adequate and effective.

New replacements were being sent to front-line squadrons from OTUs, but most of these young pilots were rushed through their training. Some had only fired their guns once; others had never fired them at all. None of them had any real idea of air fighting. These were as good as useless to an operational squadron, and had to be trained in the tactics of staying alive—as Andy Mamedoff, Shorty Keough, and Red Tobin had been by 609 Squadron—before they could be sent into combat.

There was never any shortage of fighter planes, mainly because of the energy and ability of Lord Beaverbrook, the Minister of Aircraft Production. But, unfortunately for Fighter Command, fighter pilots could not be replaced as quickly or easily as fighter planes. The shortage of trained pilots—properly and fully trained pilots—would continue to worsen throughout the battle.

On the other side of the Channel, senior German officers were watching a rehearsal of the invasion of southern England. Feldmarschall Walther von Brauchitsch and General Franz Halder saw infantrymen make landings on the French coast. The landing forces came ashore in rubber boats and specially converted canal barges. The Navy, especially Admiral Raeder, were still wary of any kind of landing, but the Army had confidence. They felt certain that they could pull it off, and were in the final stages of preparation. Now, all they had to do was wait for the Luftwaffe to make the air safe over the Channel.

Göring also had confidence. He was certain that his Luftwaffe could neutralize RAF Fighter Command, and were already well on their way toward gaining air superiority. If his bombers kept pounding the enemy's fighter fields, and his fighter pilots continued to shoot down Spitfires and Hurricanes in the same numbers, the invasion would take place, as planned. Air Chief Marshal Dowding felt the same certainty. If steps were not taken toward reversing the present trend in fighter pilot attrition, Dowding was sure that the Germans would be in England before autumn.

18 August, Sunday

For a while, it looked as though Sunday might be another lull. In fact, there were some optimists in southern England who thought that the Germans might have given up. What else was there to think? Two gorgeous days in a row, and no Luftwaffe.

People on their way home from church remarked about the inactivity—no church bells were rung; this was the pre-arranged signal that the invasion had begun. American reporters were not relieved, only puzzled. Some had seen the damage done to Fighter Command's airfields a few days earlier, and wondered what Göring was up to.

At around noon, southeast England—American reporters included—found out. Nine Dorniers of KG 76 roared over Kent at a height of 100 feet or less, startling anyone who happened to be outdoors. The bombers had not been detected by the CHL station at Beachy Head, but the Observer Corps had spotted them and reported their presence.

The Dorniers had been assigned to bomb Kenley. Along with this low-level raid, KG 76 also had some of its Do 17s approach from high altitude. The combined attack brought a hail of 50 kg. (110 lb.) bombs to the airfield; one of the aircrew saw them bounce down the runway "like rubber balls." It seemed that they had done a thorough job on Kenley. Now, all they had to do was get back home again.

Thanks to the Observer Corps' warning, Kenley's anti-aircraft gunners were at their posts when KG 76 arrived. Every machine gun on the station began firing, and the PAC (Parachute and Cable) crews began launching their rockets at the Dorniers. Each rocket carried a 500-foot length of steel cable with a parachute at each end. If an airplane ran into the cable, the two parachutes would open and send the unfortunate victim spinning into the ground. At least, that is what everybody thought would happen—nobody had actually tried them out yet.

The low-level Dornier attack was tailor-made for the PACs. And the awkward-sounding weapon worked. Much to the surprise of their crews at Kenley. A Dornier piloted by one *Feldwebel* Petersen caught its wing on one of the rocket-propelled cables. Both parachutes opened, jerking the bomber into an involuntary snap-turn. Before Petersen had time to react, his airplane crashed to earth and exploded.

While the PAC crews were doing their best to stop the low attack, Hurricanes of 32 Squadron intercepted the high-altitude attack—Do 17s escorted by Bf 110s—with a head-on rush. At least one of the Dorniers was destroyed during this charge; it fell out of formation and spun toward the ground out of control. The other bombers took evasive action, which resulted in the bomb-aimers missing their targets.

Meanwhile, the Hurricane pilots of 615 Squadron were taking on the Bf 109s that were flying top cover for the Dorniers and Bf 110s. In the ensuing melee, 615 Squadron lost four Hurricanes (and one pilot), while JG 3 parted with two Messerschmitt 109s (and one pilot).

The battle over Kenley had been intense and furious. Four Dorniers had been lost in the low-level attack alone, with several more damaged. At least one other had been shot down during the high-altitude raid. This does not take into account the Dorniers that landed at their base with their fuselage and tail section riddled with .303 bullet holes; crew members realized that they were lucky to be alive, let alone back home.

But they had left Kenley a shambles. Eight aircraft had been destroyed on the ground—including four of 615 Squadron's Hurricanes. Ten hangars were in ruins, along with repair shops and other buildings; the runway was so badly cratered that the remnants of 615 Squadron had to land at Croydon. Because of the damage inflicted, by this raid and in past attacks, Kenley would now only be able to support two fighter squadrons instead of three.

Kenley was not the only fighter base that had come under attack. Biggin Hill, Manston, and West Malling also received their share of attention from the Luftwaffe. Bombs had cratered West Malling's runway in 30 places.

At Biggin Hill, KG 76's Dorniers also came in two waves, as they had done at Kenley—a low-level rush followed by a high-altitude raid. The low attack came first—*Oberleutnant* Lamberty, pilot of the lead Dornier, released all of his bombs on camouflaged hangars. Behind him, the other eight bombers released over their targets. All nine now tried to get away before either flak or fighters woke up.

But before they could make good their escape, the Bofors anti-aircraft gunners started shooting, and "a damn carpet of some kind of rockets were being shot up"—the PAC batteries. Lamberty pulled the Dornier's nose up sharply, trying to get above the parachute cables, and flew right over two Bofors batteries.

Lamberty could hear the guns firing, and could even feel the pressure of the muzzle blast against the bomber's fuselage. He also felt a jar—one round hit his port wing, blowing a hole in the fuel tank and disabling the engine. At a height of only 150 feet, the Dornier was too inviting a target to miss.

Lamberty feathered the port engine and pushed the starboard throttle full forward. But while he was making his turn for the Channel coast, Lamberty saw a storm of machine gun bullets striking the ground just ahead—the fighters of either 32 Squadron (Hurricanes) or 610 Squadron (Spitfires) were cutting off his escape.

The Dornier's crew heard something that sounded like a handful of peas hitting the bomber—.303 machine gun bullets. Then the port side was on fire; they could feel the heat. Lamberty looked for a good field to make a wheels-up landing.

There was not a lot of time left—the Dornier was already so low that one of its stabilizers touched the top branches of a tree. As Lamberty picked out a place for a crash-landing, local Home Guardsmen started shooting at the bomber with their Enfield rifles. The bomber touched down and skidded across the field. Its clear perspex nose shattered, sending a shower of dust and dirt into the the plane.

Lamberty and another crewman, *Hauptmann* Roth, scrambled out of the burning aircraft. Both had suffered burns, but could walk without any difficulty. Some of the Home Guard unit came at them with rifles and shotguns, but they seemed more afraid of Lamberty and Roth than the two Germans were of them.

While the two sides were sizing up each other, the high-level attack arrived—about 20 minutes late. Everyone fell flat on the ground, and stayed there until the bombing ended.

The Home Guard took the two Germans into a town, probably Biggin Village. From there, they were taken to the sick quarters at Biggin Hill airfield, and then to a hospital. Lamberty learned that the other three members of his crew had jumped from the Dornier at low level rather than stay with the buring bomber, and that they had miraculously survived. Two had fractures of the skull and thigh; the third only had minor lacerations on both hands.

Biggin Hill had survived also; at least, it had got off a lot more lightly than Kenley. But this was not because of lack of determination on the part of the Luftwaffe. The defenses—especially those unnerving PAC batteries—were so sudden and intense that pilots and bomb aimers missed their targets. Of the nine low-level Dorniers, one was shot down with all hands killed; Lamberty's was shot down, the crew captured; two crash-landed in the Channel, their crews rescued by motor launches;

three crash-landed in France; one made it back to base with a dead pilot; and the ninth landed at base with no casualties.

Most of the bombs missed Biggin Hill completely, and landed on the nearby golf course. Several hit the airfield and failed to explode. Sergeant Joan Mortimer, Women's Auxiliary Air Force, decided to give a helping hand to the bomb disposal units. While she was busy marking each live bomb with a red marking flag, one of them exploded a short distance away. In spite of the explosion, she carried on with her work. Sgt. Mortimer was awarded the Military Medal for what she had done, acting with calm and bravery in spite of the obvious danger—an award that she never really felt she deserved.

For Biggin Hill, however, this would only be a temporary reprieve. During the next two weeks, the station would be attacked on an almost daily basis.

Besides Kenley and Biggin Hill, Manston and West Malling also received visits from the Luftwaffe. West Malling escaped without any further damage, the result of inaccurate bombing. But Manston's runway was cratered thirty times, and the station's new hangars were hit by bombs.

During the early afternoon, the Luftwaffe threw a second major attack across the Channel. This time, the objectives were Portsmouth and Gosport; the air station at Thorney Island in Hampshire; the Fleet Air Arm station at Ford, in Sussex; and the CH station at Poling.

At Gosport, eyewitnesses saw "at least a dozen" Ju 88s plunge out of the sky, drop their bombs, and disappear. But the main attack was carried out by Stukas of StG 77. Twenty-two of the dive bombers fell on Gosport; the rest attacked Ford, Thorney Island, and Poling.

These attacks were, as usual for the Stukas, murderously accurate. About 90 bombs hit Poling, knocking it off the air and keeping it out of action until the end of August—the second station after Ventnor to be disabled. Thorney Island and Ford also found out how lethal the Stuka's near-vertical dive bombing could be.

The Junkers Ju 87 Stuka was an excellent dive bomber, used to great effect on targets in Poland, the Low Countries, and in France. It had the capability of putting a bomb on its target with incredible accuracy and, with screaming siren attached, was the terror of the Continent. But the Stuka was also slow and vulnerable. It was mauled by Spitfires and Hurricanes, and had to be withdrawn from the Battle.

When the Stukas formed up for their trip back to France, they were intercepted by Hurricanes of 43 Squadron and Spitfires of 152 Squadron. This time, the murder came from the other side. The rear gunners of the slow and vulnerable bombers fought back, but it was a totally one-sided fight. Between them, the two RAF fighter squadrons shot down 12 Stukas.

Sergeant Hollowes of 43 Squadron "caught up with 5 Ju 87s in-line astern, opened fire" on one of them and watched the crew bale out. Over Thorney Island, he caught another Stuka after it pulled out of its dive. "I gave it three short bursts," and watched it break in two and fall to earth.

Spitfire pilots of 152 Squadron had the same experiences—charging at the slow dive bombers, coming within firing range, and chopping them to pieces with their eight .303 Brownings. "The British fighters gave no quarter," noted the author of the *Luftwaffe War Diaries*.

Following their decimation at the hand of RAF fighters on 18 August, the Stuka units were withdrawn from the battle. On this day, a total of 30 Stukas had either been shot down, or had limped back to France sieved with .303 bullet holes. When these losses were added to those of previous days, it became obvious that the Stuka could not survive against determined fighter attacks. Sending them against Spitfire and Hurricane pilots would only mean a waste of both machines and their crews.

At around 5 pm., the next phase began—CH stations at Dover and Rye began plotting large enemy formations heading for Kent. Another large plot looked as though it would be making for the Thames Estuary; it seemed that Hornchurch and North Weald would be their objective.

Dorniers of KG 2 and Heinkel He 111s of KG 53, a grand total of over 100 bombers, were intercepted by Hurricanes of 501 Squadron and 85 Squadron. But the weather also intervened; the clear morning sky had deteriorated into murky overcast by afternoon. Pilots had trouble finding their objectives because of the cloud cover; they flew to within the general vicinity of their assigned targets, unloaded their bombs, and hoped for the best. Twelve Bf 109s hit Manston at tree-top height and destroyed two Spitfires on the ground. But most of the late afternoon strike missed its mark. Residential areas had been bombed, including parts of southeastern London, instead of fighter bases. Fighter Command was given a brief respite, at the expense of civilians.

Peter Townsend and the rest of 85 Squadron, based at Debden, were in the air over Essex. Debden would be the home of the U.S. 4th Fighter Group, which would destroy more than 1,000 German aircraft between 1942 and 1945 and would be nick-named "The Debden Gangsters" by Propaganda Minister Josef Goebbels. But during the Battle of Britain, the station guarded the Thames Estuary and the eastern approaches to London.

Squadron Leader Townsend admitted that he had "qualms about leading my little band into the midst of a vast horde of the enemy," because today would mark his debut. He had already been in combat—in February, he had a hand in shooting down a Heinkel He 111 near Whitby, Yorkshire—and had been shot down himself. But today would be the first time he would lead his little band of 12 Hurricanes against the Luftwaffe.

The Hurricanes bolted out of the clouds "somewhere over the Thames estuary." The ground controller had given them a good vector; when they broke out of the overcast, the Hurricane pilots found themselves closing in on "a massive column" of German airplanes—bombers and fighters, with Bf 109s at the top of the column. Townsend pushed his throttle forward, but before he could get close to the bombers, the Hurricanes were cut off by Bf 110s.

One of the twin-engined Zerstörers presented itself to Townsend's gunsight. The Messerschmitt looked as though it might have been trying to escape, but instead executed a slow, banking turn in front of the Hurricane's eight .303 Brownings. It was an easy shot for Townsend.

The Bf 109s were never very far away. One dived at Townsend, firing its cannons and machine guns. Townsend turned toward it; the Messerschmitt dived past, then climbed back after the Hurricane. Townsend maneuvered until he was behind it, and pressed the firing button. "When I fired, the Me 109 flicked over and a sudden spurt of white vapor from its belly turned into flame."

Another Bf 109 came after him; once again, Townsend was able to get in back of the Messerschmitt. The German pilot tried to out-turn the Hurricane—a fatal mistake. Townsend fired, and watched bits of the enemy fighter blow off. "He looked incongruous there," Townsend recalled, "a wingless body in the midst of this duel of winged machines."

Townsend claimed three enemy machines destroyed. All of 85 Squadron's pilots had fired their guns at the enemy, and all returned safely. Later in the day, Townsend received a message from the Chief of Air Staff: "Well done 85 Squadron in all your hard fighting." He also received another signal, which ordered

85 Squadron to transfer to Croydon. At Croydon, they would see the enemy often in coming days.

Sunday 18 August had been a day of unrelenting combat. Both sides went at each other with almost superhuman violence, and were able to inflict telling losses upon each other. It had been another hard day for Fighter Command: one sector airfield partially crippled for the remainder of the battle; another CH station knocked out until the end of August; 27 fighters destroyed; and, most damaging of all, ten more of its pilots killed.

But by inflicting this damage, the Luftwaffe also suffered losses. Seventy-one of its aircraft had been shot down (the original RAF claim had been 126); 28 of these had been Stukas. Göring was not happy about the number of aircraft that had either been lost or damaged. From then on, Göring ordered, more fighters would be called upon to escort the bombers. And these fighters would be required to give their escorts much closer support.

19 August, Monday

After four days of fine, sunny weather, cloud returned to southern England on the 19th. As always, Luftwaffe activity decreased as the amount of overcast intensified. Compared with the previous few days, fighting fell off sharply because of the deteriorating visibility.

Dover was strafed by fighters shortly before 1 pm., and again about an hour and a half later. (Dover was such an easy target that it was attacked whenever poor visibility prevented raids against more distant objectives.) Scattered targets throughout Kent were bombed, along with the docks at Southampton and Portsmouth. At night, small raids bombed Liverpool, Southampton (again), Hull, Bristol, Leicester, and several other cities—the force that struck Liverpool consisted of 12 He 111s. (A victim of the bombings took exception to the phrase "small raid"—"If only one bomb is dropped and it hits your house, it is not a small raid!")

Losses suffered by the RAF: 3 aircraft. The Luftwaffe lost 6 airplanes.

On this Monday, the main activities did not take place over southern England or the Channel. The most important action of the day took place at Hermann Göring's Karinhall. Göring used the poor flying weather as an opportunity to confer with his air commanders, and to tell them about changes he was about to make in their conduct of the war.

First, the Reichsmarschall icily informed everyone present, including General Erhard Milch, that he was not happy about the battle so far, or the way in which it was being fought. He thought that the Battle of Britain should already have been won. Next, he announced that the battle would now be entering "the decisive phase"—RAF Fighter Command would now be the Luftwaffe's sole target, especially the airfields of 11 Group.

The reason that the battle had not yet been won, Göring continued, was because his fighter pilots were not aggressive enough—they did not give his bombers adequate protection. In other words, everything that had gone wrong so far had been the fault of the fighter pilots. When General Milch heard this line of reasoning, he became as angry as Göring, and told the Reichsmarschall that the real problem was the Luftwaffe High Command—"they gave the wrong orders."

But the Reichsmarschall was not really interested in solving problems; he was especially not interested in accepting any of the blame for recent failures and shortcomings. He only wanted a scapegoat for what he saw as unacceptable losses among his bomber units. Although he awarded Adolf Galland and Werner Mölders the Pilot Medal with Jewels for their leadership and the number of enemy aircraft destroyed, Göring could not resist using the presentation as an occasion to say quite plainly that "he was not satisfied" with the performance of the German fighter pilots.

Göring did offer some real changes. His main alteration was to transfer *Luftflotte 3's* single-seat fighters over to *Luftflotte 2*—this increased the number of Bf 109s in the Pas de Calais area, where they would be closer to southern England. He also confirmed that the Ju 87 Stuka would henceforth be used only for special assignments, jobs where pinpoint bombing would be needed. Otherwise, the Stukas would no longer participate in the battle.

Also, there was the matter of the Bf 110s, Göring's pet *Zerstörers*. Too many were being shot down, the Reichsmarschall complained—79 of them had been lost in the previous week alone. And so, he ordered that the Bf 110s be escorted by Bf 109s in the future. This was an open admission by Göring that he had been wrong about the big twin-engined fighter—the Bf 110 was not an interceptor, and was no match for either the Hurricane or the Spitfire. (Or for any single-seat American fighter later in the war.) It was also a source of embarrassment for *Zerstörer* pilots—being told that they would need a fighter escort came as a slap in the face, since they wre supposed to be flying fighter planes themselves.

In addition, Göring announced that not more than one officer could be a member of a bomber's crew from then on; too many commissioned officers had been lost in recent days. At the same time, he promoted some of the Luftwaffe's more junior officers, including Major Werner Mölders and Major Adolf Galland, over older and more senior officers—Mölders, for instance, replaced Major General Theo Osterkamp as *Geschwader* commander of JG 51.[12]

Britain's Chain Home system was also on the Reichsmarschall's mind. He ordered attacks onthe CH network to stop, because the stations had proved such difficult targets—those damn latticework towers simply refused to fall down! This was probably Göring's most far-reaching decision of the day, and revealed his almost total ignorance of radar and what it could do. (And had been doing.) Had he been more technically-minded, Göring would have ordered the CH network knocked out by intensified attacks. His order, based upon a total disre-

---

12 Adolf Galland was not happy about being promoted, since he thought it would mean more paperwork and less flying. He asked Göring to rescind the promotion; Göring refused.

gard of technological knowledge, would cost his Luftwaffe dearly.

As for the Luftwaffe's offensive, Göring ordered that fighter and bomber units would henceforth have a freer hand in choosing targets. This meant that more RAF fighter bases would come under attack and few non-Fighter Command facilities (such as the docks at Southampton) would be targeted, since it was the Spitfires and Hurricanes that were making life deadly for German pilots and aircrew. Destroy the enemy's fighters, and operations against England would be much simpler.

Göring hoped that these measures would hasten the destruction of RAF Fighter Command. But from his own remarks at this meeting, Göring showed that he had absolutely no idea how much damage the Luftwaffe had already done. Two Chain Home stations were still non-operational, and were being covered by inadequate mobile sets. Three sector stations had been heavily damaged. And, most important of all, RAF Fighter Command was losing pilots that could not be replaced. Although the battle had not yet reached any decisive conclusion, the balance was shifting in favor of the Luftwaffe.

While Reichsmarschall Göring was holding his conference at Karinhall, the pilots and personnel of 616 Squadron RAF were moving south—from Leconfield in Yorkshire to Kenley.

The Spitfire pilots had seen combat on 15 August, when they had met the unescorted bombers of *Luftflotte 5* and gave them a very rough welcome. Now they were being sent south to relieve a battle-weary 64 Squadron at Kenley. "We drank a little more than usual at lunch time and went down to the airfield in a hilarious mood," recalled Hugh Dundas, "eager to take off for Kenley and glory."

All of their hilarity was immediately subdued when the squadron landed at Kenley, however. "Much of the station lay in ruins," Dundas said. He could see wreckage and newly-filled craters all around. He also noticed the strain in the faces of the other squadrons' pilots, pilots who had seen a good deal of the Luftwaffe in recent days. It seemed that something more than glory lay in store for him and the rest of 616 Squadron. The commander of 11 Group, Air Vice Marshal Keith Park, was also concerned for the future. His main worry lay in how to cut losses among the harried fighter squadrons within 11 Group. On 19 August, Park issued Instruction No. 4, which addressed the problem of pilot attrition.

One of Park's main points concerned the loss of pilots because of forced landings at sea. He instructed ground controllers: "Avoid sending fighters out over the sea to chase reconnaissance aircraft or small formations of enemy fighters." It was bad enough to have his pilots shot down in combat; Park wanted to avoid having them drown in the Channel or the North Sea.

Another point that Park wanted to make involved the interception of enemy aircraft. "Our main objective is to engage enemy bombers," he emphasized. The message: forget all of the knights of the air rubbish—shoot down the German bombers and leave the fighters alone. This was probably a totally unnecessary order, since most RAF fighter pilots wanted to avoid the Messerschmitt 109 as much as possible, and usually stayed well clear of them unless the enemy fighters struck first.

Besides trying to cut down on losses, Park also increased the number of pilots available to 11 Group. He released No. 1 (Canadian) Squadron, as well as two sections of 303 (Polish) Squadron, to "fully operational" status. The Poles were only to be used to patrol fighter bases, however. Park still doubted their usefulness—his reason was the Poles' limited (and often non-existent) understanding of English.[13]

These measures represented a step in the right direction. But they fell far short of solving Fighter Command's pilot shortage problem.

---

13   This might be put down as a typically English prejudice. When the first all-American Eagle squadrons were formed, some RAF officers doubted their usefulness because of "lack of discipline."

20 August, Tuesday

Cloud, wind, and occasional rain curtailed operations for the second day in a row. Dover's balloon barrage came under attack again in the afternoon, along with fighter bases at Manston, West Malling, and Eastchurch. A convoy, code-named "Agent," was bombed off the North Sea coast; one German aircraft was shot down, another was damaged.

During the morning, the Luftwaffe had flown a flurry of nuisance raids against a scattering of targets, including the Pembroke docks in Wales. Pembroke's oil tanks had been set on fire on the previous day, and would continue to burn for six more days.

Although 453 sorties had been flown by Fighter Command, only 7 German airplanes had been shot down. This was largely due to poor visibility—the fighters had trouble finding the enemy through the overcast. Fighter Command's losses consisted of two aircraft and one pilot.

Across the Channel, preparations for Operation Sea Lion took another step forward. The first group of 1,130 landing barges were shipped from their inland collection points to ports along the Channel coast. Even though the Army and the Navy were still squabbling, the official date for the invasion of southern England had been set for 15 September.

In the House of Commons, Prime Minister Winston Churchill gave an optimistic assessment of the battle to date: "The enemy is, of course, far more numerous than we are," he said, but went on to assure his audience that "our bomber and fighter strengths now, after all this fighting, are larger than they have ever been." He added that "American production is only just beginning to flow in," and predicted that Britain would be able to hold off the enemy if RAF Fighter Command could beat back the Luftwaffe.

Churchill concluded by telling the Commons that the gratitude "of every house in our island, in our Empire, and indeed throughout the world" went out to the RAF fighter pilots. He concuded his address: "Never in the field of human conflict was so much owed by so many to so few."

This sentence had gone on to become one of the great catch phrases of modern history, and has entered the literature of the English language. But at the time, it launched a thousand irreverent wisecracks, especially among RAF types. One pilot remarked, "He must be thinking of our liquor bills." Other gems include: "He must mean our back pay." and, "He must be talking about my ex-wife's brassiere size." Referring to his flying officer's pay of 14 shillings and sixpence per day,[14] Michael Appleby of 609 Squadron said, "and for so little."

Churchill's famous words were also reprinted in America, where they made a considerable impression—especially among the interventionists, those who favored sending aid to Britain. It made a lot more of an impression than the Ministry of Information's inflated figures on German aircraft losses.

American correspondents dutifully reported the numbers they wre given by the Ministry, but they did not believe them. Some of the more intrepid (or foolhardy) tried to chase down every German airplane reported shot down, but could not hope to locate all of the wrecks. Most gave up after finding only one or two, and tripping over fences, wading through streams, and driving all over southern England.

Much of the American public did not believe what they were being told, either. "If the Germans keep losing so many planes, how come they keep coming back for more every day?" one New Jersey teacher asked. "If they really lost as many as the British claim, the Germans would be out of the war by now."

Instead of convincing the American public that Britain was winning the battle, the MOI's overblown numbers were seeming to have the opposite effect—Americans were beginning to believe that the wily Brits were inflating the enemy's losses for the purpose of covering up their own.

A British biographer of Winston Churchill wrote that Americans were "foreigners who disliked the British Empire even

---

14   72½ pence in 1995 currency, or $1.20 US dollars.

more than did Hitler." This is an extremely valid point—especially since Hitler actually seemed to have admired the British Empire, and America was once a part of it. Because of this deep-seated historical prejudice, as well as ingrained isolationism, America's view of her traditional antagonist remained wary—Adolf Hitler and his evil hordes notwithstanding.

In short, Americans were still not convinced that Britain was going to win the battle.

21 August, Wednesday

The weather did not improve by Wednesday, which limited the Luftwaffe to small raids and armed reconnaissance flights over coastal objectives. These were carried out by small formations of two or three planes, and sometimes by only a single aircraft. In the course of these raids, some of the airplanes flew so low that the pilot's face could be seen by observers on the ground.

Squadron Leader Peter Townsend reported that 85 Squadron were "kept limbering up with frequent but fruitless searching for elusive raiders." But not all the searching was fruitless—14 German aircraft were shot down during the day's operations. The RAF lost one fighter, a Hurricane of 56 Squadron that was brought down by return fire from a Dornier 17.

One of the 14 German airplanes, a Heinkel He 111 of KG 53, was shot down by Pilot Officer Ted Shipman of 41 Squadron. Shipman had previously accounted for the Bf 110 piloted by Oberleutnant Hans Kettling.

Another of the 14 enemy planes was brought down by Flight Lieutenant Minden Blake, the acting C.O. of 238 Squadron. Blake had taken over the squadron when the commander, S/L Harold Fenton, and five other pilots had been lost in combat in mid-August. Following this disaster, 238 Squadron was withdrawn from Middle Wallop to St. Eval in Cornwall, so that it could be brought up to strength.

On this Wednesday, one section was scrambled to intercept enemy aircraft. Blake and the two other pilots spotted three Ju 88s approaching the north coast of Cornwall, right where the controller said they would be, and began maneuvering so they could make their attack from out of the sun. They made a good run-in toward the enemy, but began firing before they were within range—this was Blake's first look at an actual German plane, so his nervousness was excusable. The three Junkers, alerted by the premature shooting, broke and headed for the clouds below.

When the three bombers dove, Blake and the other two Hurricane pilots pushed over and went after them. Blake lost sight of the Junkers until he broke through the bottom of the cloud layer; his Hurricane was shaking from the excessive speed. He latched onto one of the bombers and tried to close with it. Had the German pilot continued to dive, he might have got away. But he began to turn, which allowed Blake to catch up with him.

The Junkers' rear gunner began shooting at the Hurricane; Blake could see the machine gun's muzzle flashes. But he had no intention of being distracted—it had been a long chase, and he was finally within the .303's range. When he pressed the firing button, Blake could see the flashes of his bullets hitting the bomber's fuselage.

Blake claimed his Ju 88 as "destroyed"—after pulling out of his dive, he was mildly astonished to find his legs shaking uncontrollably. A second pilot also claimed to have shot down a Junkers; the third pilot of the section fired his guns at his bomber, but did not hit it. Still, two out of three was not bad, especially on a first operational sortie.

Göring decided to mark the day with a visit to *Luftflotte 2's* advance headquarters at Cap Blanc Nez. Among the things he did on his day out was to observe the masts of Dover's CH station through high-powered binoculars. It would have been intriguing if he had made a few notes on his own thoughts while he looked across the Channel; maybe it would give some clue as to his ideas on the CH network, and exactly why he had stopped attacking these vital stations.

22 August, Thursday

Once again, cloud and wind interferred with operations. Most of the Luftwaffe's activities were limited to reconnaissance sorties, although Manston was attacked again during the early evening. The main action of the day took place in the Straits of Dover, when the convoy "Totem" became the target of the Luftwaffe.

Totem first came under fire by the heavy guns near Cap Gris Nez at about 9 am. The artillery batteries fired 100 shells in 80 minutes, but did not hit any of the ships. This was probably the result of a combination of poor visibility, a choppy sea, and bad gunnery.

The Luftwaffe showed up at 12:40 to try to do what the guns could not, but Totem's luck held. Spitfires from 54 Squadron arrived and caused enough trouble for the attacking Ju 88s that no hits were scored.

Night operations began to increase, in accordance with Göring's directive of 19 August. Four fighter stations—including Manston, for the second time in less than twelve hours—were bombed, as was the Bristol airplane factory at Filton. And during the early morning hours of Friday, 23 August, a single bomber released his stick of bombs on Wealdstone, a suburb of south London.

It had been a thoroughly frustrating day for both sides. The Luftwaffe failed to inflict any significant damage, either to Fighter Command or convoy Totem, although their raids had considerable nuisance value. (Especially at Manston, where nerves were already over-stretched.) The RAF lost five fighters, in exchange for three German bombers.

The day was especially discouraging to Flying Officer Hugh Dundas of 616 Squadron. He had very nearly been killed by a Messerschmitt 109 that he had not even seen.

Dundas had no idea that he was in danger until his Spitfire was jarred by several explosions; his first thought was that he had been hit by anti-aircraft fire. Immediately, the cockpit filled with white smoke, and Dundas felt himself pressed against the side of the cockpit by centrifugal force—the Spitfire was in a violent spin.

After a struggle with the jammed cockpit hood, Dundas managed to extract himself from the stricken fighter. His parachute opened; it took several minutes before Dundas came down, only two or three hundred yards away from the burning wreckage of his Spitfire. His leg was wet with blood, and his shoulder hurt "abominably."

A local farmer came over to investigate, carrying a shotgun and displaying a manner that was a good deal less than congenial. "Perhaps he did not much like having aeroplanes making holes in his fields and frightening his sheep," Dundas reflected.

Eventually, an ambulance arrived to take Dundas off to Canterbury Hospital. Because of his injured shoulder, Dundas would miss most of the Battle. But he had been lucky, and he knew it—he had been shot down by a Bf 109 and had lived to tell about it.

23 August, Friday

Cloud and showers once again limited the Luftwaffe's Air Fleets to nuisance raids by small bomber formations and to reconnaissance flights. Biggin Hill and Tangmere each received visits from a single bomber; Portsmouth, Southampton, and other places scattered across southern England also were inconvenienced. These attacks were so small that they were hardly worth the effort. But they were not intended to be disabling blows, only pinpricks to harrass the enemy and keep him from getting any relief.

The Luftwaffe lost five aircraft in these raids, including two bombers shot down at night. RAF Fighter Command lost no fighters.

The bad weather had lasted for five days, so far. Some of the pilots, both RAF and Luftwaffe, did not consider the cloud and the overcast to be bad, however, To them, it was good weather—it allowed them to get some badly-needed rest. Peter Townsend was so tired, from flying what seemed like endless sorties, that he did not even bother getting out of bed during a nuisance raid on Croydon. "It was a bad sign," he said. "I was more exhausted than I realized."

But in the early hours of 24 August, the weather began clearing. Peter Townsend looked up at the brightening sky, and it occurred to him that he would probably be getting even less rest in the days to come.

Townsend was absolutely correct. Reichsmarschall Göring had been waiting impatiently for the cloud and overcast to disperse, so that the Luftwaffe could stop flying nuisance raids and put his directive of 19 August into effect. Now, it looked like he was going to get his fair weather.

In Washington, DC, President Franklin D. Roosevelt waited for something a good deal more substantial from across the Atlantic than the weather report. The President was hoping for word that the air battle over southern England was beginning to tilt in favor of the Royal Air Force.

Roosevelt was a confirmed interventionist; he believed that America's best interests lay in helping Britain fight Nazi Germany. He wanted to send as much help as possible to Britain—he knew full well, as did Winston Churchill, that Britain could not hope to win against the German war machine without American support and financial credit.

But Roosevelt was also a professional politician. He was running for an unprecedented third term as President, and did not want to do anything that might damage his chances for re-election in November, only a few months away. And he was probably more mindful than anyone else that most Americans remained adamant about staying out of the "foreign war" for as long as possible.

If Roosevelt did anything at all that might bring America closer to war, he saw the political danger for him. One such potentially dangerous act was the plan to transfer fifty World War I vintage destroyers from the U.S. Navy to the British fleet—destroyers that were badly needed for convoy patrols and for anti-invasion precautions. But Roosevelt had his doubts about authorizing this transfer.

As one British historian put it, "Offering destroyers, which America itself would need if Britain fell, could be a futile, even suicidal, gesture."

If Britain fell. And neither Roosevelt nor anyone else in America had any assurances that Britain would win the battle against the German Luftwaffe, and had very little confidence. The Luftwaffe showed no signs of weakening; Ambassador Kennedy continued to send gloomy reports from London about Britain's chances. If his own ambassador had such pessimism, how could Roosevelt hope to persuade an isolationist Congress that Britain was worth backing with money and materiel?

Roosevelt needed some sign of assurance, some grounds for confidence, that Britain's RAF would be able to hold off the advancing Germans. No one else had been able to do it so far—not the Belgians, not the Dutch, not the Poles, not the Norwegians, and conspicuously not the French.

The coming weeks would be vitally critical—for Britain, for Germany, and for a yet-to-be-convinced America.

CAPTAIN DIXON'S EXPLODING BULLET

Pilots of RAF fighter units very quickly found out that the calibre .303 ball (solid shot) ammunition had its limitations. The .303 was actually not suited for shooting down bombers, because of its small rifle calibre, and was almost totally ineffective against self-sealing fuel tanks. The 20 mm cannon available to RAF squadrons quickly proved themselves unreliable, because of a tendency to jam. But in August 1939, the RAF received an incendiary bullet that could be fired from a Browning .303 machine gun and still penetrate a bomber's (or fighter's) fuel tanks.

A year earlier, an explosive bullet was developed by two Swiss inventors: Paul Rene de Wilde and Anton Casimir Kaufman. The two gave a demonstration of their new bullet to the Air Ministry, which was not an overwhelming success—of nine rounds fired, only three actually exploded and set fire to their target.

A small arms expert, army Captain C. Aubrey Dixon, was given the job of making the explosive bullet—which became known as the "De Wilde shell"—work. This amounted to completely re-inventing it.

Along with a chemist named J. S. Dick, Dixon developed an explosive filler for the bullet—the original filler had a tendency to explode while the bullet was still in the gun barrel. Next, they had to devise a reliable method of making the bullet explode on contact with the skin of an enemy airplane.

Dick suggested inserting a steel "anvil" in the nose of the bullet, and placing a steel ball-bearing behind it. When the bullet struck something solid, the ball would hit the anvil and ignite the explosive filling. Dixon used this idea, modifying it by softening the nose of the bullet. This lessened the resistance, allowing the ball to strike the anvil with more force and produce a surer explosion.

In August 1939, just a few weeks before the war with Germany began, Dixon tested the improved bullet. His target was a sheet of aluminum alloy, .028 inches thick. A half-filled two-gallon tin of gasoline was placed 6 inches in back of the sheet.

The first round fired penetrated the aluminum sheet, struck the gasoline tin, and set fire to its contents. He tried the same test five more times. All five times, the bullet penetrated the aluminum sheet and set fire to the gasoline.

The RAF had an explosive .303 bullet that worked—the name "De Wilde shell" was kept, primarily to deceive the Germans into believing that Fighter Command was still using the unreliable Swiss bullet.

Dixon's .303 incendiary went into production shortly after its development. It was used against the Luftwaffe over Dunkirk with telling results. The Dixon/De Wilde bullet made a bright flash on contact, which let a pilot know that his shots were hitting their target, and could bring down a German aircraft that ordinary .303 ammunition would not. During the Battle of Britain, it became available in increasing quantities.

"The incendiary ammunition known as 'De Wilde' was of excep-

tional merit," Air Chief Marshal Dowding noted. And Max Aitken, a fighter pilot during the Battle, wrote, "No aircraft that was built in the last war could stand up against it."

THREE AIRPLANES—ONE BRITISH AND TWO GERMAN—THAT COULD NOT COMPETE

Very early on during *der Kanalkampf*, it was becoming evident that two of the Luftwaffe's most vaunted aircraft had actually glaring weaknesses. The two aircraft in question were the twin-engine Messerschmitt Bf 110 fighter, and the Junkers Ju 87 Stuka.

The Ju 87 had been the terror of Poland and France. ('Stuka" is an acronym for *Sturzkampfflugzeug*, which is usually translated as "diving attack aircraft.") Their near-vertical dives, their banshee-wailing sirens, their almost diabolical accuracy in bombing, combined not only to destroy enemy targets but also to shatter enemy morale. Just the mention of the "scraming Stukas" brought fear to soldier and civilian alike during the first fatal monts of the war.

But the murderous success of the Stuka had largely been because it had not yet encountered much fighter opposition. It was a very slow airplane—about 240 miles per hour—which made life very difficult for the pilots of escorting Bf 109s. The Messerschmitts could not

stay with the slow, ungainly-looking dive bombers, but RAF fighter pilots found that the Stukas' lack of speed made them easy targets.

Major Adolf Galland, the commanding officer of *Jagdgeschwader* 26, said that "those Stukas attracted Spitfires and Hurricanes as honey attracts flies." The first inkling of trouble took place over Dunkirk; the Stukas certainly did attract Hurricanes, and came out second best.

On 11 July, a Stuka raid on Portland was attacked by Hurricanes of 601 (County of London) Squadron. After the Stukas released their bombs and pulled out of their dives, the Hurricanes jumped them and shot down two of them. Losses among Stuka units would continue to cause alarm all during July and into August.

The Bf 110 Zerstörer was another major disappointment. The Luftwaffe high command, and Reichsmarschall Hermann Göring in particular, expected great things from the Bf 110—it had two Daimler Benz 601A engines; four 7.92 mm

151

MG 17 machine guns and two 20 mm MG FF cannons in the nose; as well as a second machine gun facing aft, which was manned by the radioman.

The Bf 110's firepower was certainly impressive. S/L Peter Townsend had this to say about it; "Viewed from the wrong end, the [Bf 110's] two 20 mm cannon and four machine guns were disconcerting." Because they were so large and heavy, however, the twin-engined fighter could easily be out manoeuvered by the Spitfire and Hurricane. When attacked by the single-seat fighters, Bf 110 pilots would execute a "defensive circle"—covering each other's tails. Which, because of the plane's wide turning radius, was the best that could be done.

Later on in the war, the Zerstörer would become useful against the U.S. Army Air Force's B-17 Flying Fortresses—when it could bring its foreward firepower to bear. But against single-seat fighters, the Bf 110 simply could not compete.

But the Luftwaffe were not the only ones who suffered disappointments; the RAF also had its fair share of them. On of their earliest was the Boulton Paul Defiant. The Defiant was a single-engine fighter. Its armament consisted of four .303 machine guns mounted in an aft-facing power turret—it had no forward-firing armament at all. It speed was around 300 mph, which made it a good 55 mph slower than the Bf 109E.

One of the characters in Derek Robinson's novel *Piece of Cake* described the aircraft in accurate but not-very-charitable terms. "A Defiant's got four Brownings in a turret, which is fine as long as the enemy agrees to fly alongside for a few minutes. It's got nothing firing forward. The turret weighs an extra half a ton, not counting the gunner inside it, and there's no more power up front than a Hurricane, so it flies like a brick. They call it a Defiant because it defies comprehension."

The Defiant did have some success over France, but even this was a fluke—the German pilots mistook them for Hurricanes, attacked from behind, and met the fire from those four turret-mounted Brownings. But on 19 July, the Luftwaffe met the Defiant again. This time, the German pilots made no mistakes.

Nine Defiants of 141 Squadron, which had only recently arrived from Edinburgh, took off from Hawkinge at about 12.30. They were assigned to a height of about 5,000 feet in the area south of Folkstone.

Fifteen Bf 109s of JG 51, led by Oberleutnant Hans Trautloft, were also in the vicinity of Folkstone. Trautloft spotted nine "strange looking" aircraft with gun turrets behind the cockpits, and identified them as Defiants. He led an attack from the front, where the Defiant had no armament. Within minutes, five of the Defiants had been shot down; a sixth crash-landed near Dover. Three of the nine made it back to Hawkinge—one was so badly shot-up that its gunner had bailed out.

The Luftwaffe claimed 12 Defiants destroyed. One Bf 109 was

lost—to Hurricanes of 11 Squadron, who intervened and saved the surviving Defiants. What was left of 141 Squadron was removed to Prestwick. Another Defiant squadron, No. 264, was also moved out of the Battle, north to Kirton-in-Lindsey and then on to Manchester. The two-man fighter was later used as a night fighter with some success, but could not hope to survive against the Messerschmitt Bf 109.

Chapter IV

The Decisive Phase:
24 August - 6 September

The seriousness of Britain's situation was not lost on any-one—anyone on either side of the Channel, or on either side of the Atlantic Ocean. Winston Churchill was all too aware that RAF Fighter Command's position was deteriorating with each passing day—the shortage of trained pilots was on the verge of becoming desperate, and the Luftwaffe showed no sign of weakening. Lord Beaverbrook's production wizardry kept the fighter squadrons supplied with Spitfires and Hurricanes, but there could be no way to produce instant pilots. And if Fighter Command ran out of competent pilots, the German invasion would not be long in coming.

In a broadcast to the United States, American correspondent Edward R. Murrow used the phrase, "If the British succeed in defending these islands against the first German onslaught...." To Americans, this seemed a very large "if." The air battle had been going on for a month and a half, and the Luftwaffe seemed as strong and hardy as ever. Another "if" was also causing some anxiety among senior American military officers: If Britain surrendered, would the Royal Navy fall into the hands of the Germans?

On one point, at least, the British, the Americans, and Her-mann Göring were in complete agreement: The next few weeks would be the decisive phase of the Battle of Britain. While the Luftwaffe and the RAF prepared for the next round, Americans anxiously waited to see what would happen next.

24 August, Saturday

On this Saturday morning, the attacks began where they had left off before the lull. Chain Home stations began plotting a large raid forming up over Cap Gris Nez at about 9:00, and followed its course across the Channel.

Dover was attacked first, apparently because it was directly in the Luftwaffe's line of approach. Next, Hornchurch, North Weald, Eastchurch, and Manston were worked over. Hornchurch escaped with relatively little damage, mainly because anti-aircraft fire threw the bomb-aimers off. But Manston was devastated.

About twenty Ju 88s fell on Manston without any fighter opposition and left it, according to Peter Townsend, "a shambles of wrecked and burning hangars, a wilderness strewn with bomb craters and unexploded bombs." As soon as the raid ended, workmen began clearing away the rubble and repairing the damage—ignoring the unexploded bombs while filling in craters only a few yards away, and mending the main telephone and teleprinter cables.

They might just as well have saved themselves the trouble. At about 3 pm., another attack hit Manston, lodging more unexploded bombs throughout the station, blasting additional craters in the landing area, and blowing up the telephone cables again. All contact between Manston and 11 Group Headquarters at Uxbridge had been severed again. Almost all the buildings on the station, including living quarters, had been damaged by the blast; some had been reduced to rubble.

When communications were restored—for the second time since 9 am.—the station commander received an order to evacuate Manston. Fighter Command decided that the base was too vulnerable. Because it was in a virtual state of ruin, there was no point in keeeping the airfield operational. In the future, Manston would be used only as an emergency field.

It took a lot of .303 bullets to bring down a German bomber. This particular photo is very well-known in the vicinity of Worthing, West Sussex, where the bullet-riddled Heinkel He 111 came to rest. The bomber, number 1582, crashed at Honeysuckle Lane, High Salvington at about 10:05 hours on Friday 16 August 1940. It had been assigned to KG 55 (aircraft markings G1 + FR). Among the five crew members, two were killed (Uffz. A. Weber and Gefr. J. Moorfeld); and three were taken prisoner (Ltn. R. Theobald, Uffz. R. Hornbostel, and Gefr. H. Glaser.) The bomber had probably been intercepted by Spitfires of Number 602 (City of Glasgow) Squadron, according to George Clout, of Worthing. (Mick Plumb, **Worthing Herald***)*

The primary goal of Göring's change in tactics, his concentration on 11 Group's airfields, was to force the RAF to abandon these bases—to push Fighter Command out of Kent and Sussex, and leave the approaches to London wide open for the Luftwaffe. His plan had not been in effect for even a full day, and one of RAF Fighter Command's most foreward bases—Manston was situated on a cliff alongside the Channel—had already been abandoned.

One of Manston's Blenheim squadrons, No. 600 Squadron, received orders to move up to Hornchurch. The airfield's second unit, the 264 Squadron, equipped with Defiants had arrived at Hornchurch from Kirton-in-Lindsey only two days before. Today, they intercepted an incoming force of Ju 88s and their Bf 109 escort. The Defiants could not hope to fight with the Messerschmitts on anything resembling equal footing, and were mauled by the German fighters.

Of the nine Defiants that took off from Hornchurch, three were lost and another was damaged during the five-minute fight: six men were killed. The Defiants did no damage to the enemy.

Later in the afternoon, *Luftflotte 3*'s bombers and fighters struck at Portsmouth. Between 50 and 100 bombers of KG 51 broke throught the RAF's fighter screen and scattered their loads all over the city of Portsmouth, the bomb-aimers rattled by the sudden and intense anti-aircraft barrage. The gunfire was not only unexpected, but also extremely accurate—a retired brigadier general watched the wing of a bomber fall to earth, while the rest of the plane fell in pieces in other parts of Portsmouth.

Most of the RAF's fighters had been positioned too low to intercept the incoming raid. David Crook of 609 Squadron was impressed by the "terrific" anti-aircraft fire, which looked to him like a "a large number of dirty cotton-wool puffs in the sky," but felt nothing but frustration at his own lack of altitude.

But 609 was the only squadron on hand to intercept, so they kept climbing until they were at the same height as the German aircraft. Among the pilots positioning themselves for the attack was Andy Mamedoff, one of the squadron's three Americans. Today was Andy's twenty-eighth birthday—making him an "old man" among fighter pilots. It would also be his first combat since being pronounced operational by 609's CO, George Darley.

Maybe it was first-time jitters; maybe he was just over-eager. Whatever the reason, Mamedoff let a Bf 110 get behind him. The American was given a first-hand lesson on the destructive power of the *Zerstörer's* armament—four machine guns and two 20 mm cannon—when it could be brought to bear.

One of the Messerschmitt's cannon shells nearly blew Mamedoff's tail wheel off; another took a foot of fabric from one of the Spitfire's elevators; and still another ripped the trimming tab off. But the most damaging shell came close not only to destroying the entire aircraft, but very nearly killed Mamedoff, as well.

The cannon shell "entered the tail of the aircraft," according to the damage report, "went straight up the fuselage, through the wireless set, just pierced the armour plating" behind the pilot's seat, and ended up in Mamedoff's parachute harness. He was lucky; he got away with nothing more than a bad fright and a badly bruised back.

Because 609 Squadron had been so woefully outnumbered, they stood no chance at all of stopping the incoming attack. Much has been made over the fact that the German bombers scattered their bombs all over Portsmouth. But they also hit the dockyard—two destroyers, one being HMS *Bulldog*, were damaged. *Bulldog* had her stern blown off; her captain died five days later from wounds received during the attack.

The Luftwaffe lost 38 aircraft—most of them were fighters, since a larger number of Messerschmitts were now escorting the bombers. The RAF lost 22 fighters, including Andy Mamedoff's Spitfire, Also lost to Fighter Command was the forward airfield at Manston, which was as much a blow to morale as it was to operations.

The day's main activities did not begin until after sunset, however. Night activity was on the increase; about 170 German bombers attacked targets all over England: in the North, the Midlands, and even Cardiff, Wales. But the most important air strike of the day had not been planned—the attack, along with its consequences, was completely accidental.

A strike had been planned against the oil tanks at Purfleet and Thameshaven, miles downriver from London. But the lead navigator lost his way. The bombers overflew their target and unloaded over various sections of London. Bombs fell on

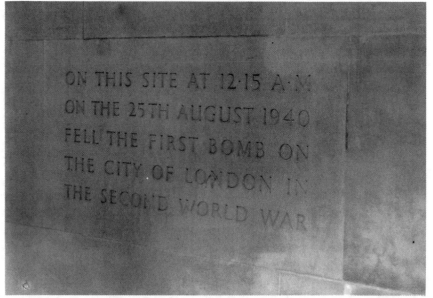

A wall plaque on Fore Street, in the City of London, commemorating one of history's turning points. The bomb that fell here, dropped accidentally by a German crew who had overflown their target, would cause Hitler and Göring to change their strategy and, ultimately, would cost the Luftwaffe the Battle.

several districts of the capital, including Islington, East Ham, Stepney, and Bethnal Green. One bomb-aimer released over the ancient City District; the damage caused by these bombs attracted the most publicity. One bomb set Broad Street Railway station alight; the fire burned for several hours. Another landed in the middle of Fore Street at 12:15 am.

It had all been a mistake. Hitler did not order an attack on London; in fact, he expressly prohibited London from being bombed. On 25 August, *Luftflotte* 2 Headquarters received a message from Reichsmarschall Göring via teleprinter; "It is to be reported immediately which crews dropped their bombs in the prohibited zone of London. The supreme commander reserves the personal punishment of the commanders in question, and will re-assign them to infantry units."

Winston Churchill did not know if it had been a mistake or not, and did not really care. Bombs had been dropped on London; Churchill wanted to hit back. He sent a note to his Chief of the Air Staff, Air Chief Marshal Sir Cyril Newall: "Now that they have begun to molest the capital, I want you to hit them hard, and Berlin is the place to hit them."

Berlin would be bombed as a reprisal on the following night. This, in turn, would lead to counter-reprisals, and a complete change of tactics by the Luftwaffe. No one realized it yet, but a turning point in the battle had been reached—a turning point that would affect the outcome of the war. And all because of a mistake in navigation.

25 August, Sunday

The Luftwaffe took the morning off—to the surprise of Fighter Command. The weather was fine and clear; plotters at CH stations had been keeping track of small numbers of enemy aircraft over the Continent all morning. But no raids formed up until afternoon.

The first major strike began forming on CH screens at about 5 pm. Several raids—50-plus from Brittany; smaller formations of 20-plus from Normandy—joined up and flew north toward Portsmouth. The number of German aircraft closing on the south coast totaled about two hundred.

To counter this threat, 10 Group sent two squadrons, which were joined by a third—36 RAF fighters against 200 German aircraft. Needless to say, the ridiculously outnumbered RAF squadrons—152 and 609 Squadrons flew Spitfires; 17 Squadron was equipped with Hurricanes—did not even come close to stopping the German onslaught. The Luftwaffe's objective turned out not to be Portsmouth, but the fighter base at Warmwell.

The Ju 88s damaged two hangars, burned out the sick quarters, and left nine unexploded bombs (UXBs) embedded in the grass landing field. Telephone and teleprinter communications were also disrupted when a bomb severed the cables. The landing runway remained in service, however, in spite of the UXBs.

But the fighter pilots did manage to get at the bombers, both before and after they made their bombing runs. Pilots of 152 Squadron claimed three German aircraft destroyed, but also lost two of their own pilots; 17 Squadron lost two Hurricanes and one pilot, Squadron Leader Cedric Williams; 609 Squadron claimed six enemy airplanes, with no losses.

One of 609's German raiders was claimed by Pilot Officer Red Tobin, from California. At 19,000 feet above Portsmouth, Tobin had his first sighting of the enemy—a formation of Bf 110s. He was having a problem with his oxygen feed line, but before he could report the problem the squadron had begun its attack. David Crook, a squadron mate of Tobin's, reported "sweeping down and curling round at terrific speed to strike right into the middle of the German formation."

Tobin pushed his throttle forward and closed with the enemy formation. One of the twin-engine fighters began a gentle banking turn right in front of him— a target too tempting to pass up. When the Messerschmitt filled his gunsight—and before the rear gunner had the chance to start shooting—Tobin pressed the firing button. He could see hits striking all along the fuselage. One of the bullets apparently hit the pilot; the airplane reared up, almost vertically, as though the pilot had yanked back on the control column involuntarily. Then it stalled out and plunged out of sight.

He was tempted to follow his victim down and watch him crash, but squadron veterans had warned him never to do this—he would be leaving himself wide open to attack. But Tobin did not have much time to think about it—he spotted another Bf 110.

Once again, he closed to within machine gun range, resisting the temptation to open fire from too far away. This time, he held his gunsight on the Messerschmitt's engine. A second or two after Tobin pressed the firing button, he saw the engine catch fire and begin to smoke. The Bf 110 rapidly began losing altitude. Tobin dove after it.

When he had descended to the same altitude as the twin-engine fighter, Tobin yanked back on his stick. But he had pulled out of his dive too abruptly; his vision faded as G-forces drained the blood from his head, and he blacked out. His Spitfire began to spin in. Tobin was unconscious; he kept spinning out of control toward the Channel.

When he finally came to, Tobin found himself flying straight and level at a height of about 1,000 feet. His Spitfire had saved his life; it had righted itself from its spin while he had been unconscious.

Tobin made it back to Warmwell, landing his Spitfire despite UXBs and bomb craters. He expected S/L Darley to give him holy hell for blacking out and nearly killing himself. Instead, everybody was glad to see him back alive—they had watched him spin, and thought that he had crashed.

In addition to the attack on Warmwell, German bombers also struck at other targets in southern England—including the RAF station in the Scilly Isles, off Land's End.

Roughly an hour after the Warmwell raid, about 100 German aircraft flew across the Channel en route to Dover and the Thames Estuary. Eleven Spitfire and Hurricane squadrons scrambled to confront the attackers. Enough of them found and engaged the enemy to discourage the bomber pilots from pressing on to their targets. It gave both sides an idea of what defending fighters were capable of doing when they were not hopelessly outnumbered.

It had not been a very encouraging day for either the RAF or the Luftwaffe. The Germans were able to inflict a fair amount of damage, especially at Warmwell, but lost 20 airplanes—bombers and fighters—in the day's fighting. The RAF lost 16 aircraft, all fighters. Nine pilots had been killed; another had been taken prisoner by the Germans.

When night came, the air war began its second phase. Luftwaffe units attacked widespread targets; their main object was to keep civilian workers in their air raid shelters and away from their factories, rather than to inflict major damage. Industrial cities, including Birmingham, were visited; the fighter base at

Montrose, on the east coast of Scotland, was attacked; and mines were dropped in coastal waters. London was studiously avoided.

But a reprisal raid for the Luftwaffe's accidental bombing of London, which had been carried out on the night of 24/25 August, was already underway. In accordance with Winston Churchill's directive, the attack was aimed at Berlin. The effect of the raid would produce effects far more significant than Churchill could ever have hoped for.

Eighty-one Wellingtons, Whitleys, and Hampdens were mustered for the raid—a fairly large force for RAF Bomber Command at the time. Their target was Berlin's industrial and transportation centers—power stations and railway stations. But night bombing is always imprecise, at best. On this night, cloud cover made accuracy even more elusive.

Only twenty-nine bombers actually dropped their bombs over Berlin; German sources claimed that only ten reached the city. Bombs fell in several sections of Berlin, including the suburb of Dahlem, where a school and a dairy farm were hit. Actual damage didn't amount to much, according to Willaim L. Shirer. But the psychological impact could not have been greater had a hydrogen bomb been dropped.

German citizens thought that the war had been won—that is what the Propaganda Ministry led them to believe. France had given up; the Low Countries and Poland had been overrun; and Britain had been humiliated at Dunkirk. Britain had not yet surrendered, but everyone had been told that the British Isles would either be invaded, or would be blockaded by U-boats and left to die on the vine. As far as the Americans were concerned ... they were too fond of luxury and soft living to cause any trouble and, besides, they were on the other side of the ocean.

Now, suddenly, the war had come to them, and with a vengeance. Göring had promised that Berlin would never be bombed, but the RAF had gotten through the defenses, dropped their bombs, and gotten back home again. Göring had been wrong; this bombing raid made everyone think. Hitler and his men did not like people to think.

Both the British and the German press concentrated on the Berlin raid in their morning editions. Of course, they told completely different stories. British papers spoke about the triumphant raid on the enemy's captital. Berlin reporters called the raid a "cowardly British attack" and played down the air strike, mentioning only light damage in the suburbs.

The most interesting reports, from a propaganda point of view, appeared in American newspapers. The battle for American public opinion was still being fought with as much determination as the battle over southern England. British communiques emphasized that RAF bomber pilots only hit military objectives, and brought their bombs back if they could not locate their targets.

A story in the New York *Daily News* gives an account that is a happy mix of half-truths and wishful thinking. It was supposedly told by one of the pilots who bombed Berlin, who insisted that he "cruised around for half an hour" before locating his target. He also said that the anti-aircraft fire was particularly hot, and that the German gun crews fired at the bombers quite accurately. William L. Shirer thought that the flak was strangely ineffective, and that the gunners fired blindly. But regardless of its accuracy, the report was taken in and digested by thousands of *Daily News* readers.

The accidental attack on London had been responsible for this raid, as well as another RAF raid three nights later. Outraged senior Nazi officials, including both Göring and Hitler, would call for retaliation against London for this attack on Berlin. The raids would escalate throughout the rest of the war, increasing in number of bombers, amount of explosives dropped, and number of civilians killed. London would be devastated, but the cities of the Third Reich would be reduced to piles of rubble by man-made firestorms and ever heavier loads of high explosives. As Winston Churchill put it in his memoirs, "Alas for poor humanity."

A Spitfire on fire and trailing smoke after an encounter with a German fighter. This was an all too common occurrence during the last week of August and first week of September—not only Spitfires, but Hurricanes were also being destroyed in record numbers. For the first time, aircraft losses were overtaking production. But even more ominous for the RAF, trained pilots were being killed and badly wounded in such numbers that the "rotation" system—the practice of rotating squadrons to quiet areas after a period in 11 Group—was in jeopardy.

August 26, Monday

The first major effort of the day began just before 11 am., when CH stations at Dover and Rye picked up plots that merged into an incoming raid—about 150 bombers and fighters heading for Kent. Biggin Hill and Kenley were the main targets.

The CH stations had given ample warning. Before the Luftwaffe could reach the coast, they were intercepted by Spitfires and Hurricanes of 11 Group—including 56 Squadron's Hurricanes and 610's Spitfires. Folkstone was hit by bombs and several of Dover's barrage balloons were set on fire, but Kenley and Biggin Hill managed to escape the Luftwaffe's wrath thanks to the efforts of the Spitfire and Hurricane pilots. The incoming raid had been broken up and disorganized before it could get very far inland. In the fighting, *Jagdgeschwader 3* lost six Bf 109s.

At around 2:30, the next incoming raid was plotted. Rye and Dover stations began picking up enemy formations of 20, 30, and 40 while they wre still over France. Had Göring been a bit more perceptive about the CH stations, he would have had second thoughts about their uselessness, as well as about his order not to bomb them.

Peter Townsend led the pilots of 85 Squadron from Croydon eastward toward Kent, and toward the Dorniers of KG 3. About 30 minutes after take-off, they spotted their target—Dorniers flying in "an impeccable phalanx in vics of three." The formation did not remain impeccable for very long—85 Squadron ran head-on toward the bombers, opened fire, and broke away by darting underneath them.

"Ease the throttle to reduce closing speed," Townsend recounted. "Get a bead on them right away, hold it, and never mind the streams of tracer shooting overhead. Just keep pressing on the button until you think you're going to collide—then stick hard forward."

The strategy worked—85 shot down four Dorniers for the loss of one of their Hurricanes.

While 85 Squadron was keeping KG 3 busy over Kent, the rest of *Luftflotte* 2 had other things to do. Hornchurch and North Weald both came under attack, but intercepting fighters were able to break up these raids before they could inflict any damage. But the airfield at Debden, Essex, was bombed; the bombers got through the Spitfires and Hurricanes, and were able to cause serious damage.

Over one hundred bombs, high explosive and incendiary, hit the sergeants' mess, the motor transport yard, the WAAF living quarters, the equipment building, and the landing field. A slit trench received a direct hit, killing the five people sheltering in it. The electricity and water mains also were damaged. The attacking Dorniers got off without any losses.

It had been a bad day for 616 Squadron, which had flown down from Leconfield only seven days before. The squadron lost seven Spitfires; five had been shot down by Bf 109s in 15 minutes. But 616, along with five other squadrons, did turn back a Luftwaffe raid that had been driving at Biggin Hill and Kenley.

Luftflotte 3's late afternoon attack began forming up at about 4:00 pm.—150 He 111s of KG 55, on their way to Portsmouth. Eight RAF squadrons—three from 10 Group joined by five from 11 Group—were scrambled to intercept.

For once, everything went the way it was supposed to. The CH stations detected the incoming raid in plenty of time to scramble the fighters; the ground controllers gave the pilots the correct height and vector; and no cloud cover interfered. In the fray, four He 111s were shot down; three others returned to base on the continent with battle damage.

Some of the Heinkel's commanders ordered their bombs jettisoned into the Channel. Portsmouth was not bombed; the Heinkels turned back before crossing the coast. The RAF lost three fighters, with four more damaged.

This would be *Luftflotte 3's* last daylight operation for a while. During the next several weeks, it would fly most of its bombing sorties at night.

The day had been one of thrusts and parries. Sometimes the Luftwaffe managed to break through the RAF's defense, notably at Debden; sometimes the RAF were able to block the bombers' thrust, as they had done at Portsmouth. The RAF flew 787 sorties, and lost 31 fighters. The Luftwaffe lost 41 aircraft.

It had not been a decisive day. But the Luftwaffe's commanders had the initiative, and they knew it. They realized that if they kept on pounding 11 Group's airfields, they were bound to win the battle. Either the RAF pilots would wear themselves down by flying several sorties every day, or the German bombers would destroy the sector airfields by overwhelming the defenses, or both.

Night operations consisted of raids against the industrial cities of Birmingham and Coventry. In addition, about 50 bombers attacked the port of Plymouth. Throughout the Midlands and southern England, nuisance raids wre directed against scattered targets—damage consisted largely of jangled nerves among the civilian population. A decoy field at St. Eval in Cornwall also came under attack; the simulated station sustained 62 bomb hits, and its false flarepath was set alight.

So far, the nocturnal bombing sorties had been limited to these small-scale raids. But the air crews were gaining experience for the time—not very far off—when their efforts would be for larger targets and more serious stakes.

27 August, Tuesday

Cloud and rain kept the Luftwaffe on the ground, except for reconnaissance units. Two photo-recon Dornier 17s were shot down by RAF fighters: one near Plymouth and another over Cap Gris Nez. A total of nine German aircraft were shot down. The RAF lost one Spitfire when its pilot made a careless attack on a Ju 88; the Junkers' rear gunner shot the Spitfire down.

Another battle of sorts was being fought on the ground. This one was between Air Vice Marshal Trafford Leigh-Mallory, the commander of 12 Group, and 11 Group's commander, Air Vice Marshal Keith Park. Park complained that 12 Group did not co-operate with him or with the ground controllers of 11 Group. When 12 Group's fighters were requested to protect airfields to the south, they did not show up.

Not only did Park complain, he did so officially, and in writing. He also instructed 11 Group's ground controllers (in a document called Instruction No. 7) to make their requests to Fighter Command Headquarters at Stanmore, Middlesex, when they needed reinforcements, and not to bother asking 12 Group for any help. North Weald and Debden both had been heavily bombed because Leigh-Mallory's squadrons failed to patrol above these stations, as Park had requested. Park, needless to say, was not happy. He always referred to 11 Group's airfields as "my airfields," and took Leigh-Mallory's lack of action personally.

Leigh-Mallory was not happy, either. He did not like Keith Park very much to begin with; now, he hated him. The rift between the two men would continue to worsen as the battle went on.

One of the major causes of friction between the two men was a basic disagreement over tactics. Each had a completely different idea of how the battle against the Luftwaffe should be fought. Park was using forward interception techniques—he was sending individual squadrons to intercept the incoming enemy raids from his fighter bases in Kent, Sussex, and Surrey. Leigh-Mallory criticized this method. He thought that his own "big wing" theory, which would confront enemy formations with massed units of fighters, should be employed, and that Park was wrong for not following his big wing method.

Fighter Command already had its hands full with the Luftwaffe. It did not need a tiff between two of its senior commanders, especially now that the battle was nearing a crisis stage.

While the RAF vice marshals feuded, Adolf Hitler tried to calm tensions between the Army and Navy regarding Operation Sea Lion. Hitler was fully aware of the Navy's reservations regarding the invasion of England. As a concession to the Navy, especially to Admiral Raeder, Hitler made the landing beaches more compact, so that transporting troops across the Channel would be less complicated. He also informed the Army that its operations "must make allowances for available shipping space, safety of the Channel crossing, and the security of the landing itself."

These instructions were certainly well-timed—the Wehrmacht already had most of its troops in place along the channel coast, waiting for orders for the invasion to start, and the transports and landing barges were being moved to Channel ports. The only item lacking was German air superiority over the Channel and the English beaches. Göring assured everyone that the Luftwaffe was already well on its way toward accomplishing this vital goal.

After the sun had gone down, CH stations along the south coast began to pick up enemy bombers over Normandy. Tonight, the nuisance raids concentrated on scattered targets between the Isle of Wight and Kent. Damage consisted mainly of broken sleep. A Heinkel of KG 1 was shot down by anti-aircraft fire at about 2:45 am.; its presumed objective was Coventry.

*   *   *

Although Britain was desperate to persuade Americans that the RAF was winning the battle, senior British officials did not want to give away any information that might prove useful to the enemy. And so the Ministry of Information assigned censors to "blue pencil" news stories sent across to America by correspondents and wire services. American reporters were encouraged to send approved stories back to the United States—just as long as a British censor saw the story first, and was able to remove any offending passages.

American correspondents in Britain marvelled at Britain's mastery of propaganda—especially "white propaganda." White propaganda was very subtle—cynical Americans would say "very British." This method of propaganda did not employ actual lies; it merely exaggerated the truth, overstating the victories of one's own side, as well as the failures of the enemy. This encouraged the home troops and allies, and also made the enemy look inept.

The British knew how to use white propaganda better than anybody—publishing inflated figures of Luftwaffe losses, for instance, without batting an eye over the exaggeration. Or by portraying all RAF pilots, including Americans, as "gallant knights of the air." (In the 1980s novel *Piece of Cake*, the pilots are crude, juvenile, and venal—anything but gallant.) And when this view of propaganda was delivered to the U.S.A. by American correspondents, this only made the stories even more convincing. Once in a while, though, the censors got in their own way by trying to be too clever. American reporter Raymond Daniell found this out the hard way. Daniell had written a story about one of the air battles over the Thames estuary, a battle that he had watched along with thousands of others. When he tried to cable the story to his newspaper, *The New York Times*, the censor blocked it—Daniell had mentioned the River Thames in his report.

A rule of censorship prohibited the mention of any exact geographic location in news stories. Daniell thought that this particular censor was taking the rule to ridiculous extremes. But, he said, he was tired and bad-tempered, and did not feel like arguing. He agreed to let the censor delete the word "Thames."

When the censor asked Daniell if he would like to substitute anything for "Thames," an idea occurred to Daniell—he asked the censor to substitute "Amazon" for "Thames."

Daniell thought he was pulling a fast one. The copy editor in New York would be certain to catch the slip-up and correct the name of the river. The staff at *The New York Times* knew full well that Daniell was in London and not South America. And so he would be able to get his story through as he had written it, and would teach the censor a lesson at the same time.

But as it turned out, the joke was on Daniell. The copy editor did not catch the word "Amazon"; the story was given to the printer as received. On the following morning, readers of *The New York Times* had an exclusive story of how pilots of the RAF intercepted the German Luftwaffe over the Amazon Estuary.

28 August, Wednesday

The Luftwaffe was up early, apparently trying to make up for the day before's loss of flying weather. Dover CH station plotted 100-plus aircraft over Cap Gris Nez at about 8:30 am.—Heinkels of KG 1 escorted by Bf 109s of JG 26—on their way to attack Eastchurch and Rochford airfields.

Four squadrons were scrambled to intercept, including the Hurricanes of 79 Squadron and Defiants of 264 Squadron. Just after 9 am., the fighters made contact but could not get through the defending Messerschmitts. Ironically, the obsolete Defiants came closest to succeeding. They maneuvered into position under the Heinkels, the machine guns of their dorsal turrets pointing upwards, when the Bf 109s, led by Adolf Galland, arrived.

The resulting combat resembled a flight of hawks taking on a flock of pigeons. Three of the Defiants were shot down; four others were damaged. In addition, 79 Squadron lost two Hurricanes. And it had all been for nothing. The Heinkels bombed their objectives, leaving both Eastchurch and Rochford a shambles.

Rochford received another visit at about 12:30. This raid was almost a carbon copy of the morning's. Several RAF squadrons scrambled to intercept the incoming raid and were prevented by the intervention of hovering Bf 109s. At least two of the Messerschmitts were accounted for by 56 Squadron's Hurricane pilots, in a battle that was visible to onlookers on the ground for miles around.

Winston Churchill happened to be visiting Manston at the time, what was left of it, and probably saw the fighting. His main concern, however, was the bomb damage at the now-abandoned airfield. He said that he was shocked to find the station still out of action, and to see that its cratered landing field was untouched by maintenance crews. The reason that the craters had been left unfilled, as any member of Manston's ground crew could have told him, was that the RAF had not been able to prevent the Luftwaffe from bombing the station at will. Keeping Manston open for most of August had been strictly for political reasons; closing it had been for practical reasons—it was too easy a target.

The Luftwaffe had done a fair amount of damage already on this day—having pasted two airfields, although one of them (Eastchurch) was a Coastal Command station, and also having shot down several RAF fighters. But *Luftflotte 2*'s commander, Feldmarschall Albert Kesselring, meant to apply as much pressure as he could to 11 Group and its airfields. Taking advantage of the fair weather, Kesselring launched yet a third attack.

At about 4:00 pm., one hundred BF 109s from JG 3 and JG 51 made a fighter sweep over Kent. They approached the coast so quickly, and at such a low altitude, that the CH stations did not have time to give sufficient warning. While the German fighters swept in at 25,000 feet, RAF squadrons were only just taking off and straining for altitude.

This would be the fourth time since dawn that 85 Squadron had been scrambled. Peter Townsend was leading at 18,000 feet when he spotted a group of Bf 109s below him, in a perfect spot for attack. Even the sun was co-operating—it was at their backs, and would be in the eyes of the German pilots.

The Messerschmitts scattered when jumped by the Hurricanes. Townsend fired a burst at one; it rolled over, streaming white smoke from its cooling system. He fastened onto a second Bf 109, but the German pilot dived away from him. Even when Townsend "pulled the tit"[15]—applied emergency power boost—he could not catch it.

After he had gained some distance, the German began climbing, giving Townsend "a long shot." He fired and missed. Townsend began to maneuver into position for another attack, and failed to notice that a Bf 109 was maneuvering behind him. His first hint of immediate danger came when a bullet smashed into his cockpit. But, once again, Townsend was lucky— he pushed the stick forward, kicked the Hurricane's rudder pedal, and managed to get out of the German's line of fire.

The pilots of 85 Squadron claimed 6 Messerschmitts, for the loss of no Hurricanes. It had been one of the RAF's better outings for the day.

The Luftwaffe's results were not spectacular, but Kesselring must have been satisfied; at about 6:45, he ordered another fighter sweep. This time, 50-plus Bf 109s of JG 54 went across the Channel to challenge the RAF fighters. In the fracas that developed, each side lost two aircraft.

Losses for the day came to 20 fighters for the RAF and 30 aircraft of all types—including a Gotha bi-plane that landed on Lewes racecourse in Sussex by mistake—for the Luftwaffe. Peter Townsend thought this was a "good bag." But the RAF also lost 9 pilots killed and another four that were seriously wounded and would not return to the battle—13 pilots lost. Fighter Command could not afford very many "good" days like this one.

---

15 Emergency power boost was so-called, according to one American smart-aleck, "because of its appearance and effect when pulled."

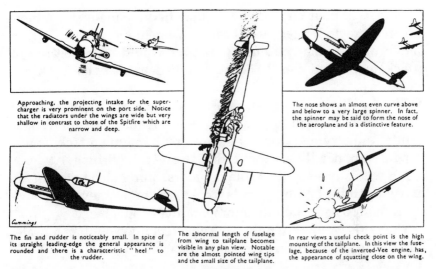

Approaching, the projecting intake for the super-charger is very prominent on the port side. Notice that the radiators under the wings are wide but very shallow in contrast to those of the Spitfire which are narrow and deep.

The nose shows an almost even curve above and below to a very large spinner. In fact, the spinner may be said to form the nose of the aeroplane and is a distinctive feature.

The fin and rudder is noticeably small. In spite of its straight leading-edge the general appearance is rounded and there is a characteristic " heel " to the rudder.

The abnormal length of fuselage from wing to tailplane becomes visible in any plan view. Notable are the almost pointed wing tips and the small size of the tailplane.

In rear views a useful check point is the high mounting of the tailplane. In this view the fuselage, because of the inverted-Vee engine, has, the appearance of squatting close on the wing.

The drawing is a British aircraft recognition leaflet, illustrating the Bf 109's most easily recognizable features for pilots and observers. The model shown is the Bf 109G, which was introduced long after the Battle had ended.

The Luftwaffe's nocturnal activities increased sharply on the night of 28/29 August. This was also in concert with the stepped-up campaign against Fighter Command in particular and against war production in general. The usual nuisance raids were carried out against Birmingham, Sheffield, Manchester, Coventry, and other targets. But about 150-160 bombers concentrated on the port city of Liverpool, dropping over 100 tons of high explosives and incendiaries.

The compliment was returned by RAF Bomber Command; Berlin was bombed for the second time in three nights. According to correspondent William L. Shirer, ten people were killed in the bombing—the first German civilians that had died in Berlin—and more damage was done than on the night of 25 August.

Compared with what was to come, the bombing attack was a pinprick. But it shook the complacency of Berliners, even more than the previous raid had done. The RAF proved that they could attack their city whenever they had the inclination; their homes were no longer safe. It came as a genuine shock—Göring had promised that no enemy aircraft would ever be able to attack them, and the RAF had bombed them twice within a week.

What William Shirer referred to as "the Nazi bigwigs" were also shaken. Instead of playing down the attack, as the Propaganda Ministry had done after the first bombing attack, newspapers ran headlines about the "Cowardly British Attack," along with stories of the brutal aviators. Shirer also noted in his diary that if the bombing raids were to continue, they "will have a tremendous effect on the morale of the people here."

The raids would not only have an effect upon civilian morale, but also upon the future course of the war.

29 August, Thursday

Just after 3 pm., CH stations began to plot German formations while the aircraft were still climbing for altitude over France. When the raid turned north and headed for the Kentish coast, the alarm went out—to Fighter Command Headquarters, to 11 Group Headquarters, and to individual fighter stations throughout 11 Group.

Inside dispersal huts at Biggin Hill, Kenley, Hornchurch, Tangmere, and satellite fields across Kent, Sussex, and Surrey, telephones rang and the "Scramble!" was shouted at the tense pilots. At Croydon, the 12 Hurricanes of 85 Squadron were sent to intercept 18 He 111s. But before they were able to reach the bombers, the Hurricane pilots were jumped by fighters—Bf 109s and Bf 110s.

Actually, few bombers were taking part in the day's operations. Kesselring's plan was to send overwhelming numbers of his fighters across the Channel to draw the RAF into combat. The number of German fighters that took part was between 200 and 500, depending upon which source is consulted. The tactic had succeeded, at least in Kesselring's judgment. He would try the same scheme again, except on a larger scale—the plan would be to swamp the defenses, and knock down RAF fighters in wholesale numbers.

Before reaching the coast, the fighters divided their force: part flew eastward, toward Ramsgate, in Kent; part headed west toward Beachy Head. Thirteen RAF squadrons were sent to head them off—including 85 Squadron.

But before most of the Spitfire and Hurricane pilots had the chance to engage the enemy, ground controllers called them back to base. Air Vice Marshal Park ordered the Messerschmitts to be left alone—he wanted his fighters to go after the bombers instead. Since the incoming raid consisted of almost all fighters—this attack is usually referred to as a "massive fighter sweep"—the RAF fighters were withdrawn from the battle before it could properly begin.

Peter Townsend apparently never heard the recall. He led 85 Squadron into the thick of an enemy formation—it seemed to him that they were 12 against 200. He was probably right—no other RAF fighters were in the vicinity of Beachy Head at the time. The Hurricane pilots kept trying to get through to the Heinkels, but either Bf 109s or Bf 110s always interfered.

Squadron Leader Townsend claimed a Bf 109 shot down—it "staggered like a pheasant shot in the wing." Another pilot of 85 Squadron also claimed a 109. Only two Hurricanes, and no pilots, were lost in this running fight, which was incredibly lucky, considering the odds.

At about 6:30 pm. another Luftwaffe fighter sweep headed across the Channel, this time on course toward eastern Kent. Air Vice Marshal Park's "leave the fighters alone" order prevailed, but 85 Squadron once again was sent up. This time, the squadron was not as lucky. It lost one Hurricane, along with its pilot; no enemy aircraft were claimed.

The Luftwaffe lost 17 aircraft. The RAF lost nine fighters; six pilots were reported missing, along with one killed.

A great deal has been made of the fact that Fighter Command was kept well-supplied with replacement fighters by the factories, as well as by civilian maintenance units. These maintenance units were able to perform near wonders, sometimes making a new Spitfire or Hurricane by cannibalizing several fighters that were beyond repair. But fighter planes need fighter pilots to fly them, and the shortage of trained fighter pilots was proving to be Fighter Command's most urgent problem.

Every squadron had lost experienced pilots in the course of the Battle. Some felt the loss more sharply than others. Since 19 August, for instance, 616 had lost 5 pilots killed or missing, along with 5 others wounded and hospitalized. Which meant that most of the young men that had flown south to Kenly 10 days before, looking for glory, were now gone. Number 54 Squadron, Alan Deere's unit, was also "in a very bad way"—no squadron commander, only four experienced pilots, and a lot of new pilots who had been rushed through training.

Replacement pilots from Operational Training Units (OTUs) were sometimes so poorly trained that they were all but useless. Some had fired their guns only once, and then only into the Channel. As the battle went on, and the shortage became more desperate, some reached operational squadrons without having fired their guns at all. Most did not know anything about flying in formation—either "finger four" or the obsolete vics. Stragglers who lagged behind the rest of the group were easy victims of watchful Messerschmitt pilots—they did not know how to defend themselves.

As desperate as the shortage was at the end of August, it would become even more acute in the days to come. RAF Fighter Command began to look for pilots outside of their own OTUs. This notice began to appear in American newspapers in July and August:

LONDON July 15: The Royal Air Force is in the market for American flyers as well as American airplanes. Experienced airmen, preferably those with at least 250 flying hours, would be welcomed by the RAF.[16]

---

16   This particular advertisement appeared in New York's *Herald Tribune*.

Luftflotte 3's night operations were launched in two attacks. In the first wave, bombers scattered small nuisance raids across southern England. Damage from these small raids, as might be expected, was negligible. The second attack, about 137 bombers, concentrated on Liverpool. One hundred thirty tons of high explosive and over 300 canisters of incendiaries damaged the port facilities and factories. Disruption of factory production was becoming a cause for concern. Along with the shortage of pilots, this situation would get worse in the coming weeks as well.

30 August, Friday

Fighting began around 9 am. when Rye and Pevensey CH stations plotted the Luftwaffe forming up over France. A heavy layer of cloud hid the enemy from ground observers, but CH plotters tracked the German aircraft right across the Channel.

The formations did not start moving north until after 10:00, however. By that time, intercepting RAF fighter squadrons had been in the air for nearly an hour; the fighters had to land for refuelling.

Enough fighters were on hand to intercept a raid of Dorniers and Bf 110s over the Thames Estuary; its target had been a coastal convoy. But this was not the main force. About 60 Bf 109s were allowed to pass over Kent unchallenged just after 10:30. This was partly in accordance with Air Vice Marshal Park's order to "leave the fighters alone," and partly because the fighters were still being re-fuelled.

When 70 bombers—Heinkels and Dorniers—came at about 11:00, escorted by about 100 fighters, 11 Group's fighter squadrons were ready. Ground controllers gave the order to scramble.

Squadron Leader Peter Townsend caught sight of the Heinkels of KG 1 from 18,000 feet; they reminded him of a swarm of gnats. He only had ten Hurricanes behind him. He gave the enemy's height, course, and numbers to the ground controller, and ordered a head-on attack. Under the circumstances, he felt that it was the best he could do.

The crew of a Heinkel He 111 runs to their aircraft. As the Battle continued, an increasing number of Heinkels and their crews were lost in operations over England; when the bombing of London began in September, losses became even heavier. During the air battle of 15 September, for instance, no fewer than eight Heinkels were shot down; their crews were either killed or taken prisoner.

Townsend took his "little band of Hurricanes" down in a shallow dive, maneuvered them into line, and headed for the Heinkels. The attack "had the desired effect," he wrote in his combat report—the Heinkels scattered, thrown into confusion by the unexpected rush of fighters.

Head-on attacks usually did succeed in demoralizing Luftwaffe bomber formations. But closing with an enemy bomber at a combined speed of 600 miles per hour (or 300 yards per second), left almost no margin for error, and was a highly risky business. Teddy Morris, a South African pilot with 79 Squadron, found out just how risky it could be.

At about 11:00, sixteen squadrons were scrambled to confront an incoming raid aimed at Kenley and Biggin Hill. One of them was 79 Squadron. Pilot Officer Teddy Morris and the other two Hurricanes of his section went after the leading Heinkels in the formation. Another section of Hurricanes interfered with the escorting Bf 109s.

The three leading Heinkels were followed closely by another formation of three—more closely than Morris had thought. Also, the gap between the two formations was much narrower. Morris went at the leading formation, shot through it, and was on top of the trailing Heinkel formation before he had time to react. He crashed into one of them, destroying both the bomber and his own Hurricane.

He did not feel a jarring crash—just a thump as the right wing of his Hurricane struck the Heinkel and was torn off. The fighter went into a violent spin, making it difficult for Morris to get out of the cockpit. He did manage to extract himself from the stricken Hurricane, however, after a struggle.

While he floated down beneath his parachute, Morris could watch the Heinkel going down—both engines on fire and the outboard sections of both wings gone. Three of the bomber's crew managed to bail out, and had joined Morris in an involuntary parachute jump.

When he landed, the first thing that Morris had to do was to convince a group of farm laborers that he was not a German—one of the men had a pitchfork, and the other had a shotgun. He accomplished this by the usual method—swearing a blue streak at his persecutors in flawless English.

A Canadian army unit was contacted by telephone. The Canadians collected Morris, gave him a good lunch, and drove him back to Biggin Hill. In his combat report, Morris laconically wrote: "One Heinkel confirmed destroyed by collision."

Kenley had escaped attack, but Biggin Hill and Lympne were both bombed. Biggin Hill had been especially punished; its landing area was cratered, and Biggin Hill Village also had been hit by bombs aimed at the nearby RAF station.

The defense of Biggin Hill had been assigned to 12 Group. Park had requested assistance from Leigh-Mallory, since 11 Group's squadrons were already engaged. The failure of 12

Group to protect Biggin Hill added to the already simmering bad feelings between Leigh-Mallory and Park. At about 1:30, the Luftwaffe came back—three raids crossed the south coast and made straight for Tangmere, Kenley, and Biggin Hill. At about the same time, the electricity supply for the south coast CH stations—Dover, Pevensey, Rye, Foreness, Fairlight, Whitstable, and Beachy Head—was abruptly cut off. Screens at all the stations went blank. The south coast was wide-open to attack.

And the next attack was not long in coming. At 3:30, about 50 aircraft—bombers with a fighter escort—crossed the Channel. An hour later, another raid approached the south coast. Neither was detected until within visual range of the Observer Corps posts. The second strike was the most destructive—it hit the Coastal Command station at Detling, a few miles east of West Malling, and left it a total ruin. The station would stay shut down until the following day.

With so many raids developing in such quick succession, sometimes overlapping one another, Park had his hands full trying to intercept each one. He had no choice but to send small numbers of fighters to confront the incoming Luftwaffe. Sometimes, only one squadron would be available. If he sent too many fighters to meet one raid, there might not be any available for the next one. This sometimes meant a half dozen Spitfires or Hurricanes trying to intercept 50 or more German aircraft.

But after today, Park would have one additional squadron to send up, and a first-rate squadron, at that. The Poles of 303 Squadron shot down their first German airplane on the afternoon of 30 August, and had been pronounced "operational."

Neither the shot-down German airplane nor the transfer to operational status had been planned. The Poles had been on another training exercise—to familiarize themselves with the Hawker Hurricane and to get the hang of RAF gound-to-air spoken English. They were to rendezvous with six Blenheims over the town of St. Albans, Hertfordshire, and make practice attacks; after the exercise, the Poles were to go home. While on their way to meet the Blenheims, one of the pilots spotted 60 Dorniers below, along with their Bf 109 escort.[17]

Ludwig "Pasko" Paszkiewicz announced his sighting to Squadron Leader Ronald Kellett—"bandits 10 o'clock." Kellett did not reply; now that there was an enemy formation in sight, his job was to escort the Blenheims back to base. But Paszkiewicz did not wait for a reply. He "pulled the tit" and dove for the Dorniers.

One of the German pilots saw him coming and dove away. Paszkiewicz dove after him. When he had closed to within 100 yards, he pressed the firing button. His bullets hit the starboard engine; Paszkiewicz saw it catch fire, but kept on shooting. When one of the crew baled out, he was still shooting at the bomber. He continued hitting the Dornier with .303 machine gun bullets until it finally plunged out of control. After this display of shooting and determination, S/L Kellett was satisfied that 303 Squadron had been given enough training. He telephoned Fighter Command headquarters at Bentley Priory to report what had happened, and to recommend that the Poles be pronounced operational.

Dowding agreed with S/L Kellett's recommendation. The Poles were needed; experienced fighter pilots were as valuable as gold dust. Number 303 Squadron became active, regardless of language difficulties.

But the day's fighting was not over yet. The most damaging raid, at least from Fighter Command's point of view, came at about 6 pm. Nine Ju 88s swept in toward Biggin Hill without any warning, and dropped sixteen 1,000 lb. bombs. The noise from the explosions shattered the eardrums of ground personnel; the destruction from the blast was even worse.

The Junkers did not come in from the south, as usual. Instead, they had flown up the Thames Estuary, heading west toward

---

17   This force was on its way to Luton, Bedfordshire. It would attack the airfield as well as the Vauxhall Motor Works, which would result in the death of about 50 people and damage to both objectives.

London, and then turned southwest—hitting Biggin Hill from the north. Before the Observer Corps knew that any enemy aircraft were in the area, the nine Ju 88s had already begun their bomb runs.

They left Biggin Hill ravaged and gutted. The transport yard was demolished, along with most of the station's vehicles. The armory, workshops, and barracks were in such poor condition that they were declared unsafe. A shelter had been hit; the dead were still being dug out of the rubble 24 hours later. In addition, the power, gas, and water mains had been cut, along with the telephone cables. Biggin Hill was cut off from communicating with the outside world, including its own fighter squadrons.

Biggin Hill had been effectively knocked out. Thanks to the almost frantic efforts of workers and technicians—telephone engineers, maintenance men from the gas, electricity, and water services, and RAF personnel who filled bomb craters—the station would recover in time for the next day's operations. The station's personnel would be dog tired, and the station would still be badly damaged, but Biggin Hill would be a working fighter base again.

The day's losses came to 36 aircraft for the Luftwaffe and 26 for the RAF. Another 11 RAF pilots were also killed. But for Fighter Command, even more ominous than the number of pilots lost was the fact that the Luftwaffe's attacks were not being fended off. The bombers were getting through the defenses, and inflicting serious harm to airfields and other objectives.

The battle was not proving to be easy for either side—the Luftwaffe and RAF had been too evenly matched for that. But through their constant hammering, the Germans were putting constant pressure on the RAF—ground crew, support staff, and especially pilots.

The fighting had unmistakably tilted in favor of the Luftwaffe. The RAF were losing too many aircraft, far too many pilots, and were no longer able to defend their airfields, their cities, or any other objectives that the Luftwaffe chose to attack.

* * *

That night, the Luftwaffe once again made its presence known by employing its usual *modus operandi*—109 bombers attacked Liverpool, while small, scattered raids bombed other targets. Single raiders went after airfields—including Biggin Hill, as if the station did not already have its share of troubles—but rarely were able to find their targets in the dark.

The RAF were up as well—bombing Berlin for the third time. Although the force was fairly puny compared with the Luftwaffe's effort—only about half as many bombers hit Berlin as were striking at Liverpool—this was the most damaging attack so far. Even worse than the physical destruction to the city—which was small indeed when measured against what was to come, although the Siemens factory had been damaged—was the disillusionment among Berliners.

Another feeling, a feeling of frustration, produced even more anger and bitterness among Hitler, Göring, and other high-ranking Nazis. They had believed their own propaganda, that Germany was somehow invincible from enemy air attack.

31 August, Sunday

Both Air Chief Marshal Dowding and Air Vice Marshal Park fully realized that Fighter Command's position now bordered on desperate. The Luftwaffe's constant attacks had seriously affected the efficiency of the fighter stations of 11 Group, as well as the fighting efficiency of the squadrons themselves. If the Germans kept up the pressure—and there was no sign of their letting up—no one wanted to predict the worst that could happen.

But, incredibly, evidence seems to indicate that the Luftwaffe was not aware of the extent of the damage they were inflicting. Although photo-reconnaissance aircraft took pictures of the bomb-cratered ruins of Manston and Biggin Hill, neither Göring nor any of his senior commanders appeared to have any idea that the fighting efficiency of these stations had been seriously compromised. Most of the airfields remained open, so the

"These fragments I have shored against my ruins." Full-scale models of a Hurricane and a Spitfire on display outside the Royal Air Force Museum at Hendon, north London. In November 1978, the Battle of Britain Museum opened, just adjacent the RAF Museum, to house artifacts of the 114-day Battle. Both RAF and Luftwaffe items are on display inside the Museum: everything from 20 mm. cannon shells, to bullet-shattered windscreens, to photos and full-scale displays. A replica of 11 Group's Operations Room is open to the public; its map and "tote board" can be viewed from the Controller's Gallery.

majority of German commanders concluded that bomb damage to the stations had not been very serious.

Nor did the Luftwaffe have any concrete information concerning the attrition of RAF fighter squadrons. Every day, Fighter Command was losing pilots, frequently experienced pilots that could not be replaced. The new pilots brought up from OTUs were undertrained, and were frequently shot down after only a few sorties against the Luftwaffe.

To Hitler and Göring, however, these shortcomings in the RAF's strength and efficiency were not apparent. They only knew that the enemy was always there to meet the Luftwaffe's air strikes every day. Senior officers, including Hitler himself, realized that the RAF had suffered damage in the past few weeks, but had no idea to what extent. As Peter Townsend put it, "Hitler judged by results, and the RAF was still in action."

The Luftwaffe was also having its own share of problems—problems with aircraft shortages, problems with pilot shortages, and problems with morale. Every day, bombers and fighters would return to their French bases badly damaged and riddled with bullet holes. Both pilots and ground crew could see for themselves what the guns of the RAF's fighters were doing. This was a lot different from anything they had experienced in Poland or France.

Another factor that demoralized Luftwaffe pilots and aircrew was the presence of the Channel—the "Shite Kanal." Adolf Galland stated that the Channel—having to fly over it and the very real possibility of having to land in it—had as much of an effect upon the Luftwaffe's pilots as RAF fighters. Ditching in the Channel was a thing to be feared; it meant the possibility of being taken prisoner by some bloody stinking fishing trawler, or of drowning in the freezing water.

But in spite of lagging confidence and morale, on both sides, the battle went on. On this last day of August, Luftwaffe High Command ordered another *Grosseinsatz* against the airfields of 11 Group.

The first raid appeared at about 8:00 am. Its objective was Duxford airfield, which was actually in 12 Group. Hurricane pilots of 111 Squadron, along with the Spitfires of 19 Squadron, met the bombers—about 15 Dorniers of KG 2. Their attacks rattled the Dornier crews to such an extent that they dumped their loads and turned for home before they reached their target.

This was probably the RAF's high-water mark for the day. From 8 o'clock on, the Luftwaffe would bully each raid through to its objective by sheer weight of numbers. Debden, in Essex, would be the next target. Two formations of Dorniers and Bf 110s overflew the station and dropped their bombs, cratered the runway and landing area, and killed 13 RAF ground personnel.

After Debden, the targets followed the Luftwaffe's usual litany of RAF airfields: North Weald; Eastchurch; Detling. After a brief rest, they began again: Croydon; Biggin Hill; Hornchurch. In the early evening came another effort; Hornchurch and Biggin Hill again. According to Fighter Command's summary for the day, the Luftwaffe's attacks lasted from 8 am. until 2 pm., more or less continuously, and began again at 5:30 until 7:30. About 800 aircraft were involved.

Hornchurch and Biggin Hill were probably hardest hit. At Hornchurch, the attack began at 1:15 pm, when Dorniers of KG 3 dropped about 60 bombs on the station. Except for some blown-out windows, none of the station's buildings suffered damage. The grass landing area was cratered, but not severely enough to close the station.

The station's squadrons had been scrambled to intercept; 54 Squadron was ordered off just as the bombs began to land. Nine Spitfires got clear, but the remaining three did not fare as well. This section, led by Fight Lieutenant Alan Deere, had just become airborne when exploding bombs burst underneath. All three Spitfires were literally blown out of the air. Deere's plane skidded, upside-down, for about 100 yards. All three pilots survived the experience.

Biggin Hill also was on the receiving end of an attack in the afternoon. It began at about 5:30, and very nearly put the station out of action.

The Hurricane pilots of 85 Squadron intercepted Biggin Hill's attackers. Before they could even get close to the bombers, the pilots ran into the screen of protecting BF 109s and Bf 110s. Squadron Leader Peter Townsend was in the process of closing with a Bf 110 when the 109s dived down. He positioned himself behind one of the 109s and opened fire; it slowed and rolled over, trailing smoke.

Another Messerschmitt presented itself; it was below Townsend, and so close that he could see the pilot. He took aim, and noticed a Bf 110 beyond, with its guns flashing. An instant later, his Hurricane was hit by an unexpected burst of machine gun and cannon fire. His left foot was blown right off the rudder bar—the Bf 110 had been aiming at him!

His Hurricane went into an uncontrollable steep dive, but Townsend quickly managed to regain control of the fighter and pull out. He took stock of his situation, and came to the conclusion that it was not very good: his left foot hurt; his fuel tank had been hit, with gasoline pouring into the cockpit; and his bullet-proof windscreen had been shattered by hits. (He was grateful that Dowding had insisted upon bullet-proof glass, so that his pilots would be "at least as well-protected as the gangsters of Chicago.")

Before the gasoline had the chance to explode in his face, Townsend decided to bail out. He jumped clear and parachuted into a grassy patch in a wood near Hawkhurst, Kent. That night, he was taken to Croydon General Hospital, where the big toe of his left foot was removed. When he returned to operations on 21 September, 85 Squadron had been withdrawn to the Midlands and turned into a night fighter unit.

Peter Townsend was well aware that he had been lucky. Thirteen pilots died on this last day of August; 39 RAF fighters had been destroyed. Hornchurch, Briggin Hill, and North Weald all had been damaged, and their efficiency reduced yet again. Even CH stations on the south coast had been bombed—Foreness, Dover, Rye, Pevensey, and Beachy Head—although they did not stay off the air for very long.

Dowding fully realized the peril of Fighter Command's position. For one thing, pilots were being lost faster than the OTUs could replace them—casualties were nearly double the output of the training schools. And the replacement pilots, almost all of whom were woefully undertrained in every aspect of aerial combat, had little experience in either Spitfires or Hurricanes—sometimes only seven or eight hours. Which meant that even if a squadron were kept up to strength, its fighting effectiveness would be badly watered down.

The Luftwaffe also felt the strain. Fighter pilots especially felt increased stress and fatigue, since they flew more sorties than bomber crews. And even the so-called "crack" units were not immune to their share of losses; JG 26, Adolf Galland's *geschwader*, lost six Bf 109s on 31 August, with five of the six pilots either killed or captured.

But the day had undoubtedly gone to the Luftwaffe. They had hit RAF Fighter Command hard, both in the air and on the ground—harder than Fighter Command could afford. Their new tactic of using massive fighter support to escort concentrated bomber strikes was working, and was on the verge of overpowering Fighter Command, especially 11 Group.

Liverpool was the night's main target again, with about 145 bombers making their attack. About 25 other aircraft also made nuisance raids against scattered targets throughout the country.

Berlin was bombed for the second night in a row. The raid was not a very large one; only about 20 aircraft carrying a relatively light load of bombs had been sent to harry the capital. And, once again, the main damage was to morale.

During the afternoon, while the Luftwaffe was doing its best to pulverize Fighter Command's airfield, Göring issued a directive in accordance with Adolf Hitler's ruling of the day before: the Luftwaffe would now begin a campaign of destruction against British cities. The primary target in this new campaign would be London.

During the 1920s, the Italian general Giulio Douhet published a thesis called *The Command of the Air*. His thesis was that aerial bombardment, carried out on a massive scale, would cause wholesale panic among the civilian population, in addition to substantial destruction to property, industry, and communication centers. This panic would lead to rioting and revolution; the population of the stricken city would demand that an armistice be negotiated as quickly as possible. In short, Douhet thought that heavy bombing could win wars by itself.

Hitler may have read Douhet's *The Command of the Air*; his Luftwaffe senior commanders certainly had. By switching from attacking the airfields to bombing London, they hoped that the war with Britain would be shortened—ended before the British could bring their American allies into the fighting, as they had done during the First World War. The offensive against Fighter

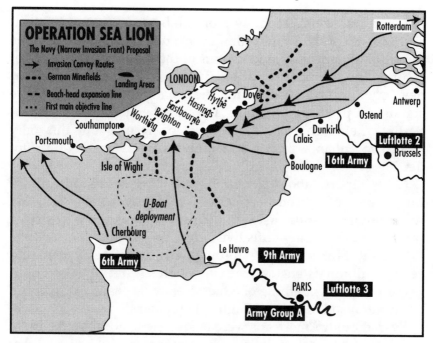

OPERATION SEA LION
The Navy (Narrow Invasion Front) Proposal
→ Invasion Convoy Routes
••• German Minefields
▬ Landing Areas
▬ ▬ Beach-head expansion line
••• First main objective line

Command was taking too long. Hitler and Göring thought that a knockout blow against Britain's most populous city was now called for.

A joint agreement between the Army and Navy had finalized plans for Operation Sea Lion. According to the agreement, landings would be limited to narrow fronts on the Kent and Sussex coasts. From the Calais area, elements of the *16th Army* would land between Folkstone and Hastings. Units of the *9th Army* would cross the Channel from Normandy, landing near Brighton. Paratroops would also be dropped near Brighton, as well as north of Dover.

Another set of instructions had been issued, as well: these concerned the terms of occupation by German forces. Among the items covered in these instructions was the arrest of about 2,300 people who might prove troublesome to the occupation forces—including Winston Churchill, other leading politicians of both parties, and various notables, including writers and academics.

Americans were becoming more understanding toward Britain and its predicament, almost in spite of themselves. The public at large still wanted no part of the war, and was dead-set against American participation. But a grudging admiration had developed, an admiration for the way that the British were standing up to the Germans and had begun hitting back at Berlin. Their fight seemed to be a losing one, but this only served to enhance Britain's standing—Americans love an underdog.

News reports about the battle were largely responsible for this change of attitude—American correspondents in London were almost unanimously pro-British—as was the Ministry of Information's highly effective white propaganda campaign. Edward R. Murrow, of the Columbia Broadcasting System, told several million listeners in the United States that "the defense of Britain will be something of which men will speak with awe and admiration so long as the English language survives."

Even though Americans were beginning to admire Britain for its courage and determination, however, they still believed that the British wre going to lose the war. (A good many broadcast reports from England sounded ominously like Dunkirk—another heroic defeat in the making.)

A British general who had been sent to the U.S. to buy weapons came back to London with disheartening news. He thought that Americans were doubtful of Britain's "capacity to survive." The Americans, he continued, were "shy of starting production of weapons for a country which might 'go under' at any moment"—weapons that might be captured by the Germans and eventually used against Americans.

At the very beginning of the Battle of Britain, Winston Churchill and his government were faced with two major tasks. The first was to turn back the Luftwaffe and prevent an invasion. The second was to convince Americans that Britain could indeed fend off the Germans and their air force. But by the end of August, it was becoming evident that Britain was failing in both of these tasks.

1 September, Sunday

One year had passed since German forces had invaded Poland, and had precipitated the war. Berlin radio used the occasion to boast of the brilliant military successes on all fronts during the past 12 months: Poland overrun in the autumn of 1939; Norway and Denmark seized early in 1940; and the six-week blitz through the Low Countries and France in May and June. The Reich had broken out of its pre-war encirclement in a series of dazzling victories unsurpassed in the history of warfare, the media went on. Only Britain remained, and she could not possibly hold out much longer. As for the Americans—they were over 3,000 miles away, and were too busy with their gang wars and profiteering to get involved in the war.

High-ranking Nazis actually believed this line, and were taken in by their own propaganda. Göring calmly informed Hitler that American industry would not be a factor in the war. "They are very good at razor blades and refrigerators," Göring said, but Americans could not produce airplanes. It was a conclusion based solidly upon wishful thinking. By 1943, U.S. manufacturers turned out 86,000 airplanes—more than the Third Reich ever thought possible.

In Berlin, and throughout Germany, people sincerely hoped that the authorities were right this time. The past year had seen a lot of fighting, but the war had been away from Germany and had not distrupted their lives. Now, the war was coming closer to them; the RAF attacked at night, in spite of Göring's promise that no enemy would ever bomb the Reich. Germans wanted to believe that the war would be over before long. William L. Shirer wrote, "They long for peace. And they want it before winter comes."

The day was fine and cloudless; Fighter Command braced itself for more attacks. The attacks were not long in coming.

About 120 German aircraft formed up over France before heading across the Straits of Dover to Kent and its fighter bases. The docks at Tilbury, down river from London, were also attacked, but this raid was intercepted and scattered by RAF squadrons. Eastchurch and Detling airfields also were raided; why the Luftwaffe persisted in bombing these Coastal Command stations remains one of the mysteries of the Battle. And Biggin Hill received its sixth visit in three days from *Luftflotte 2*—more damage was added to the station, which was already in shambles.

Fourteen RAF squadrons were sent up to meet the incoming raiders, including 54 and 72 Squadrons (Spitfires), and 85 and 1 Squadrons (Hurricanes). Because of the nearly overwhelming number of fighters at the disposal of *Luftflotte 2*, the Spitfires and Hurricanes ran into a hornets' nest before they could get anywhere near the Heinkels and Dorniers. The results were predictable: 72 Squadron lost four Spitfires destroyed and another four damaged. Only one pilot was killed, however.

Biggin Hill received its second visit at 1 pm., and still another during the late afternoon, around 5:30. By this time, there was little left to destroy. Every hangar had been wrecked. The Operations Room was a ruin—a 500 lb. bomb had punched through the roof, caromed off a steel safe, and exploded inside the defense teleprinter room.

The operations room switchboard had been manned by WAAFs throughout the raid, even after the alert had sounded. Corporal Elspeth Henderson and Sgt. Helen Turner stayed at their board as long as they could, diving under a table just before the operations hut blew up. For their single-mindedness and determination under fire, both were awarded the Military Medal.[18]

To those on the ground, the raid seemed to go on for hours. Actually, it only lasted about 20 minutes, from the alert to the all clear. To some, the first warning of the attack was the throbbing roar of the incoming bombers. Others did not hear the planes coming at all. Then came the ear-numbing explosions as bombs

---

18   In 1974, both Helen Turner and Elspeth Henderson had streets named in their honor in Biggin Hill.

burst on the landing area, in the hangars, and on the other buildings around the station.

When the raiders had finally gone, the most common recollection was of sudden silence. Only a few minutes before, exploding 500 kg. bombs had threatened to burst everyone's eardrums; afterward, the stillness seemed eerie. Knowledge that the enemy might return at any time, and begin the awful ritual all over again, did not help to calm anyone's stomach. A WAAF corporal compared these days at Biggin Hill to living on top of a volcano. An officer thought it must be like a 20th century Dante's inferno.

For all intents and purposes, Biggin Hill was finished as a fighter station. Gas and water mains had been broken; all telephone lines except one—out of 30—had been cut. The operations room had to be transferred to a shop in Biggin Hill Village. Only one squadron, 79 Squadron's Spitfires, could now be serviced at the field, and barely that. So many buildings had been smashed by the daily bombings that some WAAFs had to be billeted in town—much to the annoyance of a number of residents. If Winston Churchill hadn't pledged not to abandon any more fighter bases, the station would have been evacuated, like Manston.

Hawkinge and Lympne had also suffered at the hands of *Luftflotte* 2, although not to the extent of Biggin Hill. It was obvious that the bombers were getting through the RAF's interceptors with increasing frequency. The Spitfire and Hurricane pilots had to contend with too many Bf 109s to be effective against the Junkers and Dorniers.

The Luftwaffe lost 14 aircraft in action; the RAF had 15 fighters destroyed, with 5 pilots killed and one injured fatally. For the first time, the RAF lost more aircraft than the Luftwaffe.

After dark, activities were carried out on a smaller scale than on previous nights. Attacks consisted of a rash of small raids, mostly by single bombers, scattered throughout England and Wales.

The day had not been a particularly busy one for the Luftwaffe—only 640 sorties, far fewer than during the hectic days of mid-August. But it had been a highly satisfactory day. Major

Freiherr von Falkenstein of the German High Command noted: "The British fighter arm has been severely hit," and recommended that the Luftwaffe "keep up the pressure." The Luftwaffe had every intention of doing just that.

2 September, Monday

Most of the battle was being fought in full view of everyone in southeast England, especially Kent. It was fairly common to look up and see formations of German airplanes heading north or northwest, toward Biggin Hill, or Kenley, or Hornchurch, or to watch a fatally stricken fighter or bomber plunge to earth trailing a long stream of black smoke. Farmers working in the fields could usually count on at least one fight occurring within visual range each day.

A ten-year-old boy in Ashford, Kent, vividly recalls watching a fight between a Hurricane and a Bf 109. The boy was bicycling to his friend's house when he saw the two airplanes circling, heard the sound of machine gun fire, and watched as the German fighter disappeared, smoking, beyond the trees with the Hurricane still behind it.

"I could see the black crosses on the Messerschmitt," he recalled. "The plane was painted dark grey. The underside of the hump-back Hurricane looked white. The Messerschitt was definitely in trouble; it was smoking, and too low for the pilot to use his parachute. My friend Vern and I went off on our bicycles looking for the crash site, but couldn't find anything."

American reporters watched the battle, as well, but from a more detached vantage point. Representatives of all the major news services, as well as most of the leading American newspapers and broadcasting services, went on filing their stories on the strange new kind of war that was being fought—hundreds of feet above the earth, by a relative handful of men on either side. By the beginning of September, most American journalists had given up on Britain and the RAF. They could see for themselves which way the battle was going. Edward R. Murrow of the Columbia Broadcasting System was, in the words of his wife Janet, "one of the few who felt that somehow, by some miracle, they were going to win." Most of Murrow's fellow reporters would have agreed that the RAF needed nothing short of a miracle.

Reporters in England were not the only Americans who had given up: many back in the U.S.A. also held little hope. Newsman Vincent "Jimmy" Sheehan was asked to do an article for an American magazine—the editor wanted 25,000 words describing the entry of German occupying forces into London. Sheehan turned down the offer; when Hitler arrived in London, he did not plan to be there.

The fighter pilots of 11 Group did not have either the time or the luxury to think about what the future might have in store for them. The realities of each day were enough to keep them occupied.

The reality of this day, 2 September 1940, was that the Luftwaffe had been plotted over France at 7:15 am., and were on their way across the Channel with another load of havoc. About 100 aircraft—40 bombers escorted by 60 fighters—split up and attacked Eastchurch, North Weald, Biggin Hill. Five RAF squadrons, including 54 Squadron, intercepted the raiders and shot down 3 BF 109s of JG 51. The attack on Eastchurch was turned back. Most of the raid managed to break through to their assigned airfields, however, and added to the damage of previous days.

A second raid began forming up just after noon—about 250 fighters and bombers. The Hurricanes of 43 Squadron were up over Kent, and ran into the Messerschmitt 109s of JG 2. Sergeant Pilot Jeffreys maneuvered behind one of the Bf 109s, closed until the enemy fighter's wings spread right across his gunsight, and pressed the firing button. Hit with the combined fire of eight machine guns, it staggered and quickly lost height. The Messerschmitt crashed a short distance from Ashford, with the pilot seiously wounded.

Biggin Hill had not been a target for this particular raid, but Debden received its second major attack in three days. On 31 August, about 100 bombers had raided the station, wrecking the barracks and workshops, cratering the grass landing area, and injuring 12 ground crew. On this day, 2 September, Debden received another going-over. More buildings were hit, and the landing field was cratered again. The station remained operational, however.

At about 3:15, another 250 enemy aircraft began their trip northward across the Channel. Biggin Hill and Kenley were targets again, but the Coastal Command field at Detling was hardest hit. In addition, six bombs were dropped on Hornchurch, causing relatively light damage. Hornchurch owed its good luck to the RAF fighter squadrons that had intercepted the Luftwaffe—if every Dornier in the formation had unloaded over Hornchurch, the station would have suffered 100 hits. But the harrying of the fighters, including Hornchurch's own 222 Squadron, unnerved the German bomb-aimers, causing most of them to miss.

Actually, both Hornchurch and the RAF pilots owed their luck, and their survival, to the limited range of the Bf 109. By the time the Messerschmitts had flown as far north as Hornchurch, Essex, the fighters only had enough fuel left for a few minutes of combat. The German pilots had to turn back for France, low on fuel, leaving the bombers on their own.

The day had not been all that bad for RAF Fighter Command, in spite of the Luftwaffe's best effort. Two airfields had been heavily bombed. But these stations, Detling and Eastchurch, were Coastal Command installations; the damage done to them had no effect upon 11 Group or its already overextended resources. Luftwaffe intelligence apparently had no idea that these were not fighter fields, or their *Luftflotten* would never have been so lavish in their attention.

Although damage to airfields had not been as severe as it might have been, losses of aircraft and pilots were another matter. Fighter Command lost 31 Spitfires and Hurricanes. Eight pilots had been killed, and seven wounded.

Pilot losses, even more than the loss of fighter aircraft, continued to be unacceptably high. Training units could not hope to supply replacements at such a rate.

The death of so many experienced pilots, and their replacement by new and inexperienced trainees, had diluted the strength of most RAF fighter squadrons. This diminishing strength had not gone unnoticed by German bomber crews and fighter pilots. *The Luftwaffe War Diaries* remark that "for the first fime, violence of British fighter defence was slackening." A report from KG 1 mentioned, "Slight enemy fighter resistance easily contained by our own escort."

Veteran RAF pilots were so tired and overtaxed that they were missing opportunities to attack, and missing their target when they got themselves in position to make an attack. New replacements, fresh out of OTUs, did not yet have the fighting skills needed to be effective against experienced German pilots.

The Luftwaffe lost 35 aircraft during this day. In addition to the strikes against the airfields, bomber units had also damaged the Short Brothers factory in Rochester, Kent. The factory, which produced the four-engined Stirling bomber, had its drawings office destroyed.

Night activities included light, scattered raids against targets throughout the country, as well as minelaying off the coast of East Anglia.

3 September, Tuesday

Exactly one year before, Britain had gone to war with Germany. The war had gone well for the Germans to date. Following a series of spectacular military victories, their forces controlled the continent of Europe. A year later, the way things were going for the Luftwaffe, it looked as though German forces would also be occupying Britain before long.

Once again, for the fifth day in a row, the weather was clear and fine. And, once again, CH stations in Kent began plotting Luftwaffe formations over France late in the morning. As usual, the plots formed up, turned northwest, and headed for the airfields of 11 Group.

Hawkinge received the first blow, delivered by six Bf 109 fighter-bombers. At about 10:45, Biggin Hill was bombed. Both stations remained open and fully operational, however, even though the attacks did nothing to help the morale of the ground staff. The morning's most devastating attack fell on North Weald.

About 30 Dornier Do 17s of KG 2, escorted by 50 Bf 110s, dropped nearly 200 bombs on North Weald from above 15,000 feet. The hangars of 151 and 25 Squadrons were set on fire, along with the airplanes inside them. Barracks and living quarters, along with most of the other buildings on the station, were blown up. One bomb fell on the new operations block, but no damage at all was done to the building's interior. The station remained in service, although landing became tricky since the grass runway was cratered in many places.

One of the attacking Dorniers was shot down by intercepting fighters. Unfortunately, three Blenheims of 25 Squadron were also attacked by Hurricane pilots, who mistook them for enemy bombers. One was shot down; the other two were damaged.

The day's second attack began at around 2 pm. Debden received the brunt of this assault. The station remained in action despite a landing field that was described as "lunar" because of the number of bomb craters.

Luftflotte 2 once again succeeded in getting through to its objectives, even though Fighter Command did its utmost to stop it. Sixteen airplanes were lost to RAF fighters, including three Bf 110s shot down by the Czech pilots of 310 Squadron (Hurricanes). The Czechs were as filled with hatred for the Germans as the Poles, and were just as determined. They would close to within almost point-blank range, waiting until the enemy airplane practically bulged out of the gunsight, before pressing the firing button. In the same action, two more Zerstörers collided and crashed, giving 310's Czechs something else to celebrate.

Not very many in RAF Fighter Command had anything to celebrate. Losses for the day had been 16 fighters destroyed, and six pilots killed. One of the pilots was Flight Lieutenant H.B. Hillcoat of No. 1 Squadron. F/Lt. Hillcoat was an experienced pilot; in mid-August, he and two pilot officers from the squadron had accounted for a Dornier Do 17. Fighter Command could not spare men like this, but they were losing such pilots every day. Air Chief Marshal Dowding and other senior officers knew that they could not afford the loss.

While Fighter Command continued to fight for its life, an event was taking place on the other side of the Channel that would have a permanent effect upon the war and on its outcome.

The event was a meeting that took place at The Hague. Göring had called a conference with his senior commanders and staff officers; he wanted to discuss the air strategy to be followed in the final days before Operation Sea Lion. Among those present were Feldmarschall Hugo Sperrle of *Luftflotte 3*, and Feldmarschall Albert Kesselring, chief of *Luftflotte 2*.

Wehrmacht High Command had already set a timetable for the invasion. The earliest date for the invasion fleet to set sail would be 20 September, with the landings themselves to take place the next day.[19] Final orders for the invasion would be issued ten days prior to D-Day, on or about 11 September. The Navy was still not terribly enthusiastic about the operation, but Admiral Raeder seemed more or less resigned to it.

Göring wanted to know the current state of RAF Fighter Command—was it still a force to be reckoned with, or was it on its last legs? Both Kesselring and Sperrle gave their considered opinion. Their two answers could not have been more different, or more contradictory, if the two men had been talking about different wars in different centuries.

Because of his bright manner and his optimism, Kesselring had been given the nickname "Smiling Albert"; he certainly lived up to it on this occasion. The RAF was "finished as a fighting force," Kesselring told Göring. Because they had lost so may aircraft and pilots, they would not be able to carry on the fight for very much longer. Kesselring, in common with Göring

---

19   The invasion fleet, assembled at Channel ports on the Continent, consisted of about 2,000 barges, 170 transports of various types, over 400 tugs, and about 1,600 escort vessels.

and many other officers, believed the inflated Luftwaffe claims of enemy fighters damaged and shot down.

Hugo Sperrle was the antithesis of Kesselring, both physicaly and in manner. A large man, Sperrle is frequently described as "bear-like," and generally photographed wearing a monocle and a scowl. His view of the situation was also just the opposite of Kesselring's; Sperrle insisted that the RAF was far from finished. And went on to say that they still had about 1,000 fighters at their disposal, in spite of what all the official reports insisted. He would bet a good dinner on it, in fact. He advised Göring to keep attacking their airfields; this was the most effective way of knocking the RAF out of the battle.

Kesselring disagreed. He said that the attacks on the RAF sector stations were all but useless—the enemy's fighters could never be destroyed on the ground. "We must force their last reserves of Spitfires and Hurricanes into the air," he emphasized. And the one way to bring the fighters up would be to bomb London—the RAF would have to defend their capital.

This was just the sort of thing that Göring wanted to hear. Adolf Hitler had already approved the start of reprisal raids against London—a subtle hint that he wanted the Reichsmarschall to begin paying back for the raids on Berlin. Now, the commander of one of his *Luftflotten* was suggesting that London be bombed; recommending it, even, as the sure way of finally disposing of the RAF. Göring never liked to listen to reality if he could have rose-colored optimism instead.

Sperrle tried to return the meeting to reality. If Göring had his heart set on bombing London, Sperrle suggested that his *Luftflotte 3* attack the East End docks at night. *Luftflotte 2* would then be able to continue its pounding of 11 Group's airfields by day.

But Kesselring once again appealed to Göring's over-developed sense of optimism. Even if the RAF were wiped out, he insisted, the enemy would simply withdraw to airfields north of London. The one sure way of destroying the enemy's fighter force would be to shoot them out of the air. And the best way to draw them up would be to attack london.

Göring was convinced. By ordering bombing raids on London, he would be accomplishing two things: forcing a depleted enemy to defend a vitally strategic target; and pleasing Hitler by staging reprisal raids. The Reichsmarschall announced that he was going to switch targets—from now on, the main assault would be against London. What was more, he was going to command the assault against London personally.

Actually, Göring was in no condition to make such a judgment. For one thing, his nurse reported that he was in a state of nervous exhaustion—decisions made under such circumstances would be rash, and made without much thought behind them. Also, he was taking paracodeine and other drugs—Göring had been a drug addict since the early 1920s—which further inhibited his powers of reason. The drugs tended to make him see things the way he wanted them to be, not the way they really were—which is why Kesselring's optimism appealed to him.

Under such circumstances, and in such a state of mind, the commander-in-chief of the Luftwaffe ordered a change in tactics—from attacking and harrying the enemy's fighter bases to bombing his largest city. It was certainly one of the more curious decisions of the war, and was made almost on the spur of the moment, without the advise or consultation of any of his senior commanders. Göring's judgment would decide the outcome of the battle and eventually the outcome of the war itself.

On the night of 3/4 September, *Luftflotte 3* once again concentrated its efforts on Liverpool. Other targets were also bombed. About 90 bombers, mostly Heinkel He 111s, took part in the raids.

4 September, Wednesday

Göring's order to begin attacking London did not go into effect at once; there were still many preparations to be made for the change in targets. First raids on this Wednesday were aimed at 11 Group's airfields.

The Coastal Command field at Eastchurch was bombed again, and its grass field was cratered in about a half dozen places.

Lympne also received a going-over. Both stations remained in operation.

In the afternoon, another raid headed for the Kentish coast and the airfields inland. Fourteen RAF squadrons scrambled to intercept. At the same time, 14 Ju 88s followed the railway to the Vickers Armstrong factory at Brooklands, Surrey. Brooklands produced the twin-engine Wellington bomber, one of the main-stays of RAF Bomber Command.

An aviation enthusiast attached to an anti-aircraft battery at nearby Brooklands airfield recognized the planes as German. The enthusiast, an RAF sergeant, ordered his battery to open fire. The gun's very first shell burst between two Ju 88s, damaging both of them.

The other twelve Junkers pressed on with their attack. Al-though the anti-aircraft fire—surprisingly accurate—made some of the bomb-aimers miss their marks, six of the 550 kg. bombs did not miss; they scored hits on the machine shops and assembly areas. Eighty-eight people were killed, and more than 600 injured. Many of the dead had been killed by blast, and did not have a wound, or even a bruise, to be seen. Some of the bodies were carried out of the ruins on assembed wings of Wellington bombers.

Hurricanes of 253 Squadron scrambled to intercept, and ran into the Bf 110s of ZG 76. It was not a pleasant encounter for the Zerstörers; sixteen of them, from both ZG 76 and from *Lehrgesch-wader 1* and 2, were shot down, chopped to pieces by the single-seat RAF fighters. Bullet-holed wrecks of the big, twin-engined fighters littered the landscape of Surrey. Souvenir hunters from miles around pillaged the wrecks, taking anything from machine gun bullets to engine parts.

The success against the Zerstörers did not help matters at the Vickers factory. Production of Wellington bombers was inter-rupted for the better part of a week; dead bodies were pulled out of the bomb ruins for the next several days.

Rochester's Short Brothers factory was also bombed, along with the long-suffering Coastal Command field at Eastchurch. None of these targets—including the Vickers factory at Brooklands—had any connection with Fighter Comand or with the production of fighters.

The Luftwaffe lost 25 aircraft during the day's operations, the majority of which were Bf 110s. The RAF lost 17 fighters, as well as nine pilots killed, badly wounded, or missing. Hardest hit was 66 Squadron, which lost 3 Spitfires during the morning's attack and three more in the early afternoon melee over Kent.

At night, about 200 bombers of *Luftflotte 3* made their presence known over England. Liverpool and Bristol were the main targets, although other cities were bombed, as well (including Manchester and Nottingham). Flares were dropped over the London docks, apparently in preparation for the raids to come.

Two Heinkels were trailed and shot down by night-fighter Blenheims of 25 Squadron. One of the bombers crashed in Suffolk at 1:10 am.; the other managed to fly across to Holland before going down. In addition, another Heinkel was brought down by anti-aircraft fire. Three enemy bombers in a single night was very encouraging for the defenders at this stage, when just being able to find an enemy bomber was considered a huge boost to morale.

Just before midnight—"punctually at fifteen minutes before midnight," according to William L. Shirer—RAF Wellingtons once again dropped their bomb loads over Berlin. But the day's major story from the German capital concerned Adolf Hitler, and what he said in a speech at Berlin's *Sportspalast*.

Hitler's appearance had been kept secret until the last minute. He was to address an audience of female social workers and nurses at the opening of the 1940 *Winterhilfe* campaign—winter relief for the underprivileged. But the real reason for the speech was to mark the opening of the Luftwaffe's *Zielwechsel*—target switching.

"I have rarely seen the Nazi dictator in a more sarcastic mood," correspondent Shirer wrote 20 years after the fact. Hitler made some snide remarks about Winston Churchill, and then addressed the question of the invasion of Britain: " In England, they're filled with curiosity and keep asking, 'Why doesn't he come?' Be calm. Be calm. He's coming! He's coming!" (He might have mentioned that everyone in the United States was almost as curious.)

The audience laughed on cue. Then Hitler approached his main topic: retaliation for the recent RAF raids on Berlin. "You will understand that we are now answering night for night. And when the British air force drops two, or three, or four thousand kilogrammes of bombs, then we will drop 150, 230, 300, or 400 kilogrammes in one night." This met with wild enthusiasm from his audience, who reacted with hysterical applause.

After the noise died down, Hitler came to the point: "When they declare that they will increase their attacks on our cities, then we will raze *their* cities to the ground!" More applause.

There was a bit more to the speech than this. Hitler also said, among other things, that Britain would collapse but National Socialist Germany would survive, as well as other items designed to please the audience—for nurses and social workers, that night's crowd in the *Sportspalast* seemed a fanatical lot.

Hitler had declared his intention—massive retaliation for the RAF's raids on Berlin. (He failed to mention that there were also military reasons for this change of targets.) The speech was broadcast to the nation two hours later. If British Intelligence listened to the broadcast, they were not able to learn any specific details regarding the date and time of the impending change.

5 September, Thursday

Army commanders throughout Britain received a warning that the German invasion might come at any time: "Conditions are most favourable for an invasion about 12 or 13 September, but the possibility of a change in the present fair weather period might help the Germans to decided to act at any time after 6 September." The memo went on to say, in a minor masterpiece of understatement, that "the attack will be carried out ruthlessly with every means available."

The day's aerial activities began at about 10:00 am., when the Luftwaffe made for 11 Group's airfields in Kent and Surrey:

Croydon; Biggin Hill; North Weald and Lympne; and poor Eastchurch again. Fourteen squadrons went up to intercept, and ran into the Bf 109 escort. The next few minutes were bedlam gone amok—six Messerschmitts were shot down, and five RAF fighters were either damaged or destroyed.

All of this took place in full view of onlookers on the ground. Ten-year-old James McCurdy watched the fighting from his back garden near Maidstone. The airplanes were too high for him to identify them, or to tell which were RAF and which were German, but he could see them twisting and turning in the sky overhead.

While he was watching, a clatter of machine gun cartridge cases bounced off the roof of his parents' house and landed in the garden—exactly 37 brass .303 cases, which young James quickly collected and put into a box. Over a half century later, he still had them, in the same box.

The day's first effort was not spectacularly successful; RAF fighter attacks managed to spare the airfields from another pulverizing. But the second raid had better luck, or maybe it just benefitted from better planning. After noon, a high flight of Dorniers made for the oil tanks at Thameshaven, far down the Thames Estuary, as well as for Biggin Hill. The bombers came in at such an altitude that all the early warning systems, apparently including the CH network, failed to detect them. Thameshaven's oil tanks were hit and set on fire, and Biggin Hill received yet another load of German bombs.

A diversionary fighter sweep, Messerschmitt 109s from JG 3 and JG 53, darted across Kent looking for trouble. They found it when the Poles of 303 Squadron intercepted.

These Polish pilots were among the fiercest in Fighter Command—Zdzislaw Kranodebski, Waclaw Lapkowski, Kazimierz Wunsche, and the others of the squadron, including the Czech sergeant Josef Frantisek. Most had at least 500 hours in fighters—although most of the fighters they had flown were hopelessly obsolete, such as the P.Z.L. P-11c, which was over 100 mph slower than the Bf 109—and had fought against the Luftwaffe in Poland.

Anything that the Poles lacked in skill was more than compensated for in determination—a determination to kill Germans that sometimes bordered on the obsessive. All of them fought with no regard for their own lives; they had seen what the Nazis had done to Poland, knew that they could not go back while their country was occupied, and realized that they had nothing to lose.

Over Kent, the Poles pounced on the 109s—closing within 100 yards or less before pressing the firing button. Sometimes, a particularly single-minded pilot would hold his fire until only 20 yards—60 feet— away, ensuring that the full impact of the Hurricane's eight .303s would be brought to bear.

Sgt. Frantisek closed to within point-blank range of his Messerschmitt; when he fired, he could see pieces of the enemy plane shoot past his cockpit. He followed the German down, still shooting; he wanted to make absolutely sure that this BF 109 was dead. If the German pilot in the cockpit was dead, as well, that would be even better.

Another Messerschmitt got behind Sgt. Frantisek, and hit his Hurricane with cannon and machine gun fire—he had forgotten the basic lesson: Never Follow an Enemy Airplane Down. Frantisek was able to fly it back to Northolt, where it was repaired. (If a Spitfire had sustained as much damage, it probably would have been written off.) Flying Officer Lapkowski, his squadron mate, also was jumped by a Messerschmitt, but was not as fortunate as Frantisek. Lapowski had been forced to bail out of his Hurricane, and was admitted to the hospital for burns and a broken leg.

The pilots of 303 Squadron had certainly lived up to their growing reputation as one of the best fighter units in the RAF. In exchange for one Hurricane destroyed and another damaged, the Poles had destroyed at least two Bf 109s and damaged at least three others.

The Luftwaffe's losses came to 23 aircraft. The RAF lost 20 fighters, as well another eight pilots. Pilot losses had put Fighter Command in a desperate situation; the strain on the surviving pilots was so great that many were almost at the breaking point.

But in spite of all the grimness and foreboding, Prime Minister Churchill had good news for Parliament. He told the House of Commons that the Destroyers-for-Bases Deal with the United States had been brought to a successful conclusion—the U.S.A. had agreed to exchange 50 World War I vintage destroyers for 99-year leases on naval and air bases in the Western Hemisphere.

What this actually meant was that the United States was now a co-belligerent against Nazi Germany. Britain was no longer at war alone. America was now a British ally.

Night operations by *Luftflotte 3* included attacks on about 40 scattered cities and towns throughout England and Wales. Main targets were Liverpool, Manchester, and London. Sixty-eight bombers dropped 60 tons of high explosives and incendiaries on London's docks—a portent of things to come in the not-too-distant future. Only one bomber was lost—KG 1 had one of its Heinkel He 111s shot down by a Blenheim night-fighter of 25 Squadron. The Luftwaffe were very much the masters of the night sky, and were coming close to becoming masters during the day, as well.

6 September, Friday

The RAF were fighting a losing battle against the Luftwaffe. Robert Wright, Dowding's personal assistant, recalled that "those last two weeks were the worst for us"—meaning the last week in August and the first week in September. Fighter Command was not ony losing fighter aircraft faster than the Luftwaffe, but faster than the factories could produce them. In addition, six out of the seven sector airfields of 11 Group had been pounded into near ruins. Worst of all was the constant attrition of pilots.

The pounding continued on 6 September, beginning at about 8:30. About 250 German airplanes headed for several points in Kent, including Kenley. Two RAF squadrons intercepted; 303's Poles and 601 Squadron—formerly the Millionaire's Squadron, until most of its original members had either been killed or put in the hospital.

But the two squadrons were brutally outnumbered—"only two of our squadrons in the area, and a hundred Germans," wrote one of the Polish pilots. Besides having superior numbers, the German pilots also had the advantage of height. Two Hurricanes were lost and four were damaged, in exchange for one Dornier. It had not been a good day for the Poles of 303 Squadron.

The pilots of 601 Squadron fared just as badly. One of the pilots killed by cannon fire from a Messerschmitt was Flight Lieutenant Ray Davis. F/Lt. Davis was an American who had renounced his U.S. citizenship in 1932; on his 21st birthday, he signed a document which made him a British subject. Both of Davis's parents were American: Carl Davis Sr., was born in Cleveland, Ohio; and Mary Wood Davis came from Flint, Michigan.

C. Ray Davis was born in South Africa, and is usually named as a citizen of that country. He had a brother and a sister who remained U.S. citizens; one of his sisters lived in Morristown, New Jersey, where Jimmy Davies went to school. But Ray Davis decided to become a British citizen, and joined the RAF Auxiliary in the mid-1930s. By the time he was shot down and killed, Davis had been credited with 11½ German aircraft destroyed, and had been awarded the Distinguished Flying Cross.

In the early afternoon of 6 September, Biggin Hill and Hornchurch came under attack again. Neither raid was particularly devastating; the bomb-aimers missed their mark. But some of the bombs that overshot the airfield at Biggin Hill managed to do their fair share of damage just the same; the near misses knocked out the telephone cable for about the dozenth time in the past few weeks.

The Luftwaffe's next attack was not directed at 11 Group. The recipient of *Luftflotte 2's visit were the oil tanks at Thameshaven, in a raid that began at about 5:30. Once again, the bomb-aimers discovered that fuel oil burns beautifully; smoke from the fires was visible for miles.*

This was the third and final raid of the day. Even from this sketchy account of the Luftwaffe's, it should be evident that the bombers and their Messerschmitt escort had no trouble reaching their targets, regardless of RAF interceptions. Senior Luftwaffe commanders knew it. And both Air Vice Marshal Park and Air Chief Marshal Dowding knew it, as well.

The RAF lost 23 fighters, against 35 aircraft for the Luftwaffe. Seven more RAF pilots were killed. One landed in France, and was taken prisoner, and at least two others were injured severely enough to keep them out of the rest of the battle. Andy Mamedoff of 609 Squadron said that "the loss of one experienced guy is worse than six Spitfires." And the bombers still got through.

The King and Queen visited Bently Priory, the headquarters of Fighter Command, on the afternoon of 6 September. They were escorted through the command center by Air Chief Marshal Dowding. Members of Dowding's staff remarked on how tired and strained Fighter Command's chief looked that day. But it was small wonder that he looked run-down, considering the amount of stress he had endured for the past two weeks.

Since 24 August, Fighter Command's airfields had taken a severe and steady pounding. Its fighter strength had been severely depleted, and its pilots had been decimated. A British historian wrote, "the battle in the air ... was being decisively won by the Luftwaffe. If this continued, there would be no fighters left, or at any rate not enough to put up an effective defense." Dowding knew the situation, and the desperate crisis faced by Fighter Command, better than anyone else.

During the late 1960s Laurence Olivier played Dowding in a film called *The Battle of Britain*. During the course of the film, a conversation takes place between Dowding, Park, and Leigh-Mallory. Actually, it is not so much a conversation as an argument between Park and Leigh-Mallory over Leigh-Mallory's Big Wing theory.

Dowding interrupts by saying, "We don't need a big wing, or a small wing. We need pilots. And a miracle."

Air Chief Marshal Sir Hugh "Stuffy" Dowding, Fighter Command's first Commander-in-Chief; he was appointed to the position in 1936. During the early 1930s, as Air Council Member for Supply and Research, Dowding had been responsible for the establishment of Britain's coastal RDF (Radar) network, and also oversaw the transition from the bi-plane fighter to the Spitfire and the Hurricane.

Whether or not Dowding ever said such a thing is not known, but he was probably thinking it. At this point, a miracle was what was needed to save the ebbing RAF. No one knew it at the time, but something resembling a miracle was less than a day away.

DOWDING, PARK, AND THE "BIG WING" CONTROVERSY

As the battle wound down into its final days, the two senior officers usually credited with Fighter Command's success found themselves in an awkward situation—they had to defend the tactics and methods they used against the Luftwaffe to achieve this success.

On 17 October, at a meeting to discuss "Major Day Tactics in the Fighter Force," Air Chief Marshal Dowding and Air Vice-Marshal Park were called upon to justify themselves and their methods to a board of senior RAF officers. This panel consisted of Air Vice Marshal Sir Quentin Brand, commander of 10 Group; Air Vice Marshal Sir Trafford Leigh-Mallory, commander of 12 Group; Air Vice Marshal Sir Sholto Douglas, Deputy Chief of the Air Staff; and five other members of Air Staff. Also present, among all these marshals, was Squadron Leader Douglas Bader, the legless leader of 242 Squadron.

The real reason behind the meeting, however, was not the discussion of aerial tactics. It was called mainly to examine the "Big Wing" theory, which was advocated by both Leigh-Mallory and S/L Bader, and to determine the failure to adopt this method of deploying fighters by both Dowding and Park.

The "Big Wings" became a matter of controversy in late August, when squadrons from Leigh-Mallory's 12 Group responded too slowly to 11 Group's call for re-inforcements. (At least in Air Vice Marshal Park's opinion.) Park complained that the "Big Wings"—three squadrons, up to 60 fighters, flying in one huge formation—took too much time to assemble. By the time 60 fighters had formed up and moved south to intercept the German raiders, the enemy had already bombed their targets—usually 11 Group's airfields—and turned for home.

Leigh-Mallory countered that Park's tactics were wrong, not his. Park's deploying of single squadrons against the Luftwaffe usually left 11 Group's pilots far outnumbered, which allowed the German bombers to push through to their targets.

But Park did not have the time, at least 20 minutes, to group three squadrons into formation—the German raid would be on top of them before they could ever hope to assemble. Park maintained that he deployed his squadrons so that they could intercept the enemy as far from their targets as possible, preferably over the Channel. He wanted to attack the enemy before they bombed 11 Group's airfields, not afterward. Big Wings required too much assembly time to accomplish this, and were too impractical.

This argument went on for several weeks, with bad feeling building between Park and Leigh-Mallory. And, to Leigh-Mallory's annoyance, Dowding agreed with

Park and refused to order him to adopt Big Wing tactics.

The adjutant of S/L Bader's squadron, Flight Lieutenant Peter Macdonald, was a Member of Parliament of some influence. He took the Big Wing argument—at least Leigh-Mallory's and Bader's side of it—to two of his colleagues in Parliament, as well as to the under Secretary of State for Air and Prime Minister Winston Churchill. This august group had more than enough power and influence to force the Chief of Air Staff to take some sort of action. The 17 October meeting was the result.

This meeting, which has been described as a "trial," turned out to be a disaster for both Park and Dowding. Park emphasized the scarcity of time for 11 Group to intercept incoming German aircraft and insisted that Big Wings took too long to become airborne and gather into formations. Leigh-Mallory replied that he could get his Big Wings into the air in six minutes. Douglas Bader backed Leigh-Mallory, telling the gathering that the Big Wing was the main reason for 12 Group's impressive number of enemy aircraft shot down. (Post-war records show that most of these numbers were highly exaggerated.)

Sholto Douglas summed up the meeting on a conciliatory note, urging more cooperation from both 11 Group and 12 Group. But Leigh-Mallory and Bader had simply made a better presentation than Park and Dowding, and the tide of opinion

went against them. Both men would very soon feel the result.

Technically, Dowding was not "dismissed" as chief of Fighter Command, but retired on 25 November 1940. He had held the post since July 1936, and was the most senior officer in the RAF; he had been up for retirement three times, and had been asked to postpone his retirement three times. But it was the manner in which Dowding was informed of his final retirement that left him with bitterness—a notice giving him 24 hours to vacate his office. His post was occupied by Sholto Douglas.

Keith Park was removed from command of 11 Group, and replaced by his antagonist Trafford Leigh-Mallory. He went to a training command, and then to command the fighter forces on Malta, where he used his Battle of Britain tactics to good effect once again—the RAF held off the Luftwaffe's onslaught and prevented an invasion by the Wehrmacht.

A variety of reasons have been given for the indignity to which Park and Dowding were subjected, in spite of their record against the Luftwaffe: petty jealousy; personality clashes. Politics, not suprisingly, is most often mentioned. But author Len Deighton probably comes closest to the mark. "Dowding and Park," Deighton wrote in *Fighter*, "had committed an unforgivable sin in the eyes of the Air Ministry and their other critics: they had proved their theories right."

AMERICAN ISOLATIONISM—NO FOREIGN WARS

Shortly before France surrendered, London correspondent Mollie Panter-Downes remarked, "Now the universal question is, 'Will the Americans come in?'"

The Americans soon made it quite clear that they had no intention of "coming in" with Britain against Germany, and also that they resented the question. They felt that they had been given short shrift by the British for America's role in the First World War—the most frequently voiced British opinion was that U.S. forces did not contribute very much toward winning that war. Many Americans now had the feeling that Britain would somehow try to drag them into this war, as well. (A feeling that, as it turned out, was fully justified.)

Throughout the United States, men and women of all backgrounds and occupations believed that Britain would lose the war, and that the British would somehow try to involve them in the fighting to save themselves. It looked like a repeat of the First World War, and would probaby have the same result for Americans if the British succeeded with their plan.

Everybody from janitors to U.S. Senators shared this opinion. When a member of President Roosevelt's cabinet called Britain a "good risk," Missouri senator Bennett C. Clark publicly expressed his astonishment at the remark. A New Jersey factory worker put it even more bluntly:

"Let the British fight their own war this time. They need us. We don't need them."

There were those who opposed helping "the redcoats" because Britain had always been America's traditional enemy, or because they resented the fact Britain was trying to pull Americans into "the British war." But the most widespread sentiment was pure isolationism, deeply ingrained into the American character—"Whatever the British do, 3,500 miles away, is none of our concern."

As the Battle of Britain went on, Americans emotionally argued over "all aid short of war" versus Thomas Jefferson's warning about "entangling alliances." But the vast majority of the country—sixty four percent, according to a Gallup Poll taken in May—favoured staying out of the fighting. The war against Nazi Germany was a foreign war; most Americans wanted no part of it.

Charles Lindbergh summed up the isolationist point of view in a speech in 1940: "We believe that the security of our country lies in the strength and character of our own people, and not in fighting foreign wars." (In Britain, a speech by "Lindbergh" was seen to be as much of a menace as several German divisions.)

Winston Churchill knew that he would have to change this point of view—American participation in the war against Adolf Hitler was absolutely vital. He also knew enough about the United States and its occupants to realize that changing America's public opinion would be a formidable job. Success would require nothing less than the complete re-education of the American public. Churchill set about this task with typical energy and ruthless determi-

nation, but could see that he would be needing all the help he could get.

NOTES

1. Mollie Panter-Downe's *London War Notes*
2. Lindbergh's speech in *Alistair Cooke's America*
3. Gallup poll statistics in Manchester

THE EFFECTS IN EUROPE WERE PROFOUND

In spite of what conventional widom has to offer, the United States did not enter the Second World War on 7 December 1941, when Japanese aircraft attacked the U.S. Pacific Fleet at Pearl Harbor. America became an active participant in the war 15 months earlier, in September 1940. On 5 September, Winston Churchill informed Parliament that the Destroyers-for-Bases deal with the United States, a deal that he had been negotiating since May, had finally been concluded.

The agreement sent 50 mothballed American destroyers, which had been built during the First World War, to the British fleet in exchange for 99-year leases on British naval and air bases in the Western Hemisphere. The deal represented a personal triumph for Churchill, who had begun to petition President Franklin D. Roosevelt for the "loan" of these destroyers less than a week after he became Prime Minister. Ne-

gotiations had run into snags and delays on several occasions, mostly caused by American isolationists. But during the first week of September, Churchill could report that a "memorable" transaction had been concluded, "to the general satisfaction of the British and American peoples."

Far more was achieved by this agreement than simply sending 50 American warships to Britain, however. What the Destroyers-for Bases swap really accomplished was to end U.S. neutrality—in spite of the fact that the Neutrality Acts were still in effect. American historian William Manchester put it this way: "The swap wasn't even legal, and it made the U.S. a nonbelligerent ally of Britain."

Churchill arrived at one of his most urgent goals by bringing the destroyers deal to a successful conclusion: he had convinced Franklin Roosevelt that Britain could win the

Battle, especially with American help—in spite of the fact that Britain was losing the Battle! Also, by convincing Roosevelt to send warships to Britain, Churchill brought the U.S. one reluctant step—one large reluctant step—closer to war.

Americans did not seem to recognize the significance of the agreement. Isolationists opposed it because isolationists opposed any involvement in the "European war." Some people objected because it helped Britain; one protester carried a sign that said, "Benedict Arnold helped England, too." But few realized what it meant to Berlin. The Nazis saw the deal as nearly tantamount to a declaration of war, which made the U.S. only slightly less belligerent than Britain.

"The Germans say it is a breach of neutrality, as it is," wrote William L. Shirer from Berlin, "but they're not going to do anything about it, not even protest." He might have said: "they're not going to do anything about it *yet...*"

Winston Churchill viewed the situation with a bit more clarity. "I have no doubt that Herr Hitler will not like the transferrence of destroyers," he said to Parliament, "and I have no doubt that he will pay the United States out, if he ever gets the chance." He knew full well that the chance would come, and that Hitler would jump at the chance to exact his measure of vengeance against the United States. And at that time, Churchill also knew that the U.S. would become an active belligerent against Germany and a fully-committed ally of Britain.

"The effects in Europe were profound," Churchill said about the destroyers deal. It was a prediction as much as a statement. But another prediction, this one by Admiral Wilhelm Canaris, chief of German intelligence, also comes to mind. On 3 September 1939, the day that hostilities began between Germany and Britain, Canaris predicted that Germany would lose the war. He knew that the British would talk the Americans into joining the fight, somehow and by some way. Germany could not hope to win against both the British Empire and her American ally.

Chapter V

Strategy and Fortune Change
7 September - 17 September

"*T*he destiny of Britain had become a national obsession for
the multitudes of interventionists," American historian William
Manchester said about the mood of his countrymen—or at least
a segment of them—in the late summer of 1940. Isolationists
were just as concerned about Britain's fate, but for motives that
were vastly different.

From what they were reading in their newspapers and magazines, and from what they were hearing in news broadcasts, the
American public knew that all was not going well for the RAF,
or for Britain. Surprisingly—or maybe not so surprisingly—the
average American had a truer picture of the battle than most
Britons. Strict censorship kept the British public from knowing
anything that the Ministry of Information did not want them to
know.

Neither isolationists nor interventionists were reassured
about Britain's future. Senior U.S. military officers were not
reassured, either. General George C. Marshall, U.S. Army Chief
of Staff, and Admiral Harold "Betty" Stark, Chief of Naval
Operations, opposed aid to Britain. Both had been against the
Destroyers-for-Bases deal. Britain seemed on the brink of defeat;
any warships and weapons sent to aid Britain would soon wind
up in the hands of Nazi Germany. (For a variety of reasons,

President Roosevelt chose to ignore his senior military advisors.)

Had Göring kept to his strategy of hammering Fighter Command and its airfields, this gloomy prediction almost certainly would have come true. But the Reichsmarschall had no idea that his strategy was working so well. And so, he decided to change his plan of attack.

With the full support and approval of Adolf Hitler, Göring decided to send his Luftwaffe to bomb London, the enemy's capital, instead of RAF fighter bases. He hoped that this would bring the Spitfires and Hurricanes up in record numbers, which would thus allow his Bf 109 pilots to shoot them down in record numbers. Bombing London should finally bring the battle to a close; it had gone on for too long.

On 7 September, the Reichsmarschall arrived at Cap Gris Nez. From there, he watched his fighters and bombers fly overhead to deliver, he hoped, the final attack in the Battle of Britain. But he had not come just as an observer. He had made his intentions known in an unscheduled radio announcement: "I have taken personal command of the Luftwaffe's Battle for Britain myself."

7 September, Saturday

Practically no Luftwaffe activity took place before noon, even though the day was sunny and cloudless all morning. The only action of the morning took place at about 9 am., when three Spitfire pilots of 266 Squadron chased a snooping Dornier reconnaissance aircraft across the North Sea. The three fighter pilots finally caught it over the Netherlands, which was too close to the Luftwaffe's fighter aerodromes for comfort, and shot it down over Walcheren Island.

The lull ended at 3:54 pm., when Chain Home stations began picking up plots of German planes over France: 20-plus became 80-plus and 150-plus, and went on growing until the massed formation numbered more than two hundred aircraft. This was clearly a heavier-than-usual raid. In fact, it was too large to be classified as a raid; this was a maximum effort.

The word went out from Fighter Command headquarters at Bentley Priory: it looked as though the Luftwaffe had planned a knockout blow against 11 Group's fighter fields. Ground controllers passed the height and course of the incoming attack to intercepting fighter squadrons, and placed them in position to protect the fighter bases.

But the attacking formation did not split into smaller groups, with each group going after a fighter airfield, as was the usual procedure. The formations continued on toward the Thames Estuary. It soon became evident that the Germans were not aiming for the airfields—their target was London. And Fighter Command had everything up covering 11 Group's sector stations.

Civilians on the ground could hear the approaching aircraft before they saw them. The droning of hundreds of engines made pedestrians all along the Thames Estuary look up. The bombers, which are frequently described as looking like either toys or miniature models, did not seem threatening at all to onlookers.

Just after 5 pm., the first bombs fell on Woolwich Arsenal, a genuine military target, as well as the oil tanks at Thameshaven. London's docks were next—the West India Docks, and the sprawling Surrey Commercial Docks. Residential districts, streets of cheap and flimsy houses in West Ham, Poplar, Stepney, and Bermondsey, collapsed from fire and explosion.

Because the RAF's squadrons were protecting 11 Group's airfields, the Dorniers and Heinkels could hit their targets without any interference. After dropping their loads, however, the bombers were set upon by the Spitfires and Hurricanes of both 11 Group and 12 Group. Douglas Bader's renowned Duxford Wing—242, 19, and 310 Squadrons—did their best to come to grips with a group of Dorniers and their Bf 109 escort. Only 242 Squadron's pilots were able to bring their guns to bear, however; the other two squadrons did not have enough height to jump the German airplanes.

The Poles of 303 Squadron found a formation of Dorniers in a perfect position for attack—just ahead, and about 3,000 feet

On 7 September, the Luftwaffe changed its tactics. Instead of attacking the airfields of RAF Fighter Command, as it had been doing with savage success for the past two weeks, the German formations flew past 11 Group's bases and bombed London. The photo shows warehouses in the area of St. Katherine's Dock, just east of the Tower of London and Tower Bridge, burning furiously during the late afternoon.

below their Hurricanes. The Dorniers were so numerous that nobody took the time to count them.

They charged the enemy as only the Poles could—with chilling determination and single-minded fury. Corporal Wojtowicz maneuvered behind a Dornier that had strayed from the formation, fired a burst at it from his .303s, and watched it go down. Another Dornier flew in front of him—he gave this victim six short bursts before it blew up.

The other pilots were just as determined, and just as good at shooting. They chased the Dorniers as far as the coast, when Messerschmitts arrived to spoil the fun. But they had destroyed or damaged ten of the bombers—about a quarter of the formation—before the Bf 109s intervened.

The day had been a triumph for the Poles, but it also had been a time for reflection. The sight of the raging fires in East London reminded Corporal Wojtowicz of what he had seen in Poland, just a year before, when the Germans had bombed Lublin.

This daylight bombing convinced the chiefs of staff in Whitehall of one thing—the feared German invasion was not far off. The chiefs assumed—correctly—that the anticipated landings would be immediately preceded by a major attack on the capital. Added to this were recent reconnaissance reports which disclosed that landing barges were being massed across the Channel, which meant that preparations were almost completed.

Shortly after 7 pm., the All Clear sounded. About an hour later, troops in southern England received this communique from the commander of Home Forces:

HOFOR LONDON TO C-IN-C S AND E COMMANDS. CROMWELL ALL INFORMED.

CROMWELL was the code for "attack is imminent." Issuing of this code caused all sorts of hell to break loose. Rumors started that the Germans had landed on the south coast and were surging north toward London, murdering civilians as they went. Another rumor was that the invasion had failed, and 20,000 Germans had drowned when their ships were sunk. In some areas, the authorities ordered church bells to be rung—the signal that German paratroops had landed.

In fact, the nearest German soldier was still on the far side of the Channel. The Wehrmacht had received no alert and no landing instructions. When CROMWELL was issued, most of the Wehrmacht were in their barracks, preparing to turn in for the night.

At about 4 pm. that afternoon, while the massed Luftwaffe formations surged toward London, Air Vice Marshal Keith Park and Dowding were in conference at Fighter Command headquarters, Bentley Priory. The two were trying to come up with a more effective system of defending 11 Group's airfields. On the great table map of southern England, Park and Dowding

223

The night of September 7, the Luftwaffe returned and laid waste to London's docks. The photo above, taken from approximately the same vantage point on London Bridge as the picture taken a few hours earlier, gives some idea of the fires and destruction that the German bombers inflicted.

watched the WAAFs as they plotted the incoming raid. As they watched the girls move the colored disks across the face of the map, they realized that today's target would not be Biggin Hill, Kenley, Hornchurch, or Tangmere. While 11 Group's fighters were guarding the airfields, Park and Dowding could see that the raid was going straight to London.

According to Group Captain Frederick W. Winterbotham, one of the RAF's senior Intelligence officers, Churchill and Dowding knew of the massive raid on London on 5 September, two days before it happened. Winterbotham said that Göring radioed Kesselring about the maximum effort on 5 September, ordering a 300-bomber attack to be launched on 7 September, and that Ultra picked it up immediately. Churchill and Dowding were notified of the impending raid at once.

But in no account of the battle does this Ultra interception get any mention. This is possibly because Dowding was trying to protect Ultra, which was still highly secret. (Ultra transcripts remained unavailable to the public until many years after the war had ended.) It has also been stated, however, that Dowding had not been placed on Ultra's privileged list of informants until October, when the battle was nearly over. Which, in that case, would mean that Dowding did not have advanced knowledge of the 7 September mass attack on London.

And thus, Dowding and Ultra—how much he knew and when he knew it—has become another of the Battle of Britain's perplexing (and maddening) myths.

The sweeping change in tactics had been ordered partly because of revenge—perhaps even largely because of revenge—and partly because of widely-held beliefs on the bombing of civilians.

During the 1920s and 1930s, air strategists believed that heavy aerial bombardment of cities could win a war. The theory was that bombers would not only knock out the enemy's roads, railways, utilities, and infrastructure, but would also demoralize the civilian population to the point of inciting an armed revolt against the government. In setting the Luftwaffe against London, Adolf Hitler strongly believed that he could stir the population of London to riot. He had used terror raids against Warsaw and Rotterdam, and had achieved the results he had anticipated. As a British author has pointed out, Hitler "was switching to those methods of terror and brutality which had won him such spectacular victories both in his own country and abroad."

The Japanese attache in London seemed to re-inforce Douhet's—and Hitler's—thoughts on this type of warfare. The attache commented on the favorable effect of the Luftwaffe's bombing. In Washington, DC, the German attache, General Friedrich von Boetticher, was moved to comment: "The morale of the British population has been greatly shaken. Indications of major stress. All good feelings and optimism have gone. The heart of London has been hit like an earthquake. Heavy damage to public utilities."

But one of the overlying motives for attacking London was revenge—revenge for the RAF bombing of Berlin. Göring had watched the bombers and fighters pass overhead on their way to London, along with Kesselring and other senior Luftwaffe brass. The Reichsmarschall approached a broadcast correspondent and impulsively snatched the microphone out of his hand, telling listeners of the *Grossdeutsche Rundfunk*, "*Es um historichen Augenblick geht*"—"this is a historic moment." His fighter and bombers had delivered the enemy "a blow right to the heart"—"*die dem zuersten Male mitten ins Herz Hineinstiessen*."

Göring also hoped that targeting London would persuade Americans that the Luftwaffe could not be beaten—it might convince them to be a bit more friendly toward Germany than they had been since the war began. He wanted to demonstrate that his *Luftflotten* could still strike at the enemy's largest city at will, even after two months of fighting with the RAF. It would also be a fittingly dramatic ending to the war—burning London was much more suited to the Reichsmarschall's garish style than the grinding attacks against Fighter Command's airfields. Also, he hoped, more persuasive for neutral America.

Unfortunately for Göring, he did not see that his relentless attacks against Fighter Command's sector airfields were producing the desired results, slowly but surely. "Slowly but surely" was not a phrase that suited Göring's flamboyant personality, however. His bombing attacks on London would quickly prove to be counter productive. Winston Churchill called the abrupt changing of targets, from airfields to London, "a foolish mistake."

The mistake was actually more Hitler's doing than Göring's. Hitler, as absolute dictator of Nazi Germany, had the final word on all military decisions. But Göring willingly went along with his Führer's decision and, as chief of the Luftwaffe, deserves equal blame.

The RAF lost 28 fighters in its attempt to stop the Luftwaffe's attack on London; 9 pilots were killed, with 2 missing. Forty-one German aircraft were shot down.

To many of the RAF's pilots, the day's hammer-blow at London seemed to mark the end of the battle—the Germans were still able to put up massive numbers of fighters and bombers, in spite of weeks of fighting. (The actual figure was about 1,000 aircraft, one-third of which were bombers.) "The formation looked like a vast black storm cloud," a British author noted, "for it was nearly two miles high, and covered about 800 square miles."

Some civilians also began to have the same idea: the Germans were not to be stopped. Today, they had ploughed their way right through to London, brushing aside any attempts at interference by RAF fighters, and proceeded to unlead their bombs and go back home again. The fires they started were visible from as far away as the Channel coast. The fact that the Luftwaffe was still able to carry out such an operation must mean that there was no hope of stopping them.

Air Vice Marshal Park saw the smoke over London, as well. He had other ideas as to its meaning, however.

Following his conference with Dowding at Fighter Command headquarters, Park went to Northolt airfield, a few miles from Stanmore, and took off in his personal Hurricane. He circled over London, taking a good look at the fires and the havoc below. But instead of lamenting over the bomb damage, Park hoped that it would continue.

To Park, the bombing of London signified hope—hope that 11 Group would be given respite, and that it would be able to recover and rally for the next phase of the battle.

If the Luftwaffe kept attacking London, they would have to leave his airfields alone. Which meant that the stations, including Biggin Hill and Tangmere, so badly shattered during the past two weeks, could be repaired and restored. And his harried and depleted fighter squadrons would have time for replenishment and reinforcement.

For about an hour and a half, from just before 7 pm. to just before 8:30 pm., the sky over the Greater London region was clear of enemy aircraft. But at about 7:45, the south coast Chain Home stations began sending ominous reports to Fighter Command Headquarters—another raid was building. By the time the bombers arrived over eastern London, the time was about 8:20.

Combined forces from *Luftflotte* 2 and *Luftflotte* 3 returned to the East End of London. They could hardly miss their target—the fires started that afternoon could be seen for miles away and made a brilliant bull's eye.

Unlike the massed bomber formations of the afternoon, which had rattled windows with the throb of engines, the evening attack arrived as a slow but steady procession of bombers. The Heinkels and Junkers came as solitary raiders, or sometimes in pairs. They had no need to hurry—there were no RAF night fighters to contend with, and the anti-aircraft fire was not very accurate.

Only one squadron of RAF Blenheims were up over London. The chances that the Blenheims' crews would even catch sight of a German bomber, much less get in position to attack one, were so slight as to be non-existent. An anti-aircraft battery actually had the good fortune—fantastically good luck is more like it—to bring down one Heinkel. Apart from this single instance, the Luftwaffe's air fleets went where they wanted to go, and did what they wanted to do.

What they did was to bring havoc to the residents of East London. For eight hours, from 8:20 pm. to 4:30 am., about 450 bombers dropped over 300 tons of high explosives and about 450 canisters of incendiaries. Well over 1,000 fires were started, including 9 that were officially labeled conflagrations by the London Fire Brigade—these called for the attention of 100 fire engines each.

This was a new kind of warfare—new to Britain, at least, but not new to the inhabitants of Warsaw or Rotterdam. Civilians were killed, injured, and made homeless by an impersonal enemy thousands of feet above them. When the homeless moved to a neighborhood shelter, taking as many possessions as they could carry, the shelter was also bombed.

In the district of West Ham, entire streets had been set on fire. A school was taken over as a temporary rest center for those who had lost their homes in the bombing. Then the school was hit by a bomb, killing about 450 homeless.

Fighter Command was being given a desperately needed reprieve. But their respite came at the expense of civilian homes and civilian lives—including the 450 in the West Ham rest center.

8 September, Sunday

"We wondered what old Adolf was up to now," a former Army private recalled. "We heard various rumours—the bombing of London would come first, then the invasion. That's the way the Germans did it in Holland and in Poland—bomb first, then invade. We didn't have the slightest clue what was happening—first we got the signal CROMWELL, then we heard that the invasion had been postponed. Nobody gave us any news at all. We only had rumours. All kinds of rumours."

It was just as well for Britain that the Germans did not invade. This private, along with the rest of his unit, had been assigned to guard the Sussex coast. Neither he nor any of his mates had a radio—if they spotted the German fleet approaching, one of them would be detailed to run a half-mile to the nearest telephone coin box to report the sighting. (He has often wondered what would have happened if he had sighted the enemy fleet, run at full-speed to the telephone—and discovered that he had no change to make the phone call!)

The invasion still had not been given the go-ahead by Adolf Hitler. But Göring remained convinced that his "area attacks" on London would be decisive, and would indeed be the preliminary to the landings on England's south coast. Because he thought that the bombings would be so vital, Göring ordered the raids to be intensified and expanded.

London was divided into two zones: A Section, which included the docks and eastern London; and B Section, which took up the rest of the city. Both A and B Sections would soon feel the Reichsmarschall's full wrath.

German newspapers were filled with stories of the "vengeance and reprisal" attack on London—an attack that was retribution for the RAF's raids on Berlin. The official communique reported: "Tonight, one great cloud of smoke extends from the centre of London to the mouth of the Thames."

The American news media also reported on the bombing—newspapers, magazines, and newsreel cameramen all sent stories and photos back to their home editorial offices. The Blitz, as it would come to be known, would prove a turning point in Britain's propaganda campaign in the United States. Pictures of ruined buildings and homeless refugees, stories about stout-hearted Cockneys who carried on in spite of the German air raids, helped recruit support and sympathy for Britain. (Censors made very sure that only positive stories were released, and blocked any and all references to rumors of panic in badly bombed areas.)

With the start of the Blitz, the Ministry of Information had a lever by which they could manipulate American sympathy. Before the bombing, broadcasts and news stories to the United States had mainly involved aerial combat—the daily fighting over southern England. While the American public was interested in the stories about the RAF versus the Luftwaffe, these news items did not elicit very much sympathy for Britain.

Even when Americans began to be persuaded that Britain could conceivably win the battle—and this took some doing—the mood of the country was still not terribly sympathetic. The British might be brave, courageous, and all that, but a lot of Americans still held a great many historical prejudices against their traditional foe.

The Blitz altered this mood, at least temporarily. When the Germans bombed London, the Ministry of Information made certain that photos of civilian targets, especially churches and hospitals, were given prominence; mention of military objectives was forbidden. Given a steady diet of such stories, Americans began to think of the Nazis as Huns, just as the British had been calling them all along.

In other words: Americans may not have been pro British, but the Blitz news stories were making them anti-Nazi. Which, from the Ministry of Information's point of view, was almost as good.

By shifting his main offensive from 11 Group's airfields to London, Göring not only allowed Fighter Command time to recover from the pommeling of the past two weeks, but, just as important, he also gave the Ministry of Information a priceless propaganda coup.

A few days before the Blitz started (on 4 September, to be exact), representatives from the MOI, the Air Ministry, and Home Security and Censorship (American Division) met to discuss how news stories and broadcasts could be more effective "in persuading America to give more help to this country." The bombing of London gave them the solution: allow American broadcasters and reporters to describe how ordinary working people had their lives changed and disrupted by the Blitz. This was a calculated move to make Americans more sympathetic toward Britain and her plight. If Americans became more sympathetic, they would also be willing to send more aid and assistance.

Just a year earlier, neither the Air Ministry, nor the Ministry of Information, nor anyone else in Britain, gave a damn what the Yanks thought of them. Now, American public opinion was as vital to the war effort as Fighter Command's supply of Spitfires and Hurricanes.

Luftflotte 2's bombers and fighters struck at 11 Group's airfields again—West Malling, Gravesend, and Hornchurch—as well as the towns of Sevenoaks, Gravesend, and Dover. These seemed to be only half-hearted efforts, though. West Malling reported sporadic raids throughout the day. Bombs fell on a road outside the airfield; telephone service was knocked out for the next 48 hours.

Between 12:15 and 12:30, Fighter Command lost five aircraft; two pilots were killed. Three of these were Hurricanes of 46 Squadron, as was one of the pilots. But the squadron was also credited with at least one Dornier of KG 2, which blew up near Maidstone. Two other Dorniers, also of KG 2, were shot down by anti-aircraft fire.

The Luftwaffe's main effort was aimed at London. Beginning at about 7:30 pm and continuing until five o'clock in the morning 247 twin-engine bombers unloaded their cargoes of high explosive and incendiaries over the city, almost at leisure. Over 330 tons of high explosive and 440 incendiary canisters landed on rail stations, power stations, the Natural History Museum, St. James Park, and streets filled with houses in East London's Dockland. More than 400 civilians were killed; hundreds more joined the ranks of the homeless—"bombed out" was the phrase.

The city had been injured—there was no question about it. Gas, water, and electricity services had been cut for entire districts. Rail services to the south were badly disrupted. But the blow had not been a mortal one. An official report to the War Cabinet commented: "While considerable damage had been done, the intensive bombing had comparatively little effect on undertakings engaged in war production."

Göring did not see a copy of this report. But even if he had seen it, he probably would not have paid any attention to it. The Reichsmarschall believed only what he wanted to believe. And he remained convinced that the only way to win the battle was by bombing London.

9 September, Monday

No air strikes at all were directed against Fighter Command. During the morning, the Luftwaffe did not fly any operational sorties. The first enemy formations of the day were plotted by Chain Home stations at about 4:20 pm., in groups ranging from a dozen or so bombers to more than 50 fighters.

Park received the CH warnings at 11 Group's headquarters in Uxbridge. He ordered nine squadrons to patrol the vicinity of Canterbury, as well as other points over Surrey, Essex, and Kent. Park had also been tipped by Ultra, and knew that the Luftwaffe

Articles and photos in American popular magazines reflect the change that had taken place in the United States by September. An illustrated piece in Life Magazine, called "Tactics In The Air War," clearly made the Germans seem the aggressors and showed the RAF as determined defenders of their country—a decided switch since July and August.

were on their way to London again; he was positioning his fighters to block the incoming raid.

Park's fighters were in the right place, but the bombers' Messerschmitt escort missed their rendezvous. The fighter pilots blamed the bombers for this failure to communicate, and vice versa.

As a result, the Spitfires and Hurricanes fell on the German bombers, in the words of a civilian onlooker, "like avenging angels."

The bombers radioed their plight to ground controllers in France. These messages were received as clearly in Kent as by the Luftwaffe controllers on the French coast. In response, the controllers gave formation leaders permission to turn away from their approach "if defences are too strong, or if fighter protection is too weak."

The defenses were definitely very strong. "The sky was full of roundels," KG 54's Kommodore Hans Trautloft said. "For the first time, we had the feeling we were outnumbered." In the course of this action, KG 54 lost only one Heinkel to fighters; that pilot was able to fly back to France, where he crashed outside of Paris. Other units were not as fortunate, however.

Spitfires of 66 Squadron shot down a Junkers of KG 30. Altogether, KG 30 lost 5 Junkers to the fury of the attacking Spitfires and Hurricanes.

For the rampaging fighter pilots, the kills were almost too easy—it was sometimes simply a matter of lining up the target, keeping out of the way of the bomber's rear gunner, and thumbing the firing button. Then, a half-roll and a dive out the bottom of the formation. If there was any ammunition left, the pilot would climb back up and do it again—always looking over his shoulder for Bf 109s, which kept themselves mysteriously absent.

Douglas Bader and his Duxford Wing also were on the scene. Bader had been ordered to patrol the Hornchurch-North Weald area, but decided to ignore the order. Instead, he took his wing—242 and 310 Squadrons' Hurricanes and 19 Squadron's Spitfires—south into Kent, climbing to 22,000 feet.

When he first caught sight of the bomber formations, Bader split his fighters—Spitfires to fly top cover, Hurricanes to attack the bombers. "Line astern, we're going through the middle," he announced to his Hurricane pilots.

Bader's Big Wing did its job—the concentrated attack of 24 Hurricanes rattled the bomber pilots into breaking their formations, jettisoning their bombs, and turning for France. Hundreds of tons of bombs were scattered across Kent, Sussex, and Surrey; the walled cathedral city of Canterbury was hit. The London districts of Wandsworth, Chelsea, and Lambeth also received some German bombs from individual aircraft that managed to evade the Spitfires and Hurricanes.

Even though strong complaints were lodged by the commanders of the bomber units about the lack of fighter cover, there were fighters up over southern England. The Spitfire pilots of 92 Squadron found this out the hard way. Six of 92's pilots were scrambled to intercept a formation of bombers on their way to London. Somewhere near Canterbury, they were jumped by Bf 109s.

This was the Squadron's first combat of the Battle, and served to be a very nasty initiation. Before anybody knew what had happened, two of the six Spitfires had been shot down. Another returned to Biggin Hill badly damaged. Two pilots had been wounded; none had been killed.

But from the Luftwaffe's point of view, the day had been a total waste. They lost 28 aircraft (the RAF lost 19 fighters), and had accomplished exactly nothing for their efforts. They did not bomb their objective; they did absolutely nothing at all to hinder the RAF's ability to wage war. Göring's plan to bring a quick victory by bombing London was certainly not having its desired effect. On this particular day, it was a total failure.

For the third night in a row, London came under a steady and determined attack from *Luftflotte 3*. For eight and a half hours, a total of 195 bombers toggled their loads over the city. Usually, they flew singly or in small groups. Nobody worried about night fighters.

For Oberleutnant Dieter Heibing of KG 51, the switch from bombing 11 Group's airfields to London was a great relief. Every time he had to attack the airfields, he was always scared stiff—those damn Spitfires were always around, and he was afraid that one of them would kill him. His Junkers had been shot up on two occasions. The first time, he crash-landed near Calais when his hydraulic system had been shot up. No one had been hurt, but that was just luck.

The second time had not been as lucky. They had just dropped their bombs on Biggin Hill and were straining for altitude when the Tommys struck. The guns of the fighters put several bullet holes through the clear perspex of the nose, killed the navigator outright, and hit the port engine. He brought the Junkers back to base on the one good engine—Heibing was sure that this was luck, as well.

But for the past three nights, Oberleutnant Heibing had not faced any danger from the defenses. None of his crew had even

A barrage balloon floats over the towers of the Houses of Parliament, against the glow of fires from a night bombing attack.

seen a night fighter. Anti-aircraft fire had been wildly inaccurate. He and the rest of his crew hoped that Reichsmarschall Göring was right, and that the bombing of London would bring a quick end to the war. Maybe then, he would live to see the end of it.

That night, 370 Londoners died in the bombing. The main damage was, once again, to the Docks and East End, but other districts were also damaged by scattered bombs. Hundreds more had been made homeless and, what was worse, none of the authorities were quite sure what to do about them.

In short, the Luftwaffe's bombing campaign against London was doing real damage to the city, and was also having a demoralizing effect upon its population. But it was not helping to pave the way for Operation Sea Lion, and was not doing anything to destroy RAF Fighter Command. The *Kriegsmarine* commented on this; the naval staff even went on to suggest that the ports of Dover be bombed instead of London. This might help to eliminate any threat by the Royal Navy to the imminent Sea Lion campaign.

But Göring insisted that the large-scale attack on London would make Sea Lion unnecessary. He still entertained the notion that RAF Fighter Command would send their Spitfires and Hurricanes up in large numbers to defend their capital, and that they would be shot down in large numbers by his *Jagdgeschwadern*. After this happened, the population of London would riot and demand an armistice, since this would be the only way to stop the bombing.

Adolf Hitler listened to this line from his friend, the Reichsmarschall. Whether he believed what he was hearing is another question. It is just possible that he had already half given up on the idea of an invasion—he already had his eyes turned toward the east.

In a broadcast to the United States on 9 September, Edward R. Murrow described the after-effects of the raid to millions of listeners. He noted that he had seen "men shovelling mounds of broken glass into trucks" from blasted windows, and that he had come across "the largest crater I've ever seen" from a bomb that smashed windows five or six blocks away. He also mentioned that the RAF "shot down three of the night bombers last night," which was a pipe dream.

One of his comments on the raid would have been pertinent for Hermann Göring: "This night bombing is serious and sensational. It makes headlines, kills people, and smashes property; but it doesn't win wars."

10 September, Tuesday

The Luftwaffe launched air strikes against RAF Fighter Command on this Tuesday, but these were mainly nuisance raids carried out by single bombers. The fairly heavy cloud helped the raiders by providing them with cover—the bombers stayed alone in the overcast, attacked their objectives, and then climbed back into the safety of the fleecy grey stuff again.

Nothing at all happened until about 5 pm. West Malling was bombed by a single raider; Tangmere was bombed and strafed, also by a lone German aircraft. The RAF lost its only fighter in action at around this time, when Pilot Officer Males of 72 Squadron became careless while trying to dispose of a Dornier Do 17.

P/O Males approached the Dornier from astern, deliberately holding his fire until he was well within machine gun range. This also brought him into the range of the Dornier's rear gunner, however. Males saw the muzzle flashes of the German machine gun, and felt his Spitfire shudder from hits an instant later.

Instead of trying to bail out, Males elected to attempt a crash landing. Luckily for him, a farmer's field presented itself; Males lowered his wheels and prepared for a rough landing. The landing turned out to be rougher than he expected when the Spitfire's notoriously delicate undercarriage collapsed—the strain of rolling through the soft earth at high speed proved to be too much. P/O Males walked away from the wreck, but his Spitfire was beyond repair.

About half an hour later, seven other small raids were picked up by coastal CH stations. Only one amounted to anything—a strike aimed at Biggin Hill. The station was such a ruin by this time, after weeks of bombing attacks, that it was a wonder that the Luftwaffe bothered anymore.

Actually, Biggin was attacked by only one bomber, a Do 17 of KG 76, and the crew of that aircraft did not enjoy their little triumph for very long. The pilot apparently tried to get away by flying a west-by-south course, instead of making straight for the Channel. He was intercepted by fighters and badly shot up over Sussex. As the pilot skimmed the ground, desperately pushing toward the coast, the Dornier was hit by ground fire. It crashed far short of the Channel coast; two of the crew were killed, the other two taken prisoner.

It had been a curious day. The Luftwaffe lost four airplanes, plus eight that had been blown up on the ground in an RAF raid. (The RAF lost one fighter: P/O Male's Spitfire.) The weather had not been much good for flying. For all the damage it inflicted upon Fighter Command, the Luftwaffe might just as well have stayed on the ground.

Reports from Fighter Command had been encouraging during the past few days—it had been enjoying its four-day respite, and was using the breathing space to make some much-needed repairs. Prime Minister Churchill told the War Cabinet this news in an early afternoon meeting, but also went on to warn that a powerful armada was being deployed by the Germans to invade Britain.

During the same meeting, steps were also discussed on how to thwart the invasion. Among the items mentioned were: re-inforcing shore defenses; increasing air strikes against German installations on the Continent; and increasing requests to America for aid and assistance.

London was bombed again after dark—this time by 148 bombers dropping 176 tons of high explosive and 289 incendiary canisters. The East End caught the brunt of the attack again—meaning, of course, the residents of the flimsy row houses in the vicinity of the docks.

The crisis that General Douhet had predicted—that the residents of a city would panic and revolt when they became targets of aerial bombing —was beginning to look like a grim possibility. The residents of West Ham and other East London districts were not yet on the brink of revolt. But they were very angry and resentful that the authorities had not done more for them in the way of building emergency shelters. Many had been bombed out and had nowhere to go except the most primitive rest centers.

Many of these rest centers had only the barest of essentials for housing the homeless; some did not even have mimimum amenities. Most had inadequate washing facilities, little bedding, not enough furniture, and few facilities for cooking. Inevitably, they were overcrowded. Plumbing was something that was non-existent—people simply used pails for latrines. The pails were not emptied until morning; by then, they were frequently overflowing.

Morale in the badly bombed areas was very low, to put it mildly. People grumbled that "something better be done." But before the situation got completely out of hand, volunteer workers took over and made the rest centers more livable—getting food from charities; sometimes borrowing utensils from church halls and schools; and sometimes cooking meals. Eventually, the government stepped in, and the crisis passed. But the first days of the Blitz were very nearly a catastrophe.

11 September, Wednesday

In spite of the fine, clear weather, the Luftwaffe stayed on the ground during the morning hours. In the afternoon, however, they made up for their lack of early activity.

The Hurricane pilots of 46 Squadron intercepted a raid over the Thames Estuary at about 3:30. In the resulting fight, three of the Hurricanes were lost, with one pilot killed and two injured.

At about the same time, 253 Squadron was giving another raid a hearty welcome over Sussex. The Hurricane pilots shot down two Bf 109s of JG 51; one of 253's Hurricanes was damaged.

A total of about 250 German aircraft, bombers and fighters, were making their push toward London. Some of the bombers jettisoned their loads over Kent. The determined Poles of 303 Squadron went after some Bf 109s while 229 Squadron, their partners for the day, dove after a formation of Dorniers and Heinkels. Sgt. Wojtowicz shot down one of the German fighters; moments later, he was shot down and killed himself.

But the Germans were numerous enough, and determined enough, to hack their way through to London. The East End and the docks received the loads of about 100 bombers.

While all this was going on, a small group of bombers from *Luftflotte 3* was making a shambles of the Supermarine plant at Southampton. They came in very low—one eyewitness estimated a height of only 100 feet—dropped their bombs, and zoomed off in the general direction of France.

Because they had come in so low and so fast, there had been no time to sound an air raid warning. Several bombs hit the

Plan view of Spitfire, showing the characteristic "elliptical" wings.

brand-new Cunliffe Owen plant, and effectively destroyed it—the factory had not even been officially opened yet. The roof over the airplane assembly area collapsed; steel girders crashed on top of one another. Among the debris were the bodies of the dead—the official count stood at 50, but some of the workers thought that the real total was nearer 70.

Following this—probably about an hour later—a gaggle of Bf 109s shot up the Dover barrage balloons—Dover had not been visited for a while, so they were probably overdue. Also, the coastal convoy Peewit was dive-bombed; the escort destroyer *Atherstone* was hit and damaged in this action.

It had been an afternoon of furious activity. Even though none of Fighter Command's airfields had been attacked, the Luftwaffe definitely got the best of the RAF. Twenty-nine fighters had been shot down; 17 pilots were killed, with an additional six injured. The Luftwaffe lost 25 aircraft, six of which were Bf 109s. (Nine Bf 110s also were shot down.)

Losses among RAF fighters probably would have been even higher if the Messerschmitt 109's range had been longer. The Bf

109 carried enough fuel for only about 15 minutes of combat in the London area. After this, the red warning light came on, and the pilots had to make straight for base before their fuel ran out.

Göring said that this would happen when London became the Luftwaffe's primary target—the RAF would come up in strength to defend the city, and would be shot down in droves. Luftwaffe intelligence made the day a bit more successful than it really was when it stated that 56 RAF fighters had been shot down—an overestimation of 27 aircraft.

But in addition to the 29 fighters shot down, one hundred German bombers had also struck at London. Also, the Supermarine plant at Southampton had been knocked out—which meant fewer brand-new Spitfires reaching RAF fighter squadrons. All in all, a highly satisfying day from Göring's point of view.

A decision would have to be made regarding the invasion of England, and would have to be made quickly. If an invasion were to be attempted in 1940, it would have to be launched by the end of September; otherwise, the weather would interfere with the landings. A tentative date for the invasion had been set for 21 September, which meant that the decision to go (or not) would have to be made today—it would take ten days for the Navy to clear enemy mines and make other preparations.

Hitler decided to postpone his go/no go decision for six days, until 17 September. This would give the Navy enough time to make its preparations, and would also give the Luftwaffe enough time to destroy the RAF, once and for all. Old Göring was always boasting about how marvellous his pilots were, and that they were always on the brink of destroying RAF Fighter Command. Today, the Reichsmarschall had a good day. This would give him six more days to live up to his boasting.

Hitler left it at that. On 17 September, he would make his decision on whether to invade Britain or not. Until then, it was up to Reichsmarschall Göring and his Luftwaffe.

The Prime Minister realized the urgency of the situation as much as Hitler. "This effort of the Germans to secure mastery of the air over England is, or course, the crux of the whole war," he said in an address. He went on to advise that for Hitler "to try to invade this country without having secured mastery of the air would be a very hazardous undertaking."

He went on to tell the public—American as well as British, since he knew that his speech would also be released in the United States—that an assault force was being gathered in harbors all along the Continent's northern coast, "all the way from Hamburg to Brest." He also gave a warning that "no one should blind himself to the fact that a heavy full-scale invasion of this island is being prepared with all the German thoroughness."

In summing up, Churchill used an inspiring blend of history and drama: "Therefore, we must regard the next week or so as a very important period in our history. It ranks with the days when the Spanish Armada was approaching the Channel, or when Nelson stood between us and Napoleon's Grand Armee at Boulogne."

One hundred eighty bombers dropped another 217 tons of HE (High Explosives) on London during the night, as well as 148 clusters of incendiaries. The docks and the old City district—the old square mile that surrounded St. Paul's Cathedral—received the brunt of the attack, although other areas also felt the Luftwaffe's hand.

During the day, the air raid sirens had already sounded several times. The night raids were an added ordeal. Some Londoners were growing resigned to the raids. Everybody wanted to hit back at the raiders.[20]

On this particular night, the guns of Anti-Aircraft Command put up more than their usual effort—the guns of London fired about 13,500 rounds of ammunition. To Londoners, this was just what they had been waiting for. The noise of the guns was ear-shattering, even at a distance of several streets. But Londoners loved it.

---

20   Several Londoners said that they never "got used to" the raids; they just
      endured them.

Actually, the anti-aircraft shells were doing more damage to buildings in the city than to the Luftwaffe. Splinters from bursting shells broke skylights, and sometimes even damaged roofs. But the guns gave the illusion of getting back at the raiders—they might have been ineffective, but they were good for morale. And the exploding shells sometimes did make the bombers fly higher, which only served to scatter their loads over a wider area.

12 September, Thursday

Cloud and rain kept the Luftwaffe on the ground, except for a few small raids. When these raiders presented themselves, Spitfire and Hurricane pilots went after them. Two Ju 88s of KG 1 were intercepted in the course of a raid. One made it back to base with two injured crew members; the other Junkers crashed, with loss of life to all four crew.

Total losses came to four bombers for the Luftwaffe. The Chain Home station at Fairlight had been bombed, although the station stayed on the air and no one had been killed in the attack. The RAF lost one fighter, a Hurricane of 213 Squadron, in a flying accident, along with its pilot. No aircraft were lost as a result of enemy action.

London was bombed again at night, although weather curtailed the Luftwaffe's activities. Between 40 and 45 bombers took part—numbers vary, depending upon which source is consulted—and about 50 tons of high explosives were dropped.

One of the bombs came to earth next to St. Paul's Cathedral. It missed the southwest tower by a few feet, and began to sink into the soft earth until it imbedded itself underneath the Cathedral walls. If it blew up, it would destroy St. Paul's—not only destroying one of London's most famous landmarks, but also further damaging the city's already shaky morale.

The bomb disposal squad set to work excavating the thing—it had slipped to a depth of 28 feet beneath the ground. The squad, commanded by Lieutenant Davies of the Royal Engineers, erected a system of pulleys to haul the bomb to the surface. It slipped back during their first two attempts, but on the third attempt they succeeded.

Lt. Davies and his squad carefully loaded the bomb onto a flat vehicle, and packed it so that it would not roll or slide. It was eight feet long, carried a ton of high explosives, and was probably a naval mine, designed for use against ships at sea. Davies drove the bomb through London to Hackney Marshes—he refused to take anyone else with him. When it was exploded a few hours later, it blew a crater 100 feet across.

News services wanted to spread the word about how Lt. Davies saved St. Paul's—especially to the United States, where it would have made an excellent propaganda piece. But the censors stopped it—naming specific places or locations was strictly forbidden, since it might be useful to the Germans.

At about this time, the Air Ministry came up with an idea involving the American pilots on service in the RAF: why not form an all-American squadron? Even if it served no other purpose, an all-American squadron would be a gold mine for propaganda. The three Yanks of 609 Squadron—Red Tobin, Andy Mamedoff, and Shorty Keough—received more publicity in the United States than all the other fighter squadrons in the RAF combined. If three Yanks were worth that much to the American press, an entire squadron of 12 Yanks should be worth at least four times as much.

By September, enough Americans were serving with operational units, or were training in OTUs, to form a full squadron. The Air Ministry's original idea apparently was to change 609 Squadron into the first squadron composed entirely of Americans—or at least almost entirely.

Chesley Peterson had been one of the three young Americans stopped by the FBI on their way to Canada and given a choice—go back home, or go to jail. He tried again; this time, he made it across to Canada and into the RAF. By September 1940, he was assigned to an OTU at Hawarden, learning how to fly a Spitfire.

On 20 September, Pilot Officer Peterson was on a readiness flight from Hawarden, and took part in the destruction of a Heinkel He 111 near Liverpool. "As a wingman I observed but did not participate ...the flight leader did the shooting," he said.

Peterson remained at Hawarden for about another month, when he was posted to 609 Squadron. By that time, Tobin, Keough, and Mamedoff had been sent to join the brand-new 71 (Eagle) Squadron. Before he had a chance to join 609, Peterson was also transferred to the first Eagle Squadron, based at Church Fenton, Yorkshire.[21] The Eagles would prove to be a colorful, irritating—and highly publicized—group of rugged individualists, who annoyed senior RAF officers as much as they harried the Luftwaffe.

Whether anyone liked it or not—and there were any number of people on both sides of the Atlantic who hated the very idea—the Yanks in the RAF were there to stay.

13 September, Friday

Rain and cloud intervened for the second day in a row, limiting the Luftwaffe's operations.

About 1:30, small raids attempted to harrass the Fighter Command fields at Tangmere and Biggin Hill. The raiders were intercepted by RAF squadrons near the Channel coast. A Ju 88 of *Lehrgeschwader 1* encountered Hurricanes of 501 Squadron, and was badly shot up. The pilot managed to fly the Junkers back to base, but it was too badly damaged to be repaired.

In the same action, 501 Squadron lost a Hurricane when its pilot, Sgt. Lacy, was hit by machine gun fire from a Heinkel's rear gunner. The Hurricane's radiator was damaged by the German gunner's accurate fire; Sgt. Lacy baled out, slightly burned.

---

21 Chesley Peterson would transfer to the U.S.Army Air Force in September 1942, when the three Eagle Squadrons—71 Squadron, 121 Squadron, and 133 Squadron—became the 4th Fighter Group, USAAF. Eventually, he would become a Brigadier General in the U.S. Air Force.

The Spitfire pilots of 609 Squadron reported sighting Ju 87 Stukas on their way to bomb Tangmere. One of 609's pilots claimed to have attacked the starboard bomber in a formation of three, diving from 3,000 feet above the formation. His target caught fire, turned over, and went down.

London had been the subject of attacks by single aircraft during the morning. One of the bombers made a deliberate attack on Buckingham Palace; both the King and Queen were in residence, and were only about 800 yards from the nearest explosion.

In a famous quote, Queen Elizabeth said, "I'm glad we've been bombed," because it made her feel that she could "look the East End in the face."

The bombing of the Palace provided an excellent source for propaganda, both at home and in the United States. But, once again, the censors intervened—naming specific locations in news releases was strictly forbidden. This time, though, Prime Minister Churchill had something to say. "Dolts, idiots, stupid fools!" Churchill shouted. "Spread the news at once. Let it be broadcast everywhere. Let the humble people of London know that the King and Queen are sharing their perils with them."

The news was spread. East Enders did find some comfort in knowing that other parts of London had been bombed, even the Royal Family in the Palace. But the word was also spread to the United States, for entirely different reasons.

British propagandists were still hard at work to convince Americans that the RAF was winning the battle. Since the Blitz against London began, they also had another goal—to show the U.S. that Britain would not crack under the strain of German bombing.

Some American newsmen had expressed doubts that London would be able to hold out against the German Blitz. They fully realized that the Luftwaffe was a formidable opponent, and remembered what the German air force had done to both Warsaw and Rotterdam. Reporters and correspondents from the United States had to be shown positive images of London under fire, and the Buckingham Palace bombing was made to order—photos and stories appeared in the American press of a cheerful King and Queen bravely inspecting the damage done to their London home.

Britain would continue to use white propaganda against the United States, to prove to Americans that the British were worthy allies, and to show that they were not about to be subdued by the beastly Huns. Churchill was determined to bring the Yanks into the war, whether they liked it or not; at this stage, the best method was to coax them with propaganda. The Blitz would provide him with many opportunities.

Apart from the propaganda war, the day was a minor event in the battle. The Luftwaffe lost four aircraft. The RAF lost one fighter: Sgt. Lacy's Hurricane.

14 September, Saturday

Rain and cloud once again put a damper on operations. But the Luftwaffe could not afford to let up its offensive. During the morning, ground crews throughout northern France prepared aircraft, both fighters and bombers, for sorties against Britain. Because of the weather, air strikes would have to be limited. But there would be air strikes, and the main target would be London.

The first raiders did not make their presence known until mid-afternoon. Just after 3 pm., formations of fighters and bombers approached London from the south and east. The RAF sent fighters from both 11 Group and 12 Group to intercept.

Above Kent, and over the Thames Estuary, dozens of individual combats broke out as the German pilots tried to break through to London. Thousands of observers watched from the ground.

One ten year-old boy recalled the air fighting that afternoon:

> "It was my tenth birthday. My friend Billy and myself were outside watching the German planes flying north, presumably toward London, when a bunch of our fighters dove on them. I thought they were Spitfires, but Billy, who was our expert on aircraft identification, said they were Hurricanes.

An early model of the Messerschmitt Bf 109, taken before the war. Although the Bf 109 had its faults—mainly its narrow undercarriage, which was the cause of numerous take-off and landing accidents—it was the Luftwaffe's fighter mainstay throughout the war, and had undergone many modifications by 1945.

"The fighters shot at the bombers, and one of them started to smoke and lose height. The German plane remained on course, but kept on losing height until it was out of sight beyond the trees.

"Later in the day, another friend gave me an empty brass machine gun casing. I thought it was the best birthday present I ever had!"

The next wave of raids began at about 5:30, with a series of small attacks—between 10 and 35 aircraft each. Their target was London, but the goal of the combined bomber-fighter forces also was to harrass RAF Fighter Command as much as possible. They succeeded in both of their aims—not only did the bombers get through to London, but the escorting Messerschmitts gave intercepting RAF fighters a very nasty shock.

At about 6 pm., 253 Squadron lost two Hurricanes over Kent—both to Bf 109s. One of the pilots was able to jump clear, but had to be hospitalized because of his injuries. The second pilot was still in the cockpit when his Hurricane smashed into the ground and blew up.

In the same action, Spitfires of 72 Squadron and Bf 109s of LG 1 also went at each other. The Spitfire pilots shot down a Messerschmitt, which crashed near Ashford, Kent; the German pilots accounted for one of 72 Squadron's Spitfires.

The day had not been a good one for the RAF. Although the Luftwaffe lost 14 aircraft, Fighter Command also had 14 fighters destroyed, and lost six pilots, as well. (The Luftwaffe had only four fighters shot down, all Bf 109s.) And the main thrust toward London had not been stopped, in spite of the losses and the efforts of 860 sorties flown.

Adolf Hitler had not been greatly impressed by the RAF's performance; their defense of London seemed ragged and not very co-ordinated. Maybe Göring's optimistic appraisal—that Fighter Command was on the brink of burning itself out—was right, after all.

Hitler met with Luftwaffe Chief of Air Staff Hans Jeschonnek, Army Commander-in-Chief Walther von Brauchitsch, and *Grossadmiral* Raeder to talk about Operation Sea Lion, and what to do about it. Hitler had lost much of his enthusiasm for the invasion, largely because RAF Fighter Command did not seem to be falling apart the way that Göring said it would. But Admiral Raeder insisted that the landings were indispensable—a surprising change of mind. And the latest Luftwaffe figures showed that *der Dicke* might not be as full of hot air as everybody thought.

"A successful landing, followed by an occupation, would win the war," Hitler rightly concluded. He did not want a long war, and wanted Britain neutralized before either the Russians or the Americans could involve themselves in the fighting. Everything was in position for the invasion—the Navy was ready; so was the Army. Only the Luftwaffe still had its work cut out.

"The air attacks against London will be continued, the target area to be expanded," Hitler ordered. As for Operation Sea Lion: "A new order will follow on the 17th. All preparations to continue."

In other words, the invasion was still on—but everything depended upon the Luftwaffe. Sea Lion had been postponed for three more days, to give the air force more time to winnow down the RAF. The weather forecast was for a bright, sunny day tomorrow, 15 September, and the Luftwaffe had another *gross-einsatz* scheduled. Hitler decided to wait and see what tomorrow would bring, and then make his final decision concerning Sea Lion.

15 September, Sunday

"I say, better wake up." Red Tobin stirred, groggily and reluctantly, and found squadron mate John Dundas shaking his shoulder and staring into his face.

Tobin had spent the previous night in a pub with his fellow American, Shorty Keough, and did not feel much like either rising or shining. The hut was dark and cold, and he was still half asleep. He asked Dundas exactly why the hell he should get out of bed at that particular moment, when the world was still dark and he could not even open his eyes.

"I'm not quite sure, old boy," Dundas replied, "they say there's an invasion on or something."

This struck Red as being a very good reason—although he was as impressed by Dundas' nonchalant reply as by his information. He got out of bed and looked outside the hut for any sign of any activity. He could just see the silhouettes of 609 Squadron's Spitfires against the faintly brightening sky, along with a few other huts scattered around the station at Warmwell. There was certainly no sign of anything as dramatic as a German invasion.

As it turned out, Red Tobin had grounds for complaining about being rousted out of bed at dawn. Except for the usual early reconnaissance flights, the Luftwaffe did not stir until late in the morning.

Ultra had picked up heavy radio traffic from Luftwaffe aerodromes, which tipped Fighter Command that they could expect a major effort later in the day. But CH stations along the Channel coast did not begin plotting German formations until 11:00 am.: 40-plus, followed by a smaller formation; then another 40-plus. At about 11:30, the first enemy aircraft began moving north, toward the coast.

The warning gave 11 Group about 30 minutes to get ready. By the time the Luftwaffe had formed up and turned toward the Channel, seventeen RAF squadrons were in position—including a Big Wing from 12 Group: five squadrons led by Douglas Bader.

At 11 Group Headquarters, the excitement had begun an hour before the first warning; Prime Minister Winston Churchill dropped in for an unexpected visit at about 10:30. The Prime Minister went down the Hole, the nerve center of 11 Group that was situated under fifty feet of ground, just off Hillingdon Golf Course, to see if anything was happening. At 10:30, no one was sure exactly what was going to take place. But by noon, the enemy had shown his hand.

The first raid, about 200 aircraft, began crossing the south coast just before noon. Prime Minister Churchill watched the incoming raid's course being plotted on the great table map, and said to Air Vice Marshal Park, "There appear to be a great many aircraft coming in." Park instantly replied, "There'll be someone there to meet them."

And there was someone there—five squadrons of Spitfires and Hurricanes, including 609 Squadron from Warmwell. Red Tobin heard Squadron Leader Darley's voice over his headset: "Many, many bandits at 7 o'clock." Red himself saw 50 Bf 109s several thousand feet above, and 25 Dorniers about 1,000 feet below. Tobin's flight, Red Section, was preparing to attack the Dorniers in spite of the Messerschmitts overhead.

Red was assigned the unenviable position of Ass-End Charlie again, weaving behind the leader and his wingman to protect their tails. The leader had already told Tobin, "OK, Charlie, come on in." But before joining up, Tobin executed one more weave. As he swung his Spitfire, he caught sight of three yellow-nosed Bf 109s charging in from astern.

"Danger, Red Section! Danger! Danger! Danger!" Tobin shouted into his microphone—loud enough, he thought, to be heard back in Kansas. His leader dove to starboard, the wingman climbed to port, and Tobin threw his Spitfire into a 360° turn. He knew that the German pilots would never be able to pull out of their dive; if he kept turning, they would not get him.

The Messerschmitts shot past, as Tobin had calculated. As the last one passed, Tobin was able to get his gunsight on him. He fired a burst, and saw smoke trailing from it as all three of the Bf 109s disappeared. Red felt his blood pounding; it had been a close call.

The bombers, escorted by Bf 109s and Bf 110s, pressed steadily toward London. To some onlookers on the ground, the approaching aircraft reminded them of swarms of insects. Fighter pilots saw the enemy aircraft from a different point of view, however; they were overwhelmed by the sheer number of them. Red Tobin could see 100-plus German airplanes. Within minutes after the first interception, the sky over Kent was filled with individual fights, falling airplanes, and parachutes.

Among the squadrons that had its hands more than full was 609. John Dundas, who had shaken Red Tobin awake a few hours before, shot down a bomber over Kent, made another attack on a Dornier, and managed to evade several Bf 109s—all within a few minutes. Andy Mamedoff and Shorty Keough, Red Tobin's fellow Americans, shot up a Dornier with four other Spitfire pilots; each claimed one-sixth of the bomber.

Red Tobin's fight had not ended after his altercation with the three yellow-nosed Messerschmitts. After pulling out of his 360° turn, Red caught sight of a Dornier making a shallow dive—the pilot had spotted Red's Spitfire, and was heading for the saftey of cloud cover. Red pushed the stick forward and went after the bomber—he knew that he would never be able to find it if it reached the clouds.

He pulled out of his dive gently—remembering what would happen if he yanked back on the stick—and lined up the bomber in his gunsight. Immediately after pressing the firing button, Tobin saw the Dornier's port engine take several hits. White smoke began pouring from the stricken engine—either the radiator or the glycol tank had been punctured.

He lost the bomber momentarily, and had to come round again. This time, he came in on the Dornier's starboard side. He held the gunsight on the starboard wing, held the firing button down for several seconds, and watched as bits of aileron and wing blew off.

The stricken Dornier dove through the clouds. Tobin chased it through the layer of overcast, and saw it crash-land in a field. The bomber hit the ground, ploughed its way across the grass, and come to a bone-jarring stop. As Red circled the wreck, three crew members made their way out of the fuselage and sprawled across the starboard wing.

But Red was not absolutely sure that this was the Dornier that he had brought down. He had lost sight of his victim as it passed through the clouds, and he could see another Dornier in another field a quarter mile away. He could also see the wreckage of a Spitfire, a Hurricane, and a Bf 110. Beyond these, he could see other wrecks from other combats.

There were certainly enough individual fights going on at the same time as Red Tobin's. The entire southern route to London, from the Channel coast to the city's southern outskirts, seemed a whirling melee of aircraft. Contrails criss-crossed the sky in an insane pattern of white brush strokes. Sixteen-year-old Michael Bennett rode his bicycle to the top of a hill and watched—everywhere he looked, he could see descending parachutes and falling airplanes.

Most of the bombers reached London, as they usually did, and unloaded their bombs. Explosions could be heard throughout the city. One bomb ruined the Queen's apartments in Buckingham Palace; neither she nor King George were in residence.

By this time, the Bf 109s were starting to run low on fuel. The red warning lights were coming on, telling pilots that it was time to turn back toward France. As the Messerschmitts pointed

Contrails over London. This photo, taken on 15 September, gives an idea of the ferocity of the fighting on that day—a chaos of white contrails against a blue background, as hunter pursued hunted. More than 200 RAF fighters were in the air over London, and at least that many Luftwaffe fighters as well. The foreground silhouette is the dome of St. Paul's Cathedral.

their noses southeastward, they left the bombers very much on their own. For the pilots and crews of the Heinkels and Dorniers, the timing could not have been worse. At about the same time that the Bf 109s began breaking for home, Douglas Bader's Big Wing from 12 Group arrived on the scene: five squadrons, 59 fighters. They arrived late—moving five squadrons as a unit required a lot of time for grouping and maneuvering and, as Keith Park had been insisting, was not really a practical way to attack the enemy. (Bader complained that he was late because he had not been given enough warning.)

All of the Messerschmitts had not yet withdrawn when Bader and his Wing reached Kent. Squadron Leader Jack Satchell of 302 (Polish) Squadron observed that "a number of 109s" were still with the bombers, and that they "attacked us as soon as we arrived." But they soon had to turn back, as well, allowing the Duxford Wing to pounce.

One of the most famous air combats of the day, which also became one of the Ministry of Information's most prominent propaganda successes, was led by one of the Duxford Wing's squadrons. Flight Lieutenant Jeffries of 310 (Czech) Squadron, attacked a Dornier of KG 76 along with three other Hurricane pilots. F/Lt. Jeffries set the bomber's port engine on fire. His three squadron mates followed close behind, chopping away with bursts of machine gun fire.

With one engine out, the Dornier, piloted by Oberleutnant Robert Zehbe, was now easy prey. Spitfires of 609 Squadron, flown by P/O Keith Ogilvie and his wingman, also went after the bomber.

At this time, two of the crew wisely elected to abandon the aircraft; the gunner either dead or wounded, remained on board. Oblt. Zehbe was still at the controls when Sgt. Ray Holmes of 504 (Hurricane) Squadron came across the stricken airplane and also attacked it. Zehbe bailed out during Sgt. Holmes' attack.

Very shortly after Zehbe jumped, the now-abandoned Dornier (except for the presumably dead gunner) went into a violent spin and broke in half. The tail section fell on the roof of a building on Vauxhall Bridge Road in Westminster—not "just outside a Pimlico public house," as was later reported. The foreward half, minus the outboard segments of both wings, crashed into the forecourt of Victoria Railway Station.

Sgt. Holmes' Hurricane also went into a spin immediately after firing his burst at the Dornier. He baled out, landing either in a garbage can in Ebury Bridge Road, Pimlico, or on a rooftop in Chelsea, depending on which source is consulted. Oblt. Zehbe parachuted into the London district of Kensington, where he had to be rescued from a bunch of outraged civilians. He died of injuries received during the air battle.

The press made much of this incident, with the full help and co-operation of the Ministry of Information. The story released was that Oblt. Zehbe's Dornier was the same airplane that had bombed Buckingham Palace. Pilot Officer Keith Ogilvie was given a personal commendation by Queen Wilhelmina of the Netherlands; she had been a guest at Buckingham Palace, and wanted to thank P/O Ogilvie for his concern over her personal safety.

Photos of the crashed Dornier's remains appeared in newspapers and magazines throughout Britain and the United States, along with a dramatic photo of the bomber, its tail section and outboard sections of both wings clearly missing, as it plunged toward Victoria Station. One of the American releases identified the wrecked bomber: "believed to be the plane that bombed Buckingham Palace on the 15th"—another propaganda attempt at American sympathy.

Thus was yet another myth created about the Battle of Britain. This time, the facts were distorted deliberately—in the name of propaganda— to sway the opinion of neutral America.

By this time, the Spitfire and Hurricane squadrons were returning to base for re-fuelling and re-arming; although four squadrons still had enough fuel and ammunition left to harrass the retiring German bombers all the way to the Channel coast. As the fighters touched down, the "At Readiness" lights on the tote board of 11 Group Headquarters began to go out. Prime Minister Churchill, watching the scene from the gallery, asked Air Vice-Marshal Park, "What reserves have we?"

Park replied, "There are none."

If Sperrle and Kesselring had launched another strike at this time, while most of 11 Group was on the ground, the Luftwaffe would have had the upper hand. Such a strike would have left their airfields in France before the RAF squadrons could have become airborne. The bombers would have been halfway to their targets before the fighters could have been scrambled. When they had finally been serviced and took off to intercept, the Spitfires and Hurricanes would have been jumped by Messerschmitts.

But the Luftwaffe had no attack prepared. The fighter and bomber units remained at their bases in France, waiting to see what was going to happen next. The Messerschmitt *Geschwad-*

ern, like their RAF counterparts, were replenished with fuel and ammunition.

Red Tobin approached the grass landing area at Warmwell with a destroyed Dornier to his credit and seven gallons of gasoline in his tank. He made a good approach, but did not see the crash wagon charge out from behind a hangar and into his path. One of his wheels hit the top of the vehicle, snapping it back into the well in the fuselage.

The landing wheel was jammed in the "up" position. Red had no choice but to land on one wheel—he did not have enough fuel to do anything else. The one-legged landing badly damaged the Spitfire. It would fly again, but not before undergoing some major repairs. Red was grounded, at least for the rest of the day—Warmwell was only a satellite field; there was no extra Spitfire on the station for him to fly.

At bases throughout 11 Group, as well as at Debden in 12 Group, the pilots straggled in. The ground crews for each individual fighter were quick to check whether or not the guns had been fired; some pilots side-slipped to make a distinctive hollow sound as air passed over the open gun ports (the same noise that is made by blowing into a bottle). After they landed, the pilots returned to their dispersal hut to report their activities, as well as any aircraft shot down, to the Intelligence Officer, and to fill out combat reports.

While this was going on, the airplanes were being looked after by their fitters, riggers, mechanics, and armorers. Fuel tanks were re-filled by squat gasoline tankers called "petrol bowsers"; armorers replenished the .303 Brownings with long belts of ammunition. Also, the aircraft was checked for any bullet holes and battle damage.

Everyone was certain that the Luftwaffe would be back. The pilots tried to relax by reading or kicking a football around, or vainly to get some sleep. But when the loudspeaker made its first metallic click, even before any announcement was made, the pilots' nerves jarred them to full alertness.

About an hour after the last of the Luftwaffe raiders departed for France, CH stations began plotting another German build-up over the Continent. The announcement to scramble came at about 1:45 for twelve squadrons, sending the tense pilots sprinting for their Spitfires or Hurricanes.

By the time the pilots reached their aircraft, the engines had already been started. Then it was onlly a matter of clipping on parachutes and, a minute later, they were in the cockpits, rolling across the grass at full throttle.

The usual scramble took only a couple of minutes, from the first terse announcement to actual take-off. As a matter of fact, a group of high-ranking American military and naval officers had been at Hendon that morning, to see how long it actually did take.[22] They used stop watches to time 504 Squadron's Hurricane pilots in their rush to intercept. The 12 Hurricanes got away in 4 minutes and 50 seconds.

The Luftwaffe's formations began crossing the coast at about 2:15. Each formation consisted of between 30 and 40 bombers and twice as many fighters, both Bf 109s and Bf 110s.

In spite of the fighter escort—or maybe because so many of the escorting fighters were the lumbering Bf 110s—the Spits and Hurricanes managed to break through to the bombers. The Hurricane pilots of 605 Squadron closed with Dorniers of KG 3 near Maidstone, Kent. Pilot Officer Michael Cooper-Slipper felt his Hurricane shudder when one of the German gunners hit its fuselage. He reached the conclusion that his airplane had been destroyed, and that he would attack the Dorniers by the only method he had left—ramming.

Very calmly and deliberately, not thinking of the possible consequences to himself, Cooper-Slipper aimed his Hurricane at the middle aircraft of a three-Dornier formation. He flew straight into the bomber, and was surprised by the easiness of the bump—not a violent collision at all, just a dull thud. The Hurricane's port wing flew off, and Cooper-Slipper bailed out.

---

22 Generals Strong and Emmons, U.S. Army Air Corps, and Admiral Gormley, USN.

As he vacated the fighter's cockpit, he had a fleeting impression of the Dornier falling away.

It took more than 40 minutes for him to descend 20,000 feet by parachute. He came down in a hops field, and was nearly lynched by farm hands who thought he was a German. When the police arrived to take charge, the field hands fought to keep Cooper-Slipper in their own custody—by that time, they had discovered that he was an RAF pilot, and did not want to give him up.

Eventually, Cooper-Slipper was taken back to Croydon. His kindly chauffeur stopped at every pub between Kent and Surrey. And at every pub, the patrons bought him drinks—it wasn't every day that they got the chance to drink with a real, live fighter pilot. By the time P/O Cooper-Slipper arrived back at Croydon, he was so drunk that he could hardly walk.

A second wave of German aircraft reached the coast at about 2:30; the third wave arrived about 10 minutes later. Each wave was made up of at least 60 aircraft, and each formation made its way directly toward London.

This time, the intercepting RAF squadrons found the bombers protected by a very determined escort of Bf 109s. Spitfire and Hurricane pilots tried to press through, but the Messerschmitts would not allow them anywhere near the Dorniers and Heinkels. Within five minutes, 303 (Polish) Squadron lost two Hurricanes and one pilot killed, as well as five more Hurricanes damaged. By the end of the day, only four of the squadron's fighters would still be serviceable.

Sgt. Leslie Pidd of 238 Squadron had his Hurricane shot up by a Bf 110, and bailed out over Kenley. While he was descending by parachute, Pidd was machine-gunned by a German fighter. He was dead when he landed.

Shooting men in parachutes was just the sort of thing expected from "the Hun;" Sgt. Pidd's squadron mates were understandably outraged. But Dowding's reaction to this very delicate subject comes as something of a surprise.

After the battle was over, Dowding commented on the ethics of machine gunning pilots and crew who bailed out of their airplanes. Germans who parachuted over Britain were potential prisoners of war, Dowding said, and should be immune to such treatment. But RAF pilots were still combatants—they could be driven back to their bases, and be back in combat the same day. As such, German pilots were "perfectly entitled" to shoot at RAF airmen in parachutes. (This opinion was written in 1941 but, wisely, not published until 1946, after the war was over and tempers had been given time to cool.)[23]

But many of the bombers had missed their rendezvous with their fighter escort, and began circling in the vicinity of Maidstone—apparently waiting for the Messerschmitts to appear. When they began moving north toward London, it took the bombers a half hour to travel the 60 miles between the Channel coast and London.

By this time, many more RAF squadrons had arrived to intercept—including the five squadrons of Douglas Bader's Big Wing. An estimated 170 Spitfires and Hurricanes were in position to attack before Bader arrived with 60 more fighters. And, once again, the hated red warning lights were beginning to appear on Bf 109 instrument panels—indicating only 15 minutes of fuel left.

Many of the bombers had reached London, as they always did, and hit scattered districts throughout the city. Specific targets were not pinpointed; apparently, the bomb-aimers were releasing their loads at random. Train service in and out of London was slowed to a near crawl; telephone and telegraph lines were damaged; hundreds more Londoners were made homeless by bomb blast and fire.

But the formations were being shot to pieces by the RAF pilots. *Kampfgeschwader 53* had six Heinkels destroyed and two more damaged; one badly shot-up Heinkel crash-landed at West Malling airfield. *Kampfgeschwader 2* lost eight Dorniers, with four more damaged. Group Captain Stanley Vincent, a veteran

---

23   When a former U.S. Air Force pilot was shown this statement, he roared that
      this was a "ridiculous overdevelopment of so-called 'British fair play," and that
      only a British officer could "come up with such a half-assed reaction."

of the First World War who was now Northolt's station commander, broke up a formation of eight Dorniers by attacking head-on. The eight bombers turned for France, shaken by his single-handed attack.

Spitfire and Hurricane squadrons attacked the bombers over London, and harried them when they scattered and broke for the Channel. The chasing and harrassing went on until after 4 pm., when the last of the German bombers reached the safety of France. Many of them landed with dead and wounded on board; some of the airplanes would never fly again.

The day was not quite over, however. Just before 6 pm., about 20 Bf 110 fighter-bombers of *Erprobungsqruppe* 210 attacked the Supermarine plant at Southampton. The pilots of the twin-engined airplanes showed steely determination, diving straight through a murderous anti-aircraft barrage. The airplanes came down in fast, shallow dives, in two waves of 10 planes each. After dropping their bombs, they zoomed away, re-formed, and disappeared.

Eyewitnesses on the ground were greatly impressed by the flying skill of the German pilots—they had obviously been well-trained, and flew as a highly disciplined and co-ordinated team. Their flying ability was a lot more impressive than their marksmanship, however—none of their bombs landed anywhere near the Southampton factory.

All of *Erpro* 210's twin-engined Messerschmitts returned to their French bases without any damage at all. But in spite of their fancy flying, and their unquestioned bravery, the pilots had not accomplished a thing; production and delivery of Supermarine Spitfires suffered no interruption, except for a few minutes when factory workers took cover in air raid shelters.

Erpro 210's departure for France marked the end of fighting on 15 September.[24] The thrusting and parrying between RAF

---

24   At about 3 pm., Heinkel He 111s of KG 55 attacked the docks at Portsmouth, and were set upon by RAF fighters. One of the bombers was shot down; another returned to base badly shot up.

Fighter Command and the Luftwaffe had been hard and intense, but not as hard as it had been in late August and early September. The RAF lost 26 fighters and 13 pilots; several squadrons were demoralized by the day's losses, including 303 Squadron's Poles. It seemed as though the killing would never stop.

Now that the fighting had ended for the day, at least, the propaganda battle of 15 September began. The Luftwaffe claimed 78 of the RAF's fighters as destroyed, a figure that the Propaganda Ministry broadcast throughout Germany and its occupied territories.

Britain's Ministry of Information also threw itself into high gear. The RAF claimed 185 German airplanes shot down; the MOI released this claim not only throughout the British Isles and Commonwealth countries, but also made certain that the American press received it. This claim, as it turned out, was just as inflated as the Luftwaffe's. The postwar British total was given as 60 German aircraft destroyed; postwar German records show that the Luftwaffe lost 56 airplanes, with 2 missing.

But in wartime, truth plays a minor role, at best. The number 185 sounded a lot more impressive than either 56 or 60, so this was the number that was released. Newspapers and magazines, on both sides of the Atlantic, published the story that 185 German raiders had been shot down. Even War Cabinet ministers were regaled with the news that 186 enemy aircraft had been shot down—no one has ever attempted to explain where the additional German airplane came from—along with 46 probables. The figure did not have to be accurate, just dramatic.

In the United States, this line of propaganda and misinformation was having its desired effect. Even Britain's arch-bogeymen, the isolationists—including the America First Committee—were becoming convinced that the British were able to hold their own against the Luftwaffe, even though they were still unwilling to send anything in the way of aid or assistance. American interventionists used the news of 185 German aircraft destroyed as an argument for coming into the war on Britain's side. Their argument was: because the RAF were clearly winning the air war over Britain, the United States owed it to herself to declare war on Germany as soon as possible. By forming an Anglo-American alliance, the argument went on, the German-held continent could be invaded by combined forces of both countries, and the war could be brought to a quick end.

President Franklin D. Roosevelt took note of both the isolationist and interventionist lobbies. Although Roosevelt intended to do everything in his power to send as much aid to Britain as possible—he had given up all pretense of neutrality with his Destroyers-for-Bases deal—there was not very much more that he could do until after the presidential election in November. He was too much the professional politician to risk the election by doing anything controversial. But headlines like "185 German Raiders Shot Down" encouraged Roosevelt to campaign against isolationists in Congress. His line was that the British really *were* a good risk, since they were more than holding their own against Nazi Germany —and the Nazis might very well become enemies of the United States one day.

On the evening of 15 September, Prime Minister Churchill sent a message regarding the outcome of the air battle that day. It was supposedly meant for Air Chief Marshal Dowding, but was actually issued for propaganda purposes:

> Aided by Czech and Polish squadrons and using only a small proportion of its total strength, the Royal Air Force cut to rags and tatters separate waves of murderous assault upon the civil population of their native homeland.

The RAF certainly gave the Luftwaffe an unexpected setback on 15 September. But the propaganda coup that the fighter pilots gave to the Ministry of Information was just as important—it formed another step toward convincing Americans that Britain was not losing the war, was fully capable of stopping Hitler and the Germans, and would be a worthy ally of the United States.

The Luftwaffe was taken aback by the resistance put up by RAF Fighter Command, in spite of their heroic claims of enemy aircraft shot down. Intelligence had been boasting that the

RAF's fighter squadrons were weakening. The most famous remark heard by both fighter and bomber units, which would come back to haunt, was that the enemy had been reduced to their "last fifty Spitfires." But today's show of force convinced even the most confirmed optimist that Fighter Command was a long way from the verge of extinction.

In his *Luftwaffe War Diaries*, German writer Cajus Bekker pointed out that the German air force learned two harsh lessons from the fiqhting on 15 September:

> —So far from being knocked out, the British fighter defense appeared to be stronger than ever before.
>
> —The close escort of the bomber formations by their own fighters had turned out to be only partially successful. Tied to their slow charges, the Messerschmitts had been unable to exploit their flying attributes and so were in a poor position to repel the Spitfires and Hurricanes,

These realizations would convince senior German officers—- as well as Adolf Hitler himself—that a change of tactics was essential in the air war against Britain.

In Britain, 15 September would become known as Battle of Britain Day, acknowledged as the turning point of the battle and as one of the turning points of the war. But no one realized this at the time. During the evening of 15 September, the topic of conversation was still the threatened German invasion. In his broadcast to the United States, Edward R. Murrow mentioned that "much of the talk" he had heard throughout London concerned the invasion.

16 September, Monday

It is certain that the Luftwaffe would have put up another maximum effort, in spite of the previous day's activities (and losses), if the weather had not intervened. Rain and overcast limited the number of sorties. In some places, in Britain and on the Continent, the ceiling was down to 300 feet. Today's offensive would be confined to nuisance raids throughout Britain.

Individual bombers, mostly Ju 88s, used the cloud cover to their advantage—staying in it for cover, diving out of it to attack the target, and disappearing back into the impenetrable grey again. Two pilots of 616 Squadron, Colin MacFie and Philip H. Leckrone, came across a Junkers that was busy stalking a convoy off the coast of East Anglia. Flying convoy patrols was usually a boring job; it meant flying in circles over a bunch of ships and not doing much else. Once in a while, though, a prowling German bomber would present itself, and the boredom would vanish instantly.

Pilot Officers Leckrone and MacFie maneuvered into position to attack the solitary Junkers, all the while looking over their shoulders for Messerschmitts. Their luck held—no Bf 109s showed up to spoil the fun. While the Junkers was stalking the convoy below, they stalked the Junkers. Both of them fired at it, both of them watched it crash into the sea, and each was credited with half of an enemy aircraft destroyed.

"Zeke" Leckrone was an American, from Salem, Illinois. In about a month, he would join 71 (Eagle) Squadron. In January 1941, he would be killed on active service in the RAF—nearly a year before his country entered the war.

Göring called a meeting of his senior commanders to discuss the action of 15 September. Included, of course, was the usual Göring tirade against the fighter pilots for letting him down—"The fighters have failed!" he shouted.

The Reichsmarschall would not listen to any defense of the *Jagdgeschwadern*. It was pointed out to him that the fighters were placed at a disadvantage because they were not allowed to venture very far from the bomber formations—fighter pilots sometimes said that they were *kettenhunde*, chained dogs. Göring was not impressed. Oberst Theo Osterkamp argued that the RAF was concentrating large numbers of Spitfires against the German bombers. Göring bellowed his favorite line on that particular subject—everyone should be happy about the situation, because if the enemy comes up in large numbers, they can be shot down in large numbers!

It was a phrase that Göring had used before, and made no more sense now than it had previously. Osterkamp and everybody else in the room decided to save themselves the aggravation of arguing. There was no point in trying to discuss anything with *der Dicke* when he was determined to be unreasonable—as he usually was these days.

After his outburst, Göring came down to business. There would be changes, he promised. One change would be to reduce the size of bomber formations, which would increase the ratio of fighters per bomber—he wanted as many fighters as possible to cover his Heinkels and Dorniers. London would continue to be the main target, but large formations would only be sent up on cloudless days.

In Göring's mind, this was a way of returning to his attack against RAF Fighter Command—luring the Spitfires and Hurricanes into the air with small groups of bombers, and then proceeding to shoot the enemy down in large numbers by ambushing them with massed formations of Messerschmitts. He still thought that his Luftwaffe would make an invasion of Britain unnecessary by destroying the RAF's fighter shield, as well as by demoralizing the British public by massive air raids.

* * *

Air Vice Marshal Keith Park also planned to make some changes, changes which were outlined in a memo known as Instruction No. 18. Even though 11 Group had scored a resounding success on 15 September—he knew better than to believe the figure of 185 destroyed—he saw ways in which the fighters might be made even more efficient.

In his Instruction No. 18, which was issued to 11 Group's ground controllers, Park criticized the vectoring of single squadrons to intercept large incoming raids; the assigning of intercepting squadrons to the wrong altitudes (usually too low); and the delay of sending paired and multiple squadrons to intercept raids. Park also criticized the pilots themselves: for attacking Messerschmitts and letting the bombers get through; and for failing to rendezvous with other squadrons.

He also instructed the three Tangmere squadrons and the three Northolt squadrons to operate as wings—each station sending squadrons up as a unit. The CH stations on the south coast usually gave enough warning to allow these wings to get in position before the Luftwaffe arrived.

Park's criticisms made a lot more sense than Göring's, and were also a lot more constructive. Park's main object was to stop the enemy. Göring's sole purpose seems to have been to make himself look good in the eyes of Adolf Hitler, and to deflect blame for changes in tactics toward his subordinates.

On paper, at least, the invasion was still on; troops were still training in preparation for it. A force of RAF bombers surprised a training exercise off the French coast, sinking several landing barges and causing heavy casualties.

Two days later, the German wounded—mostly burn victims—arrived in Berlin by hospital train. American correspondent William L. Shirer described it as "the largest Red Cross train I've ever seen." On the 16th of September, Shirer had heard stories that a landing had been attempted on the English coast, and had been given "a good pummeling." The rumor going round was that the burned soldiers on the Red Cross train had received their wounds during this failed invasion, and that many troops had been drowned, as well.

The night air attack on London was carried out in force, in spite of the light air activity during the day. The sirens sounded at about 7:40 pm.; the All Clear was not given until 4:30 am. In between, 185 bombers dropped nearly 200 tons of high explosives. Liverpool and Bristol also were bombed.

The Luftwaffe lost 9 aircraft resulting from enemy action, including a bomber that hit a barrage balloon cable. The RAF lost one fighter, and no pilots.

17 September, Tuesday

Once again, cloud and rain interfered with operations. The Luftwaffe waited until afternoon to launch its only effort of the day—about 250 aircraft, mostly fighters, began forming in groups over France. Their height was about 15,000 feet—high enough to be detected by CH stations well before they turned north toward Kent. They could have swept in at low altitude, but their object was to be picked up by CH—this would then bring up the RAF squadrons. Hopefully, the ensuing battle would result in many enemy fighters being destroyed.

The resulting combat did not quite produce the results that Göring had expected. The RAF did send up its fighter squadrons to intercept—28 of them. But in the whirlwind that followed, the Luftwaffe was so preoccupied by fighting for survival that they could not advance very far inland from the Kentish coast.

The German formations advanced in waves, with between 30 and 35 aircraft in each wave. The first group of German aircraft crossed the coast shortly before 3 pm.; the last departed at about 5:45. Air combat was sharp and determined, but not particularly costly for either iide. The Luftwaffe lost four Bf 109s and two bombers. The RAF had eight fighters shot down, along with many others damaged, and also three pilots killed.

Some of the bombers did manage to get through to London. One of the bombs fell on Marble Arch Underground Station, killing twenty and wounding twenty others.

But by this time, the most important event of the day had already taken place.[25] During the morning, Ultra intercepted a message from the German General Staff: Adolf Hitler had authorized the dismantling of all "air unloading equipment" at airfields in the Netherlands—equipment that would be essential for the invasion of Britain. This news was relayed to Prime Minister Churchill immediately, along with an explanation of the significance of the message—it looked as though Operation Sea Lion had been called off.

---

25   The Luftwaffe also returned after dark, as they had done every night since 7 September. The bomber force consisted of 268 aircraft, which dropped 334 tons of high explosives and 91 canisters of incendiaries.

Later in the day, Hitler himself issued a directive that confirmed Ultra's interception. The German Admiralty made this note on the afternoon of 17 September:

> The enemy's air force has not been defeated; in fact, it appears to be stronger than before. Also, the weather forecast does not give any cause for optimism regarding calm conditions any time soon. As such, *der Führer* has decided to postpone Operation Sea Lion indefinitely.

But even though Sea Lion had been postponed, the naval staff was advised to maintain a high level of readiness—the invasion might still be launched at any time. If the weather co-operated, and the meteorogical bureau could predict a series of calm, clear days, the invasion might still be launched sometime in October.

Hitler obviously did not know which way to jump. He did not want to invade Britain without good weather and, even more important, complete air superiority. At the same time, he did not want to call off the invasion completely. But the communiques he sent on 17 September are generally regarded as the end of any serious invasion threat, and the end of Operation Sea Lion.

Just ten days before, on 7 September, the Luftwaffe looked to be on the verge of decimating the RAF, wearing it down to the point where it would no longer be an effective fighting force. But just a week and a half later, the RAF had re-inforced itself. Fighter Command had caught its breath and come back from the edge of extinction.

By switching their main objective from the vital sector fields to the sprawling mass of London, Hitler and Göring allowed the RAF fighter squadrons to recover, and set the stage for the startling comeback of 15 September. After being told about the losses suffered by the Luftwaffe on the 15th, Hitler knew that his air force would not be able to make the Channel secure for an invasion, at least not this year, and so he called off the landings.

In other words, the Luftwaffe almost won the battle, and would have if its leaders had not changed their strategy and, by attacking London instead of fighter airfields, allowed the exhausted RAF to recover.

But the battle was not over yet. The Luftwaffe still occupied bases just across the Channel, and would continue to strike at southern England, especially London. The RAF would not have any respite, regardless of Sea Lion's cancellation. And the propaganda campaign against isolationist America was still a long way from being won.

THE ULTRA CONTROVERSY

A year before the Battle of Britain began, British Intelligence gave RAF Fighter Command an immeasurable advantage over the Luftwaffe—an advantage that would be put to significant use during summer of 1940.

In July 1939, Colonel Gwido Langer, of Poland's Cipher Bureau, gave British Intelligence a replica of the secret German code machine, called Enigma, along with some technical drawings. Since the 1920s, the German armed forces had been using the Enigma machine as its main instrument for encoding and deciphering secret messages. The Poles managed to smuggle an Enigma out of Germany years before—they had been intercepting and de-coding German messages since at least 1934—and Colonel Langer considered himself an expert on the machine. Now, Britain would also have a copy of it, and would also be able to read and interpret secret German signals.

An increasing number of these secret messages were being sent via radio. Radio was not only more convenient than the telephone; in the case of communicating with airplanes in the air, it was essential. Operation Ultra concerned the interception and de-coding of these radio signals.

"Put in the simplest possible terms," wrote Ronald Lewin in *Ultra Goes To War*, "the operation called Ultra involved intercepting enemy signals that had been mechanically enciphered, rendering them intelligible, and then distributing their trans-lated texts by secure means to appropriate headquarters."

One of the "appropriate headquarters" was Bentley Priory—Fighter Command Headquarters. Ultra intercepts gave the RAF advance warning of the Luftwaffe's intentions on many occasions. Group Captain Frederick W. Winterbotham, one of Ultra's founders and author of the ground-breaking book *The Ultra Secret*, noted that German signals were being intercepted at the rate of "one, two, and three hundred a day" at the height of the Battle.

Among the hundreds of signals picked up and de-coded by Ultra were Göring's "Operation Eagle" order of 8 August, and his directive of 5 September ordering Kesselring to launch a 300 bomber raid against London on 7 September.

But there has been some controversy raised over how useful Ultra's intercepts had really been, and how much warning was actually supplied by Ultra. In their "Jubilee History" of the Battle of Britain, Richard Hough and Denis Richards insist that the role of Ultra in the Battle has been overrated. They cite author Martin Gilbert as mentioning that Air Chief Marshal Dowding did not actually begin receiving Ultra signals until late October, when the Battle was almost over. Hough and Richards also offer an opinion that Dowding often received secret information too late to do any good.

But these two writers also point out that Dowding and Fighter Command were often "kept informed of anything important" from Ultra. One such communique was an Ultra "Most Secret-Officer Only" transcript from 25 August 1940:

"It is reliably reported," the transcript reported, "that air attacks are to be expected during the course of today, 25th August 1940, on WARMWELL, LITTLE RISSINGTON, and ABINGDON aerodomes, and reconnaissance of aerodromes by single aircraft in the area of SOUTHAMPTON-ALDERSHOT-BRIGHTON."

That afternoon, Warmwell was bombed, as the Ultra transcript had warned. "Syren sounded at 14.25 hours an enemy attack commenced," Warmwell's Operations Record Book records. "Approx. 20 bombs were dropped."

The Ultra intercepts were not infallible. Neither was RDF, for that matter. In his dispatch on the Battle of Britain, which was not published until 1946, Dowding admitted, "Although Secret Intelligence sources supplied the information available, it is possible that on days of heavy fighting complete formations may have escaped recorded observation altogether." But Ultra did indeed give Dowding and Fighter Command advance warning of the Luftwaffe's intentions.

Along with RDF, Ultra gave the RAF another vital edge over the Luftwaffe. It is still not entirely clear just how important Ultra's contribution actually was—the majority of the Ultra transcripts are still kept secret from the public. But there can be no doubt that Ultra did play an active part in the Battle of Britain, in spite of what cynics or "revisionists" might say to the contrary.

NOTES

The main sources for Ultra were Winterbotham and Lewin.

Hough and Richards' view are from their Jubilee History.

Dowding quotes is from his report on the Battle.

Ultra transcript quote are from the Public Records Office in Kew, Richmond, Surrey, UK.

WILLY MESSERSCHMITT AND THE Bf 109

Germany's most talented aircraft designer was Willy Messerschmitt, Germany's equivalent to R.J. Mitchell and Sidney Camm. In the autumn of 1938, during a vistit to Germany, American aviator Charles Lindbergh met Messerschmitt; Lindbergh described him as "a young man, probably about forty, and undoubtedly one of the best designers of airplanes in the world. He has a stong face and honest eyes. An interesting and likeable character."

Willy Emil Messerschmitt was born in Frankfurt in 1893. He became interested in flying as a child; during the First World War, he became involved in building and flying gliders. With the help of his friend Friedrich Harth, a well-known flyer who was 18 years older, young Willy built his first glider in 1915.

Following the First World War, Messerschmitt and Harth continued to experiment with gliders—powered aircraft were prohibited in Germany by the hated Versailles Treaty. He married the daughter of a wealthy businessman; with the financial help of her family, he was able to buy the Udet-Flugzeugbau in Augsburg, the aircraft works begun by the First World War fighter ace Ernst Udet. The firm, now known as BFW—Bavarian Aircraft Works—produced several civilian transports. The most famous (or infamous) of these machines was the M 20.

In August 1928, two M 20s crashed. In one of the crashes, eight Reichswehr officers were killed; one of the officers was a personal friend of Erhard Milch. Milch was the head of Lufthansa and was in charge of purchasing aircraft; he would one day be a Luftwaffe Feldmarschall. He blamed Messerschmitt for the crashing of the two M 20s, citing negligence; he also cancelled an order for ten more M 20s by Lufthansa. This led to the bankruptcy of Messerschmitt's firm, and to lifelong animosity between Milch and Messerschmitt.

He had to start his firm all over again, from scratch. But by the 1930s, in spite of the Depression, Messerschmitt and BFW were still producing civil aircraft. In 1934, the year after Adolf Hitler came to

power, BFW's main design was a small, low-wing monoplane called the Bf 108 Taifun (Typhoon), The Taifun was well-liked because of its design, its hardiness, and its ease of handling—in the 1930s, it was known as a "progressive" (roughly the same thing as "state of the art") machine. Quite a few Taifuns were exported throughout Europe; the Royal Air Force bought three of them for communications aircraft.

But the German government had its eyes on things beyond well-designed pleasure aircraft. The German Air Ministry was looking for specifications for a monoplane fighter—a fighter armed with two machine guns mounted in the fuselage, and possibly a third gun that would fire through the propeller hub. Several firms were invited to submit designs for such an aircraft, including Heinkel, Fiesler, Focke-Wulf, and BFW. Messerschmitt and his staff used their experience in designing civil aircraft to meet the Air Ministry's specifications. They submitted their design during the summer of 1934.

The resulting aircraft was the Messerschmitt Bf 109. Drawings of the Bf 109 show a distinct resemblance to the Bf 108 Taifun: both are low-wing, all-metal monoplanes with retractable landing gear, and were both considered to be very much ahead of their time.

In keeping with the Air Ministry's specifications, Messerschmitt designed his new fighter with thin wings. This would give the Bf 109 better airspeed and would not interfere with its armament, since only

274

two fuselage-mounted machine guns would be required.

But when the Air Ministry found out that the RAF had two new fighters armed with eight wing-mounted machine guns, they changed their minds about the Bf 109's armament. They also changed their specification. Wing-mounted 7.62 mm machine guns would now be required—one machine gun each wing. This meant that the wings of the Bf 109 would have to be re-designed to accomodate the machine guns, as well as to house an elaborate ammunition feed for each gun. Each ammunition belt had to travel the entire length of the wing—out to the wing tip, over a roller and all the way back to the fuselage, and finally out to the machine gun. It was not an ideal set-up, but it had to do the job if the Air Ministry was to have its damn wing-mounted guns.

When flight trials began in the autumn of 1936, Messerschmitt's only rival was the Heinkel He 112—all the other competitors had dropped out of the running. The trial flight between the two aircraft has become something of a legend.

At the trials, each fighter was required to do ten spins to port and ten to starboard, but the Messerschmitt test pilot decided to give the judges something to remember. He did seventeen spins to port and twenty one to starboard; then, he took the Bf 109 to a height of 24,000 feet and executed a power-dive that did not level off until nearly zero feet. The judges certainly were suitably impressed, and Messerschmitt's fighter was chosen

as the standard single-seat fighter for the Luftwaffe.

By this time, the Luftwaffe was no longer masquerading as a civilian/commercial airline, or as a flying school for civilian pilots. The *Enttarnung*, or "de-camouflaging," had taken place in 1935; the German air force had come into the open, and the Versailles Treaty was officially defunct. The development of new warplanes would now be done without any cover-up or pretext.

The Spanish Civil War, which began in 1936, would give Messerschmitt, and the Luftwaffe, an oportunity to test the Bf 109 in combat. Hitler formed the Condor Legion, an air contingent made up of Luftwaffe pilots, in response to a request from the leader of the Spanish Fascists, Francisco Franco. Spain's Civil War was tailor-made to fit the plans of both the Nazi regime and the Luftwaffe—it gave Hitler the chance to suport Franco and his Fascist regime; it gave Luftwaffe pilots of the Condor Legion actual combat experience; and it gave the Luftwaffe the opportunity to test its aircraft and its tactics in actual air fighting.

The first aerial skirmishes involving the Condor Legion began late in 1936. The German fighter of the Legion was the Heinkel He 51, a biplane. But the Soviet-built Polikarpov I-15, flown by opposing Republican pilots, outclassed the He 51. So in December 1936, experimental Bf 109 V4, V5, and V6—"V" meaning "Vsuchsserie," or "test series"—were sent to Legion pilots in

Spain. (A total of 136 of them would be used during the Civil War.)

These experimental Bf 109s were flown against the Russian I-15s, and proved themselves to be a much better machine. After two months in Spain, these Bf 109s were returned to Germay for further testing—reports from Spain would be put to good use by engineers at BFW in Augsburg during future modifications.

The first Luftwaffe unit to be equipped with the Bf 109 was Jagdeschwader Richthofen, which had originally been designated JG 132 but was later changed to JG2. Adolf Hitler had named the squadron himself; he hoped that naming the Luftwaffe's first modern fighter unit after Germany's most famous fighter pilot of the First World War, Manfred von Richthofen, might prove to be a good omen.

But testing the Bf 109 went on. In 1938, the Bf 109E was introduced. The "E"—called "Emil"—would be the model flown in the Battle of Britain. It featured a Daimler-Benz 601A engine, which gave an additional 400 hp over the Jumo engine that it had replaced. The 601A was a 12-cylinder, inverted-vee, liquid-cooled engine. Some Emils also featured an engine-mounted 20 mm. cannon, which fired through the airscrew hub. This "nose cannon," which is one of the Emil's best-remembered features, turned out to be more trouble than it was worth; it was finally scrapped, in favour of two wing-mounted cannon, which caused troubles of their own.

The Messerschmitt Bf 109E was the Luftwaffe's principal fighter in the Battle of Britain. Great things had been expected from Messerschmitt's "other" fighter, the twin-engined Bf 110, which was called the Zerstörer (destroyer). But the Bf 110 was a much heavier aircraft than either the Spitfire or the Hurricane, and almost always came out second-best in a fight with either British fighter. In the coming air battles over southern England, the Bf 109 would bear the brunt of the fighting.

GERMAN BOMBERS

Junkers Ju 87-B "Stuka"

Engine: Junkers Jumo 211-D.
Max Speed: 232 mph at 13,500 feet.
Range: 370 miles.
Armament: Three 7.9 mm machine guns.
Bomb Load: 1,100 lbs.

The Junkers Ju 87 was developed by Ernst Udet, after he had flown a U.S. Navy Curtiss Hawk in 1933. Udet was greatly impressed with the Hawk, and with the idea of bombing a small target by attacking it from a near-vertical dive. He thought the Luftwaffe outght to be developing something similar to the U.S. Navy's version, and asked Berlin for the funds to buy two of them. Money was sent, and the Curtiss Aircraft Co. willingly sold Germany two of its factory-fresh Hawks.

Senior Luftwaffe officers shared Udet's enthusiasm, especially after they had seen Udet demonstrate the Hawk's ability to dive almost vertically, and issued bids among several firms to develop a dive bomber. The winning design was Junkers' Ju 87, which was based upon an already existing airplane called K-47. It was called *Sturzkampfflugzeug*— plunging battle aircraft—and was certainly a formidable aircraft, within its limitations.

Its basic drawback was its slowness—only 232 mph, it had no hope of outdistancing even obsolete biplane fighters. But it handled well, was said to be accurate to within 100 feet of its target (depending, of course, upon the steadiness of the pilot), and had an automatic pullout device connected to the altimeter. Pilots loved the Stuka, especially since so much prestige and publicity was attached to flying this ungainly-looking but highly practical bomber.

It certainly proved itself to be practical for hitting small, obscure targets, as Udet had envisioned. The Stuka was not seen as a naval bomber, to be used against ships at sea, but for hitting individual objectives that would be too small for conventional horizontal bombers—bridges, tanks, artillery emplacements, buildings, airplane hangars.

In Poland, France, and the Low Countries, the Stuka was certainly

the Luftwaffe's terror weapon. Not only could it hit small targets with terrifying accuracy, it was also fitted with a screaming siren that demoralized civilians and soldiers alike. The Stuka became the Wehrmacht's "flying artillery," able to hit targets well beyond the range of even the heaviest howitzer.

Heinkel He 111

Engines: Two Junkers Jumo 211
Maximum Speed: 247 mph at 16,000 feet.
Range: 1,200 miles.
Armament: Between 3 and 6 7.9 mm machine guns
Bomb Load: 4,400 lbs

The Heinkel He 111 was laid down both as a civilian airliner and as a medium bomber. As a civil transport for Lufthansa, the Heinkel carried ten passengers—four first-class passengers in the forward cabin, and six more in the aft cabin. In between was a smoking compartment, which became the bomb bay in the military version.

When the Heinkel He 111 first appeared in 1935, it was the latest word in modern bombers. But by the time of the Battle of Britain, it was beginning to show its age. It was slow, and the heaviest bomb it could carry was 550 lbs.—bombs were loaded vertically in the bomb bay. To compensate for its slowness, the Heinkels were given more armor and machine guns—which made them even slower. It remained in service throughout the Battle, but was limited to night air strikes against British cities after the day-light sky became too hazardous.

Dornier Do 17 "Flying Pencil"

Engines: two Junkers Jumo 211-B.
Maximum Speed: 265 mph at 16,000 feet.
Range: 205 miles.
Armament: Between 6 and 8 7.9 mm machine guns.
Bomb Load: 2,200 lbs.

This slim, elegant airplane also began as a civil aircraft; it first made its appearance in 1933 as a Lufthansa transport mail carrier. The Dornier carried six passengers, as well as air mail letters, on express service between the major centers in Europe. When the Luftwaffe began preparing for the coming war, it ws re-designed as a medium bomber.

By the beginning of the Battle of Britain, the Do 17 was not only obso-lete, but was also out of production. It was simply too small, carried too limited a bomb load, and was too slow. But the Flying Pencil was well-liked by its air crew; it handled well, and had a reputation for being reli-able.

Photo-reconnaissance units were equipped with specially modified Dorniers; the airplane's most impor-tant service to the Luftwaffe may very well have been its reconnais-sance flights over southern England. Its background made it much more suitable for this role; its small bomb load and slowness limited its useful-ness as a medium bomber.

Junkers Ju 88A

Engines: Two Junkers Jumo 211-B-1.
Maximum Speed: 280 mph at 18,000 feet.
Range: 1153 miles.
Armament: between 3 and 6 7.9 mm MG 15 machine guns.
Bomb Load: 4,000 lbs.

Unlike the Dornier Do 17 and the Heinkel He 111, the Junkers Ju 88 never carried either mail or passen-gers. By the time it was designed, in 1936, the Luftwaffe was no longer a secret organization; warplanes were being developed without having to appear as airliners or mail carriers.

When it first appeared in 1937, the Ju 88 was labeled the "wonder bomber"—it could reportedly carry more bombs than any other German medium bomber, and the experts said that it could outrun any enemy fighter. Propaganda insisted that it did not need a fighter escort because of its speed.

This might have been true when the RAF's principal fighter was the Gloster Gladiator bi-plane. But it soon became evident that the Junkers could not outrun either the Hurricane or the Spitfire. Machine guns were added for defense, along with other modifications that re-duced its speed.

It was still faster than either the Dornier or the Heinkel, however. In fact, the Ju 88 was one of the best medium bombers of the Second World War. Although no longer billed as the "wonder bomber," it was certainly the most modern bomber employed by the Luftwaffe during the Battle of Britain. The Junkers could be employed either as a horizontal bomber or as a dive bomber, and proved to be highly effective in both capacities.

Heinkel He 177: The Luftwaffe's Wasted Advantage

The Luftwaffe had a four-engined bomber capable of carrying heavy bomb loads, up to 4,400 lbs., for distances of one thousand miles or more. This same bomber also had the capacity of taking smaller loads for much greater distances—over 4,000 miles. But because of poor judgment by senior Luftwaffe officers—lunatic decisions, based upon technical ignorance—this airplane had no impact on any of the Luftwaffe's campaigns and ended as a total fiasco.

The bomber was the Heinkel He 177, a four-engined airplane with the on-paper capacity of hitting targets anywhere within the British Isles with potentially massive loads of explosives. In other words, it was the strategic bomber that the Luftwaffe consipcuously lacked. But senior Luftwaffe officers, including Ernst Udet, could not see beyond a short-duration war and doubted the need for a long range bomber.

Udet, the leading proponent of dive-bombing, also had little faith in horizontal bombing—in his mind, releasing bombs at heights of 15,000 or 20,000 feet was a waste of time and bombs, since it was nearly impossible to hit any target from that altitude. And so Udet, with the backing

of Luftwaffe High Command, ordered that the He 177 be designed with the capability of dropping its bombs while in a dive. In short, the He 177 was to be a four engined dive bomber.

The problem was that the He 177 was too large and too heavy to be used as a dive bomber—a dramatic Stuka-like plunge would probably result in the breakng off of its wings and tail section. One of the engineers at Heinkel got the idea that the He 177 might be able to recover from a step dive if all drag was reduced to an absolute minimun. One way of reducing drag would be to cut the number of engine nacelles, since these engine housings added significantly to the amount of air resistance.

And so the He 177 was designed to have two engines in each nacelle—it would look like a twin-engined bomber, with an engine housing on each wing, but would actually have two engines in each housing. The engines—Daimler-Benz 600 twelve-cylinder engines—would be linked together by a complex system of gears and linkages. It sounded awkward, but the design seemed practical and was built as an experimental bomber.

When the bomber was tested, however, it showed itself to be anything but practical. The connecting rods were susceptible to breaking; fuel dripped out of carburetors onto the hot engines, causing fire; oil leaked out of the crankcase, causing the engine to seize up and catch fire. And the two engines were jammed together so closely that fire walls could not be installed.

More than 40 of the huge bombers were lost during test flights. Either the engines caught fire and exploded, or the airplane broke up while in a thirty-degree dive. Senor officials at Heinkel tried to convince the Luftwaffe that the He 177 would probably be a very successful bomber if that odd two-in-one engine coupling system could be abandoned and a conventional four-engine system be employed—which would rule out diving.

But Ernst Udet was adamant: the airplane must be a dive-bomber, regardless of the cost.

Had the He 177 been available to Luftwaffe units during the Battle of Britain, the results probably would have been decisive. An attack on the Supermarine works, for instance,

would have been disastrous for RAF Fighter Command. These bombers would probably heave destroyed not only the factory building, but also the Spitfires inside it, as well as the machinery. Deliveries of new Spitfires to fighter squadrons would have stopped just when they were needed most. The same situation would have applied to bombing attacks on the Rolls Royce factory, and any other target of strategic importance.

But the threat to British industry never materialized. The Heinkel He 177 was kept from being the Luftwaffe's strategic striking bomber by short sightedness and total lack of technical understanding concerning aircraft design. Instead of the bomber that turned the tide of the Battle, the He 177 became a spectacular failure.

Chapter VI

The War Would Be a Long One
18 September - 31 October

Most accounts of the Battle of Britain end in mid-September, either 15 September, "Battle of Britain Day," or 17 September, when Hitler postponed Operation Sea Lion indefinitely. But the battle did not end suddenly in the middle of September, and the Luftwaffe did not vanish as though by magic. The fighting went on throughout September and October, although it changed in its scope and objective.

Even though the threat of an invasion in 1940 waned with each passing day, as the days grew shorter and the weather worsened, the next phase of the battle was still critical. Especially critical was the propaganda campaign being waged to turn American opinion, which was also entering a new phase.

The goal of this campaign was no longer to convince Americans that Britain could win the battle; that stage had passed. Now, the object was to show Americans that Britain's war against Nazi Germany would soon be America's war, and that it was in the best interest of the United States to send as much material aid as possible—as well as some soldiers.

But the real motive behind the public relations effort was very simple: Britain was broke. The British treasury did not have the resources to buy any more American goods—it had already bankrupted itself paying for war supplies. And so the new task would be to persuade the United States to send all manner of war materiel—everything from paper clips to bombers.

Fortunately for Britain, President Franklin D. Roosevelt had already been persuaded, and had a plan of his own.

For the Luftwaffe, the goal was still the same: destroy the RAF. Even though Operation Sea Lion had been postponed, it would certainly be revived in the spring—which would mean that the Battle of Britain would begin all over again. And an RAF pilot shot down in late September would be one less to face in May or June.

18 September, Wednesday

The Luftwaffe began early—the day was fine, and it was best to strike while the weather still held. Starting at about 9:00 am., CH stations on the south coast began plotting the first raid. Most of the German aircraft in this strike were fighters, which were intercepted above the coast of Kent. The RAF came out second best; this fighter sweep left 72 Squadron with three of its Spitfires damaged before the Messerschmitts began running low on fuel and had to return to their French bases.

The routine for the rest of the day was set by this sweep—formations of 150-plus German aircraft headed for Kent, which were intercepted by RAF squadrons. At about 1:00 pm., another fighter sweep met Hurricanes and Spitfires from several squadrons. *Jagdgeschwader* 27 lost four Bf 109s during the fighting over Kent, while 46 Squadron had two of its Hurricanes damaged and another shot down.

Late in the afternoon, at about 5 pm., a full-scale raid against the London docks began to take shape—bombers escorted by fighters. The bombers got through the RAF fighters and hit their objective, but the squadrons of the Duxford Wing had enough time to form up and charge at the Luftwaffe's formations.

And charge they did, right at the bombers. Kampfgeschwader 77 lost nine Ju 88s in this action. A Hurricane piloted by a sergeant named Paterek of 302 Squadron opened fire at a Junkers at such

A Junkers Ju 88 about to take off on an air strike against targets across the Channel. The Ju 88 was one of the best—perhaps the best—medium bomber of the Second World War. Although faster than either the He 111 or the Do 17, it was not able to outrun the RAF's single-engine fighters.

close range that his fighter was damaged by debris from the disintegrating bomber. Big chunks of fuselage began flying off the stricken Junkers, pelting Sgt. Paterek's Hurricane and quickly crippling it. He was able to make a controlled wheels-up landing in a field, and was also able to claim a Junkers Ju 88 destroyed.

The pilots of the Duxford Wing got carried away with themselves when making claims, as they frequently did, and put in for a grand total of 30 enemy aircraft destroyed. Actually, the Luftwaffe only lost 19 aircraft throughout the entire day, losses that were about equally divided between fighters and bombers. Losses among Fighter Command's squadrons totalled 12 fighters, with several others suffering various degrees of damage, and three pilots killed.

It had not been a decisive day for either the RAF or the Luftwaffe. Albert Kesselring, the commander of *Luftflotte* 2, was mainly concerned with the good flying weather, and with launching as many air strikes as possible while it lasted. Today's raids were not meant to be knock-out blows, just solid attacks to inflict as much damage as possible while the clear skies permitted.

The nighttime bombing sorties continued at full fury, weather notwithstanding.

This day's edition of the Blitz began when the sirens sounded at 7:30 pm., and ended when the All Clear was heard at 5:30 the following morning. Bombs were scattered all over London, causing still more damage to residential districts. Sections of Kent, Surrey, and Middlesex—the counties immediately south and west of London—also received random loads of high explosives and incendiaries.

RAF Bomber Command returned the compliment with attacks on the invasion ports. Aerial reconnaissance showed that the number of invasion barges being transported to the Channel ports was still on the increase—an indication that Hitler was still keeping his options open.

19 September, Thursday

Kesselring knew that he had been correct in ordering yesterday's attacks against RAF Fighter Command. He had made a good guess regarding the weather. Today turned out to be rainy and nasty, not suitable for any large-scale operations. His pilots and air crews would be able to make good use of the day, however, to rest and recuperate.

Operations were limited to the usual dirty-weather detail—single aircraft making individual attacks.

In London, the air raid alert sounded when lone raiders entered the Civil Defence zone. One particularly zealous pilot machine-gunned the district of Hackney at roof-top height.

The most exciting incident of the day took place when a Ju 88 made a forced landing at Oakington airfield, near Cambridge. The bomber came down intact, in spite of having had engine failure, to the surprise of everyone at Oakington; its crew was taken prisoner.

Five German aircraft, all bombers, were shot down by fighters in the course of the day's operations. Several others crash-landed at their French bases, with hydraulic systems shot away and other combat damage inflicted. The RAF lost no fiqhters.

Rain also hampered *Luftflotte* 3's night operations against London, although a few bombers did manage to take off in spite of the weather. A Heinkel He 111 of KG 55 was shot down by anti-aircraft fire north of London, over Hertfordshire.

Ultra intercepted another communique regarding Operation Sea Lion; this one was from Adolf Hitler himself. In his memo, Hitler ordered the invasion fleet to be moved inland from the Channel ports, and gave instructions that no more landing barges were to be moved to the coast. His reason: RAF Bomber Command was doing too much damage to the barges.

The message indicated that Hitler had finally made up his mind: Operation Sea Lion would not be staged in 1940.

* * *

At Church Fenton, Yorkshire, the Air Ministry's Great Experiment was about to begin—Number 71 (Eagle) Squadron, the RAF's first all-American fighter unit, had been created. Today, its first three members arrived. This entry was made in 71 Squadron's Operations Record Book:

> 19.9.40. Arrival of the first group of pilots for Eagle Squadron No. 71 — P/O E. Tobin, P/O A. Mamedoff, and P/O V.C. Keough, having been posted from No. 609 Squadron where each had had about 50 hours operational service on Spitfires. These three officers had been evacuated from France, where they had qone to join the French Air Force.

In some high-ranking circles within the RAF, the formation of a squadron manned by nothing but Americans was not looked upon with much enthusiasm. Yanks were regarded as irresponsible cowboys, damned renegades, and overgrown children. A

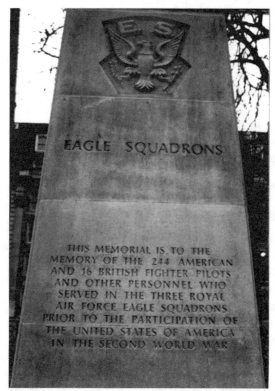

EAGLE SQUADRONS

THIS MEMORIAL IS TO THE
MEMORY OF THE 244 AMERICAN
AND 16 BRITISH FIGHTER PILOTS
AND OTHER PERSONNEL WHO
SERVED IN THE THREE ROYAL
AIR FORCE EAGLE SQUADRONS
PRIOR TO THE PARTICIPATION OF
THE UNITED STATES OF AMERICA
IN THE SECOND WORLD WAR

This monument to the all-American Eagle Squadrons, in which more than 200 U.S. citizens served in the Royal Air Force, was unveiled in 1986 in London's Grosvenor Square, adjacent to the U.S. Embassy and across the Square from the statue of President Franklin D. Roosevelt.

number of senior officers wanted nothing to do with them, including Air Vice Marshal Trafford Leigh-Mallory, the commander of 12 Group. Leigh-Mallory stated that he was "very strongly opposed" to having a squadron of Americans in the RAF, and especially to having it in 12 Group. He had experience with Americans during the First World War, and had not been impressed with their performance. He considered Americans to be charming as individuals, but on the whole they were completely undisciplined. Some of Leigh-Mallory's colleagues shared his opinion, but were usually not so blunt about it.

There were many Americans—including American Ambassador Joseph P. Kennedy—who were just as set against a squadron of American volunteers serving in the RAF. They did not like the idea of U.S. citizens fighting with the armed forces of a foreign country, especially British forces. For an American to fight on the side of the Bloody Redcoats, the same people who burned the White House and perpetrated the Boston Massacre, was tantamount to high treason.

As it happened, the three Yanks of 71 Squadron were not very happy about their situation, either. They arrived at Church Fenton expecting to find a fully operational squadron—airplanes, men, equipment, and everything else needed to run a fighter unit. What they actually found was nothing—no other squadron members, no commanding officer, no ground support personnel, and no airplanes. (Actually, there was one airplane—a Miles Magister trainer that would not fly.)

Things would get worse before they got any better. When the Squadron's first fighters arrived, they turned out to be obsolete U.S. Navy Brewster Buffalos. These were deliberately wrecked, by order of the Squadron's commanding officer; otherwise, Messerschmitts would have made short work of them, and their pilots.

By this time, the squadron not only had a commanding officer, they had two co-commanders. Someone at the Air Ministry had the idea of assigning an American squadron leader, who would be more or less a fugurehead, and a Briton, who would be the actual commander. (Since an American, in the Air Ministry's eyes, could not be trusted with that much responsibility.) To compound the problem, the two co-commanders did not like or get along with each other.

Eventually, the experiment worked. The first of the Eagle squadrons became operational early in 1941, after a great many teething troubles, and after finally being equipped with Hawker Hurricane fighters. Some senior RAF officers still did not like the idea. But as far as propaganda value was concerned, the pilots of 71 Squadron were worth their weight in gold dust.

The Eagles would be deluged by writers, reporters, photographers, and newsreel cameramen from both the U.S. and Britain, and would become the beneficiaries of every form of promotion and publicity except neon lights. All of this was to prove to the Great American Public that their fellow countrymen were al-

Grosvenor Square, with Eagle Memorial in foreground; American Embassy in background; and Franklin Roosevelt Memorial to the right, across the Square. Grosvenor Square has been London's "Little America" since the end of the War of Independence, and has many connections, both real and sentimental, with the USA.

ready engaged in the war against Hitler, and to persuade them to be more sympathetic toward their British cousins.

20 September, Friday

At about 10:30 am., south coast CH stations began plotting German activity over France. The first of three formations crossed the coast shortly after 11:00. The other two formations followed at about 11:20 and 11:40. These consisted mainly of fighters, escorting a fairly small number of bombers. The total number of German aircraft came to about 65.

When the Spitfire and Hurricane pilots of 11 Group came up, they found themselves overwhelmed by Bf 109s. In the furious combat that followed, four Messerschmitts were shot down; a Bf 109 of JG 27 crashed into the Kentish countryside with its pilot still in the cockpit, in full view of several eyewitnesses. In spite of the Messerschmitts, however, the RAF pilots forced their way through to the bombers, and shot down four of them.

This was the only air action of the day. The RAF lost seven fighters and four pilots. Major Werner Mölders of JG 51 accounted for two of the fighters. German losses on the day also were seven aircraft destroyed.

That night, London was bombed again. It was not a major effort, however. No specific targets were attacked; the air crews of *Luftflotte* 3 scattered their bombs across the city, disrupting transportation and communication lines, and keeping factory workers in their air raid shelters.

On the other side of the Atlantic, Britain managed to stage yet another propaganda coup. Brigadier General Strong, U.S. Army, who had been sent to Britain to observe the Luftwaffe's offensive against the RAF, gave his report on these observations. And an astonishing report it was! It could just as well have been written by someone in Britain's Ministry of Information.

General Strong was either extremely gullible, or else he possessed the eternal optimism of Pollyana on her best day. In his report, he actually told his superiors that the Luftwaffe's offensive since July had not seriously affected the strength of the RAF, and had inflicted only minimal damage to military targets.

Which meant that General Strong had either been kept away from RAF sector airfields during his stay in Britain, or he had not been given access to information—or, at least, not to accurate information—concerning either the battle or the Blitz.

By concocting this sunny report, General Strong made an admission that he had absolutely no idea of what had been happening in Britain during the past two months—incredible, coming from a general officer. He said that he did not know that RAF Fighter Command had been decimated in August and early September; he said he did not know that airfields, such as Manston and Biggin Hill, had been crippled by the Luftwaffe's attacks; and he said that he did not know that strategic targets, such as the London docks, had been seriously damaged.

It is difficult to believe that an officer of such senior rank could have been hoodwinked to this extent. One possible explanation might be that General Strong was under orders from President Franklin D. Roosevelt to make a favorable report even if he had to make up a purely fictitious report. President Roosevelt was committed to American involvement in the war by this time. He would certainly not have been above ordering General Strong to produce a report on the British situation that would have been optimistic to the point of lying. A realistic assessment might have hurt Roosevelt's campaign against isolationists in Congress and throughout the country. It would not have been the first time an American president turned to subterfuge to get what he wanted, and certainly would not be the last time.

21 September, Saturday

The Luftwaffe did not launch any major efforts on this day, even though the weather would have been perfect for a large-scale air strike. Operations were limited to scattered attacks by single raiders.

Among the objectives that were attacked was the Hawker Aircraft factory at Brooklands. The raider did not lack either skill or daring, but was short on luck; he hit the Hawker works, but did not do any serious damage either to the production or the assembly areas of the factory.

German losses came to five bombers and one fighter, including a lone raider shot down over Liverpool. The RAF lost a Spitfire from 92 Squadron. It seems strange that senior Luftwaffe officers did not take advantage of the good flying weather to create more havoc across the Channel.

* * *

Luftflotte 3 was back over London again after the sun went down. And at BBC Broadcasting House, American correspondent Edward R. Murrow of the Columbia Broadcasting System was back on duty with his microphone, giving the word to millions of listeners in the United States. During the radio

Royal Observer Corps volunteer early in the war, with St. Paul's in the background. In addition to binoculars and helmet, he is equipped with a gas mask container on his chest.

program *London After Dark*, Murrow's listeners actually heard the air raid in progress: the faint droning of airplane engines; the dull boom of anti-aircraft fire; and the shrill warning of police whistles.

They also heard Murrow calmly describing the raid. "I am standing on a rooftop looking out over London," he announced from the roof of Broadcasting House. "You might be able to hear the sound of guns in the distance, very faintly, like someone kicking a tub."

A moment later, he was describing how the local searchlights were trying to pinpoint German bombers in the vicinity. "More searchlights spring up over on my right," he said. "I think probably in a minute we shall have the sound of guns in the immediate vicinity. The lights are swinging over in this general direction now. You'll hear two explosions. There they are! ... Just overhead now the burst of anti-aircraft fire."

Murrow's tone of voice was always level and matter-of-fact. He never shouted, and he never showed any pro-British bias. He made the people of London seem heroic by understating their predicament.

But he also made it clear that Britain's situation was perilous, and that the German Blitz showed no signs of letting up. His unspoken message: British heroism by itself would not win the war against Hitler.

"It was the *War of the Worlds* come to life," wrote one of Murrow's biographers, "the rooftop observer reporting on the life and death of cities .... This was the real thing, broadcasting's first living-room war."

Every night, Murrow delivered his subtle message from London to millions of Americans: Britain was in a fight to the death, and must not be abandoned. If Britain lost, what was now happening to London might happen to New York in the not-too-distant future. The Ministry of Information realized that these broadcasts did more to sway American opinion than all their overdramatic propaganda messages and all the second-rate war films put together.

22 September, Sunday

The Luftwaffe's attack had definitely changed dramatically, at least for the time being. Emphasis was now on night bombing, particularly against London. Daylight operations had been cut back sharply.

In the course of the day's activities, the Luftwaffe lost one bomber, a Ju 88. The squadrons of Fighter Command flew only 158 sorties—few flights were needed because few enemy raiders came over. RAF Fighter Command lost no aircraft.

But that night, air activity picked up. *Luftflotte* 3 sent 123 bombers to attack London—not exactly a *grosseinsatz*, but a lot more aggressive than *Luftflotte* 2's daylight activities had been. The All Clear did not sound until the early hours of 23 September. As on previous nights, the German bombers wandered above the city at will, dropping their bombs when and where they pleased.

Also as on previous nights, neither night fighters nor anti-air-craft defenses accounted for any of the German bombers—-which is why they were able to roam about at leisure. Overall, the night defenses were just about useless. Once in a while, the pilot of a night fighter would be able to stalk one of the intruders and shoot it down, or anti-aircraft gunners would pick off one of the bombers. But this was the result of luck as much as anything else.

23 September, Monday

A fine early autumn day brought the Luftwaffe up from its French bases —the Luftwaffe's fighters, at any rate. CH stations in Kent began plotting enemy aircraft over the Pas de Calais by 9 am. The planes arrived over Kent shortly before 10 o'clock; most of them were Messerschmitt 109s.

For about an hour, from 10:00 to 11:00, intercepting RAF fighters and Bf 109s made impressive contrail patterns in the blue sky over Kent as they chased and tried to kill each other.

And kill they did—within a few minutes of 10 o'clock, five Bf 109s and four RAF fighters crashed to earth: nine airplanes in five minutes. By the time this fighter sweep ended, and surviv-ing German pilots turned toward the French coast, twelve Messerschmitts and eleven Spitfires and Hurricanes had left their wrecked remains in the fields of Kent.

The battle had not been conclusive. Although the German fighter pilots had succeeded in bringing the RAF up in force and in shooting down nearly a dozen fighters, they had also lost a dozen of their own. The next time the weather permitted, the *Jagdgeschwader* pilots would try their luck again.

Another fighter sweep crossed the Kentish coast at about 5 o'clock in the afternoon. This second sweep turned out to be a very curious affair, however. Instead of engaging the RAF fighters as they came up to intercept, which is the whole point of a fighter sweep, the Messerschmitt pilots seemed determined to elude the Spitfires and Hurricanes.

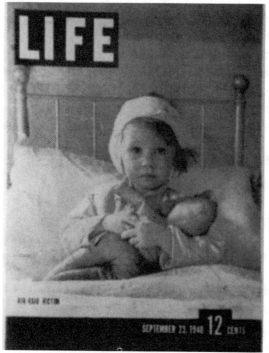

A highly effective example of British propaganda appeared on the cover of Life *Magazine's 23 September 1940 edition. The photo is of Eileen Dunne, three years old, hospitalized as the result of a German air raid; the caption is simply "air raid victim." The message was: If we lose, sooner or later the Germans will also do this to your children. Photos like this were highly influential in changing the American point of view toward Britain.*

The German fighters swept over Kent in five separate formations, remaining over British soil for the better part of an hour, and turned back again to their bases in France without engaging the RAF squadrons. This was a nuisance raid in the truest sense—the German pilots seemed content to make their presence known, to stir up the defenses, and then to go home again.

* * *

London came under attack once again after nightfall. According to Edward R. Murrow, the alert sounded at about 8:00 pm., and was still on at 4:00 am. Over 260 bombers of *Luftflotte* 3 dropped their explosives over the city at large.

In his nightly broadcast, Murrow said that "the raid appears to be routine." Actually, tonight's attack was quite severe; heavier damage was done than on the previous night, when the

raiders caused widespread destruction. Once again, the defenses did not bring down any of the German attackers.

The only positive note about these night bombing raids for
Britain was the broadcasts of Ed Murrow and his fellow American journalists; their words were slowly changing the outlook of
Americans toward Britain and the war. Otherwise, the raids
meant only destruction and frustration. Not only were the
Germans pummelling London every night, but there did not
seem to be anything that could be done to stop it.

24 September, Tuesday

Fog and cloud over northern Europe dissipated by 8:30 am.,
allowing the Luftwaffe to launch a morning strike. Formations
of both fighters and bombers arrived over Kent at about 9
o'clock. Intercepting RAF fighters did not fare very well in the
resulting combat. Between 9 o'clock and 9:30, six Spitfires and
Hurricanes were shot down; no German aircraft were lost.

The next action took place after one o'clock, when twenty
bomb-carrying Bf 109s attacked the Supermarine factory at
Woolston, near Southampton. The Messerschmitt pilots came in
low and made a good approach, but they missed the factory
with every one of their bombs. Each of the 550-lb. bombs came
down on the surrounding neighborhood, however, knocking
out gas and water for local residents. Also, about 100 Supermarine factory workers and staff died when their air raid shelter
received a direct hit. The local First Aid post, which also had
been hit, was pressed into service as a mortuary; as the bodies
were pulled out of the demolished shelter, they were piled on
the floor inside the post.

After dropping their cumbersome bombs—fighter pilots
cursed having to carry them—the Messerschmitts circled over
Portsmouth for about 20 minutes. Ground observers could not
tell if the pilots were trying to find a particular target to strafe,
or if they were just showing off. As they overflew the city,
however, they became a bit careless. Anti-aircraft fire caught one
of the fighters, sending both the plane and its pilot crashing to
earth.

Just when this raid was ending, another formation crossed the coast and was intercepted by fighters of 11 Group. Two bombers were badly damaged by the interceptors. Both managed to make the trip back to France, but had to make forced landings short of their bases. Losses to the RAF consisted of two fighters destroyed.

For the second time in two days, the Luftwaffe had increased its pressure on RAF Fighter Command. Today, their tactics brought them the results they wanted. Nine RAF fighters had been shot down, for a loss of eight German aircraft—fighters and bombers combined.

No one outside the very top ranks of Churchill's government had any idea that Operation Sea Lion had been called off. This new flurry of activity by the Luftwaffe kept everyone guessing about what Hitler was up to next.

London's air raid sirens sounded early in the evening; the All Clear was not heard until 5:30 the following morning. In between, *Luftflotte* 3's bombers fell to their usual routine: bombing at random and causing widespread damage and destruction. Anti-aircraft gunners accounted for one of the raiders—a Heinkel He 111 of KG 26, which crashed at about 1:30 am.

25 September, Wednesday

It seemed a fair bet that the Luftwaffe would be coming over today, and probably in force. The day dawned fine and cool, which provided excellent visibility throughout the south of England. During the mid-morning hours, Ultra picked up signals from bomber and fighter bases in France, heavy radio traffic that confirmed all suspicions.

But this time, the attack was not aimed at London. The Luftwaffe's main thrust was aimed at the Bristol Aircraft Company's factories at Filton, just outside Bristol. Both the Beaufighter, a twin-engined night-fighter, and the Blenheim, which served both as a night-fighter and a light bomber, were manufactured at Filton.

Eyewitnesses saw between 60 and 70 German airplanes approach from the southwest. The Alert sounded; factory workers went to their shelters before the bombers arrived. About 90 tons of high explosives fell on or near the factories, blowing apart machine shops and assembly areas, and killing 72 people outright. Another 19 died later from their injuries.

This time, the bombers had hit their mark with a vengeance. Buildings had been shattered; production had been set back by several weeks. Also, rail and road transport in the area was brought to a standstill; telephone cables had been destroyed; and gas and water mains were shattered. The bombers had done a thorough job.

After dropping their bombs, all the German raiders had to do was get back home again—and the pilots and aircrew were to find out that it was much more difficult to get out of Filton than it had been to get in. Three squadrons from 12 Group had been scrambled to intercept, and caught the retreating bombers before they could reach the coast. Five He 111s of KG 55 were shot down at around 12 noon, within minutes of each other.

One of the squadrons that confronted the Filton raiders was 152 Squadron, which lost two pilots and two Spitfires in this action, as well as three more Spitfires damaged. At least one of the escorting Bf 110s was shot down by the Spitfire pilots of 609 Squadron.

At about 4:30, two other raids were intercepted. One was on its way to Plymouth, the second on course for London. The German raiders, or at least some of them, got through the fighters and bombed their targets.

Losses for the day came to four RAF fighters and 13 German airplanes. But despite its losses, the Luftwaffe came out ahead—the German high command would gladly give up thirteen of its airplanes in exchange for the Bristol factory at Filton. They considered it a bargain price, in fact.

London was the object of *Luftflotte* 3's attention again at night. But, according to Edward R. Murrow, "Tonight's attack against the central London area has not been as severe as last night's; less noise, fewer bombs, and not so many fires." So, he told his American radio audience about last night's raid, when two or three German planes "came boring in through the barrage every five minutes."

It was another romantic broadcast, designed not so much to inform his fellow countrymen across the Atlantic as to persuade them.

Murrow spoke about Londoners as being stubborn and determined—two traits that Americans prize—people not about to let the Nazis get the best of them. He saw the staff of bombed shops "doing business in the open air," carrying on with their lives in spite of the German bombs, and reported what he had seen. The message: the Germans were not going to beat these people, regardless of the great Nazi armies and air fleets.

An American writer said that Murrow "brought home to Americans the horror and the thrill of air power" better than any other correspondent. Murrow's audience listened to his description of the Luftwaffe's air raids with total fascination. The stories of the bombed buildings, the sounds of air raid warnings and anti-aircraft fire, and sometimes the explosion of the bombs themselves were a new sensation to Americans.

The broadcasts also made Americans start thinking of something else: if the Luftwaffe could do this to London, they just *might* be able to bomb the United States as well. "After listening to Murrow," the same writer said, "Americans began to think of the Battle of Britain as a prelude to the Battle of America."

Unwittingly, the Luftwaffe was feeding Britain's propaganda machine with material that was tailor-made for an American audience. Murrow took this material and used it to tilt Americans toward the war that was coming.

26 September, Thursday

Another "blitzy day"—blue skies and fair weather—brought the Luftwaffe back to southern England in force.

A fighter sweep late in the morning cost 253 Squadron two of its Hurricanes. But the main effort was not launched until late afternoon, when 76 Heinkels and Junkers, along with their Bf 109 escort, bombed the Supermarine plant at Woolston, near Southampton—the Spitfire factory.

Air raid warnings sounded the alert, and the planes themselves could be heard as they droned in from the coast a short while later. In spite of the warning, the German bombers made their approach without any interference from the defenses. They dropped their bombs—about 70 tons of high explosives—with accuracy that bordered on the astonishing. So many explosions occurred at the same time that they sounded like one long, continuous *booom*.

The Supermarine works were literally blasted apart. Both factory buildings were destroyed. Only the office block remained intact, although it suffered damage from blast and bomb splinters. When the smoke cleared, workers emerging from the shelters could only blink at the devastation. In a matter of about two minutes, the factory had disappeared; nothing remained except heaps of debris and a tangle of steel girders. Nearby houses had been gutted by blast, and a grain warehouse had been reduced to a smoldering ruin. Over two dozen people had been killed—actually fairly light casualties considering the destruction done by bombs.

The bombers were not intercepted until after they had released their loads. One of the intercepting squadrons was 303 (Polish) Squadron, which was in the middle of an inspection by King George VI when the order to scramble was given. When the Poles first spotted the bombers, they were just making their wide turn toward their bases in France.

The Poles pushed their throttles all the way forward and ran right at a formation of Heinkels. Flying Officer Urbanowicz caught up with one of the Heinkels, which seemed to be lagging behind. A long burst from his Hurricane's .303s set the bomber on fire; F/O Urbanowicz watched it crash into the Channel.

Actually, the Poles were lucky. Most of the other fighters could not get past the escort of Messerschmitts. Within minutes of making contact, five of the intercepting fighters had been shot down before they could get anywhere near the bombers. A total of six RAF fighters were lost in this action; the Luftwaffe lost three aircraft.

It had been a highly satisfying afternoon for the Luftwaffe. They had effectively knocked out the Woolton Supermarine Spitfire factory in one concerted effort.

Although only three fully assembled Spitfires had been destroyed in the bombing, and damage to machinery—engine lathes, drill presses, and the like—was surprisingly light, the actual buildings could no longer be used for manufacturing. New production facilities would have to be found and new factories set up. Until this happened, production of the Spitfire fighter would be severely curtailed. As the result of today's raid, the number of Spitfires manufactured would be cut back by about 60%. Full production would not be resumed until the end of November. If the Woolston plant had been knocked out in July, the consequences for the RAF would have been devastating.

On the day, the Luftwaffe lost a total of 9 aircraft, and the RAF lost eight fighters. From the German point of view, it was an extremely profitable exchange—nine aircraft for the Spitfire works at Woolton. Göring wished that he could arrange such a swap every day of the week.

At night, London came under attack again. And, as had been the case for the past two weeks, damage was described as scattered and widespread.

27 September, Friday

The Luftwaffe was back again in the morning, even though the weather was not perfect for flying early on—the sky was slightly hazy and overcast. They came early, and kept coming back in numbers.

The day's first action took place just after 9:30 am. Bomb-carrying Bf 110s of LG 1, with their Bf 109 escort, were intercepted over Kent. This time, the pilots of the Bf 109s were not able to keep the Hurricanes and Spitfires away from their charges. Seven of the big, twin-engined fighter-bombers were shot down; those that managed to drop their bombs scattered them for miles around Kent.

Messerschmitt Bf 109, standard German fighter during the Battle of Britain.

At about 11:00 am. a much larger raid approached from the south. Actually, it was two separate raids—about 300 aircraft on their way to London, and about a quarter of that number headed for Bristol.

Fighters from 10 Group pounced on the Bristol raid with such determination that none of the German aircraft—about 80 planes—could bomb their target. Only about a quarter of the attacking Messerschmitt 109s and 110s managed to reach the southern boundaries of the city. The few that actually managed to reach Bristol were met by still more fighters. The twin-engined Messerschmitts jettisoned their bombs and turned for the Channel.

The attack of a Pilot Officer of 609 Squadron named Miller should give some idea of the ferocity of the RAF pilots. P/O Miller made a head-on charge at one of the Messerschmitt 110s, but misjudged his approach and collided with his intended target. The Spitfire blew up, and the Bf 110 crashed to earth. Both P/O Miller and the crew of the Bf 110 were killed.

The London raid did not fare much better. The German formations were intercepted over central Kent by several squadrons from 11 Group. When the German bomber pilots saw the Spitfire and Hurricane units maneuvering to attack, they executed diving turns and headed back toward the Channel coast—obviously, the air crews had been under a great deal of strain during the past few weeks, and the stress was now taking its toll.

Spitfire and Hurricane pilots went after the diving bombers. They caught up with several of them before they could reach the Channel. Observers on the ground watched several twin-engined German bombers, either Ju 88s or Do 17s, fall within a few miles of the coast or into the Channel.

But the fighting had not been completely in favor of the RAF. Messerschmitt 109s were flying top cover for the bombers. Although they were not quite as aggressive as they had been on previous occasions, the *Jaeger* pilots did account for some of the intercepting fighters. The Hurricanes of 1 (Canadian) Squadron were attacked by Bf 109s; one of the Hurricanes was shot down, and two others were damaged.

In the late afternoon, at about 3:30, another London-bound raid was given a going-over by the fighters of 11 Group. Several bombers were shot down, and their Bf 109 escort also came out second best—JG 52 lost six Messerschmitts in this fight.

The day had brought a complete reversal of fortune for the Luftwaffe. On the previous day, German formations had destroyed an essential military target while suffering only modest losses. Today, most of the attacking bombers did not get to within miles of their targets, and had suffered heavily for their unsuccessful effort—55 aircraft destroyed. (Against 28 fighters shot down for the RAF.)

Of course, some of the bombers did manage to push their way through to their objective, through luck, or skill, or single-mindedness, or a combination of all three. Central London was attacked by at least 20 German aircraft, which scattered their bombs across a wide area. "Scattered bombs" sounds fairly harmless, as though the bomb-aimers were throwing out handfuls of confetti. Actually, the cargoes they had unloaded blew up houses, knocked out gas lines and other utilities, destroyed offices and a warehouse filled with food, and killed about 100 people.

That night, the bombers of *Luftflotte* 3 returned to London, and did more of the same.

"It dawned on Berlin a few days ago that Britain might not be defeated at all this fall," William L. Shirer commented from Berlin. Senior German officers reached the conclusion that Britain "might still be fighting next spring, and that the American aid to Britain, especially in planes, would begin to make itself felt rather seriously."

Actually, these possibilities had dawned on Berlin a lot longer than only a few days ago—to everyone except Reichsmarschall Göring, who lived in a drug-induced dream world.

American aid to Britain—and its effect on German war aims—was becoming especially troublesome. And extremely annoying. Neutral America had sent 50 destroyers to the British fleet, bombers to the RAF, and crates filled with rifles and other small arms to Britain's Home Guard. And there was no telling what else President Franklin D. Roosevelt had in mind.

"Something must be done after all about the United States," Shirer went on to say. "What? Something to scare her and to set American isolationists loose again with a new cry about the danger of war."

What Berlin did was form an alliance with its two allies, Fascist Italy and Imperial Japan—the Tripartite Pact. The pact was signed in Berlin's Chancellery on 27 September. It formally bound the three countries together in a mutual defense agreement.

The Pact's main points were:

ARTICLE I: Japan recognises and respects the leadership of Germany and Italy in the establishment of a new order in Europe.

ARTICLE II: Germany and Italy recognise and respect the leader-ship of Japan in the establishment of a new order in Greater East Asia.

ARTICLE III: Japan, Germany, and Italy agree to co-operate in their efforts on the aforesaid lines. They further agree to assist one another with all political, economic, and military means when one of the three Contracting Parties is attacked by a power at present not involved in the European war or in the Sino-Japa-nese conflict .

The "power not at present involved" was obviously the United States; the point of the alliance was to warn Americans to stay out of the war. Senior Nazi officials did not try to deny the fact that the pact was directed at the U.S., but William Shirer's censors tried to stop him from saying so during his nightly broadcast. But Shirer did manage to get in what he described as a "watered down" mention: "There is no attempt in informed circles here tonight to disguise the fact that the military alliance signed in Berlin today ... has one great country in mind. That country is the United States."

The censors let this pass, but would not allow a more detailed analysis of the pact to be broadcast.

Actually, the Germans made more of a fuss over the treaty than the Americans, who were the object of it. And with good reason. By agreeing to a mutual protection pact with his two allies, Hitler tacitly admitted that the Battle of Britain was not going his way, and that the war would not be over this year.

American papers reported the signing, but only a few seemed to give it any significance. The American public was far from frightened by the pact; most people ignored it completely.

Prime Minister Winston Churchill did not seem to be overly excited by the Berlin-Rome-Tokyo alliance, either. In his mem-oirs, he gave it only a passing mention. He might have been a bit more enthusiastic if he could have guessed what effect the pact would have on the future, especially Britain's future, and that the agreement would eventually provide the answer to his persistent American problem.

28 September, Saturday

Senior Luftwaffe commanders were determined to take full advantage of every sunny autumn day that came along. Today, another series of air strikes were sent across the Channel—bombers escorted by massive numbers of fighters flying at great height. No one could tell how soon the winter weather would close in; the plan was to send as many air raids to southern England as possible while the weather held. The first of the day's forays began at about 9:30 am. Large formations were plotted by CH stations as the Luftwaffe formed up and headed for Kent. Most of the German aircraft were Bf 109s, escorting about 30 bombers. Spitfires and Hurricanes from several 11 Group squadrons were scrambled to intercept.

But the RAF fighters themselves were the victims of this interception. The Messerschmitts fell on each squadron that came up, keeping the attacking Spitfires and Hurricanes from reaching the bombers. Seven RAF fighters were shot down, and several more were damaged. The bomber formation turned back before reaching London, for some mysterious reason. None of them had been shot down, and there was no sign of any difficulty that might have caused them to turn for home.

At about 2:30, the next big attack of the day made its presence known. This time, the attackers set their course for Portsmouth—about 50 Bf 110s, escorted by Bf 109s. Just as happened in the morning, RAF fighters came up to confront the intruders—squadrons from both 10 Group and 11 Group. And once again, just as in the morning, the Bf 109 fighter escort stopped them dead, shooting down eight fighters for the loss of one Messerschmitt.

The day had been a tactical setback for the RAF. Fighter Command lost 16 aircraft, but could only account for three German airplanes destroyed. In spite of their losses, however, the Spitfire and Hurricane pilots did their job—they prevented the German bombers, and fighter-bombers, from attacking their targets.

A month earlier, the German bomber crews probably would have shoved their way to their objectives regardless of fighter opposition, and at least some of the bomb aimers would have found their mark. This was a sign of determination as much as of skill and ability; the pilots and air crew were committed to destroying the RAF.

But now it was the end of September, not the end of August. Göring had changed the Luftwaffe's goal: London was now the main target, not the RAF's fighter bases. Also, the stress and fear of two and a half months of air fighting was taking its toll.

*   *   *

London was bombed again, for the twenty-second night in a row. The air raid sirens sounded early in the evening; as usual, the All Clear was not heard until dawn. Bombs were scattered all over the city, with no particular targets; since the night was moonless, no individual buildings or locations could have been seen from the air.

By this time, Londoners were beginning to settle into something resembling a nighttime routine. Most people spent the night in an air raid shelter. In the morning, they got up and went to work—if their office or factory had not disappeared in the bombing of the night before.

Sometimes a person carried on working just the same, even if their office had been bombed. When the news offices of *The Times* had taken a direct hit a few days earlier, on Tuesday 24 September, production of the newspaper continued from the basement.

When the news staff arrived for work on the morning of the 25th, they found—in the words of one of the sub-editors—"most of the entire building in shambles." A large part of the day was spent in moving the editorial department—tables, chairs, reference books, and everything else—below ground. While the big move was being made, the day's edition was put together, the type was set, the pages were printed, and *The Times* made the newsstands. In fact, *The Times* made the newsstands every day during the war, without missing a single edition.

Photos of air raid shelters usually gave the impression that life below ground, especially in the London Underground, was a romantic adventure. Reality was not quite so romantic. Photos like these were published to show Americans that British morale would not break, in spite of anything Hitler might do, and were very effective in raising support and sympathy for Britain in America.

This was the sort of stuff that the American press and news media were allowed to circulate—evidence that London Could Take It, in spite of what The Huns might do. But there was another, more subtle, message here, as well: London was being bombed today, but it might be New York's turn sometime in future.

29 September, Sunday

Blue skies, and the results of yesterday's operations, made it a fairly safe bet that the Luftwaffe would be back for more daylight activities.

Two main efforts were launched, both in the afternoon. The first raid— "fortified fighter sweep" would probably be a more accurate description—crossed the coast shortly after 4 pm. As they made their way toward London, the raiders were attacked by fighters from 11 Group.

When the Hurricanes and Spitfires made contact, the resulting fight was short and explosive. One Messerschmitt was shot down, two more were damaged, and KG 1 lost two He 111s all within a few minutes. In addition, 253 Squadron had two of its Hurricanes destroyed. None of the bombers penetrated to London.

About two hours later, a second air strike made its way across western England, apparently heading for Liverpool. Over the Irish Sea, the RAF pilots intercepted the raiders, and shot down two He 111s of KG 55. During this same action, 79 Squadron lost three Hurricanes; two were shot down, one force-landed in Ireland, where the fighter was impounded and its pilot interned.

The past two weeks certainly showed a dramatic change in spirit of the German pilots, both in fighters and bombers. Their aggressiveness, so prominent in August and early September, had just about vanished. These days, their primary determination seemed to be to get back home as quickly as possible. Whether or not they did any damage to the enemy was of secondary importance, just as long as the enemy did not do any to them.

This drop in morale was understandable. It was fairly evident to anyone with a grain of sense that there would be no invasion of England, at least not in 1940, and that the RAF was nowhere near the verge of collapse—as they had been told so often. The German pilots and aircrew could see no point in their daylight trips to England. They did not seem to be doing any harm to the enemy. And if they happened to get shot down, it seemed to them a waste, not a sacrifice.

In his nightly broadcast to America, Edward R. Murrow told his audience about his two-day holiday in Somerset, in the southwest of England. Murrow reported that the countryside was very peaceful and quiet—so peaceful, in fact, that he had trouble sleeping. Instead of enjoying the change of scenery, Murrow "kept wondering what was happening in London." So he decided to cut his holiday short and go back.

After a four-hour train trip, Murrow was in London again. "It's a strange feeling to ride through dark streets lit by anti-aircraft fire," he said about his taxi drive from the railway station, "wondering if your home is still standing or whether it has become a pile of ruined rubble during your brief absence.

"As the man who shared my taxi remarked," Murrow concluded, "it's like coming back to the front lines after a short leave."

This was not news, this was propaganda. Excellent propaganda, and effective. A biographer of Franklin D. Roosevelt remarked on Murrow's subtle method of persuasion, and how much it was admired by the British. One of Murrow's fans was Britain's ambassador to the United States, Lord Lothian. Lothian did not have to revert to overt propaganda when stating the British position to Americans. Edward R. Murrow's broadcasts from London had already done most of his work for him.

30 September, Monday

The Luftwaffe decided to end September with a flourish.

Three air raids were dispatched before noon. Two crossed the coast over Kent, bound for London; the third made for the vicinity of Bournemouth, near the southwestern coast.

The first formations made their appearance just after 9 am.—between 20 and 30 bombers, escorted by about four times as many Bf 109s. About an hour later, another raid stormed the Kentish coast. This raid was smaller than the first, but it had the same mix of aircraft—bombers surrounded by many fighters.

Both of these attacks encountered an angry reaction from 11 Group's squadrons. The fight resulted in two Hurricanes destroyed; during the second raid, three more fighters were damaged. But many more German aircraft, both bombers and Bf 109s, were lost. None of the bombers reached London, in spite of their impressive fighter protection.

The third air strike, which was on course for Bournemouth, did not even fare as well as this. It consisted of Bf 110s, acting as fighter-bombers, and Bf 109s flying top cover. The Hurricane and Spitfire pilots managed to get among the fighter-bombers before anybody had time to react. Two Hurricanes of 56 Squadron were shot down after making their first pass, along with fighters from other squadrons. But the attacking Luftwaffe force was decimated; the bomb-carrying Zerstörers were sitting targets. The survivors scattered and turned back for France before they could even reach the coast.

During the early afternoon, another attack was aimed at London—over 100 bombers and fighters. This time, the Luftwaffe managed to force its way through, in spite of 11 Group's efforts. About 30 aircraft reached London and dropped their bombs on widely separated areas. A Spitfire was shot down over the capital at about 1:50 pm.

The heaviest raid of the day, at least in terms of ferocity, made its presence known to ground observers on the south coast before 5 pm. About 40 Heinkel He 111s, with fighter protection, made straight for the Westland aircraft factory at Yeovil, on the border of Dorset and Somerset. Had Ed Murrow stayed another day at his holiday hotel, he would not have had to go back to London to find some excitement.

Yeovil was partially hidden by cloud when the bombers arrived overhead; the Westland factory could not be seen at all. The attacking Heinkels were at the mercy of four RAF squadrons, and were not getting much protection from their fighter escort—the Bf 109s had already begun to run short of fuel and had turned for France; the Bf 110s were out of position. But cloud or no cloud, the bomb-aimers decided to toggle their loads and hope for the best.

The results were what might have been expected. The bomb-aimers not only missed the Westland factory, they missed Yeovil. Their bombs came down a few miles away, on Sherborne, blowing up the rail line. Having relieved themselves of their bomb loads, the Heinkel crews now had the problem of getting back home.

Actually, the Heinkel dorsal gunners gave an excellent account of themselves, shooting down several of the attacking fighters. Also, the Bf 110s finally showed up and destroyed at least one more RAF fighter. For the gunners on board the bombers, their shooting was limited to snap-shots at the darting fighters, firing whenever a Spitfire or Hurricane came into view. For the Bf 110 pilots, the problem was to maneuver behind one of the more agile RAF fighters without having a Hurricane or Spitfire do the same thing to them.

If the RAF pilots could avoid the dorsal gunners, they had a fairly easy time. Several Heinkels fell to earth or into the sea, destroyed by .303 Brownings; KG 55 alone lost four. But the German gunners knew their job, as well; eight RAF fighters were either shot down or damaged, including three Hurricanes of 56 Squadron. On the day, 56 Squadron lost five Hurricanes shot down and two damaged. None of its pilots were killed in the fighting, however.

The Luftwaffe had expended great effort and energy, and had expected a few worthwhile accomplishments in return. The day's offensive did accomplish a few items—it resulted in the destruction of 20 RAF fighters and the death of eight pilots, and scattered a few bombs on Greater London. In return, it lost a significant number of aircraft—either 47, 48, or 49, depending upon which source is consulted. Twenty-nine of these were Messerschmitt Bf 109s.[26]

The day might have been a disappointment for the Luftwaffe, but the bombers of *Luftflotte* 3 were back again that night—175 of them, to bomb London again. The night was moonless, as it had been on the previous night. And once again, as on the previous night, the bombs came down on random districts of the city. No major damage was done, but the capital did sustain another wound—more lives were disrupted, and more inhabitants were killed and injured.

---

26   One of these Messerschmitts, a Bf 109 of JG 26 piloted by Unteroffizier Horst Perez, was shipped to New York, and toured America as part of Britain's propaganda program.

1 October, Tuesday

Scattered nuisance raids by fighter-bombers began during the late morning, and continued all day long. The "tip and run" attacks put a new strain on both the Luftwaffe's *Jagdgeschwader* pilots, who flew the small pinprick raids, as well as on the Hurricane and Spitfire pilots of Fighter Command, who had to intercept them.

The day's activities marked a change in tactics by the Luftwaffe—at least for the time being. Until further notice, no more twin-engined bombers would be sent out on daytime operations. Only fighters—both Bf 109s and Bf 110s—would be sent across the Channel in daylight. The Heinkels, Junkers, and Dorniers would be reserved almost exclusively for night operations. The Battle of Britain, that is to say the Luftwaffe's offensive against RAF Fighter Command, was nearing an end; the Battle of London, the nighttime Blitz, was becoming the Luftwaffe's main offensive thrust.

This shift meant a dramatic change for German fighter units. One *staffel* out of each *gruppe*—that is to say nine fighters out of 27, or one-third of the fighters in northern France—found themselves relegated to the role of lugging 550-lb. bombs. Crews of Bf 110 Zerstörer units took this transformation with a shrug and a sigh. Their role during the battle had already been changed several times, from fighter to fighter-bomber and back again. One more alteration was not about to faze them.

But the Bf 109 pilots were no happier about carrying the extra weight than they had been before. They hated the idea of lugging 250 kilograms of high explosives, which took away from their speed and maneuverability.

But like it or not, the fighter-bomber pilots found themselves on course for Southampton and Portsmouth at about 10:30 am. They dropped their bombs, drew fighters from several RAF squadrons, shot down two Hurricanes, and created general havoc before returning to their French bases. Most of the German pilots failed to see the point of the exercise—they were not inflicting very much bomb damage upon the enemy, nor were they shooting his fighters down in large numbers.

But the entire point of the operation was not to inflict heavy damage upon the enemy, but just to harrass him. Luftwaffe High Command's objective was simply to keep RAF Fighter Command off balance—distracting the RAF, keeping it busy without putting Luftwaffe units in any great peril. The goal was now to challenge the enemy pilots and make them come up to confront these raids, and keep them from getting any rest. If some of them could be killed during the course of the day's work, so much the better.

During the afternoon, several more of these harrassing raids were launched. Most of them were intercepted over Kent and Sussex. The Luftwaffe lost two Bf 109s; the RAF had one Spitfire shot down. Bombs landed on south and central London during the mid-afternoon. After 5 pm., two more raids came over to challenge RAF pilots who, once again, rose to the occasion.

The RAF lost five fighters during the course of the day; the Luftwaffe lost four. A great deal of gasoline, ammunition, and energy had been expended, with very little to show for it.

The Luftwaffe's *nachteinsatz* began at about 7:30 for Londoners. Liverpool, Manchester, Swansea, and Glasgow also received minor visitations. In the course of the night-long raid, two bombers were shot down out of 175.

Edward R. Murrow's nightly broadcast did not concern this night's air raid. He told his American audience about the after-effects of yesterday night's Blitz, and how it affected ordinary people. The subject of this program was some soldiers who had been assigned to clear away the wreckage and bomb rubble of destroyed buildings.

"Today, in one of the most famous streets in London, I saw soldiers at work clearing away the wreckage of nearly an entire block," Murrow said. "They thought maybe people were still buried in the basement, and kept on working even after the air raid sirens sounded. They paid no attention to the bursts of anti-aircraft fire overhead as they bent their backs and carried away basketfuls of mortar and brick."

This was white propaganda at its height—soldiers trying to rescue trapped civilians from a bombed building in spite of enemy bombers overhead. The Germans sounded brutal, threatening wounded civilians; the soldiers sounded heroic. This broadcast, along with the many others in this same vein, proved invaluable in switching the American point of view from isolationism to sympathy toward Britain.

2 October, Wednesday

Formations of German aircraft—and sometimes just single machines—flew a series of scattered attacks aimed mainly at London. These were similar to the attacks carried out the day before, except that the bombers were back—although in small numbers.

The south coast CH stations began plotting the enemy aircraft at about 8:30 am. First attacks began at about 9 o'clock, and continued for the next three hours. Biggin Hill was bombed aqain, for the first time in weeks. The Spitfires and Hurricanes of 11 Group were waiting; four Bf 109s were shot down over Kent between 10 o'clock and 10:30, along with a Do 17 of KG 2.

During the afternoon, more of these small, scattered formations overflew Kent. The results were just about the same as for the morning's raids—some of the raiders dropped their bombs on London's southern outskirts, while some became tangled up with RAF fighters and did not get very far beyond the Channel coast.

Although the pilots of 11 Group were harried, flying several trips to keep up with the rash of German raids, it was the Luftwaffe that drew the short end. German losses: 11 airplanes, 7 of which were bombers. The RAF lost no fighters to enemy action.

London was the target again after dark. The sirens sounded at about 7:30, the same as last night, and the All Clear was not given until 11 hours later. The moon was now in its waxing phase, growing brighter with each passing night, but was still not bright enough to help bomb-aimers pick out anything on the ground—not even a landmark the size of St. Paul's Cathedral.

Bomber crews dropped their loads at random, blowing up rail lines, office buildings, houses, and anything else that happened to get in their way. This was especially true with "hostilities only" crews, reservists who wanted to dump their bombs and get back home again before flak or night fighters got them.

Night fighters were up and searching for the raiders, but did not claim any kills which was not surprising. Just finding a German raider was more a matter of luck than anything else, especially on a night when moonlight was practically nil. Shooting one of them down was a virtual impossibility.

Even night fighters that carried the new AI air-to-air radar sets, such as the Bristol Beaufighter, had their problems—not the least of which was the radar itself. The sets were so tempermental that any kind of vibration might knock them out, such as the recoil of the fighter's machine guns, or even the engine's shake. Sometimes, the small screen would go blank for no apparent reason, leaving the pilot with no alternative but to return to base.

Spitfires and Hurricanes, which had no radar, had almost no chance at all of spotting an enemy bomber. With a full moon, a sharp-eyed pilot might be able to see something if he happened to be in the right place—and the moon happened to be in the right position. But on a night like this, going up was almost a complete waste of time.

3 October, Thursday

Cloudy weather and poor visibility limited operations. Raids were small—one bomber flying without escort, or two fighter bombers acting as an independent unit—and were launched from bases in Belgium and the Low Countries. Northern France was closed down by bad weather.

The raiders approached from the east, attacking scattered objectives in eastern and southern England. London was not bombed, but nearby Harrow and Reading received visits. The RAF fighter station at Tangmere also had a bit of excitement when enemy aircraft showed up during the afternoon, but no serious damage was done to the base. That phase of the battle, heavy raids aimed at RAF fighter bases, had passed.

Even though the German pilots had plenty of cloud cover in which to hide from interfering RAF fighters, they were not always successful in getting to the safety of the overcast before the Spitfires or Hurricanes got to them. Nine Luftwaffe machines were shot down; the RAF lost no fighters.

Fog and rain interfered with night operations, as well, but *Luftflotte* 3 still managed to mount an effort against London. Sixty bombers—about one-third as many as on the past two nights—toggled their loads over Greater London. Anti-aircraft fire was fairly intense, but not very accurate; most of the bursting shells did not even come close to the bombers, although some of the less experienced crews were rattled by the explosions.

Most of the bombs came down on London's southern and western suburbs. The General Aircraft Factory in Feltham, Middlesex, was damaged, but private homes suffered more damage than military targets. Jangled nerves, sleep, and morale suffered most of all.

4 October, Friday

Rain and low visibility once again interfered with Luftwaffe operations, but failed to ground the day's planned air strikes. Small raids, consisting of Bf 109s, Bf 110s, and Ju 88s, flew northward above Kent throughout the late morning hours. Bombs actually fell on London at about 1 o'clock. Before that, Canterbury, Folkstone, and other towns in Kent were hit by bombs.

All this activity was putting the pilots of 11 Group under debilitating strain. Spitfire and Hurricane pilots flew several interceptions every day—sometimes as many as four. Pilots in Spitfire squadrons especially felt the pressure; incoming raids were flying at heights above 25,000 feet, altitudes which the less-sophisticated Hurricanes could not reach.

In spite of their high altitude, however, 12 of the German raiders were brought down. Anti-aircraft crews shot down a Ju 88 over London at around 5 o'clock. During the morning, Squadron Leader Robert Stanford Tuck, who had taken command of 257 Squadron's Hurricane pilots on 9 September, also accounted for a Ju 88—one of the 29 enemy aircraft he would destroy before the war ended.

Hitler, Göring, and the Luftwaffe High Command were keeping the pressure on and were also keeping everyone guessing as to what they were going to do next.

* * *

The pressure continued at night, as well; London was bombed for the 28th consecutive night. About 170 bombers dropped their loads within the wide boundaries of Greater London, keeping civilians confined to their air raid shelters. As on previous nights, anti-aircraft guns added to the din with their firing and did no damage to the raiders.

Edward R. Murrow had an unusual subject for his nightly editorial from Broadcasting House. Instead of describing the ordeal of London's common people in the Blitz, Murrow spoke about an item he had seen in the newspaper.

"In this evening's London papers," Murrow said, "President Nicholas Murray Butler, of Columbia University, is quoted as saying that any faculty member who cannot agree with the University's stand and its desire to help Britain should resign."

A leading American university had announced its full support of Britain and its war effort against Nazi Germany. What was even more striking, its president invited any of the university's teaching staff to resign if they did not agree with this point of view.

Last July, when the battle was just beginning, such an announcement would have been unheard of. But after three months of stories about ruthless Nazi attacks and unshakable British resolve, and insinuations that the United States would be next on Hitler's list if Britain surrendered—in short, after three months of a subtle but relentless campaign of white propaganda—Columbia University declared itself as pro-British. Not only pro-British, but pro-intervention—helping Britain meant becoming involved in the war.

Ed Murrow could have congratulated himself for the part he played in this change of attitude. And if Columbia University made this switch, how many other Americans felt the same way?

5 October, Saturday

The weather brightened during the early morning, making for better flying weather. Fighter and bomber units in northern France took full advantage of this improvement. An attack in force was thrown at targets in Kent, as well as at London. This series of raids began at about 11:00 am., and continued for over 2 hours.

Among the first wave of attackers were the bomb-carrying Bf 110s of *Erprobungsqruppe* 210. *Erpro* 210's target was the recently finished RAF fighter base at West Malling—a tailor-made objective for this crack unit. They made their usual expert run-in and precision attack, hitting the field several times, cratering the landing area, and leaving the brand-new base very much the worse for their visit.

Unfortunately for them, however, *Erpro* 210 ran into the Poles of 303 Squadron, who were just as expert and determined. The Poles had murder in their hearts, and murder they did. Two of the twin-engined fighters were shot down before they made their bombing attack, two more were destroyed after they released their bombs, and two others were so badly shot up that they crashed in France before they could reach their base. Eight pilots and crew were killed, including *Erpro's* new commander—their third since the battle began.

But the West Malling attack was only one raid, and it was over by about 11:45. Three others followed, including a fighter sweep by about 25 Messerschmitt 109s at about 1:15. The sky over Kent became a lattice-work of contrails, as Hurricane and Spitfire units rose to confront the attackers. Anyone in Kent could see the fighting with the naked eye—white chalk marks against a blue-grey autumn backdrop.

Between about 11:45 and 12:30, 13 Bf 109s were either shot down or damaged. Several bombers also returned to base with bullet damage; some of them never flew again. But RAF squadrons also suffered in the fighting; 66 Squadron lost three Spitfires over Kent shortly before noon. Several other units also lost fighters to the guns of German pilots.

Another raid crossed the coast before 2 pm., mostly Messerschmitt Bf 109s. Several squadrons scrambled to intercept, including the Hurricanes of 607 Squadron. Over Kent, the pilots of 607 apparently were either distracted or were half asleep. At any rate, none of them caught sight of the approaching formation of Bf 109s; the German pilots were on top of them and gone again before any of the Hurricane pilots had the time to react. Before they disappeared, the Germans shot down four Hurricanes and damaged three more—although none of the pilots had been killed. When the survivors returned to Tangmere, they were a chastened bunch. And there was still another attack to come. At about 5 pm., two formations bombed the port facilities of Southampton. None of the bombers were shot down, but several found their targets—crew members could see smoke coming from the city as they strained toward the Channel.

It had been a wild day for both sides—a half-dozen raids by the Luftwaffe; 1,175 sorties by the RAF; air fighting all across Kent and East Sussex. Incredibly, each side lost only nine aircraft.

Apart from the few privileged individuals on the secret Ultra list, no one in Britain had any idea that the invasion had been called off. This much air activity seemed to indicate that Hitler must have something sinister in mind—he wouldn't be sending all those planes over for nothing.

The active day was followed by an equally active night. London was bombed by more than 100 raiders in another dusk-to-dawn Blitz. Most of the bombs fell on the East End, setting fires in the docks.

These attacks lasted all night long by design. It did not take 10 or 12 hours for 100 or so bombers to reach their target and drop their loads. But by stretching the raid to last all night, which meant sending the bombers out either singly or in small groups at widely-spaced intervals, the strain on civilians was intensified. Staging this sort of raid every night—since 7 September, the Heinkels and Junkers had not missed a single evening—increased the tension even further.

While the Alert was on, civilians felt compelled to stay in their air raid shelters. Sleep would be lost, lives would be disrupted, and morale would be lowered. Even more beneficial to the German war effort, production in factories would drop—workers on the night shift could not do their job if they were in a shelter.

And, the bombers were sent over in a slow, steady stream. The first raiders would cross the coast at about 7:30 pm; the last would depart anywhere from 4:30 am. to 6 am. Because night fighters and anti-aircraft were both so pitifully ineffective, the German bombers could do pretty much as they pleased, and could roam over London and southern England at will.

6 October, Sunday

The Luftwaffe was forced to curtail its operations for the first time in days by heavy weather.

Rain kept the large formations on the ground. Only single bombers, or sometimes small formations of two or three aircraft, got off the ground. But even these lone raiders managed to get through to their targets, and kept the defenders from getting very much rest regardless of the weather.

These harrassing jabs were aimed mainly at RAF fighter bases—once again, shades of August. And as they had done in August, these marauding attacks did their share of damage. A single low-flying bomber located Biggin Hill, dropped its bombs, and got away in spite of alert anti-aircraft defenses. A parachute-and-cable battery fired at the airplane and claimed to have hit it; if they did, the bomber did not crash. The bomber's crew could congratulate themselves on a job well done; they severely damaged three barracks buildings, blew up a Spitfire of 72 Squadron, and lived to get back to base.

These were not major attacks, and were not meant to be—these were stinging blows to the mid-section instead of a roundhouse punch to the jaw. Many writers and historians claim that the Luftwaffe was beaten by mid-September, but this was not the case. The German air force was not about to concede defeat, even though morale did falter as the possibility of an invasion began to fade. While the weather still held, before winter storms came, the bombers and fighters went out every day, in preparation for ... no one knew what.

More raids presented themselves in the afternoon. Again, fighter fields were the objective. Middle Wallop was damaged by high explosives and by oil bombs—some sort of primitive napalm.

Toward evening, though, the weather closed in; the airfields in northern France shut down altogether by cloud and heavy rain. Further operations were cancelled for the rest of the day; both bomber and fighter units stood down.

Losses on the day: the Luftwaffe lost six aircraft; the RAF had one fighter destroyed.

Night sorties against London also were curtailed by bad weather. Rather than risk accidents caused by the rain, Luftwaffe High Command decided to cut back on the number of sorties flown. Only seven bombers raided London, a dramatic reduction. But even though no extensive damage was done—although a gunpowder factory just north of London was damaged—the Alert kept Londoners in their shelters again. Which meant more disturbed sleep and more lost production hours.

7 October, Monday

The weather still was not very good for flying when daylight arrived; clouds limited visibility, and rain still threatened. But it was better than yesterday, and the forecast predicted a steady improvement as the day went on. Luftwaffe senior commanders were encouraged enough to order another series of strikes against targets in southern England.

During the morning and early afternoon, the main objective was London. Small formations of bombers and fighters crossed the coast, made their way north, and were challenged by Spitfires and Hurricanes of 11 Group. Each side had several of its aircraft damaged by enemy gunfire. A pilot of 41 Squadron became a little too casual in his approach on a Do 17, and was shot down by return fire from the Dornier's gunner. Another Spitfire of 41 Squadron was damaged during the same encounter.

The day's second attack began crossing the Channel at about 12:15, and met with the same reaction from 11 Group. This time, the German force was slightly larger—between 150 and 160 aircraft, mostly Bf 109s, as opposed to about 130 planes in the morning attack. The intercepting force was larger, as well—10 Group squadrons at Middle Wallop were put on alert.

Later in the afternoon, with skies becoming increasingly bright, the scenario was repeated—50 Bf 109s took part in a fighter sweep across Kent. But this time, the fighter sweep was part of a larger effort. Off to the west, fighters and bombers were on their way to Yeovil again, to attack the Westland aircraft factory.

The Yeovil raid began as a melee and ended in a shambles. It came in too high for a pinpoint attack—about 27,000 feet—but high enough for the CH stations to plot it and give ample warning of its approach. By the time the formation reached the coast, the Spitfire and Hurricane pilots were in position to intercept.

Although the formation was well-escorted, a large part of the fighter screen were Bf 110s. Apparently, the lessons of the past summer had been forgotten; the far more nimble Hurricanes and Spitfires had no trouble at all in outmaneuvering the big, twin-engined Zerstörers and shooting them to pieces. Seven Bf 110s of ZG 76 were shot down within a few minutes of each other.

At least some of the bombers got through to their target. The Westland factory did receive some bomb damage, although two of the attackers were destroyed for their efforts. Seven RAF fighters were also destroyed in this fracas.

A total of 17 RAF fighters were destroyed during the day's fighting; the Luftwaffe lost 21 aircraft.

In Berlin, Göring issued a five-part directive to explain the Luftwaffe's recent burst of activity. In his guidelines, Göring called for: the steady and unrelenting destruction of London and its industry; complete air superiority above the Channel; the crushing of London's civilian population, including its morale; the wearing down of Britain's armed forces; and the complete disintegration of all activity in Britain—trade, industrial, technical, and civil.

It was typical of the Reichsmarschall that he gave absolutely no hint of how to go about carrying out these mighty objectives—probably because he hadn't any idea himself. His biographers point out that Göring was devoting most of his time to plundering art treasures from France and other occupied countries, and that he had completely lost interest in the air war by this time. His five points seem to confirm this. They have the ring of a man who has lost all enthusiasm for his work—someone who could do great and wonderful things, if only he could lift himself out of his armchair.

In spite of any loss of interest, the air war went on. After sundown, London once again became *Luftflotte* 3's primary objective, although Liverpool and other cities also came under attack. The effort was not a major one; only moderate damage was done to scattered areas throughout the city. It had been exactly one month since the Blitz against London had begun, a month that had seen the Luftwaffe make many changes in its air offensive.

At about this time, American broadcaster/reporter Quentin Reynolds was in his large apartment house in a fashionable district of London when it was hit by a bomb. He wrote about the incident for *Collier's Magazine*, and also included it in a book about his London experiences.

Reynolds was a friend of Edward R. Murrow. Friendship was about the only thing that they had in common, however; their styles were completely different. Reynolds' wanted no part of Murrow's subtle white propaganda. His accounts were blatantly pro-British and anti-German, and made no attempt at either subtlety or objectivity. In every one of Reynolds' stories, the Germans were the blackest of villains, while the British were heroic underdogs, richly deserving of American help and support.

Reynolds made the bombing of his building seem more like an enjoyable adventure than a life-threatening ordeal. When they felt the shock of the explosion, he and another reporter friend went outside to see the damage. They discovered that a fire had been started in another wing. A few minutes later, they were joined by two other American colleagues, one of whom brought along a bottle of whisky.

But the Fire Brigade had the situation under control in short order. "The fire was out," Reynolds wrote. "Two apartments had been smashed. A dozen windows had been broken. No one had been hurt. We went back into the house. Everything was normal."

One of the building staff told Reynolds, "If that's the best old Jerry can do, we've got nothing to worry about."

This was Reynolds' line—"Old Jerry" was doing his worst, but it would do him no good in the end. He continued in this vein as he described other incidents during the night's raid. According to Reynolds, the bombers "scored a direct hit on a boys' school, and a great many children ... had been killed. They had hit a hospital, and thirty women had been killed."

This was just what the Ministry of Information wanted to hear—stories all about the beastly Huns dropping bombs on orphanages and hospitals, blowing up women and children and doing no damage at all to war industry. The censors could not have come up with a better story for American consumption if they had written it themselves.

Quentin Reynolds sent a steady flow of this sort of material to the United States throughout the Blitz. He also narrated the pseudo-documentary *London Can Take It*, which is actually one of the best propaganda films of the war. In short, he played his own not-very-subtle part in coaxing his fellow Americans out of their isolationism.

Adolf Hitler may not have read Quentin Reynolds' stories, but he knew all about them—as well as about Edward R. Murrow's broadcasts. His Ministry of Propaganda kept him well informed.

He knew that there was nothing he could do about Murrow or Reynolds (as he could about William L. Shirer's broadcasts from Berlin). He also knew that their broadcasts and stories were turning Americans against him, and against Nazi Germany. By this time, Hitler realized that the United States was his enemy, or, as one writer put it, "a neutral with no pretense of neutrality."

Britain's propaganda campaign was certainly having its desired effect. And not only in the United States.

8 October, Tuesday

The Luftwaffe started early. By 9 am., 150 bombers and fighters had crossed the coast on their way to London. Although several of 11 Group's squadrons were sent up to confront the attackers, the Spitfire and Hurricane pilots apparently had been given either the wrong altitude, the wrong interception course, or both by ground controllers. Combat between German and RAF machines was almost non-existent; almost every bomber got through to London.

Almost every bomber. Joseph Danforth was on his way back to his house in Sussex when he heard an airplane approaching at very low level. From the noise it was making, it was obvious to Danforth that the airplane was in trouble—"it sounded like it was in the final stages of strangulation." He turned to look, and saw a twin-engined aircraft in a shallow dive, on fire and out of control. He knew that it was German by the black *Balkenkreuz* on its fuselage. A few moments later, the plane hit the ground and blew up less than a mile away from him.

"The explosion was massive. The ground shook," Danforth recalled. "Everybody on board was killed in the crash; nobody could have survived that." He added, "I'm sure it's not very Christian of me, but I was glad that the bastards were dead. That was one bunch of Germans that wouldn't bomb us anymore."

But their comrades were busy dropping bombs on London at that very moment. Central London felt the ground shake from another kind of explosion. Government offices, underground stations, and other strategic targets were hit, even Tower Bridge, one of London's best-known landmarks, was jarred by a blast. It was the most damaging daylight raid that the capital had endured for several weeks, and the attackers managed to get away with extremely light losses—only one bomber, (Joseph Danforth's Ju 88), and one Bf 109 were shot down, as were two RAF Spitfires.

A second and a third attack were also sent. These two raids were much smaller than the early attack; about 30 aircraft took part in the second raid, and about 25 in the third. A fourth raid, another 25 planes, crossed the Channel coast just after noon. The RAF were in a better position to intercept these later formations, and shot down 11 German aircraft.

A raid was sent to Liverpool during the late afternoon, at about 4 pm. One of the attacking bombers, a Ju 88, was lost.

Fourteen German aircraft were destroyed during the day. The RAF lost eight fighters, including two Spitfires of 74 Squadron that were destroyed in a mid-air collision. Another accident cost the RAF one of its best and most determined pilots. Czech pilot Josef Frantiszek of 303 (Polish) Squadron died of injuries after his Hurricane crashed. Sgt. Frantiszek was one of the RAF's top-scoring pilots in the Battle of Britain, with 17 confirmed victories.

Keith Park was not very happy about the lack of co-ordination that morning between 11 Group's squadrons and the ground controllers. There was no excuse for allowing 150 German aircraft to penetrate all the way to London, bomb the city, and get back home again virtually unmolested. Especially not at this stage of the battle.

To prevent a repeat of this morning's fiasco, Park issued an order, a sort of guideline, for both fighter squadrons and controllers. These guidelines set down the procedure for fighter squadrons on patrol and responsibilities of ground controllers. Specifically, the memo set down the form of attack to be taken against enemy fighters ("dive repeatedly on them and climb up again each time to regain height"); the duties of ground controllers ("keep the squadron commander informed as to the height and direction of approaching raids"); as well as other points useful to Spitfire pilots on patrol over Kent (such as conserving oxygen). Spitfire pilots were especially mentioned because the Hurricanes were expected to stay at a lower altitude and deal with the German bombers.

Along with everyone else in Fighter Command, Park had no idea what Göring could do next. He wanted 11 Group to be ready for any eventuality. The air war could go on indefinitely; even if the Luftwaffe's attacks slacked off because of winter weather, they would be sure to resume come spring.

The Alert sounded in London just after 7 pm. Nine hours later, the All Clear was given. It was the city's second big raid in less than 12 hours.

By this time, going to shelter had become a set routine for most Londoners. But spending another night in an air raid shelter was no substitute for sleeping at home. The stresses of the Blitz affected some people more than others; surprisingly, many carried on with a normal life in spite of the dangers and inconveniences of being under attack each night. But even those with the steadiest of nerves were resigned to the possibility that the bombing would go on for many months to come.

9 October, Wednesday

The Luftwaffe changed its tactics again, at least partially. In addition to attacking London, bombers and fighters also turned on the fighter bases of 11 Group.

Three separate attacks were made: about 150 aircraft came over just before 11 am.; another 150 made their appearance about two hours later; and the last wave came during the late afternoon. These formations broke into smaller groups before diving on their individual targets. In a series of short, ferocious raids, the bombers and fighters swooped down, dropped their bombs, machine gunned the fighter stations, and zoomed off in the general direction of the Channel coast.

In spite of this rage of activity, losses on both sides were surprisingly light—the RAF lost three fighters (and three pilots); the Luftwaffe had nine of its aircraft shot down. The suddenness of these attacks, many of which were carried out by bomb-carrying fighters, were mainly responsible for the low casualty rate. Five of the nine German aircraft shot down were fighters.

By shifting targets and sending low-flying raiders in large numbers, Luftwaffe High Command maintained its pressure on RAF Fighter Command—attacking London, then switching to the fighter bases, and then attacking both at the same time. But they were not giving their own pilots very much rest, either. Today's sorties were flown regardless of the fact that the weather, which was windy and rainy across northern France, was almost bad enough to suspend operations.

German pilots and crew were beginning to have doubts about the long-awaited invasion of England, and whether it was going to take place this year or not. No one had heard any word on the subject for some time. And the weather was certainly not going to get any better before New Year's. These thoughts made the raids against the RAF airfields seem even more difficult than they had been during the summer. During July and August, at least there had been a reason for these life-threatening trips across the Channel. But now there did not seem to be any real point to them.

Another all-night Alert remained in effect for London until the early morning hours. Districts throughout Greater London were hit by bombs, with varying degrees of damage in each district. Anti-aircraft gunners had developed their own air raid routine—they trained their guns toward the sound of the incoming bombers, and proceeded to blast away at aircraft they usually could not even see.

Once in a while, some battery got lucky and brought down one of the raiders in spite of the odds. A Ju 88 of KG 54 was hit by an anti-aircraft shell, and did not return to base. The gunners who fired the fatal shell were not even aware that they had actually shot down a German bomber.

10 October, Thursday

The attacks on the RAF fighter stations had succeeded so well on Wednesday that the Luftwaffe decided to try their luck again on Thursday. The weather had not improved since yesterday, however; rain clouds and fog still hampered visibility across northern France and the south of England.

A mixed force of bombers and fighters bombed and strafed Tangmere's airfield just after 8 am., cratering the landing area and damaging some of the buildings. The low cloud helped the attackers evade RAF interceptors, as it had done in the past—the bombers and fighter-bombers hid in the clouds before making their bomb run, and shot back into them again after releasing their bombs.

But the RAF pilots managed to get to some of the raiders. At least two Do 17s of KG 2 returned to base with battle damage. A Spitfire pilot from 92 Squadron was shot down by return fire from a Dornier during the Tangmere raid. Two pilots of the same squadron were killed over the airfield in a mid-air collision.

Throughout the morning and into the afternoon, small groups of bombers and fighter-bombers harrassed targets scattered throughout southern England. Warmwell aerodrome was one of the targets; the fighter station received a rude visitation from fighter-bombers that bombed and strafed the station at about 1 pm. One Hurricane was shot down while trying to intercept.

None of these strikes inflicted anything resembling major damage. The RAF lost three fighters in combat, as well as three others from accidents. Luftwaffe losses consisted of four fighters and bombers. Pilots on both sides were kept tense and tired—especially German pilots, who were not rotated to rear areas for a rest. And there was still no word about the invasion of England, although just about everyone had his own pet theory on that particular subject.

"Tonight's raid has been widespread," reported Edward R. Murrow in his broadcast to the United States. Wales, Liverpool, and Manchester were bombed as well as London. Fifteen RAF airfields also received some unwelcome attention from the Luftwaffe.

In London, the anti-aircraft gunners were back at work, hammering away at the German raiders even through the low clouds. And, once again, one of the gun crews got lucky. For the second night in a row, an enemy bomber was brought down by anti-aircraft fire. The incident took place over the London docks at about 4:30 am.; a Ju 88 was disabled by a bursting shell, and its crew bailed out.

The destruction of the Junkers happened too late to be included in a news report to America, by Ed Murrow or any of his American colleagues. Had the bomber been shot down a few hours earlier, it certainly would have been broadcast to the United States. These days, everything—certainly the destruction of a German raider—was fuel for the great Anglo-American propaganda machine.

11 October, Friday

During the night, the fog and rain of the past few days had cleared away. Morning brought fair skies and, along with them, air strikes against southern England.

About 100 Bf 109s crossed the coast shortly after 10 am. The fighters split into small groups and carried out hit and run attacks on cities and towns in Kent, including Canterbury and Folkstone. A similar number of Messerschmitts came over about an hour later. This group went after fighter fields—Kenley and Biggin Hill included.

It was almost a repeat of last summer, except for the casualties—losses were a fraction of what they had been during the July and August attacks, with each side losing only three fighters during the morning raids.

Two more raids came over in the afternoon—fighter sweeps of 100 Bf 109s attacking targets in Kent. The results were about the same as a few hours earlier: the targets, including several towns in Kent, were harrassed by light raids; losses of pilots and aircraft once again were relatively small.

Losses for the day: the Luftwaffe had seven of its aircraft destroyed; nine RAF fighters failed to return. Considering the hundreds of sorties flown by each side—nearly 1,000 were flown by RAF Fighter Command—these figures are nothing short of remarkable.

Pilot exhaustion, especially among German pilots, was largely responsible for the relatively small number of airplanes shot down. It had been a long and wearing battle. Pilots were simply missing their chances against enemy aircraft.

At bomber bases across northern France, teletype machines clacked out the message: London again tonight. The Heinkels and Junkers began their cross-Channel shuttle at about 6:30 pm. Sometime after 7 o'clock, the air raid sirens began to sound across south London.

The first bombs landed within the London Defence Region between 7:15 and 7:30. For the next nine hours, the bombers scattered their cargoes across London and its suburbs; anti-air-craft batteries fired back, but scored no hits tonight. By 4:30, the last raider had set course for France.

In the morning, Londoners swept up the broken glass and began mending the damage, while fighter pilots at RAF stations began preparing for another day.

12 October, Saturday

Autumn fog spoiled the early morning sky, but all trace of mist had disappeared by the time the first air strike of the day was ready for take-off. Targets in Kent were the objective once again—nice, easy targets, if the Spitfires and Hurricanes could be got rid of.

The raids began before 9 am. and continued almost non-stop all day long—groups of German aircraft, mostly Bf 109s, kept slipping across the Channel until after 5 pm. Squadrons from 11

Group were sent up to intercept and, given good interception courses by ground controllers, confronted the Luftwaffe formations from a favorable position. In this situation, the Messerschmitt pilots fought all out.

Three Hurricanes of 145 Squadron were shot down over the coast of Kent around 10:30, within a few minutes of each other. Just before 10 o'clock, three more Hurricanes had been destroyed by Bf 109s; their remains crashed to earth in Kentish fields. The Luftwaffe also had their own losses to contend with. Flight Lieutenant Robert Stanford Tuck, one of the RAF's leading scorers in the battle, held a Bf 109 in his gunsight long enough to bring it down with a burst from his Hurricane's eight .303 Brownings.

Several other German machines were destroyed during the morning's furious combat, as well.

During the afternoon, RAF fighter bases once again drew the Luftwaffe's attention. Biggin Hill and Hawkinge were bombed and strafed at around 4:30 pm. Two Messerschmitts were shot down over Biggin Hill, and 92 Squadron lost one of its Spitfires defending Hawkinge.

The leaders of these air strikes were very efficient in finding and hitting their targets in spite of opposition from Spitfire and Hurricane pilots. And the German fighter pilots gave as good as they got: they shot down 10 RAF fighters, while losing 11 aircraft.

It had been a good day for the Luftwaffe, almost as good as during the glory days of late August. Some Ju 88s even bombed central London. Other bombers hit the city's southeastern suburbs, giving its civil population something to remember for quite a while.

While the day's fighting was churning the sky above Kent and Sussex, Adolf Hitler gave his senior commanders a directive that they would remember for quite a while. He issued the following order, (which was actually released by Feldmarschall Wilhelm Keitel):

Der Führer has decided that from now until the spring, preparations for Sea Lion shall be continued only for the purpose of keeping both political and military pressure on Enqland.

If the invasion should be reconsidered for the spring or the early summer of 1941, orders for a renewal of operational preparedness will be issued at that time. In the meantime, military conditions shall be improved for a later invasion.

Much has been made about this directive signalling "the end of the Battle of Britain." But the battle would continue, in spite of Hitler's order involving Operation Sea Lion. His decision would have very little effect on the pilots of either RAF Fighter Command or the Luftwaffe. There was no question that the Blitz had now overshadowed the daily air fighting—both as the Luftwaffe's main offensive, and as the Ministry of Information's main focus for propaganda. Reporters had all but stopped sending stories about the RAF and its fighter pilots to the United States—except for stories about the Eagle Squadron—and were concentrating on the bombing of London. Articles about the Blitz appeared in every American newspaper and magazine, complete with dramatic photos of bomb ruins and victims. The photos were carefully censored; most of them were of blitzed hospitals or historic old places—factories, transportation centers, and any other legitimate military targets were not allowed to be published. London's message to the United States—actually, the Ministry of Information's official message to the United States—was: "We've beaten the Germans in the air. We can take whatever they hit us with in their nighttime Blitz, and give it back, too."

Air warfare was still a new form of warfare in 1940. The broadcasts, stories, photos, and newsreels made the Blitz, as it had done for the Battle of Britain during the summer just past, warfare's first media event—a carefully arranged and censored media event, orchestrated by the Ministry of Information. And it certainly did stir American sympathies. Americans were appalled by the horrors of bombing, and were genuinely moved by the tales of British resilience and bravery. But whether or not Americans had become sympathetic enough to enter the fighting on the British side remained to be seen.

13 October, Sunday

In spite of the fact that the weather was sunny all throughout the morning the first Luftwaffe appearances did not take place until early afternoon.

Today, the Messerschmitt fighter-bombers and their escort left the RAF airfields alone and concentrated on London and vicinity. Just after noon, 50 Bf 109s bombed and machine gunned the arsenal at Woolwich in East London. After doing their damage, the fighters streaked for home before their fuel ran out.

The day's second attack, about 60 fighters and fighter-bombers, approached London from several different directions at about 2 pm. Several Hurricane and Spitfire units scrambled to intercept, but most of the Messerschmitt pilots managed to avoid contact. One of the escorting fighters was shot down over Kent. Chatham's anti-aircraft defenses bagged one of its own fighters, a Hurricane of 17 Squadron, by mistake to the embarrassment of the gunners.

At about 4 pm., between 25 and 30 Bf 109s presented Londoners with their third raid. Once again, 11 Group's squadrons were scrambled and, once again, most German pilots avoided contact. In the course of this air strike, one Messerschmitt was shot down, while three Spitfires were damaged by enemy cannon and machine gun fire.

There was another cause for embarrassment, as well. A Blenheim of 66 Squadron was shot down by Hurricane pilots, who mistook it for a Ju 88; a second Blenheim was damaged during this episode. It was not a proud day for the defenses, who destroyed nearly as many of their own aircraft as they did the enemy's—five Luftwaffe aircraft did not return.

Hitler's order concerning Operation Sea Lion was not having any effect on the Luftwaffe. Invasion or no invasion, senior air force commanders, including Hermann Göring, were not about to give up on their offensive. Especiaily when the results were as favorable as they had been today— the fighter-bombers charged across Kent, hit their targets (including central London), and escaped before the RAF had the chance to inflict anything more than superficial losses. It had not been a spectacularly successful day, but it was a highly satisfying one.

But many commanders on the *geschwader* level may have wondered about the point of these raids, regardless of how successful they might have been. Maintaining political and military pressure seemed a flimsy pretext for risking the lives of pilots and aircrew if Sea Lion was not going to take place. The only other possible reason for carrying out these attacks would be if the invasion were re-scheduled for the spring of 1941, and even this seemed uncertain.

Several cities were paid nighttime visits by Heinkels and Junkers of *Luftflotte* 3, including Liverpool and Birmingham. But London, as usual, received the main force.

About 100 bombers began coming over in a steady stream "shortly after blackout time," according to Edward R. Murrow. This was a surprisingly low number of raiders, considering the fact that the moon was very bright—nearly full, in fact—which allowed bomb-aimers to see their targets more distinctly.

Seeing a target and hitting it were two entirely different matters, however, as the crew that attacked Fighter Command Headquarters at Stanmore, Middlesex, discovered. Even though they were able to pinpoint Bentley Priory—a building of that size would have been difficult to overlook, especially in bright moonlight—they missed it by a mile. Literally—their bombs fell on Stanmore Underground Station, over a mile away.

14 October, Monday

The Luftwaffe staged another day of small hit-and-run raids, which were carried out through cloud and drizzle. In spite of the enthusiasm of some senior Luftwaffe officers, the weather curtailed the number of sorties by German airplanes.

Raids were scattered throughout the south of England, and included London's southern suburbs. Because these raids were so widely spread out, and also because the cloud cover limited

Men of the London Fire Brigade at work during one of the autumn 1940 raids.

visiblity, none of the raiders were shot down—in spite of nearly 300 interception sorties by RAF Fighter Command.

Air Vice Marshal Park drafted an elaborate memo on the subject of the Luftwaffe, especially on its ability to evade RAF fighters. In his memo, Park advised pilots and controllers that enemy fighter-bombers were capable of reaching London within 20 minutes of the first warning by CH stations (something they already knew). He went on to point out that only fighters already in the air would be capable of intercepting the speeding Messerschmitts before they reached London.

The Germans seemed to have a new trick up their sleeves every day. It was becoming more and more difficult to stay one jump in front of them—necessary if their raiders were to be stopped before they could reach their targets.

London was on the receiving end of another all night raid, which lasted nine hours. The central part of the city was heavily damaged. Among the buildings hit was the exclusive conservative Carlton Club, which was blown up by a direct hit. Much was made of this particular bomb incident; the destruction of this West End club was offered as evidence that all Londoners were in the front line, not just the poor and the working classes of East London. (This point was strictly for domestic consumption; Americans neither knew nor cared about British class divisions.)

Five hundred died as a result of the bombing; four times that many were injured.

15 October, Tuesday

Action on this mad day began before 9 am., when a formation of Messerschmitt fighter-bombers and their escort streaked for London at full throttle. This time, 11 Group's squadrons were in position to confront the attackers. Each side lost several fighters in this encounter, and had several more damaged, but the German pilots managed to press through to central London again. Among other targets, Waterloo Station was bombed. Waterloo is one of London's main rail stations, and suffered considerable damage from blast and explosion.

But this was only the first attack. All morning long and into the afternoon, the fields of Kent were showered with spent machine gun cartridge cases—both .303 and 7.65 calibre—as well as by the wrecks of German and RAF aircraft and an occasional pilot in a parachute. Two Hurricanes crashed to earth near Gravesend at around 2:30; many other airplanes came down at scattered points from the south coast to the Thames Estuary. Anyone who happened to be outdoors on this clear, cool day could look up and catch a glimpse of the enemy as they sped northwards in small formations.

It had been another good day for the Luftwaffe. German pilots had accounted for 15 RAF fighters. They had also harrassed targets throughout Kent, bombed London with effect, and lost only 14 of their own planes.

Senior officers were not about to give up their offensive. They were keeping their options open for spring, and for a resumption of Operation Sea Lion.

After dark, *Luftflotte* 3 also bombed London with effect. The moon was full—the phrase "bomber's moon" had entered the vocabulary—which lit up the city almost as bright as day. "The best nights for visibility were moonlit nights after rain, particularly if the moon were not so high in the sky," a former German bomber pilot recalled. "Then with the shadows cast by the buildings and the moonlight reflected from the damp streets and squares, London below us was as clear and readable as a map."

Pilots and bomb-aimers did not have the reflection from rain-wet streets to help them tonight, but they did have the full brightness of the moon. Göring took full advantage of the situation; 410 bombers were sent to London, the largest air raid so far.

Bomb damage was predictably severe. Rail lines and roads were torn up by exploding bombs; power stations were damaged; three gas works were blown up; the historic Middle Temple was destroyed. Among the strategic buildings that were hit—targets worthy of a single precision attack—was BBC Broadcasting House.

The 9 o'clock news was in progress when the bomb landed, 550 lbs. of high explosives. It went through a window, penetrated well inside the building and finally came to rest in the music library, where it remained for about an hour. The order was given to evacuate the building, but many BBC employees decided to stay where they were—there did not seem to be any danger. The bomb squad arrived, had a look at the bomb, and were deciding what to do about it when it went off.

The blast shook the entire building. Shards of glass were blown into the ventilation system, and scattered into rooms and studios with the force of shotgun pellets. Remarkably, only seven people were killed; many more were injured, however, by blast and flying glass.

Edward R. Murrow was in the building at the time, but had been in the sub-basement and was not hurt. There is a legend that Murrow described the scene after the explosion, including the carrying of dead and wounded into the underground first aid station, in a broadcast to New York. The broadcast is not only legendary, but entirely fictitious—it never happened. Censors would never allow any broadcaster, including Murrow, to mention any specific site by name, especially any place as important as Broadcasting House.

Photos of damage done in this air raid were sent off to American newspapers and magazines, including pictures of the Middle Temple, as evidence of what the Nazis were doing to beauty and antiquity. The message was the same—London could take it. No one dared to mention the fact that nobody—not the RAF and not anti-aircraft command—was able to stop it.

The air raid provided another propaganda exercise for the Ministry of Information's American campaign. But over 400 people were killed, and about twice that many were injured. And it would take Londoners several days to get back on their feet and clean up after the devastation. The raid was further evidence that the Blitz had become more important than the daytime battle. Göring sent scattered formations up during the day, but ordered 410 bombers out after dark. Had he reversed this, as he had done in August and early September, he would have been better off. Luckily for the RAF, and the ground staff at its fighter bases, Göring never realized this.

16 October, Wednesday

After yesterday's furious activity, the fog and mist that covered northern France came as a relief. But not all German aircraft were grounded by the weather. Throughout the day, twin-engined medium bombers throttled their way above Kent in small formations, making their way toward London.

The Dorniers and Junkers were neither fast enough nor agile enough to evade the RAF fighters, which the Messerschmitt fighter-bombers could do simply by jettisoning their 550-lb. bombs. Several were brought down by the Spitfire and Hurricane pilots of 11 Group; several others were able to hide in the thick overcast and make their escape. The RAF's only loss came when P/O Lofts of 249 Squadron made the rough acquaintance of a Do 17's dorsal gunner over Kent.

Pilot Officer Lofts was obviously not as good a shot as the Dornier's gunner. He came within machine gun range, pressed the firing button, heard the muffled roar of his eight .303s, and watched his tracer miss the mark. At about the same time, the German gunner fired back. Lofts felt his Hurricane stop several 7.65 mm bullets. The fighter immediately began to lose speed. Smoke filled the cockpit, and the engine temperature began to go up.

Lofts opened the Hurricane's cockpit hood to let the smoke out, pushed the stick forward to begin his descent, and managed to bring the fighter down to a crash landing in a Kentish field. The Dornier presumably made it back to France.

Seven other German bombers were not as fortunate; they left their bullet-riddled remains scattered across Kent and Sussex.

At night, the Luftwaffe came back to London in spite of the continuing bad weather. About 200 bombers dropped their loads across the city. Pilots did not have the moon to light their way, and their marksmanship suffered in comparison with the previous night's attack. But enough damage was done to satisfy Reichsmarschall Göring, who still held hopes that his nightly attacks would intimidate Britain into surrendering.

And enough damage was done to *Luftflotte* 3 to satisfy the defenders—it was one of their best nights, in spite of limited visibility. Night fighters brought down one bomber; anti-aircraft fire accounted for a second; a third ran into barrage balloon cables and crashed. The most dramatic incident of the night occurred just before 8 pm., when a Ju 88 came down near Bishop's Stortford, Hertfordshire with bombs still on board. The bombs exploded, killing everyone on board and flattening everything in the vicinity.

This was London's 40th consecutive night under fire. The Luftwaffe showed no sign of letting up in its attack.

17 October, Thursday

Winter was closing in, slowly but surely, and bringing wet and nasty weather with it. The morning turned out misty and showery again, limiting activities to another day of small raids, mostly bombers escorted by Bf 109s, although Bf 110s took part in scattered attacks along the south coast. Cloud and poor visibility prevented sending anything larger. Several aircraft had crashed on the previous day because of fog and rain; there was no desire to repeat these accidents.

Twin-engine medium bombers were heavily employed again. In spite of their escort, several of the bombers were lost to the machine gun fire of intercepting RAF fighters. In addition, KG 1 lost two Heinkel He 111s to anti-aircraft fire.

A total of 15 Gerrnan aircraft had been destroyed, including a Bf 109 that crash-landed at Manston at about 3:45; its pilot was taken prisoner. After having been abandoned at the height of the battle, Manston was operational once again. Most of its hangars and facilities were still in ruins, however, and the station was not even close to running at peak efficiency.

On the other side, five RAF fighters were destroyed during the day, including two Hurricanes of 213 Squadron. Dornier gunners accounted for an additional two Hurricanes—one damaged, one destroyed. (Dornier units seem to have been blessed with the best shots in the Luftwaffe.) One of the Luftwaffe's leading aces, Werner Mölders, shot down a Spitfire of 66 Squadron piloted by Pilot Officer Hugh Reilley. Reilley was another American who had violated the U.S. Neutrality Act to join the RAF.

Although he was born in Detroit, Michigan, Hugh Reilley claimed Canadian citizenship for the benefit of the RAF recruiting officer. (His mother was Canadian; his father was American.) He also managed to get hold of a Canadian passport, but no one is quite certain how. Everyone involved in his little plot was sworn to secrecy; if either the Canadian or American authorities ever found out about his illegal passport, those who helped him get it would have gone to prison.

The illegal passport did its job; it got Reilley around U.S. Customs and the Neutrality Act, and across to England. In September 1940, the 22-year-old was commissioned as a Pilot Officer in the RAF and posted to 64 Squadron. He was transferred to 66 Squadron, based at Gravesend, the same month, and took part in the fighting on 15 September.

On 27 September, P/O Reilly shot down a Messerschmitt Bf 109. Three weeks later, he was shot down and killed by Werner Mölders.

Hugh Reilley is buried in a churchyard in Gravesend. His death was of no use to the Ministry of Information's American propaganda campaign—because of his illegal passport, his U.S. citizenship had been a guarded secret. Otherwise, his funeral would have been reported in every magazine and newspaper in the U.S., just as Billy Fiske's had been. But no one knew Reilley's true nationality at the time; it had been buried with him.

London was the Luftwaffe's nighttime target again. About 160 bombers hit the city, in spite of the weather.

18 October, Friday

Pilots and aircrew on both sides of the Channel got out of bed to find that the weather had worsened—visibility was so poor, in fact, that most thought that operations would be called off for the day.

Air strikes against England were not cancelled, however; they were merely postponed until the afternoon. Small formations of bombers were sent across the Channel, as well as over the North Sea to the east coast of England. These raids accomplished absolutely nothing. Because of the heavy cloud, pilots and bomb-aimers had a hard time finding their targets, let alone hitting them.

Air crew should have been given the day off because of the weather; the day's effort did not justify the losses suffered. Either 12 or 15 bombers were lost (again, depending upon which source is consulted). Two were brought down by the defenses; the rest crashed while trying to land in poor flying conditions—visibility was so poor that, in some cases, pilots could not see the ground until they were only a matter of a few feet above it.

The same conditions prevailed at RAF airfields. Six fighters were destroyed, and five pilots died, in landing accidents. The pilots either lost their bearings in the fog and ran out of fuel, or could not see the runway and overshot it.

Weather did curtail air activities at night. Raiders of *Luftflotte* 3 showed themselves over southern England at around 7 pm., as usual. But by midnight, air bases in northern France were no longer serviceable because of fog and rain.

By about 1 o'clock in the morning, the last of the raiders had departed. A woman in Barnes, south London, wrote in her diary: "The All Clear sounded a few hours early tonight, giving us all some much needed rest. Now we can all return to our beds, and not worry about whether or not we will be buried alive when a land mind blows our house over, or cremated by incendiaries. Thank you, God."

Göring and the Luftwaffe High Command were kept very well informed of the damage being done to London, as well as to other cities throughout Britain. Camera-equipped Dorniers and Junkers made daily flights over the target areas, taking sharp, clear photos of what their bomb-carrying cousins had done the day before.

Also, journalists from neutral countries supplied the Luftwaffe with a good deal of useful information. Although British (and Americans) were not allowed to mention any specific locations in their copy, neutral reporters did not allow themselves to be limited by these restrictions. Staff writers on Sweden's *Morgon Tidningen* and the Swiss *Der Bund* named districts, street addresses, and even individual buildings in their stories. Particularly on the day after a big raid—such as on 7-8 September—Swedish papers carried full particulars of bomb damage in London. These news reports very quickly wound up in the files of German Intelligence.

London was being destroyed, a little bit every day. Through German Intelligence and Luftwaffe photo-reconnaissance, Göring was well aware of what was happening to the city and its inhabitants. These reports made the Reichsmarschall believe that his campaign to bomb Britain into submission was working.

Göring's thoughts were not altogether out of place. Even though American and British reporters went on at length about the high spirits of Londoners in the face of enemy bombing, cracks were definitely beginning to show in the facade. Those who could afford to leave London took up residence in the country; some did not come back until the war was over. Those who remained endured the bombing as best they could—some stood the strain very well; others could barely carry on because of it.

"I hated the city," wrote a woman from Bow, East London. "Every time the sirens went, I would feel faint and start to shake all over. I hated walking past the bombed buildings, and wondered how much more we'd have to take. If I could have got out of London, I would have gone in a second. My husband felt the same way, but he tried to put a brave face on it."

The Luftwaffe kept the pressure on Britain, and would keep bombing cities—and sometimes airfields— throughout the winter whenever the weather allowed. If all went well, the battle would be resumed in the spring, the invasion could be launched during the summer of 1941, and the Wehrmacht would be in London, what was left of it, by autumn. But first, Adolf Hitler would have to agree that this would be the best course of action for Germany. And nobody could predict what he would do.

19 October, Saturday

Once again, weather limited the number of air strikes flown. Fog kept all but a few brave (or foolhardy) souls on the ground all morning long.

First raids did not appear until about 2 o'clock, after the sun had burned off the fog and mist. Several of 11 Group's squadrons, or at least several sections, scrambled to intercept, but no contact was made. Also, no bombs were dropped by the Luftwaffe raiders. The facts surrounding this entire action—what the Germans were doing, where they were going, and why the RAF could not find any of them—are extremely vague.

The next scramble took place about two hours later, with a fighter sweep crossed the Sussex coast. Again, the RAF squadrons intercepted. This time, some of them made contact. But the resulting combat was anything but ferocious—neither side seemed very eager to fight. None of the intruding Messerschmitts were destroyed; one Spitfire was shot down, and its pilot killed.

For all they had accomplished, the Luftwaffe might as well have stayed home. They would have saved fuel, as well as stress and strain on pilots and aircrew. No targets were bombed; no airfields were attacked, and almost no damage was done to the enemy. In the course of this day's action, two RAF fighters were lost—one through combat, the other in a landing accident. Although the Luftwaffe lost five planes, only one was the result of combat.

London was bombed after sunset, along with several other cities including Bristol. The attack on London was much more determined than any of the Luftwaffe's daytime raids. Bombs hit the central part of the city and the southern suburbs, in a raid that lasted eight and a half hours. None of the German bombers was shot down.

20 October, Sunday

During the night, the cloud cover had thinned both over France and southern England, and the fog almost completely disappeared. The resulting improvement in visibility allowed the Luftwaffe to send its first attacks during mid-morning.

At least five fighter sweeps crossed the south coast between 9:45 and 10:30—they came so closely together that it was difficult to tell where one began and the other one left off. The squadrons of 11 Group came up and, unlike the day before, a fierce and determined fight developed—actually, a series of fierce and determined fights. Two Hurricanes of 605 Squadron were shot down over Kent; at least twice as many Bf 109s added their carcasses to the growing number of crashes that littered the ground between London and the Channel. The Luftwaffe definitely came out second best in this encounter.

But the day was far from over. In the afternoon, the Luftwaffe struck out at London again; aircraft of both sides were shot down either over the capital or within sight of it. At 3 o'clock, 74 Squadron lost three Spitfires over London only minutes apart;

German machines came down in and around London all throughout the mid-afternoon, including a Messerschmitt 109 shot down over the RAF fighter base at West Malling.

The best remembered incident of the day took place just before 2 pm., when a Bf 109 blew up over Woolwich. Possibly the fuel tank was punctured and exploded, or an oxygen tank was hit by an incendiary bullet. Whatever happened, the fighter exploded, broke in half, and fell like a rock. Its burnt-out remains became the object of curiosity for everyone in the vicinity. The pilot either jumped from the airplane, fell out of the cockpit, or was blown clear by the explosion, but his parachute did not open.

The raiders did get through to London, but these were only harrassing attacks, meant to keep the enemy off balance and exhausted. The heavy stuff was left to the night bombers.

The day's activities cost the Luftwaffe 11 aircraft. The RAF lost five planes, including two Bristol Blenheims over Norway. Göring apparently thought that the effort was worth the price. He showed no sign of stopping these daylight attacks against London, or even of slowing them down.

London was indeed the target of a heavy all-night raid. (Coventry, which would endure its own ordeal in less than a month, also felt the effects of a major attack.) About 300 bombers blew up roads and rail lines, shattered buildings and homes, and disrupted thousands of lives.

It had been six weeks since the nightly Blitz had begun. American reporters were asking each other how much longer it would last, and what Hitler would do next.

21 October, Monday

The weather had reached the point where it had become as deadly as the enemy—to both sides. On 21 October, the Luftwaffe would lose six aircraft—three to enemy action; three in landing accidents. The RAF lost two fighters and their pilots as the result of accidents.

During the morning, the usual small formations made their scattered nuisance raids throughout southern England. Fog and cloud kept most of the Luftwaffe on the ground. In the afternoon, the weather improved slightly; the increase in visibility brought an increase in Luftwaffe air strikes.

London was the afternoon's main objective; the city and its fringes received another sprinkling of high explosives. This bombing was truly random, since cloud prevented bomb-aimers from picking out landmarks and individual sites.

This day's memorable incident took place well to the southwest of London, over Hampshire. One enterprising Ju 88 pilot decided to remedy the problem of low cloud by flying under it. He attacked the airfield at Old Sarum from a height of about fifty feet—some say that the pilot was pretending to come in for a landing, so that he could fool ground observers into thinking that his Junkers was a Blenheim. (RAF pilots frequenty made this mistake in reverse, shooting down a Blenheim because they thought it was a Ju 88.) The Junkers strafed the station and made its getaway at full throttle.

Two pilots of 609 Squadron (Red Tobin's, Shorty Keough's, and Andy Mamedoff's former unit) were in the vicinity. Flight Lieutenant Frank Howell and his wingman, Pilot Officer Sidney Hill, spotted the bomber and went down to investigate. F/Lt. Howard Howard was not sure if it was a Junkers or a Blenheim. When he saw the black crosses on the wings and fuselage, he knew.

Howell and Hill went after the Junkers, chasing at treetop level and sometimes below, taking quick shots at it while dodging trees and power lines. The bomber's rear gunner responded by firing smoke cartridges, which surprised the two pursuing pilots but did not make them break off their attack. Their combined machine gun fire finally took its toll; the Junkers smashed into the ground and blew up, killing the four-man crew.

This Junkers was 609 Squadron's 100th enemy aircraft destroyed. A swastika cut from the bomber's tail became one of the Squadron's prized trophies. One of the station's more artistic airmen painted its history right across the face of the diamond-shaped piece of sheet metal: the names of F/Lt. Howell and P/O

Hill, the type of aircraft, and the fact that this was a piece of 609's 100th German aircraft destroyed. It hung on a wall at Biggin Hill for many years.

Except for a few unfortunate souls who lost their homes to a stray bomb, the day had no real importance or strategic significance. But Göring was not disappointed. His major concern these days was keeping his pilots and aircrew fully prepared, and keeping the RAF under as much strain as possible. At this point, however, no one knew exactly what the Reichsmarschall was preparing for.

*　　*　　*

As foggy and rainy and the weather was, it was not quite bad enough to ground the Luftwaffe altogether. London was bombed again after dark, even though poor flying weather grounded most of *Luftflotte* 3. As had been the case during the day, no significant damage was done. But the Alert kept the air raid shelters filled, and the anti-aircraft guns broke the sleep of war workers. And an occasional bomb did find a lucky target.

A secretary with a city insurance firm, who walked past streets lined with bombed buildings every day on her way to work, made this note in her diary:

> Every day, the devastation increases. Every day, morale goes down (at least mine does). We don't seem to be able to stop any of it. American President Roosevelt says he's on our side, but will he ever send us any help? We need more than just his good wishes.

President Franklin D. Roosevelt was not going to send any help, at least not for a while. The presidential election was only two weeks off. He was not about to do or say anything that might antagonize American isolationists and jeapordize his chances for re-election.

22 October, Tuesday

Fog had settled over most of Kent during the night, which closed almost all of 11 Group's fighter bases. Only Biggin Hill,

Kenley, and Tangmere remained operational. The rest were shut down because of zero visibility.

Only a few small raids were attempted by Bf 109s during the morning. The thick fog, which went right down to the ground, prevented even low-level attacks against most areas. During the afternoon, as a rain front came through, the fog began lifting. Visibility improved, in spite of the rain. At about 2 o'clock, small formations were plotted over northern France by CH stations; by about 2:20, the German aircraft—mostly Bf 109s—had reached the Kentish coast.

Most air activity took place either over the south coast or over the Channel, beginning at about 2:30 and lasting until early evening. The fields of Kent once again became a repository of airplane wreckage, as more Spitfires, Hurricanes, and Messerschmitts left their remains along the coast.

At about 5 o'clock, a Hurricane pilot of 257 Squadron was in the middle of a fight over Folkstone when the local anti-aircraft opened fire. The Hurricane crashed, killing the pilot. It is not known whether the fighter was shot down by friendly anti-aircraft fire or by Bf 109s.

Five RAF fighters were shot down. The Luftwaffe lost six aircraft in combat, and another five because of accidents. It had been another day of little consequence.

Cloud and bad weather lessened the number of raiders that came across the Channel, but did not stop the air raids. Liverpool and Coventry were bombed yet again, as was London—for the 44th night in a row.

23 October, Wednesday

Fog and rain kept most of the Luftwaffe's fighters and bombers safely at home. Raids were sent across the Channel, but these turned out to be even smaller and more sporadic than usual. Three bombers were lost: two crash-landed in France following activities over England and the Channel; the third failed to return from an air raid against London. Another ran out of fuel and crashed. The RAF lost one Blenheim in an accident.

Once again, poor visibility failed to keep *Luftflotte* 3 from its *nachteinsatz* against London. This night's raid was heavier than last night's. Most bombs fell on central London and the docks. Morning commuters into London had their journey slowed by bombs on the railway line, and by streets closed by unexploded bombs. When workers arrived at their destinations, they sometimes discovered that their offices or factories had disappeared in the last night's bombing.

* * *

That afternoon, Adolf Hitler met with Spanish dictator Francisco Franco at Hendaye, a French border town, to persuade Franco to join the war on the Axis side. More specifically, he wanted Franco to co-operate in the invasion of the British fortress of Gibraltar, which was planned for January 1941.

Franco had no intention of joining Hitler's war, at least not right at that moment. For one thing, Spain had not yet recovered from its 1936-1939 civil war, which had put Franco in power; another war might loosen his grip on the country. Also, in spite of Hitler's assurances, Franco was not convinced that Germany had already won the war.

He avoided an armed alliance with Germany by using his own special brand of devious diplomacy. Franco agreed with everything that Hitler said, and then demanded more concessions than Hitler would ever grant— including several hundred thousand tons of grain, guns and armaments, and a demand that Gibraltar be taken by Spanish troops instead of by the Wehrmacht.

In response to Hitler's insistence that the war was already as good as over, since German triumph over Britain was by now a foregone conclusion, Franco said that he did not agree. Even though the Wehrmacht might invade and occupy Britain, Franco said, there was no guarantee that Churchill and his government would not escape to Canada and continue the war from there, with American help.

Franco had said much the same thing to Ramon Serrano Suner, his Foreign Minister (and brother-in-law). "They will fight and go on fighting, and if they are driven out of Britain they will carry on the fight from Canada. They will get the Americans to come in with them." (Apparently, everyone in the world saw this except the Germans and most Americans.)

At a state dinner that evening, Hitler once again tried to manipulate Franco into an alliance, and wound up with the same result: vague promises, but no commitment. At this point, Hitler gave up. He stormed off in disgust, calling Franco unflattering names.

Instead of indulging in an outburst of bad temper, Hitler should have listened—Franco saw the situation far more clearly than either Hitler or his senior commanders. For instance, Hitler seemed to believe that the Tripartite Pact would frighten the Americans away from active involvement in the war. And he told Mussolini, "The war is won. The rest is only a question of time."

But Franco could see this as being nothing but wishful thinking. He realized that the battle against Britain was a long way from being won and that, in all liklihood, the war would be a long one. He also foresaw, as Germany's Chief of Intelligence Wilhelm Canaris saw, that the British would bring the Americans into the war, in spite of what Hitler (or the Americans) thought.

24 October, Thursday

Although both the weather and the visibility had improved during the past 24 hours, enough morning haze remained to restrict the Luftwaffe's activities. But even after noon, when skies had cleared totally, the strikes sent out across the Channel were still only a skeleton of the August and September raids, when hundreds of fighters and bombers pulverized 11 Group's bases, and later bombed London.

Weather was only partially responsible for this dramatic reduction. Most of it was part of the Luftwaffe's plan—keep RAF Fighter Command occupied as much as possible while risking the minumum number of German aircraft.

Today's routine stuck with this basic plan. Afternoon raids were carried out by small, scattered formations against targets throughout the south of England, not causing a great deal of destruction but keeping the pilots of Fighter Command at readiness and on edge. The RAF flew nearly 500 sorties; none of its aircraft were lost in combat, but three pilots were killed in accidents. The Luftwaffe had five of its aircraft destroyed by fighters, including three Do 17s of KG 2.

These nuisance raids were certainly having their desired effect. Pilots of Fighter Command, especially of 11 Group, were forced to intercept these small formations and risk an accident. At the same time, Luftwaffe losses were being kept at a minimum.

If they could keep this up until spring, the Luftwaffe would be in a good position to renew the battle and help pave the way for the invasion of England in 1941.

The raids on London were also having their effect: disrupting lives, slowing war production, and damaging transportation and communications centers. On this night, only about 50 bombers raided the city—a small number considering that the weather was clear. It was just another small—but effective—thrust in the Luftwaffe's night campaign against Britain.

25 October, Friday

Pilots and ground crew at fighter bases throughout the south of England could see that today would be hectic. Even during the pre-dawn hours, the sky was clear blue with just a hint of haze. The Luftwaffe was certain to be over today, and in force.

They were right in their suspicions. The first raid, a fighter-bomber strike against London, crossed the coast before 9 am; it was intercepted by fighters of 11 Group. One of the Bf 109s was damaged, and crash-landed. At least some of the bomb-carrying Messerschmitts released their bombs prematurely, ridding themselves of their 550-lb. burdens to face oncoming Spitfires and Hurricanes, and blasting craters in the fields below. None of the raiders got through to London.

But there were other attempts throughout the day. The next raid came at 10 o'clock. This time, bombers were able to penetrate to London and drop their bombs on the capital. In this action, 603 Squadron lost three Spitfires to the escorting Bf 109s.

All during the afternoon, attackers pressed their way across the countryside of Kent, Sussex and Surrey in an almost endless procession: at noon; just after one o'clock; just before 2 o'clock; shortly before 3 pm.; and at about 3:45. To onlookers below, the contrails in the sky overhead looked as though the Luftwaffe were re-enacting the events of last August. Eight German fighters were shot down. Several bombers managed to reach France before crashing, severely damaged by .303 gunfire. Four RAF fighters were destroyed; several others suffered combat damage.

Another Messerschmitt exploded in mid-air, this time over Kent, to the amazement of onlookers below. Pieces of the airplane flew for miles in all directions; the bits varied in size from nuts and bolts to tires and chunks of fuselage. This time, the pilot was lucky; he managed to parachute to saftey.

Eighteen other German aircraft also were destroyed, both in combat and because of accidents. The RAF lost ten fighters.

London came under attack again, for the 49th night in a row. Bombs fell in Westminster and other parts of central London, as well as on the outskirts. One Ju 88 was lost to anti-aircraft fire.

This night's most noteworthy happening was the debut of the Italian air force, the *Reggia Aeronautica*, in the Blitz. Sixteen twin-engined Fiat bombers attacked Harwich—an event that was of major significance to the Italians, but made very little impression upon either the RAF or the Luftwaffe. One of the bombers crashed on take-off.

Actually, senior Luftwaffe officers did not want Italian units in the war against Britain. The Italians had a reputation for being under-trained. It was feared that they might be more of a liability than an asset as a partner.

But Italian dictator Benito Mussolini wanted a measure of revenge for RAF raids against Italian cities. So Adolf Hitler allowed himself to be talked into letting his Axis partner have his way.

The Italian effort was of no real consequence, but it made for stirring headlines in Rome. Saturday morning's newspapers reported that *Il Duce's intrepid eagles brought a night of terror to the cowards of East Anglia, and that the RAF had best beware.*

26 October, Saturday

The cloud and haze came back during the early morning hours. At about 10 am., the Luftwaffe also came back, in the first of several raids and fighter sweeps. In this action, two Bf 109s were damaged and one was shot down over Kent.

These days, German pilots usually did not have any specific objectives—not assigned to destroy any individual fighter bases, or even any single target within London. Their only real assignment was to harrass the RAF, to cause as much trouble as possible on the other side of the Channel, and to get back to base in one piece. Since the Luftwaffe was not trying to accomplish anything in particular, it was not very surprising that they were not doing very much damage to the enemy.

"By the end of October, my main concern was not getting killed," a former RAF Pilot Officer said. "Particularly not in a landing accident in the fog." He had been flying operations since late September, and could see that there would be no German invasion this year. Many other pilots—on both sides—- certainly felt the same way.

Four RAF fighters were destroyed during the day's fighting, including two Hurricanes shot down while strafing a Heinkel seaplane off the coast of Normandy. Luftwaffe losses totalled nine aircraft from accidents and enemy action combined.

The day's lackluster operations were followed by relatively light activity against London. The moon was now waning, and was not much help to pilots or bomb-aimers. One Heinkel was brought down by anti-aircraft fire in spite of poor visibility.

27 October, Sunday

As though trying to atone for yesterday's showing, the Luftwaffe began its attack early and made a more determined effort. By 9 o'clock in the morning, London had already received its first bombing raid. Workers arriving at their offices or factories were sent to an air raid shelter. Also, the countryside of Kent received the shot-up wrecks of four more fighters: two Spitfires and two Messerschmitts.

Later in the morning, and again just before noon, more raiders were picked up on CH screens and, a short time later, by ground observers in Kent and Sussex. Formations tended to be larger than during the past few weeks—between 40 and 50 Bf 109s per sweep. Fighters from 11 Group responded in force. A furious fight erupted over Kent at about 12:30, and again just after 2 pm., both visible to hundreds of eyewitnesses on the ground through breaks in the cloud. More fighters crashed into Kentish fields, or straggled back to base with battle damage.

This Sunday's last raids against London and Southampton began at about 4:45. The RAF base at Martlesham Heath also received an unwelcome call from Messerschmitt fighter-bombers. Among the RAF's losses were three Hurricanes, which had been shot down by Messerschmitts over the Isle of Wight.

It had been a fairly successful day for the German pilots. They had penetrated the RAF fighter screen several times, bombed London and Southampton, and managed to stir up trouble elsewhere, including at Martlesham Heath. In the process, they shot down 10 RAF Spitfires and Hurricanes, while losing 15 of their own aircraft.

London, Liverpool, Bristol, as well as other targets in the south of England and the Midlands, were bombed after dark. Just as their *kamaraden* had done during the day, pilots and crews of Heinkel and Junkers units showed much more aggression than they had recently. In addition to London and other cities, the Luftwaffe also attacked several RAF bases, including Hawkinge, Coltishall, and Kirton-in-Lindsey.

American correspondents sent glowing reports back home about the bravery and courage of the British people. By this time—51 consecutive nights of bombing, without let-up—many had expected London to be a bomb-gutted wilderness, and its residents either cowering in the countryside or demanding that Churchill surrender to the Germans.

The fact that neither of these things had happened greatly impressed these highly influential reporters, and convinced them—Raymond Daniell of *The New York Times*, Quentin Reynolds of *Colliers*, Drew Middleton of the Associated Press—-that Britain deserved the full backing and support of the United States. They communicated these beliefs—in a highly effective and persuasive manner—to their millions of readers in America.

28 October, Monday

Once again, autumn weather cut back on operations. Low cloud and poor visibility grounded most Luftwaffe aircraft during the morning, when only a few single aircraft took off for the far side of the Channel. But when afternoon arrived, and the fog began to burn off, activities picked up dramatically.

At about 2 o'clock, a formation of about 40 Bf 109s crossed the coast in two waves and headed for London. But RAF Group's fighters intercepted, shooting down at least two of the Messerschmitts and preventing the rest from even coming within sighting distance of their objective.

Later in the afternoon, another formation made an attempt. This was followed by yet another 100 Bf 109s. Both raids were intercepted by 11 Group's pilots. Through a combination of good positioning by ground controllers and just plain luck, the RAF pilots got in among the German fighters, and shot down several without loss to themselves. The survivors had to jettison their 550-lb. bombs and, low on fuel, turn for France.

The day turned out to be one of total frustration for the Germans. They did not get anywhere near London, much less drop any bombs on it, and lost 11 aircraft for their efforts. The RAF lost no aircraft from any cause.

Hendon's Messerschmitt Bf 109E-3/B, a fighter-bomber, flew with JG 52 during the Battle, and had a very active and exciting career. The aircraft was shot up over the Thames Estuary on 27 November 1940; the pilot made a wheels-up landing at Manston, and was taken prisoner.

London's air raid sirens—"Moaning Minnie" was among the more polite names for the Alert—sounded at about 7:30. "I wonder what it would be like to go to sleep without the sirens?" a woman in south London wrote to a relative in America.

29 October, Tuesday

Yesterday afternoon's weather held for the Luftwaffe. Visibility was slightly limited by hazy cloud, but not enough to keep the Bf 109 fighter-bombers on the ground.

The first raid of the day crossed the Channel coast at about 10:45. The fighters of 11 Group confronted the raiders and shot down five of them, but two escaped and got through to central London. These two pilots apparently tried to bomb Hungerford Railway Bridge, which crosses the River Thames and leads into

Charing Cross Station. They missed, though both 550-lb. bombs landed near the station itself, blowing out windows in the vicinity.

The next attack appeared at around 12:30, and promptly ran into another bunch of RAF fighters—better co-ordinated than the morning's, if not more determined. Ground controllers put the interceptors in the right place at the right time and the right altitude. Four Hurricane squadrons came at the fighter-bombers—100-plus Bf 109s—from four different directions, shooting down at least four of them.

Other squadrons also closed in on the frantic Messerschmitt pilots, who were beginning to run low on fuel. As they made their 180-degree turns and set course for France, the Hurricane and Spitfire pilots followed them and shot down four more of the Messerschmitts. Pilots of 602 (City of Gloucester) Squadron claimed eight Bf 109s in this action.

London had not been the fighter-bombers' only objective. Portsmouth also came under attack. The fighter base at North Weald was bombed at about 4:40 by pilots of *Erprobungsaruppe 210*, which employed their usual low-level tactics and hit their target with its usual accuracy. About 20 people were killed by blast and splinters from about 40 1,100-lb. bombs, and a building that had been rebuilt after last summer's raids was demolished.

But the Bf 110s were intercepted before they could get away. Two of the twin-engined fighters were shot down, including the lead airplane of *Erpro* 210's leader. Oberleutnant Otto Hintze, was able to bail out and was taken prisoner.

The *Reggia Aeronautica* also put in another appearance, this time over Ramsgate, Kent. Fifteen twin-engined BR.20 bombers, escorted by 70 Fiat CR.42 bi-plane fighters, approached from the east, unloaded their bombs in the general vicinity of the target, and wheeled back toward home again. Anti-aircraft fire opened up on the stately formation, but scored no hits.

Luckily for the Italians, no RAF fighters were in the vicinity. The Fiat bi-planes, festive in their vivid blue and green camouflage, were no match for either the Spitfire or the Hurricane.

This Supermarine Spitfire Mk I, on display at Hendon's Battle of Britain Museum, served with 609 (West Riding) Squadron, based at Warmwell, during the Battle. On 21 October, while flown by Pilot Officer S.J. Hill, the fighter was given credit for one half of a kill—a Junkers Ju 88. At Hendon, it is marked with 609 Squadron's identification letters: PR.

With their open cockpits and fixed undercarriages, they were 100 mph slower than the Hawker Hurricane, and even slower in comparison to the Spitfire.

It had not been a good day for the Luftwaffe. Eighteen German aircraft had been destroyed. Except for the damage done to North Weald, the results did not justify the cost. The RAF lost seven fighters.

London was the main objective again after the sun went down. One Heinkel 111 was lost; the crew bailed out after losing their bearings. This brought Luftwaffe losses to 19 on the day.

30 October, Wednesday

Cloud, rain, and general poor visibility kept German aircraft on the ground until nearly noon, when two fighter sweeps headed for London. About 80 Bf 109s made their approach from the east; about 100 more, in two groups of about fifty each, came in from Kent. Several of the fighter-bombers reached London, dropped their bombs, and returned to base in spite of the intervention of six RAF squadrons. Between 12 noon and 1 pm. several more fighters on each side came to a violent end over Kent; several others were damaged.

Later in the afternoon, after 4 o'clock, several formations of Bf 109 fighter-bombers approached London; their total number was about 130. Again, RAF squadrons came up to block their approach; and, again, a number of them managed to reach the capital just the same. Several released their bombs and disappeared into the bleak grey overcast, shattering windows and nerves below. A Bf 109 of JG 3, shot down in flames at 4:15, probably has the distinction of being the last Messerschmitt shot down in the Battle of Britain.

Heavy rain began moving in after dark, interfering with *Luftflotte* 3's plans for London. The steady downpour soon reduced the unpaved airfields in France to mud, making for hazardous take-offs and landings. By about 11 pm., the fields had become unsafe for operations; no further take-offs were attempted after this hour.

31 October, Thursday

The bad weather of the day before carried over to Thursday, dramatically cutting back on Luftwaffe activities.

Only about 60 sorties were flown, all by Bf 109 fighter-bombers. No interceptions were attempted by any RAF units, and neither side suffered any losses.

It must have been pride that made the Germans send any airplanes across the Channel at all—it certainly could not have been for any practical reason. Flying was not only impractical, but hazardous. The day's entire effort was a complete waste.

For the fifty-fifth night in a row, London was *Luftflotte* 3's target. Weather also curtailed the night's efforts, but did not stop the raiders altogether. Air raid sirens sent Londoners to their shelters once again, and bombs were scattered across the city. It might not have been a major effort, but it was another damaging blow to London and its residents.

* * *

Although the air fighting over southern England coutinued until the end of November, and the Blitz against London went on until May 1941, the Battle of Britain was now officially over. The Air Ministry's dates for the battle run from 10 July until 31 October 1940—114 days.

These arbitrary dates annoy many individuals, especially some veterans of the battle who point out that pilots killed in the November fighting, or in the fighting prior to 10 July, have been treated with injustice. Just because these pilots were killed outside the Air Ministry's official dates, they say, is no reason to exclude their names from the Battle's Roll of Honour. The air fighting went on for nearly another month. Why should the men killed during this time be forgotten simply because of what one letter writer to *The Times* called "a historiographical absurdity"?[27]

These individuals have a point. But bureaucrats and historians like neat, tidy endings. As such, the last day of October 1940 serves as a convenient cut-off date for the battle. Pilots killed outside the official dates are excluded from membership in The Few, in spite of any objections.

---

27   Two of the pilots who fall outside of the official dates are John Dundas, the brother of Hugh Dundas, who was shot down on 28 November; and Jimmy Davies of Bernardsville, New Jersey, who was killed in June.

Chapter VII

Winners and Losers

"The Royal Air Force won the Battle of Britain," narrator Laurence Olivier rather pompously declared in the highly-praised television series *The World at War*. Actually, however, the RAF did not win the battle as much as the Luftwaffe lost it.

The Luftwaffe should have won the Battle of Britain. The German air force came perilously close to crippling Fighter Command, which would have left the Channel and the south coast vulnerable to anything the Luftwaffe and the Kriegsmarine wanted to accomplish—from harassment of the Channel ports to a full-scale invasion. No one knew this better than the commander-in-chief of Fighter Command, Air Chief Marshal Dowding.

"The last week in August and the first week in September—these two weeks were the worst for us," recalled Robert Wright, Dowding's personal assistant. "Fighter Command was nearly on its knees ... [Dowding] was wondering how much longer he could hold out."

During this two week period, 103 of Fighter Command's pilots were killed; another 128 were wounded seriously enough that they would be on the ground for the remainder of the battle. This represented 16 per cent of the RAF's Spitfire and Hurricane pilots. (Nearly 500 Spitfires and Hurricanes also were lost, but fighter planes could be far more easily, and quickly, replaced than pilots.) Also, six airfields either had been put out of action by bombing, or had been so badly damaged that they could no longer carry on with normal operations.

A few more weeks of such losses, and this kind of damage to fighter stations, would have meant disaster for RAF Fighter Command. But Adolf Hitler wanted revenge for the bombing of Berlin. And Göring became impatient and decided to bomb London instead of continuing to attack the airfields—he thought London was a more strategic target, and that the RAF would deplete itself in trying to defend it.

And so a winning strategy became a hopeless muddle. Fighter Command was able to catch its breath, and the Luftwaffe never regained the initiative. All because of Hitler's bad temper and Göring's short attention span.

It has been well documented that the decision to bomb London cost the Luftwaffe the battle—up to 7 September, the Luftwaffe very clearly was winning; from 7 September to the end of the battle, Fighter Command gradually regained its strength and was able to prevail.

This fatal change of tactics can be blamed on Hermann Görings impatience as much as on Hitler's desire for revenge. (And ranks with his equally fatal decision to stop bombing the vital CH stations.) His Luftwaffe had benefited from easy victories in Poland, France, and the Low Countries—the enemy's outmoded fighters could not catch the Heinkels, Dorniers, and Junkers, and were not fast enough or heavily armed enough to deal with the Messerschmitt 109s. And the German Stukas massacred enemy troops and blew up individual targets with impunity— again, the enemy fighters were not modern enough to stop them.

Coming after this series of quick and relatively easy victories, Göring was totally unprepared for the hammer-and-tongs fight that the Luftwaffe encountered over southern England. For the first time, his Air Fleets ran into modern fighters that were a match for his Messerschmitt 109s, and that could blast his bombers to bits—indeed, they forced the Stuka to be withdrawn from the Battle.

During the First World War, Hermann Göring was one of Germany's best-known fighter pilots. He was awarded the coveted Pour le Merite *after shooting down 20 enemy aircraft, (his final score was 22), and was the last commander of the famous Richthofen* geschwader. *This photo dates from 1915, before Göring won his* Pour le Merite *but after he had been awarded the Iron Cross First Class.*

The war against France and the Low Countries lasted six weeks, from 10 May to the end of June; this campaign was made up of a series of brilliant victories that climaxed in the fall of Paris. The German *blitzkrieg* accomplished more in a month and a half than the Kaiser's armies had done in over four years between 1914 and 1918. But when the Luftwaffe turned against England, the quick victories came to an end.

Even though the RAF was being steadily worn down by attrition, this sort of fight came as a disappointment to Göring, who expected another lightning win. When the battle began to drag on, through July and August and into September, he began to look for another way to conduct the Luftwaffe's operations against southern England.

Adolf Hitler gave Göring the order to bomb London. But the Reichsmarschall did not register any objection. In fact, he seemed to be all for switching targets. This, he felt certain, would bring the RAF up in force—they would have no choice but to defend their capital—and the Luftwaffe would then shoot the Spitfires and Hurricanes down in record numbers. Bombing London would hasten the death of RAF Fighter Command—that, at least, was Göring's theory.

Hermann Göring plainly did not know the situation, either with the RAF or with his own Luftwaffe. He was addicted to drugs, and spent much of his time during the summer of 1940 in acquiring works of art that had been looted from the art museums of Europe.

Both of these activities diverted his mind from the battle, and also kept him separated from reality.

But even if Göring had been against switching from the airfields to London—as he stated after the war—Hitler wanted to bomb London to avenge the bombing of Berlin by RAF Bomber Command.

Also Göring simply was not up to the job of leading the German air force through such a difficult time. Royal Air Force intelligence compared Göring with a student trying to do a particularly difficult mathematics examination; he fumbled his way from one problem to another, without finding a solution to any of them. A biographer said that Göring failed "because he did not seriously recognize the complex nature of the operational problems he had set himself."

And so Reichsmarschall Göring changed tactics, which failed miserably. Hitler did not seem particularly worried over this setback, and took no disciplinary action against Göring. He was satisfied with his revenge against London, and shortly became pre-occupied with his planned invasion of Russia. RAF Fighter Command retained control of the air over southern England. The Wehrmacht never got any closer to the beaches of southern England than Normandy.

The Germans miqht have had a chance if the battle had been resumed in the spring of 1941. Although the RAF became stronger throughout the winter of 1940 and 1941, so did both the

Adolf Hitler was glad to have an authentic war hero in his Nazi party; Göring gave the Nazis some much-needed prestige. He was wounded in the 1923 Munich beer-hall "putsch," and became a close associate of Hitler. His appointment as head of the Luftwaffe was based more upon this association, and upon his reputation from the First World War, than upon his knowledge of modern air strategy. Göring's grasp of fighter tactics and air power had not evolved beyond 1918.

Luftwaffe and the Wehrmacht. But this is purely an academic argument. Hitler decided to invade Russia instead.

In his dreams of Russia, Hitler became another victim of the German victory disease. Just as Göring had predicted a quick victory against the RAF, Hitler anticipated an easy time in the east, and expected to come back to finish Britain after polishing off the Soviets. But things did not work out as simply in Russia as they had in Poland.

"Operation Barbarossa," the code name for the German invasion of the Soviet Union, began on 22 June 1941. (Exactly one year after France had asked for an armistice.) This attack has frequently been compared with Napoleon's offensive in 1812. It certainly had the same disastrous result.

Hitler never got the chance to return to his offensive against Britain. Russia ate up his Wehrmacht and decimated his Luftwaffe. When the United States entered the war, it was only a matter of time before Germany was crushed to death between the two giants.

Had Göring not changed his tactics, and had Hitler set a firm date for invading England and kept to it, the war certainly would have turned out differently. An invasion of southern England in 1940 probably would have succeeded—the British army left most of its equipment on the beaches of Dunkirk, and had not been re-supplied by late summer. And the Americans were too divided, and too unprepared, to have done anything at all.

With Britain occupied, Russia would have felt the full brunt of German might without any hope of assistance from the West. And with no airfields in England for its Air Force, the U.S. would have had no way of attacking Germany's war industry, and the Western Allies would have had no base for its invasion of the German-held Continent in 1944 .

But, of course, no one realized this in 1940 or the early part of 1941. During the winter of 1940-1941, with the German armed forces winning on every front and seemingly unbeatable, British novelist C.P. Snow thought that only a miracle could help Britain to win the war against Germany—such as the United States entering the war, or a German attack on Soviet Russia. But Snow did not believe that Hitler was stupid enough to antagonize either country.

Historians like to play the game of "What would have happened if … ?"

Favorite questions regarding the Second World War and its consequences include: "What would have happened in Europe if Franklin D. Roosevelt had not died in April 1945?" Or: "What would have happened if Pearl Harbor had not been attacked?" These questions are so intriguing because they do not have an answer—nobody knows exactly what would have happened if

Franklin Roosevelt had been alive during the Potsdam conference, or when the United States would have entered the war if
Japan had not bombed Pearl Harbor.

One "What would have happened if ...?" question has a
definite answer, however: What would have happened if the
Luftwaffe had not lost the Battle of Britain? If the German air
force had won the battle, there can be no doubt that the outcome
of the war—probably including the ultimate winners and losers
of the war—would have been far different.

*   *   *

German comments on the Battle of Britain, by participants as
well as historians, generally concern themselves with explana-
tions of why the Luftwaffe lost the battle. A lot of these are
actually excuses—a search for a scapegoat, someone or something to blame for such an unexpected loss.

Many Luftwaffe officers, as well as German writers and
historians, blame the limitations of their machines—the absence
of a four-engined bomber from their air fleets, which had been
abandoned in 1937 so that the Stuka dive bomber could be
developed; the lack of range of the Messerschmitt Bf 109, which
had only about twenty minutes flying time over southern
England; the unsuitability of the Bf 110 as an escort fighter,
which had the necessary range but not the maneuverability
needed to face Spitfires and Hurricanes.

Very few blame the short-sightedness of Adolf Hitler for not
seeing a war with Britain and making plans for it during the
1930s, which is why the Luftwaffe had no long-range fighters
and no four-engined bombers in the summer of 1940.

There are also a number who keep themselves in a complete
state of denial where the Battle of Britain is concerned, to the
point where they will not even acknowledge that there was such
an event during the summer of 1940.

Hugh Dundas, who had been a Spitfire pilot with 616 Squadron during that time, recalls a dramatic instance of this denial.
In September 1960, Dundas took part in a television program to
commemorate the twentieth anniversary of the battle. Among

the others who were present was Hugh Dowding and a person that Dundas describes only as a "distinguished German fighter pilot." (Leonard Mosley discloses that the pilot was none other than Adolf Galland, who was one of the Luftwaffe's foremost apologists for its failure to destroy RAF Fighter Command.)

According to Dundas' account, the "distinguished German pilot" said that no one had either won or lost the battle because it never took place—there never was anything called the Battle of Britain. "All that happened was that we made a number of attacks against England between 1940 and 1941," Leonard Mosley recalls of Galland's comments. "Then we discovered that we were not achieving the desired effect, and so we retired. There was no battle, and we did not lose it."

In Galland's mind, the Luftwaffe simply found their air offensive against Britain to be counter-productive, so they stopped their attacks and went on to something else. It was not a matter of winning or losing, but merely of the Luftwaffe cutting its losses.

Hugh Dowding did not agree with this assessment at all, and rather disdainfully voiced his disaproval of it. "Let him say that the Germans stopped the battle if that's what he wants," Dowding said. "Very well, they did stop the battle. Certainly they stopped it. They stopped it because they had failed in their objective, which was to clear the RAF out of the skies so that they could invade this country. They stopped it because they were beaten. And that is another way of saying that we won."

A more logical argument would have been that the Luftwaffe had been cheated out of their nearly-successful campaign, by a number of factors. Our "distinguished German fighter pilot" might have argued that they lost the battle because of bad luck—not altogether invalid, since the Luftwaffe flight commanders had to contend with almost as much interference from Berlin as from the RAF. But the Battle of Britain was a fact—a very hard fact, from the Luftwaffe's point of view, and a very hard loss from which they never really recovered.

Another battle which Britain won hands down, with no argument from anyone, was the battle for American opinion.

This was a campaign that was as hard fought as the air battle over southern England. It was also just as important to Britain as the RAF's fight against the German Luftwaffe, and only slightly less trying. And, if anything, it was even more success-ful.

At the outset of the battle, 64% of Americans polled said that they were against sending aid to Britain in any form—they did not know anything about the war in Europe, and really did not care. But in November, a few days after the official end of the battle, 60% of Americans told the same poll that now they were in favour of sending Britain help—even if it meant that the United States would become involved in the war as a result.

The most immediate and tangible result of this propaganda victory was the passing of the Lend-Lease bill. Lend-Lease was introduced in Congress in mid-December—after Franklin D. Roosevelt had safely been re-elected to a third term as presi-dent—and was voted into law early in 1941. Roosevelt now had the authority to aid "any country whose defence the President deems vital to the defence of the United States."

Not that all Americans were in favor of Lend-Lease. The isolationists and "America Firsters" were still highly critical of any kind of involvement in the European war, even though there were a lot fewer of them than there had been two and a months before. Former ambassador Joseph P. Kennedy, who had re-signed his post in London in October but continued to criticize Roosevelt's policies to assist Britain, offered to be the opening witness for the opposition in a hearing on the Lend-Lease bill.

But the bill became law, in spite of opposition from Joseph P. Kennedy and the America Firsters. In July, before the Ministry of Information's media blitz, it never would have got out of Congress, not in the country's isolationist mood. If the public's feeling had not changed, Roosevelt would not even have intro-duced it. He was politician enough to have known Abraham Lincoln's adage on public opinion: You can do anything with it, and nothing without it.

The Ministry of Information's campaign was carried out with the willing participation of American journalists and report-

This wall plaque commemorating 600 (City of London) Squadron is displayed in the Lady Chapel of St. Bartholomew the Great, a 12th century church in London's City district. Number 600 Squadron flew Bristol Blenheims during the Battle, and lost 9 of its members during the fighting.

ers—willing and vital participation. The broadcasts of Edward R. Murrow, the stories of Quentin Reynolds, and the reports of Raymond Daniell and his colleagues gave Americans the word about German aggression—if Britain lost the battle, sooner or later the United States would have to face Hitler alone.

American journalists convinced the American public that the war against Hitler was not only necessary, but was also justifiable—the Nazis had to be stopped, and American money and resources would be needed in order to stop them. It was not just a matter of national defense, these writers and broadcasters implied; Americans also had a moral obligation to fight the Nazis and everything they stood for.

Since Winston Churchill first described the pilots of Fighter Command as The Few, the phrase has gone on to become a cliche. It has been used in countless book and film titles—*The First of The Few, Churchill's Few, The Last of The Few, The Leader of The Few, One of The Few*—and formed the basis of a thousand jokes and wisecracks (including many of which are uproariously unprintable). But like most cliches, the phrase had more than just a hint of fact in it.

The battle was fought by an incredibly small number on both sides, but the number of fighter pilots of the Royal Air Force was so small as to be almost unbelievable—only about 1,450 Spitfire and Hurricane pilots took part in the Battle of Britain.

Compared with other pivotal battles in history, such as Waterloo and Gettysburg, this is next to miniscule. At Gettysburg, the Union had a force of about 82,000, and the Confederates had about 75,000. Napoleon's army at Waterloo came to roughly 75,000; Wellington commanded a combined force of about 67,000. Luftwaffe and RAF Fighter Command forces make up only a minor fraction of any one of these armies, even when combined.

This is one reason why the study of this battle has been so popular over the years—it appeals to the romantic in every reader. (Or viewer, in the case of films and television.) Like the Armada, and the Marne, and Midway, the Battle of Britain involves a greatly outnumbered force prevailing over hopeless odds and overwhelming numbers. Everyone loves an underdog, especially an underdog that wins in the end.

U.S. Army Chief of Staff George C. Marshall would describe the battle of Midway, during which an even smaller number of U.S. Navy pilots beat back the Japanese fleet and turned the tide of the Pacific war, as "the closest squeak and the greatest victory." He might have used the same phrase for the Battle of Britain.

The Blitz continued throughout the winter—which one British writer referred to as "the winter of the bombs." But Adolf Hitler decided not to resume the Battle of Britain in the spring of 1941. Instead, he became preoccupied with providing *lebensraum*, living space for Germany, in the east. "When we speak

600 Squadron commemorative banner at St. Bartholomew's church. The banner displays the Squadron's eight World War II battle honors and its badge, which combines the shield of the City of London and the RAF insignia.

of new territory," he had written in *Mein Kampf*, "we must think of Russia.

The Luftwaffe's bombing attacks on London and other cities throughout Britain, the Blitz, was called off on the night of 2 November because of bad weather—after 57 consecutive nights. The raids began again on the following night and, with occasional breaks because of rain and fog, continued until May 1941. (The last maximum effort against London took place on the night of 10/11 May; survivors say that this was the worst of them all.) But from the point of view of their ultimate contribution to the German war effort, the raids never should have begun.

The Blitz did not accomplish anything positive for Germany and, in the long run, did considerable damage. The air raids did none of the things that Göring thought that they would: They did not demoralize the British public to the point of demanding an armistice with Germany; they did not cause enough damage to industrial targets to affect long-term production. Most important for the Luftwaffe, the bombing of London did not induce Fighter Command to overextend itself, or to resort to some foolish tactic in a desperate attempt to defend the capital.

What the bombings did accomplish was to divert the Luftwaffe from successfully wearing down RAF Fighter Command, with frustrating raids on London. Also, they succeeded in turning American public opinion against Nazi Germany.

It can only be guessed at what would have happened if that lost German air crew had not accidentally toggled its bombs over London's City district on the night of 24-25 August. That first bomb on London, which landed in the middle of Fore Street, reverberated in Berlin, throughout occupied Europe, and eventually in the United States.

By the autumn of 1940, even before the Battle of Britain had officially ended, Adolf Hitler's mind was already on the broad steppes of Russia. As far as he was concerned, the war in the west was already won. France and the Low Countries were occupied by German troops, and, except for minor raids by RAF Bomber Command, Britain was in no position to attack Germany.

Hitler's plan for his Russian campaign was simple: he would overrun the country with a blitzkrieg even more overwhelming than the offensive against France, Belgium, and Holland. After the Soviets had been subdued, he would turn his attention to Britain once again. With Russia out of the way, he would be able to finish Britain off at leisure.

But the fighting in Russia did not go his way. And at the end of 1941, an event on the other side of the world give his plans another unexpected, and ultimately fatal, twist.

HERMANN GÖRING'S FATAL DECISIONS

The pounding of the Chain Home stations during August played havoc with the RAF's early warning network, knocking stations off the air and severely compromising Britain's defense system. But Reichsmarshcall Göring ordered strikes against the CH stations to stop.

The air raids against RAF fighter stations, particularly against 11 Group's airfields, were wearing down Fighter Command to the point where it was nearing collapse. Had the Luftwaffe continued to concentrate on these airfields, they might well have won control of the air over southern England and the Channel. But Göring switched targets, and London became the main objective.

Why did Hermann Göring make these two disastrous decisions?

The reasons are varied and many: petty jealousies within the Luftwaffe, to which Göring was a party; Göring's suspicion of new technology, including RDF; and a nagging knowledge that he was not really up to the job as head of the Luftwaffe. But one reason stands out above all the others: Göring's trembling fear of Adolf Hitler.

All senior officers who were close either to Hitler or Göring were aware of this fear; they had observed that the Reichsmarschall would begin to shake any time that Hitler spoke sharply to him. Göring himself admitted that he was afraid of Hitler. "I often make up my mind to say something to him," he once

said, "but then when I come face to face with him, my heart sinks into my boots."

Göring made a point of getting on Hitler's good side—always agreeing with whatever Hitler said, and going out of his way to make a good impression. One sure way of impressing Hitler would be to show that the Luftwaffe could destroy British resolve, and British defenses, without any assistance from either the army or the navy. Winning the war almost single-handedly would assure him more honors and accolades, and would ingratiate him further with Hitler.

To accomplish this, Göring assumed that he would have to wage another lightning campaign, like the ones against Poland and France. A drawn-out battle of attrition did not fit into his plans, regardless of how successful it might be.

Bombing the RDF stations seemed too slow and indirect a way of destroying the RAF. For one thing, the tall lattice-work masts refused to fall, regardless of how many bombs were dropped on them. And this new type of warfare—radio waves, electronics, early warning gadgets—were beyond him. He preferred ways and weapons of the First World War, when men relied upon their own eyes for sighting enemy aircraft, and flying was a matter for pilots instead of scientists.

Göring did not grasp the fact that the coastal RDF stations were vital to Britain's home defense. As far as he was concerned, these sites were nothing more than a waste of time, as well as bombs. And so, he ordered them to be left alone—save the bombs for other, more important, targets.

Similarly, attacking the airfields of RAF Fighter Command was too slow and deliberate for his taste. He wanted to wipe out the enemy's air force at once, not in a matter of weeks or months. And in his state of mind at the beginning of September, after eight weeks of sending his Luftwaffe out against the RAF almost every day, he actually believed his own propaganda. Göring really believed that the enemy was down to their "last fifty Spitfires."

The decision to bomb London may have originated with Hitler, as a reprisal for the RAF bombing of Berlin, but Göring endorsed it. On the afternoon of 7 September, in fact, Göring went to Cap Blanc Nez to watch his fighters and bombers fly off toward London, and announced, "I myself have taken command of the Luftwaffe's battle for Britain."

Even if he had opposed Hitler's reprisal raid, Göring would not have had the nerve to confront Hitler and argue with him. But there is no evidence that Göring ever had any misgivings about switching from attacking the airfields to bombing London. He was fully in favor of it, and backed the idea with such enthusiasm that it might have been his own.

Bombing London seemed a short cut to winning the Battle—the depleted RAF would have to defend its capital, and the Luftwaffe would overwhelm the Spitfires and Hurricanes when they came up. This would both impress and please Hitler, who would be certain to repay Göring with more medals, more praise, and perhaps even another title to go along with the newly-created rank of Reichsmarschall. But the main reward would be the satisfaction of Adolf Hitler—if Hitler was happy, he would not be carping or finding fault with ihm.

Feldmarschall Erhard Milch made this observation concerning Hermann Göring: "For him, the important thing was to enhance his own position with Hitler." He might have added that equally important with Göring was to avoid a confrontation with Hitler. Göring's sense of what was important was certainly misplaced, and he let it affect his judgment. His desire to please Hitler, which was rooted in a fear of Hitler, prompted him to make decisions that cost the Luftwaffe the Battle.

NOTES

"I often make up my mind" ...in Roger Manvell's and Heinrich Fraenkel's article "Göring."

Milch quote in Mason's *The Rise of the Luftwaffe*

AFTERWORD

With Unparalleled
Stupidity...

*F*irst reports of the Japanese air attack on the U.S. naval base at Pearl Harbor, Hawaii, did not reach Britain until the evening of 7 December 1941. The impact of the event was recognized at once. It meant that the United States, with all of its money and resources, had finally entered the war on the side of Great Britain.

Winston Churchill was at Chequers, his country residence in Kent, when he heard the news. He and his American house guests, Averell Harriman (Franklin D. Roosevelt's Special Representative in Britain) and Ambassador John Winant (Joseph P. Kennedy's successor) had been listening to the nine o'clock news; when the short announcement came on regarding "an attack by the Japanese on American shipping at Hawaii," the three of them instantly became alert. Ambassador Winant telephoned President Roosevelt to ask him exactly what had happened; after Winant was finished, Churchill picked up the phone.

"Mr. President, what's this about Japan?" Churchill asked.

"It's quite true," Roosevelt replied. "They have attacked us at Pearl Harbor. We are all in the same boat now."

At long last, the Americans were in the war "up to the neck and in to the death." Churchill was overcome with relief and joy.

"England would live; Britain would live; the Commonwealth of Nations and the Empire would live!" He recalled former Foreign Secretary Sir Edward Grey telling him that the United States was like a gigantic boiler—"Once the fire is lighted under it, there is no limit to the power it can generate."

"Being saturated and satiated with emotion and sensation," he wrote in his memoirs, "I went to bed and slept the sleep of the saved and thankful."

The British public had been hoping for just such an event for over a year and a half, ever since the evacuation of the British army from Dunkirk. But the news of Pearl Harbor did not cause any widespread rejoicing. The Mass Observation Opinion poll noted that the most common reaction was "a feeling, sometimes verging on sadistic pleasure, that the Americans had been blasted into the war."

The United States may have been blasted into the war, but Americans were not in the same boat as the British. Although they certainly were at war, they were not at war with Nazi Germany.

The attack on Pearl Harbor galvanized the United States into action, and unified the divided country in a fight against a common enemy. But that common enemy was Japan, not Germany. In his famous "Day of Infamy" speech on 8 December, President Roosevelt asked Congress to declare war on Japan. Nothing was said at all about Germany, not even in passing. On Monday 8 December 1941, the United States and Nazi Germany were still at peace.

After Churchill's initial burst of enthusiasm, the mood in London turned to worry. The main fear now was that America would become totally pre-occupied with the war against Japan, and would cut back on aid to Britain. "They won't be able to spare so many ships for us," was one man's point of view. "Strikes me that they will help us less, and help them more," said another.

It was a particularly frustrating turn of events. The long hoped-for happening had finally taken place. The United States had entered the war, after long months of maddening neutrality.

But it looked as though there would be no advantage in it for Britain after all. If anything, the Pearl Harbor raid might have made Britain more alone than ever.

But there was nothing that Churchill could do about it. There was nothing Franklin D. Roosevelt could do, either, for that matter. The next move would be up to Adolf Hitler.

At this stage, Hitler was not really sure what he wanted to do—he was as surprised by Japan's attack on the U.S. fleet as the Americans. His generals and military advisors urged him to use moderation, and to remain at peace with the United States—Germany already had its hands more than full with the British in the west and the Russians in the east.

For three days, Hitler and his staff argued over the future course of the war. His advisors admitted that the United States had acted the part of the belligerent—American destroyers had been "loaned" to the British fleet; U.S. destroyers manned by American crews had attacked U-boats; and there were American citizens in the British armed forces. But they also pointed out that the Wehrmacht and the Luftwaffe already were close to being overextended, and that the Third Reich certainly did not need another belligerent.

Hitler listened to these arguments, but was not convinced. He reminded his generals of the Tripartite Pact, which had been signed on 27 September 1940 by representatives of Germany, Japan, and Italy, and bound the three countries together in a mutual defense pact. Japan was now at war with the United States, Hitler said; therefore, Germany must declare war on the Americans, as well.

His advisors were well aware of the existence of the Tripartite Pact. But they went on to remind Hitler that the alliance had no bearing in this case. The pact stated that Germany was bound to come to Japan's aid only if Japan had been attacked—the three signatories agreed to come to each other's assistance "when one of the three Contracting Parties is attacked by a power at present not involved in the European war or the Sino-Japanese conflict...."

But Japan had attacked the United States, not the other way round. Therefore, Germany was under no obligations to come to Japan's assistance.

But Hitler was determined to go to war against the United States, in spite of all attempts to talk him out of it. He had agreed to the terms of the pact, he said, and intended to live up to them.

Shortly after the war ended, Foreign Minister Joachim von Ribbentrop was questioned about Hitler's actions and motives throughout the war. Among the topics discussed was the reason that Hitler decided to declare war on the United States in December 1941. Ribbentrop cited the Tripartite Pact as the reason. A U.S. Army lieutenant asked the former foreign minister: "Why was that particular treaty the first one you decided to keep?"

Ribbentrop's reply was not recorded. But before he formally declared war, Hitler gave his own reasons: in his mind, the United States and Germany were already at war.

One reason Hitler gave was that "the United States was already shooting at our ships"—a reference to the depthcharging of the German submarine U-652 by the destroyer USS *Greer*. Also on his mind were: the Destroyer-for-Bases deal; Lend-Lease; the U.S. citizens in the Royal Air Force and other branches of Britain's armed forces; and the general sympathy of Americans for Britain, accompanied by growing hostility toward Germany, since the summer of 1940.

Hitler's resentment toward Americans, and their attitude toward Germany, had been building for a year and a half. In December 1941, it finally had its release.

"They have been a forceful factor in this war," Hitler said, "and through their actions have already created a situation of war." To his way of thinking, the United States had already attacked Germany. Now, it was time to strike back.

Which means that the activities of Britain's Ministry of Information; Churchill's protracted propaganda campaign to sway American opinion in Britain's favour; the efforts of Edward R. Murrow, Quentin Reynolds, and their fellow reporters to convince Americans that Hitler was an enemy of the United

States; as well as the presence of Hugh Reilley, Billy Fiske, and all their fellow American volunteers in the Royal Air Force, had more of an impact—in Germany as well as in the United States—than even Winston Churchill ever could have hoped for in the desperate days during the Battle of Britain.

All these people, and their varied activities, did far more than just convince Americans that Hitler was an enemy who eventually would have to be faced—which was a formidable enough job by itself. They also managed to convince Hitler of the same idea—that he would have to fight the United States sooner or later in a full-scale war. (American economist and writer John Kenneth Galbraith, who worked in Washington, D.C., during this period, called this point of view "incredible." Which gives some idea of the effectiveness of this concerted effort.)

With Japan already at war with the United States, this seemed a golden opportunity for Germany to declare war on the Americans. The U.S. would then be faced with a long, expensive, and very difficult Atlantic-Pacific two-front war on its hands. Hitler was not really interested in helping Japan fight the Americans; what he really wanted was for Japan to help Germany by dividing American strength and resources.

And so, on Thursday, 11 December, four days after Pearl Harbor, Hitler opened formal hostilities against the United States. He went before the Reichstag and, in a bitter tirade against Franklin D. Roosevelt and America, demanded a declaration of war. In Washington D.C., Congress reciprocated on the same day. The U.S. and Germany were finally at war.

It might be argued that hostilities between the two countries had begun 18 months earlier, when Winston Churchill began to look for ways to enlist American support, and that the opening rounds of the conflict had been supplied by the Ministry of Information. Hitler had probably never even heard of Bismarck's remark that the most important factor of the last century—and this one—was that Americans spoke English. It was a bit of ignorance that would one day kill him and his Third Reich.

In a single stroke, Adolf Hitler had simplified all of Churchill's problems—the Americans were no longer just suppliers of aid and encouragement, but active participants in the war against Nazi Germany. By this one act of anger and frustration, Hitler had done what Churchill had not been able to accomplish in a year and a half. Dean Acheson, who would one day become U.S. Secretary of State, thought that Hitler was an absolute fool, and had played right into the hands of Churchill and the Allies.

"At last," Acheson wrote, "our enemies, with unparalleled stupidity, resolved our dilemmas, clarified our doubts and uncertainties, and united our people for the long, hard course that the national interest required."

RAF SLANG—BROLLY-HOPS, BLACK-OUTS, AND BUS DRIVERS

Pilots of the Royal Air Force took pride in being unique, different from the other branches of the armed forces. It is fitting, then, that they found a way of expressing themselves that was theirs alone, not understandable to outsiders.

RAF slang was one "tradition" that American volunteers found particularly appealing. It reminded them of the hearty, home-grown lingo they had left behind, a product of Indian fighters, fur traders, explorers, and sodbusters. Much of it had a comic element to it, as well as a down-to-earth urgency—also in common with American slang.

There is no "standard" RAF slang. Definitions of words and phrases varied between different RAF Commands—Fighter, Bomber, and Coastal—as well as between individual stations, and sometimes between individuals. This listing of RAF slang phrases is not meant to be the last word on the subject. But according to a semi-reliable source, it should be regarded as pukka gen.

Big noise: A self-important bore; a windbag.
Black-outs: WAAF issue panties, particularly the navy blue winter weight variety. Also known as "passion killers."
Blitz buggy: Ambulance.
Brolly hop: Parachute jump. (Brolly = umbrella)
Bus driver: Bomber pilot.
Cheesed: At a loss.
Crab along: Fly close to the ground.

Dead-beat: Non-flying personnel. Ground staff.
Dud: Unfit, especially weather. Lousy.
Erk: Aircraftsman, lowest RAF rank, equivalent to army private.
Fan: Propeller
Flap: Fight; any kind of fuss or excitement.
Gen: (Pronounced: jen) News information. Pukka gen: reliable information. Elsan gen: dubious information. ('Elsan" was the trade name of the chemical toilets inside bombers,)
Glamour boys: Fighter pilots.
Gong: Medal.
Gravy: Gasoline.
Hedge Hop: Same as "crab along."
Jink: Sudden, sharp evasive action.
Kite: Airplane.
Kipper Kite: Airplane flying protective cover for fishing fleets in North Sea or Irish Sea. Mostly Coastal Command.
Kiwi: Another name for non-flying personnel.
Milk train: Early morning reconnaissance flight.
Office: Cockpit of an airplane. Also known as the pulpit.
Peeping Tom: Reconnaissance pilot looking for enemy aircraft or shipping through broken cloud.
Play pussy: Using cloud as a hiding place.
Prang: Crash-land an airplane; go to bed with a girl.
Ring the bell: achieve the desired effect.

Shoot a line: Exaggerate, especially a person bragging about his own accomplishments. American equivalent: throwing the bull.

Sprog: New recruit; newly commissioned officer. For married personnel: a baby.

Station master: Commanding Officer of an RAF station.

Stooge about: Flying a patrol, especially flying over a particular area looking for trouble.

Tear off a strip: Reprimand severely; read the riot act.

Train driver: Officer leading more than one squadron.

U.S.: Unservicable. Applied to anything not "operational"—aircraft, vehicle, weather, even sick personnel.

Bibliography

Unpublished Sources

Operations Record Books, Squadron Record Books, and Station Record Books of RAF Fighter Command Squadrons 10 July 1940 to 31 October 1940. Public Records Office, Kew, Richmond, Surrey.(Air 16, Air 27, and Air 28).

Luftwaffe Operations from 10 July 1940 to 31 October 1940. Bundesarchiv/Militararchiv, Freiburg, Germany.

Mass Observation Archives: Opinion Poll reports on various subjects, ranging from attitudes toward the United States to war jokes to thoughts about the war itself during the summer and autumn of 1940.

Television Script: *Someone Else's War*. Courtesy Television South.

Various declassified documents, dated during the summer and autumn of 1940 and the first half of 1941, from the Air Ministry in London.

History of the 336th Fighter Squadron, 4th Fighter Group, USAAF.

Constance Miles' War Journal.

Declassified letters of Eagle Squadron Pilots.

Interviews with, and/or letters from, the following individuals: Jerry McCurdy, Peter J. Stafford, Oblt. Dieter Heibing, KG 51, James Goldsmith, Ronald Joyce, Joseph Danforth, Margaret Swope, Janet Moore, Denys Tuckett.

Published Books and Magazine Articles

This listing represents the most useful and most frequently consulted of the more than 1,000 items referred to in researching this book.

"America's Spitfires" in *Air Enthusiast*, August-November 1981.

"An American Fighter Pilot in the RAF" *Air Log*, June 1940.

Anonymous. *A Short History of 151 (F) Squadron*. St. Andrews, 1954.

Ashworth, Chris. *Military Airfields of the South West*. Cambridge: PLS, 1982.

——*Military Airfields of Central, South, and South East England*. Cambridge: PLS, 1985.

"Battle of Britain 1940" in *Air Force Magazine*, September 1980.

Bekker, Cajus. *The Luftwaffe War Diaries*. NY: Doubleday, 1968.

Beschloss, Michael R. *Kennedy and Roosevelt*. NY: Norton,1980

Billingham, Mrs. Anthony. *America's First Two Years*. Murray,1942.

Boebert, Earl. "The Eagle Squadrons" *AAHS JOURNAL*, Spring 1964.

Bowyer, MJF. *Airfields of East Anglia*. Cambridge, PLS, 1979.

Braybrooke, Keith. *Wingspan* (RAF Debden). Saffron Walden, Essex: WH Hunt & Son, 1956.

Calder, Angus. *The People's War*. London: Hutchinson, 1972.

Charmley, John. *Churchill: The End of Glory*. NY: Harcourt Brace and Co.

Caldwell, Donald. *JG 26*. New York: Orion Books, 1991.

Cherry, Alex. *Yankee RN*. London: Jarrolds, 1951.

Childers, James Saxon. *War Eagles*. San Francisco: Eagle Publishing, 1983.

Churchill, Winston. *Their Finest Hour*. Boston: Houghton Mifflin, 1949.

——*The Grand Alliance*. Boston: Houghton Mifflin,1950

Collier, Basil. *The Defence of the United Kingdom*. London: HMSO 1957.

Collier, Richard. *Eagle Day*. London: J.M. Dent, 1980.

——*1941*. London: Hamish Hamilton, 1981.

——*The Sands of Dunkirk*. New York: Ballantine Books, 1959.

Cooke, Alistair. *Alistair Cooke's America*. NY: Knopf, 1974.

Crook, David. *Spitfire Pilot*. London: Faber & Faber, 1942.

Daniell, Raymond. *Civilians Must Fight*. Garden City, NY: Doubleday Doran, 1941.

Davis, Burke. *War Bird*. Chapel Hill, N.C.: University of North Carolina Press, 1987.

Deere, Alan. *Nine Lives*. London: Hodder & Stoughton, 1959.

Deighton, Len. *The Battle of Britain*. London: Cape, 1980.

——*Fighter: The True Story of the Battle of Britain*. London: Cape, 1977.

Donahue, Arthur. *Tally Ho! Yankee In A Spitfire*. London: Macmillan, 1942.

Bibliography

Douglas, Sholto. *Years of Command*. London: Collins, 1966.

Dowding, Air Chief Marshal. "The Battle of Britain," in *The London Gazette*, 10 September 1946.

Dundas, Hugh. *Flying Start*. NY: St. Martins, 1989.

"The Famous Fourth" in *Air Britain Digest*, November 1952.

Freeman, Roger. *The Mighty Eighth*. New York: Doubleday, 1970.

Galbraith, John Kenneth, "After the Air Raids," in *American Heritage*, April/May 1981.

———*A Life In Our Times*. Boston: Houghton Mifflin, 1981.

Galland, Adolf. *The First and the Last*. London: Methuen, 1955.

Gallico, Paul J. *The Hurricane Story*. NY: Doubleday, 1960.

Gelb, Norman. *Scramble!* London: Michael Joseph, 1976.

Goodson, James. *Tumult in the Clouds*. London: Wm. Kimber, 1983.

Hagedorn, Hermann. *Sunward I've Climbed*. NY: Macmillan, 1942.

Hall, Grover C. *1,000 Destroyed*. Dallas, Texas: Morgan Aviation Books, 1946.

Halpenny, Bruce. *Airfields of Greater London*. PLS, 1982.

Harmetz, Aljean. *Round Up The Usual Suspects*. London: Weidenfeld & Nicolson, 1992.

Haugland, Vern. *The Eagle Squadrons*. Newton Abbot, Devon: David & Charles, 1979.

Hough, Richard and Richards, Denis. *The Battle of Britain: The Jubilee History*. London: Hoder & Stoughton, 1989.

"J. Kenneth Haviland Is Alive And Well..." in Air Force *Magazine*, December 1980.

James, Brian. "I Gather It Was You Who Shot Me Down" in *The Times Saturday Review*, 14 July 1990.

Johnson, David. *The London Blitz*. Chelsea, MI: Scarborough Books, 1990.

———*V-1 / V-2*. Chelsea, MI: Scarborough, 1991.

Johnson, David Alan. "Divided by a Common Language" in *Heritage Magazine*, December 1989.

Kennerly, Byron. *The Eagles Roar*. Wash. DC: Zenger, 1980.

Knightley, Philip. *The First Casualty*. NY: HBJ, 1975.

Lee, Asher. *Goering: Air Leader*. London: Duckworth, 1972.

Lee, Raymond E. *The London Observer*. London: Hutchinson. 1941.

Longmate, Norman. *How We Lived Then*. London: Hutchinson, 1975.

———*The GI's*. NY: Scribners, 1975.

Manchester, William. *The Glory and the Dream*. Boston: Little Brown, 1973.

389

Manvell, Roger and Fraenkel, Heinrich. "Göring," in *History of the Second World War*, Part 2. (Periodical) Marshall Cavendish USA Ltd., 1973.

Mason, Francis. *Battle Over Britain*. London: McWhirter Twins Ltd., 1969

Mason, Herbert Molloy. *The Rise of the Luftwaffe*. NY: Ballantine, 1973.

McCrary, John. *The First of the Many*. London: Robson, 1981.

McKee, Alexander. *Strike From the Sky*. NY: Lancer, 1967.

Mencken, H.L. *The American Scene*. NY: Knopf, 1965.

Mitcham, Samuel. *Men of the Luftwaffe*. Presidio, 1988.

Mitchell, Gordon. *R.J. Mitchell: Schooldays to Spitfire*. Olney, Bucks: Nelson & Saunders, 1986.

Mosley, Leonard. 1971. *Backs To The Wall*. NY: Random House, 1971.

——*The Battle of Britain*. Time-Life Books.

Moulton, Tom. *The Flying Sword*. London: Macdonald, 1964.

Murrow, Edward R. *This Is London*. NY: Schocken, 1969.

Nomis, Leo, "Fighting Under Three Flags," in *Defence International Update*, Nos. 47 & 48.

"No. 601 (County of London) Squadron," in *Air Reserve Gazette*, No. 9, 1947.

Orwell, George, *The English People*. London: Collins, 1947.

Panter-Downes, Mollie. *London War Notes*. London: Longmans, 1972.

Parkinson, Roger. *Summer 1940. The Battle of Britain*. New York: David McKay, 1977.

Quill, Jeffrey. *Spitfire: A Legend Is Born*. Washington: Smithsonian Institute Press, 1991.

Ramsey, Winston G. *The Battle of Britain Then and Now*. London: Battle of Britain Prints Ltd., 1980.

Rawlings, John. *Fighter Squadrons of the RAF*. London: Macdonald and Janes, 1969.

"Return of the Eagles," in *RAF News*, 11 Sept. 1976.

Return of the Eagles," in *Air Clues*, Nov. 1976.

Reynolds, Quentin. *The Wounded Don't Cry*. NY: Dutton, 1941.

Rhodes, Anthony. *Propaganda: The Art of Persuasion: World War II*. New York: Chelsea Publishers, 1976

Robinson, Derek. *Piece of Cake*. NY: Knopf, 1986.

Settle, Mary Lee. *All the Brave Promises*. NY: Delacorte Press, 1966.

Shirer, William. *Berlin Diary*. NY: Knopf, 1941.

Bibliography

———*The Rise and Fall of the Third Reich*. NY: Simon & Schuster, 1960.

"605 Squadron," in *Wing, Victory Number*, Jan. 1946.

Smith, WWG. *Spitfire Into Battle*. London: Murray, 1981

Sperber, Ann M. *Murrow: His Life and Times*. NY: Freundlich Books, 1986.

Springs, Eliot White. *War Birds*. London: Temple Press, 1966.

Thompson, Robert Smith. *A Time For War*. NY: Prentice Hall, 1991.

'Tips From An Eagle Pilot,' USAAF Pamphlet. No date.

Tobin, Eugene (Red) with Low, Robert. 'Yankee Eagle Over London,' in *Liberty Magazine*, March-April 1941.

Toland, John. *Adolf Hitler*. NY: Doubleday, 1976

———*The Flying Tigers*. NY: Random House, 1963.

Townsend, Peter. *Duel of Eagles*. NY: Simon & Schuster, 1970.

'US Eagle Feature Section,' in *UK Eagle*, 22 July 1960.

'US Eagle Squadrons' in *Air Pictorial*, September 1979.

Van Ishoven, Armand. *Messerschmitt: Aircraft Designer*. Garden City NY: Doubleday, 1974.

Wallace, Graham. *RAF Biggin Hill*. London: Putnam, 1957.

Wehlen, Russel. *The Flying Tigers*. London: Macdonald, 1943.

Willis, John. *Churchill's Few*. London: Michael Joseph, 1985.

Winterbotham, Frederick W. *The Ultra Secret*. NY: Harper and Row, 1974.

Wood, Derek and Dempster, Derek. *The Narrow Margin*. London: Hutchinson, 1961.

'The Yanks of the Eagle Squadron,' in *The Airman*, Oct. 1965.

Ziegler, Frank. *Under The White Rose*. Macdonald, 1971.

Notes

Foreword
The Most Important Factor
Lindbergh quote in Cooke.
Göring's "even if you don't like us" quote in Asher Lee.
Opinion poll data in Manchester.
Deighton quote in *Fighter*.

Chapter One
A Landing Operation Against England ...
Shipman-Kettling information in Brian James.
Jodl quote in Shirer *Rise and Fall*.
Shirer's observations in his *Berlin Diary*.
Hitler's "Directive No. 16" can be found in a number of sources, including Shirer's *R&F*.
The romantic American writer is Bobert; the rhapsodic participant in the Battle is Hugh Dundas. Richard Collier quote from his *Eagle Day*.
Jeschonneck quote in Mitcham.
Dowding's "heavy air attack" quote in Parkinson.
Shipman's and Kettling's remarks in Brian James.
Jimmy Davies' biography from the *Air Log* article written by himself. George VI observation in Gelb.
The possibility that P/O Davies may have become a British subject comes from the editors of *Aviation Magazine*. While the editorial staff were at work on my "Who Was America's First

393

World War Two Ace?" in the magazine's March 1996 issue, they unearthed this bit of information.

OKW directive in Parkman.

Chapter Two
Der Kanalkampf

Fleet Air Arm pilot's remarks in McKee.

Grigg quote, ibid.

Townsend in *Duel.*

Gallup Poll data in Manchester.

Lindbergh quote in Cooke.

Kennedy quote in a number of sources, including Manchester.

The American social historian is Aljean Harmetz.

Galland quote in *First and the Last.*

Page in Collier's *Eagle Day.*

Middleton quote in Sperber.

Quotes from Hitler's 31 July meeting in Shirer *R&F.*

1 August directive also appears in many sources, including Shirer's *R&F.*

Göring quote in Townsend.

The author has been compiling material on the Yanks in the RAF for a number of years, and has a fairly extensive collection. Many of the details of Tobin's, Keough's, and Mamedoff's rocky road into the RAF are in Tobin's (and Robert Low's) *Liberty Maqazine* article. Other details come from a wide array of sources. Shorty Keough's "Dook" conversation is from Crook.

A note on sources, and information contained therein. The author discovered that "official" sources are completely unreliable while he was researching his very first book. British sources disagree with German sources, and vice versa. Air Force and Navy figures rarely agree—on the number of ships in a convoy, or on any other detail. When the United States entered the war and contributed their own sources, the situation became even more complicated. In this case, RAF statistics and Royal Naval statistics do not agree on the number of ships in Convoy "Peewit," which is not unusual.

Malan quote in McKee.

Chapter Three
Very Soon, The Big Lick

Account of 54 Squadron in Deere.

The account of the attack on the CH stations is based mainly upon primary sources, although both McKee and Collier were also consulted. Comments on 609 Squadron's activities in Crook.

Quotes by Geoffrey Page in "It Was Their Finest Hour," in *Daily News* (New York), 8 July 1990. Page also wrote his own memoirs, *Tales of a Guinea Pig*.

Donahue's account in his magazine article in the *Saturday Evening Post*.

"Very soon, the big lick" quote from Townsend.

Tobin's account from his magazine article. Largely because of this magazine piece, as well as by his well-publicized exploits as a member of the first Eagle Squadron, Tobin and his friends Mamedoff and Shorty Keough are probably the best-known of all the Yanks in the RAF.

Deichmann's decision of 15 August, and the quote about its results, in Bekker.

Account of 616 activities on 15 August in Dundas; 54 Squadron in Deere; 85 Squadron in Townsend; 609 in Crook.

To illustrate how badly fighter pilots tended to exaggerate claims of enemy aircraft shot down, the number of German planes actually shot down in mid-August are directly compared with RAF claims. The "Actual" column indicates the true number of German aircraft brought down (based on post war records), and the "Claims" column represents the number of Luftwaffe planes claimed by RAF pilots during this period.

	CLAIMS	ACTUAL
Aug 13	78	45
14	31	9
15	188	55
16	75	45
17	1	00
18	152	71

As bad as the RAF's exaggeration turned out to be, the Luftwaffe's rate of inflation was even worse. And when the United States entered the fighting, their claims of enemy aircraft shot down over the Continent would be just as prone to wishful thinking.

Tommy Thompson's activities on 16 August in Townsend.

Action of 601 Squadron in Tom Moulton's *The Flying Sword*. Details of 601 Squadron in McCrary. Following the publication of the author's article "Americans in the Battle of Britain" in *World War II Magazine* (1990), Richard Perkins of California wrote to say that he had been hired by Billy Fiske's nieces to prove that Fiske was the only American killed in the Battle of Britain. Such are the foibles of the wealthy.

Nicolson's exploits have been recorded in many articles and published acounts. His treatment at the hands of the Home Guard was not untypical; these were amateur soldiers, with a tendency to shoot first and worry about the consequences afterward.

The German writer complaining about the weather and its prejudices is Bekker.

The Luftwaffe intelligence quote in Parkinson. Townsend's quote in his account of the Battle.

Details of the raid on Biggin Hill in Wallace. Account of 85 Squadron in Townsend.

The author interviewed many survivors of the Blitz, as well as of many "small raids," while researching his book about the raid on the City of London of 29 December 1940.

Göring's complaints about his fighter pilots in Townsend.

Dundas is the source for 616's move south.

Churchill's remarks in his memoirs. The New Jersey teacher's remarks are from an interview with the author. The British biographer is John Charmley.

Statistics of artillery barrage against Convoy "Totem" in Wood and Dempster.

Details of the Biggin Hill attack in Wallace.

Falkenstein quote in Bekker.

Observations of 10-year-old boy on 2 Sept. in interview with author.

Janet Murrow's comments in Sperber.

Details of the meeting between Göring and his commanders, Kesselring and Sperrle, in Townsend.

Shirer's comments on Hitler's speech at Berlin's Sportpalast in September in Shirer *R&F*.

"Conditions are most favourable" communique of 5 September in Parkinson.

Jerry McCurdy's observations in interview with author.

Details of 303 (Polish) Squadron's activities from several sources, including Deighton, Townsend, and Wood & Dempster.

"Those last two weeks" in *The World At War*. (Video).

Information on Carl Davis in a letter from Richard Perkins, who had researched his biography (along with the biographies of other Americans in the RAF) for Billy Fiske's nieces.

"The battle in the air ..." in McKee.

Chapter Five
Strategy and Fortune Change

Observations of the 7 September raid on London were given by both civilians and members of the London Fire Brigade, when the author was researching his book on the City fire blitz of 29 December 1940. Among those who recalled that Saturday were James Goldsmith of the Fire Service.

The British author who commented on Hitler's methods is Peter Townsend. Von Boetticher's comments from Washington, D.C. in Thompson.

"Vast black storm cloud" in Deighton.

Army private's "old Adolf" quote on 8 September from author interview.

Recall order of 9 September. "if defences are too strong" in Wood & Dempster. Trautloft quote in McKee.

Deiter Heibing's observations from author interview. Quote Murrow broadcast in Murrow.

Biggin Hill attack on 10 September in Wallace.

Rest center information in Fitzgibbon.

Churchill quote in his memoirs.

Lt. Davies and the St. Paul incident in Fitzgibbon, also from the recollection of the Cathedral's librarian, Mr. Fuller.

Formation of the first Eagle Squadron from many sources, including Ziegler, Haugland, Townsend, and Red Tobin's article with Bob Low. Entries in 71 Squadron's ORB also were consulted.

Bombing of Buckingham Palace, and Churchill's reaction, in Mosley. Also, the incident was covered by virtually every newspaper and magazine in both Britain and the US.

Impression of 10-year-old boy on his birthday, 14 September, from interview with author.

Meeting on Operation Sea Lion in Franz Halder's *The Halder Diaries*. Washington D.C.: *Infantry Journal*, 1950.

Tobin observations on 15 September from his magazine article and from Collier. Churchill visit to 11 Group Hq. from many sources, including Collier. Details of Duxford Wing fighting from McKee.

U.S. Air Force officer's comments on Dowding "ethics" from author interview.

Churchill quote in 15 September in Deighton.

Göring's remarks in Townsend. Park's Instruction No. 18 in Wood and Dempster. Shirer's observations in his *Diary*.

Ultra's interception of 17 September in Winterbotham.

Chapter Six
The War Would Be A Long One

Ultra intercept on 19 September in Winterbotham.

Eagle Squadron details in Tobin, Haugland, Douglas, and Boebert.

General Strong's report of 20 September in Wood and Dempster.

"London After Dark" commentary in Murrow and Sperber.

Details of the raid on Filton of 25 September in McKee.

Murrow broadcast in Murrow and Thompson.

Shirer's comments on American assistance in *Diary*. Details of the Tripartite Pact in Thompson.

Details of the adventures of *The Times* in a letter to the author.

Murrow broadcast of 29 September in Murrow. Biographer of Roosevelt is Thompson.

Broadcast of 1 October in Murrow.

Broadcast of 4 October in Murrow.

Göring's directive of 7 October in Wood and Dempster.

Quentin Reynolds' story in Reynolds; "neutral with no pretense" in Sperber.

Joseph Danforth comments on 8 October from author interview. Keith Park's guidelines in Wood and Dempster.

Keitel's order of 12 October in Wood and Dempster.

German bomber pilot's quote (15 October) in Fitzgibbon. Details of the bombing of Broadcasting House in Sperber.

Explosion of German bomber on 16 October from author interview.

The author discovered Hugh Reilley's story while researching the "Americans In The Battle of Britain" article for *World War II Magazine*.

Comments of resident from Bow from author interview.

The shooting down of the low-flying Ju 88 on 21 October in Ziegler. Diary excerpt of City secretary from letter to author.

Details of Hitler-Franco meeting of 23 October in Toland.

"I wonder what it would be like..." from a letter to author.

Chapter Seven
Winners and Losers
Olivier quote in *The World At War* (video), Vol 4: "Alone." Wright quote from the same video.

Göring's biographer is Asher Lee.

Dundas' remarks on Dowding's 1960 commentary in his memoirs; Leonard Mosley's observations in the Time-Life "Battle of Britain."

Opinion Poll percentages in Manchester.

"Winter of the Bombs" author is Constantine Fitzgibbon.

Afterword
With Unparalleled Stupidity
Churchill on Pearl Harbor attack in his memoirs.

"Won't be able to spare us" from Mass Observation Archives.

"Why was that particular treaty..." in Galbraith.
Acheson quote in Manchester

Index

BATTLE OF BRITAIN